S0-AHF-293

The Only Wonderful Things

The Only Wonderful Things

The Creative Partnership of Willa Cather and Edith Lewis

MELISSA J. HOMESTEAD

OXFORD
UNIVERSITY PRESS

OXFORD
UNIVERSITY PRESS

Oxford University Press is a department of the University of Oxford. It furthers the University's objective of excellence in research, scholarship, and education by publishing worldwide. Oxford is a registered trade mark of Oxford University Press in the UK and certain other countries.

Published in the United States of America by Oxford University Press
198 Madison Avenue, New York, NY 10016, United States of America.

© Oxford University Press 2021

All rights reserved. No part of this publication may be reproduced, stored in a retrieval system, or transmitted, in any form or by any means, without the prior permission in writing of Oxford University Press, or as expressly permitted by law, by license, or under terms agreed with the appropriate reproduction rights organization. Inquiries concerning reproduction outside the scope of the above should be sent to the Rights Department, Oxford University Press, at the address above.

You must not circulate this work in any other form and you must impose this same condition on any acquirer.

Library of Congress Cataloging-in-Publication Data
Names: Homestead, Melissa J., 1963– author.
Title: The only wonderful things : the creative partnership of
Willa Cather and Edith Lewis / by Melissa J. Homestead.
Description: New York, NY : Oxford University Press, [2021] |
Includes bibliographical references and index.
Identifiers: LCCN 2020016655 (print) | LCCN 2020016656 (ebook) |
ISBN 9780190652876 (hardback) | ISBN 9780190652890 (epub) | ISBN 9780190652906
Subjects: LCSH: Cather, Willa, 1873–1947—Relations with women. |
Lewis, Edith, 1881–1972. | Authors, American—20th century—Biography. |
Women authors, American—20th century—Biography. |
Lesbian authors—United States—Biography.
Classification: LCC PS3505.A87 Z667 2021 (print) |
LCC PS3505.A87 (ebook) | DDC 813/.52 [B]—dc23
LC record available at https://lccn.loc.gov/2020016655
LC ebook record available at https://lccn.loc.gov/2020016656

1 3 5 7 9 8 6 4 2

Printed by Sheridan Books, Inc., United States of America

Contents

Acknowledgments

Over the eighteen years I spent researching and writing this book, I accumulated many debts, some of which I have certainly forgotten and fail to acknowledge here.

This book began as a collaborative project with Anne L. Kaufman. Although our collaboration faltered and I carried on alone, I am grateful to her for urging me to take up this work. I thank the many conference audiences who showed interest and asked important questions, and particularly the community of the biennial Willa Cather International Seminar. At the 2003 seminar, where Anne and I first presented a paper at the very beginning of this research, the late Charles Mignon seriously entertained the idea that Edith Lewis was Willa Cather's literary collaborator before I had even examined the evidence. I am grateful for his confidence in the project at such an early stage. Not long before her own death, Susan Rosowski suggested that researching Edith Lewis's life with Cather might "restore the integrity of Lewis's grief" in the wake of Cather's death, and this suggestion proved formative even though I did not write about Lewis's grief until many years later.

At Oxford University Press, Brendan O'Neill acquired the book, Sarah Pirovitz Humphreyville gave advice and encouragement until finally the project was handed over to Norm Hirschy, who got me through the final year and a half by promptly answering questions from the substantive to the most tedious.

Thanks to those hardy souls who read and commented on the whole thing: Andrew Jewell, Janis Stout (who kept urging me to stop referring to it as "my damn book"), Maureen Honey, and an anonymous reader for the Press (two additional anonymous readers read the proposal and introduction). Thanks also to those who read single chapters: Courtney Lawton (expert on all things New Mexican), Emily Rau, Robert Thacker, and Matt Cohen. The introduction and Chapters 1 and 2 were read by members of the Midwest Nineteenth-Century Americanists Writing Group (Laura Mielke, Jill Anderson, Steffi Dippold, Juliana Chow, Randall Fuller, Matthew Smalley, Etta Madden, and Kathryn Dolan). Chapter 1 was presented at a workshop conducted by the Interdisciplinary Nineteenth-Century Studies group at the University of Nebraska–Lincoln (UNL). Shouts out to Geneva Gano, my companion footstepping Cather and Lewis in New Mexico, my go-to conference roomie, and my expert on horses; to Amber Harris, who cared for my animals during many of my research trips and toured William Jennings Bryan's Fairview with me, hunted through Wyuka Cemetery with me for the gravesites of Edith Lewis's siblings who died as children, and took one memorable research trip to central Nebraska with me to find the truth about Henry Lewis's ranch; and to Amy Struthers, a real live professor of advertising, for listening to me babble endlessly about Edith Lewis's advertising career.

A National Endowment for the Humanities (NEH) Fellowship, NEH Summer Stipend, two UNL Faculty Development Fellowships, and a University of Connecticut Humanities Institute External Faculty Fellowship provided releases from teaching. I thank those who wrote letters of support for my many fellowship applications: Sharon O'Brien, Ellen Gruber Garvey, Marilee Lindemann, Linda Karell, Jaime Harker, John Plotz, Andrew Jewell, Janis Stout, Francesca Sawaya, and Alex Ross. As director of the Cather Project, Guy Reynolds arranged for two course releases and made funds available for research travel. The Center for Digital Research in the Humanities at UNL supported the creation of my digital edition of *Every Week* magazine, which was crucial to my recovery of Edith Lewis's magazine editorial career, and the UNL English Department assigned me many M.A. students as research assistants.

Portions of several chapters were published in *Cather Studies* and *Western American Literature* and are included here by permission of the University of Nebraska Press. An earlier version of Chapter 3 appeared in *Studies in the Novel* and portions of Chapter 5 in *Scholarly Editing*.

I could not have carried out this research without the help of many libraries and archives and the people who work in them, including the Smith College Archives (Nanci Young), the Mortimer Rare Book Room at Smith College (Karen Kukil), the University of Pennsylvania Kislak Special Collections Center (John Pollack), the Beinecke Library at Yale University, the Lilly Library at Indiana University, the Houghton Library at Harvard University (Leslie Morris and the service desk staff), the Harry Ransom Center at the University of Texas at Austin, Dartmouth College Special Collections, the New York Public Library, McGill University Special Collections, University of Vermont Special Collections, the Palace of the Governors Photo Archive (Hannah Abelbeck), Bryn Mawr College Special Collections, the Wisconsin Historical Society, the Archive of the National Willa Cather Center (Tracy

Tucker), Drew University Special Collections, the Minnesota Historical Society, Bowdoin College Special Collections, and, of course, University of Nebraska–Lincoln Archives & Special Collections (Katherine Walter, Mary Ellen Ducey, Pete Brink, and Josh Caster). I received support for travel to the institutions housing these collections in the form of grants and fellowships from the Oklahoma Humanities Council, the Smith College Archives, the John W. Hartman Center for Sales, Marketing, and Advertising History at Duke University, the Harry Ransom Center, the Lilly Library, and the Houghton Library.

My work as associate editor of the *Complete Letters of Willa Cather: A Digital Edition* delayed my completion of this book, but by being able to interact with the letters in electronic form, I was able to cite them much more easily in my book and finish my project. Thanks to the editorial team, past and present, including Andrew Jewell, Janis Stout, Emily Rau, Gabi Kirillof, Kari Ronning, Caterina Bernardini, Jessica Tebo, Samantha Greenfield, Lori Nevole, Paul Grosskopf, Hannah Kanninen, Gayle Rocz, and Simone Droge.

People outside the academy have played crucial roles. The late Ruth Lewis Trainor (a Smithie—that's how I found her) and her family shared Lewis family history, documents, and photographs. Francis Picard Holt, Achsah Barlow Brewster's granddaughter, preserved her grandmother's legacy and made it possible to recover her lifelong friendship with Edith Lewis. Anyone reading my notes will discover that I rely heavily on collections donated to my university by Cather family members, namely Charles Edwin Cather, and Helen Cather Southwick, and the family of Roscoe and Meta Cather—indeed, I ultimately realized that the Southwick and Charles Cather donations were, essentially, Edith Lewis's papers. George Brockway shared family letters and photographs, including a letter from Edith Lewis to his mother after Willa Cather's death that made me cry. Caroline Schimmel, granddaughter of Cather's late-life physician, provided information that transformed my understanding of Cather's final years and facilitated my research concerning Cather's death and its aftermath. Laura Buckley shared Whale Cove history and documents. Thomas Reese Gallagher walked me around Greenwich Village and devised a special personal tour of all of Edith Lewis's offices around Manhattan. All of you Smithies in the cloud, your interest kept me going, and I hope you won't be disappointed.

I must acknowledge the crucial part played by my many dogs (Brownie, Florence, Helen, Laci, Tessa, Simon, and Roberta) and cats (Isobel, Grace, Betty, Ingeborg, Marjorie, Magnus, Tom, Bessie, Annabelle, Bob, and John), who have shared my life since 2003. Helen and Laci even spent a week in Cather and Lewis's Grand Manan cottage with me in 2012.

Kelly Payne, Janel Simons, Susan Malcom, and Lindsay Andrews, if you hadn't invited me into your writing group in 2017, grief might have derailed me. I can't thank you enough.

I dedicate this book to the memory of my parents, John Arthur Homestead (1927–2017) and Carolyn Holt Homestead (1930–2017), in honor of their fifty-eight years of marriage.

Introduction

I first encountered the New Hampshire gravesite of novelist Willa Cather in the fall of 1984, when I was a senior at Smith College in Massachusetts and was writing an honors thesis on Cather. On October 3, a beautiful autumn day, I awoke to the ringing of all the bells on campus, signaling Mountain Day, an unannounced holiday from classes. I jumped out of bed, dashed to the hall phone, and managed to reserve one of the few rental cars available in Northampton so that I could drive to Jaffrey to make a pilgrimage to the Cather-related sites, including the Old Burying Ground. In the days before GPS and without even a map, I somehow found my way to Jaffrey and fixed on the town public library as an appropriate source of information. The library staff members eagerly showed me their Cather treasures, including a letter, and gave me directions to Mt. Monadnock, the Shattuck Inn (where Cather had often stayed to write—it was abandoned but still standing and visible from the road), and the cemetery.

The year before, anticipating that I would write a senior thesis on Cather, I bought all the Cather books I could find on the final day of the annual college library book sale, when hardbacks were marked down from one dollar to fifty cents. One of the items in my haul was *Willa Cather Living: A Personal Record* (1953), by Edith Lewis. After I bought the volume, I discovered that it was inscribed by the author, "For Mary Virginia with affectionate greetings," but I had no idea who Lewis was. I soon read Phyllis Robinson's trade biography *Willa: The Life of Willa Cather* (1983), the first biography to out Cather as a lesbian, and I learned that Lewis, the woman with whom Cather had shared homes in New York City for nearly four decades, was a Smith College graduate. I thus made my first attempt at archival research, presenting myself at my college archives to inquire whether there was any information available about Edith Lewis, class of 1902. The archivist, who looked the part with a cardigan draped over her shoulders and her reading glasses on a chain, pulled an index card from a drawer and read aloud from it: "Companion to Willa Cather. Not for publication." "Well, that says it all," she quipped, "doesn't it?"

I had come out as a lesbian a year earlier, and I planned to make Cather's sexuality the center of my interpretation of her fiction in my honors thesis. Sharon O'Brien's academic journal article "The Thing Not Named: Willa Cather as a Lesbian Writer" (1984) articulated the historical grounds for identifying Cather as a lesbian and became the foundation of my project. The rationale articulated in this article would become central to O'Brien's biography of the first half of Cather's life, *Willa Cather: The Emerging Voice* (1987). From what I had read and from the enigmatic notation on a card in the archives bearing information about Lewis, I believed that Cather would not have been pleased with my plans. I thus fancied that I was making my pilgrimage to Cather's grave in Jaffrey to seek her permission—or perhaps her forgiveness—for my junior scholarly enterprise. The historic Meeting House is located right on the Jaffrey town common, and I walked into the adjacent Old Burying Ground, where, in a corner, next to the stone wall, I found the gravesite. When Lewis died in 1972, twenty-five years after Cather's 1947 death, she was buried at Cather's side. What I saw in 1984 and what other pilgrims to Jaffrey had seen since late 1977, however, was a large headstone for Cather and a small flat marker for Lewis at the foot of Cather's grave. I explain in my epilogue how this misleading marker for Lewis came to be placed five years after her death. Its location at what appeared to be Cather's feet became fodder in debates over the sexuality of the dead novelist, including the character of her relationship with Lewis.

Cather and her fiction look quite different when we learn to see what should have been obvious all along—Lewis's instrumental presence at Cather's side rather than at her feet. On the basis of many years of research, I argue in this book that Lewis was both Cather's life partner and her literary collaborator. Before turning to the story of their life together in the chapters that follow, in this introduction I begin to explain how Cather biography and criticism made Lewis vanish, and I lay out the terms on which I define her relationship with Cather and make her visible again.

* * *

This book is not a biography of either Cather or Lewis individually, nor is it a biography of both. Instead, I present a series of scenes from their partnership in chapters organized both chronologically and thematically. Nevertheless, I recover previously invisible events in Cather's life and reframe others as lived in partnership with Lewis. Although I do not present a full biography of

Lewis, I make visible her life as a modern career woman who is interesting in her own right.

The image of Willa Cather as an autonomous artist, detached from the market and from the contemporary social world, has made it difficult for Cather biographers and critics to see Edith Lewis. When I first saw the index card about Lewis in the Smith College Archives in 1984, I myself fell into the trap of not seeing her or of misperceiving what I saw. I later came to understand that the card had been kept by the secretary for the class of 1902, who corresponded with her fellow alumnae to put together class notes for publication in the *Smith Alumnae Quarterly*. In 2003, early in my renewed research on Lewis and Cather's relationship, I encountered this index card again, and I realized that in 1984 the archivist and I had been so transfixed by the one mention of Cather that we failed to see the wealth of information about Lewis's early employment history in book publishing and magazine editing also recorded there. I realized as well that I had slightly misremembered the transfixing bit about Cather: the class secretary's note did not say "companion *to* Willa Cather," as I had remembered, but rather "companion Willa Cather," a slight variation that makes a substantial difference. Was Lewis, as the former suggests, Cather's companion, which might mean a sort of social secretary or personal assistant? Or did the latter (and actual) phrase signify that Cather was *Lewis's* companion? My telling of Cather and Lewis's life together resembles the class secretary's index card in that Lewis is often the primary figure and Cather is secondary or subordinate. Put another way, Cather appears inside Lewis's life rather than vice versa. Lewis's presence has so often been muted in Cather biography that it is valuable to see Cather's life from this new angle, to recognize the ways that Lewis's presence shaped both Cather's life and her art.

In the wake of both Robinson's and O'Brien's biographies, some who were not pleased with their identifying Cather as a lesbian used the markers on the Jaffrey gravesite as ammunition for their denials of Cather's sexuality. In her preface to a reprint of *Willa Cather Living*, Marilyn Arnold described the appearance and location of the "upright and tastefully engraved" marker on Cather's grave and the "modestly flat and plain" marker on Lewis's and argued that the placement of Lewis's stone "indicates that . . . the remains of Edith Lewis were squeezed in at the foot of the first grave." The placement of Lewis's remains as part of the combined gravesite, she elaborated, "tells a story." Mildred Bennett, who founded the Willa Cather Pioneer Memorial and Education Foundation in Cather's Nebraska hometown of Red Cloud in the 1950s, interpreted the gravesite as evidence of how Lewis saw herself both during Cather's lifetime and after Cather's death as her literary executor: "I think Miss Lewis deliberately put herself at Willa Cather's feet and gloried in her position there. And after Miss Cather's death she rose to guardian of the legends Miss Cather had insisted were fact."[1]

Through the gravesite, Bennett and Arnold thus characterized Lewis as unimportant to Cather in her lifetime—a functionary or a useful appendage, no more—and as claiming power to which she was not entitled after Cather's death. Denying Lewis's importance, then, was a means to deny Cather's lesbian sexuality. More recently, Joan Acocella, a staff writer at the New Yorker, has been the most vocal critic of scholars who identify Cather as a lesbian and who read her fiction through her sexuality. In Willa Cather and the Politics of Criticism (2000), a revised and expanded version of a 1995 New Yorker article, Acocella took feminist and queer critics to task for their failure to provide "evidence" of Cather's lesbianism and portrayed them as committing acts of aggression against an essentially conservative author whose life and works displeased them.[2]

Those who read Cather's fiction in the context of lesbian and gay studies or through the lens of queer theory approach sexuality historically. They locate the emergence of identity categories defined by sexuality in the late nineteenth century, when sexologists, a new category of scientific researchers and therapeutic practitioners, began theorizing lesbian identity. Sexologists defined lesbianism as a pathological condition. Paradoxically, they also provided women with a new way to think about themselves and a new identity to claim (sexologists understood male homosexuality differently, but the dynamics were similar). Of course, the particular sexual acts that came to be associated with heterosexual and homosexual identities weren't invented in the late nineteenth century. Instead, individuals from earlier eras engaged in these sexual practices without understanding them as defining who they were, whether heterosexual (normal) or homosexual (deviant). According to O'Brien, it was precisely at this transformative moment in the history of sexuality in the 1890s that a college-age Willa Cather confronted her sexual desires for other women and came to understand that she was a lesbian. If Cather had been older, the age of her mentor, the writer Sarah Orne Jewett, who lived in a partnership with Annie Adams Fields, then perhaps Cather might have entered into a "Boston marriage," a socially—but not legally—sanctioned union between two women. However, so the story goes, the rise of sexology simultaneously made the

Boston marriage impossible and made modern lesbian identity (including the social stigma attached to it) possible.[3]

Cather did not write any fiction featuring lesbian characters or romantic relationships between women. Perhaps because of this, many queer readings of her fiction are premised on the idea that Cather experienced her sexuality as a shameful secret. Eve Kosofsky Sedgwick, a founding figure of queer theory, published an influential interpretation of Cather's novel *The Professor's House* (1925). In this formally complex novel, Cather presented the first and third sections from the point of view of the title character, Godfrey St. Peter, while in "Tom Outland's Story," the second section of the novel, Godfrey remembers an occasion when Tom (killed in World War I) told him of the rise and fall of his friendship with Roddy Blake. According to Sedgwick, the structure of the novel and Cather's focus on bonds between men register "the shadows of the brutal suppressions by which a lesbian love did not in Willa Cather's time and culture become freely visible as itself." Building on Sedgwick's reading, Christopher Nealon maintains that characters in Cather's fiction create "affect genealogies" "linking the lonely dreamers who populate her fiction *within* their privacy." Nealon links this fictional dynamic to Cather herself, "who also knew the pathos of secrecy." In *Feeling Backward: Loss and the Politics of Queer History*, Heather Love places Cather's fiction in a tradition of other "dark, ambivalent texts [that] register their authors' painful negotiation of the coming of modern homosexuality" and which thus emphasize "feelings such as nostalgia, regret, shame, despair, *ressentiment*, passivity, escapism, self-hatred, withdrawal, bitterness, defeatism, and loneliness." Love argues that these "feelings are tied to the experience of social exclusion and the historical 'impossibility' of same-sex desire." These critics presume, then, that Cather lived her life in the closet, a presumption that informed my undergraduate honors thesis, which I titled "The Lesbian Writer Finding a Voice: Willa Cather's Use of Male Narrative Perspective in *My Ántonia* and *A Lost Lady*." Writing with nothing like the sophistication of these later queer critics, I read Cather's fiction through a text-subtext model, arguing that Cather expressed a lesbian sexuality that she otherwise kept hidden by writing about women through the eyes of male narrators.[4]

Other women who were Cather and Lewis's contemporaries seemingly lived their lesbian lives more openly than they did. Take, for example, the American women who lived as expatriates in Paris and were allied with avant-garde aesthetics. Gertrude Stein, who lived in Paris with her partner

Alice B. Toklas, wrote radically experimental prose, conducted a salon, and collected modernist visual art. Stein wore her hair in a severe, short hairstyle, while Toklas's gender presentation was more conventionally feminine. In *The Autobiography of Alice B. Toklas* (1933), Stein depicted herself as conversing with the (male) geniuses, while Toklas sat with the wives of the geniuses. Writing in the voice of her partner, Stein thus portrayed herself as the husband and Toklas as the wife. Djuna Barnes, also part of the expatriate Paris lesbian scene, wrote *The Ladies Almanack* (1928), a roman à clef about the lesbian network centered in the salon of Natalie Clifford Barney. Cather experimented with fictional form, but her aesthetic grew out of the nineteenth-century tradition rather than breaking radically with it, and her prose was conventional. Cather and Lewis were also conventional in their styles of dress and grooming. Cather's conservatism has been overstated. Nevertheless, during the height of her fame as a novelist, she was a middle-aged woman who styled her hair in a bun and wore dresses and skirts (she reserved trousers for rugged recreation in remote locations).[5]

Cather and Lewis lived together in Greenwich Village for twenty years, and yet they were as strikingly different from other female couples in this New York neighborhood known for political and sexual freedom as they were from the expatriate lesbians of Paris. Take, for example, Elisabeth Irwin and Katherine Anthony, Cather and Lewis's near neighbors. Irwin was Lewis's contemporary at Smith College, graduating in 1903. She began her professional life in New York as a social worker, but in order to put the educational theories of John Dewey into practice, she founded the Little Red Schoolhouse on Bleecker Street in the Village. Anthony also started out as a social worker and social researcher in New York but then became a prolific and popular biographer, applying the psychological theories of Sigmund Freud to the lives of the women she took as her subjects. Both Irwin and Anthony belonged to Heterodoxy, the famous feminist women's luncheon club, where they and other lesbian couples were welcomed and recognized as such, and during World War I they were members of the radically pacifist New York chapter of Women's Peace Party. Irwin and Anthony raised adopted children together, and punning on the Connecticut town where they had a summer home, they called themselves "the gay ladies of Gaylordsville."[6]

In many respects Irwin and Anthony were precisely like Lewis and Cather. Lewis and Irwin were both Smith College graduates and New York professional women, while Cather and Anthony both became full-time authors. From 1913 to 1927, Lewis and Cather lived at 5 Bank Street, while around

1913, Irwin and Anthony moved into 23 Bank Street, one block away, and lived together there until Irwin's death in 1942. Despite the fact that Cather and Lewis were career women who lived in partnership rather than marrying men, however, they quietly followed convention rather than flouting it, while Irwin and Anthony were prototypical Greenwich Village radicals. Considering their many points of connection, the two couples certainly had at least a glancing acquaintance with each other, and yet they were not friends and seemingly lived on different cultural planets rather than a block apart. To some contemporary observers in Greenwich Village, Cather's conventionality looked like a form of closeting. Gus, an aspiring ceramic artist who was Kansas-born and Ohio-bred, kept voluminous diaries of his years living in the Village and perceived Cather this way: he wrote that she was "Sapphic; keeps herself hidden." Unlike Anthony and Irwin, Cather and Lewis left no explicit traces of self-identification as lesbians. As in all things, it is possible that such documentary traces exist and I have not found them. I hasten to add, however, that the oft-repeated stories that the two women routinely destroyed letters—stories that have contributed to the notion of Cather as closeted—are wildly exaggerated.[7]

In *To Believe in Women: What Lesbians Have Done for America* (1999), a study of late-nineteenth- and early-twentieth-century feminist reformers who had romantic relationships with other women, Lillian Faderman distinguishes between "lesbian" as a noun and as an adjective. While she concedes that most of her subjects never claimed "lesbian" as a noun, "used as an adjective" the term "accurately describes their committed domestic, sexual, and/or affectional experiences." "Lesbian" as an adjective accurately describes Cather and Lewis's long relationship, and given their time and place, it is the right category for their individual identities. Some have wanted to define Cather as heterosexual based on traces of what might have been brief romantic episodes with or brief periods of heightened feelings toward particular men, so why shouldn't Cather's intimate domestic partnership of nearly forty years with Lewis define her as a lesbian? Faderman has been the most thorough chronicler of lesbian life in the U.S. In *Surpassing the Love of Men: Romantic Friendship and Love Between Women from the Renaissance to the Present* (1981), which I first read in college, Faderman put Cather's life forward as testimony to the decline of the Boston marriage after the teachings of sexology took hold. In *Odd Girls and Twilight Lovers: A History of Lesbian Life in Twentieth-Century America* (1991), Cather appears briefly as an example of a woman navigating the new regime of secrecy: Faderman claims that "Cather became very secretive about her private life around the turn of the century because she was cognizant of the fall from grace that love between women was beginning to suffer."[8]

Faderman relies on published biographies of Cather, in which Lewis appears as little more than a shadow. When Cather biographers mention Lewis at all, they mostly characterize her as a nonentity or a mystery, or they draw thumbnail sketches of a fussy, slightly hysterical woman. Hermione Lee, for example, devotes a mere three pages to Lewis, describing her as "a mere shadow," "the faithful Boswell" to Cather's Samuel Johnson, and "affectionate, emotional, anxious, rather fussy." Lee, like other biographers, gives far more space and more respectful attention to Isabelle McClung, in whose family home in Pittsburgh Cather lived for several years before she moved to New York in 1906. McClung married violinist Jan Hambourg in 1916 (an event at which Cather felt aggrieved). The fact of McClung's having entered into a heterosexual marriage seems to have made her comparatively more attractive to some Cather biographers. Lee, for example, caps off her backhanded portrait of Lewis with a reading of the Jaffrey gravesite: "in the end, [Lewis] would be buried at [Cather's] feet: not—at a guess—a position that Isabelle McClung would have wanted to assume for eternity." McClung's decision to marry a man also looks like evidence of the decline of the possibility of socially sanctioned romantic relationships between women in the early twentieth century.[9]

However, what I have come to believe is that Cather and Lewis lived in something like a Boston marriage well into the twentieth century. Indeed, the degree to which their relationship resembled a marriage made biographers and critics anxious after Cather's death, and these anxieties are the subject of my epilogue. Their partnership was also, however, more open and flexible than marriage as traditionally constructed for women (at least for white middle-class women like Cather and Lewis). That Cather continued her relationship with McClung after she and Lewis first began living together in 1908 testifies to this openness. Cather and Lewis also maintained independent lives and spent months at a time apart while Cather was traveling and Lewis's professional responsibilities (first as a magazine editor and then as an advertising copywriter) kept her in New York. Nevertheless, both women valued their partnership enough to maintain it for more than thirty-eight years, despite the pressures of their separate lives that sometimes threatened to dissolve it. Choosing a life together in the early twentieth century was, as it was for the reformers whose lives Faderman documents in *To Believe in Women*, a creative way for both women to combine sharing, love, and intimacy with autonomy and a devotion to their own careers. My adoption of the term "creative partnership" reflects this understanding of their relationship.[10]

Cather and Lewis's relationship was, in many contexts, visible rather than hidden. To return to the copy of *Willa Cather Living* I fortuitously purchased at the college library book sale, I eventually realized that Lewis had inscribed it to one of Cather's nieces, Mary Virginia Auld (later Mellen), who graduated from Smith in 1929. When Mary Virginia died in 1983 she left her Cather books to her alma mater, but because the library already had a copy of *Willa Cather Living* on its shelves, her inscribed copy was put in the book sale pile with other duplicates. Lewis's inscription was one of my earliest pieces of evidence that Cather and Lewis's relationship was visible to Cather's family.

Despite the "not for publication" notation on Lewis's index card in the Smith College Archives, this document similarly testifies to the visibility of their relationship (Figure I.1). Notably, a date is embedded in the information about Lewis and Cather's relationship: "Companion Willa Cather 1931 (not for publication)." In the November 1931 *Smith Alumnae Quarterly*, the 1902 class secretary reported, "Achsah (Barlow) Brewster and her artist-husband are living in the south of France, to be near their daughter Harwood,

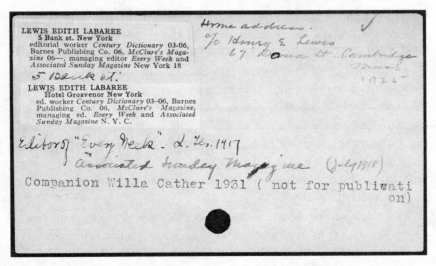

Figure I.1 The index card on which the secretary of the Smith College Class of 1902 recorded information about Edith Lewis. Courtesy Smith College Archives.

who is in school in England. Edith Lewis visited them last summer." Achsah Barlow (late Brewster) and Lewis were roommates at Smith and became life-long friends. The class secretary did not retain the letter from Brewster in which she reported Lewis's visit (although other such letters are in Brewster's file), but I suspect that she wrote something like this: "Edith Lewis and her companion, Willa Cather, visited me and my husband in the South of France last summer—don't put the part about Miss Cather in the class notes, she wouldn't like the publicity." Cather's name did *not* appear in the *Quarterly* note (it was "not for publication"). Nevertheless, two people who knew Lewis (Brewster and the class secretary) shared with one another the fact that a member of the class of 1902 had as a "companion" the distinguished novelist. Furthermore, the class secretary felt no compunction about recording the information on a card documenting Lewis's life for future reference and in-formal sharing with others—it was not for publication, but it was not a secret.

I doubt the word "lesbian" (or "homosexual" or "gay") appeared in Brewster's report to the class secretary, and I doubt that the word was ever spoken by Cather's and Lewis's friends and families. Still, I have found abun-dant evidence that many people implicitly recognized that the partnership between the two women was marriage-like. Perhaps those who withheld the word "lesbian," whether Cather and Lewis themselves or those who knew them, were practicing a form of discretion. Such discretion, however, is not the same thing as living in the closet. As George Chauncey argues in *Gay New York: Gender, Urban Culture, and the Making of the Gay Male World, 1890–1940*, the "metaphor of the closet" was an invention of the 1960s. In his reconstruction of the experiences of men in late-nineteenth- and early-twentieth-century New York, Chauncey finds not a closet but "a highly vis-ible, remarkably complex, and continually changing gay male world that encompassed a wide variety of identities and practices." No one has repli-cated Chauncey's work with a focus on women, but I have come to believe that rather than living closeted lives, Cather and Lewis lived in one of many ways that women in same-sex relationships in the early twentieth century might have lived.[11]

My understanding of the history of sexuality is not whiggish, then: I do not see society as moving out of darkness in a continual march toward freedom and tolerance. Instead, as Cather and Lewis's case suggests, his-tory develops unevenly and features reversions and losses as well as gains and progress. I also am not offering Cather and Lewis as a model for em-ulation in the present (the era of legally authorized same-sex marriage) or as a lens for interpreting all other intimate relationships between women in the past. I take seriously the queer critique of the rush to same-sex marriage as a potential trap that obscures other possible models of queer affiliation. Furthermore, as white, middle-class, college-educated women, Cather and Lewis had a privileged status that doubtless protected them and allowed them to make choices that other women could not. Nevertheless, because the marriage-like character of their relationship so powerfully formed—and deformed—perceptions of Lewis after Cather's death, it is important to recognize how aspects of their partnership aligned with this powerful social institution. I also have chosen "lesbian" over "queer" as the appropriate category for them and their relationship. As a noun or an adjective, "queer" is generally understood to be a broader category that might encompass lesbian as well as other identities. As a verb in queer theory, "queering" entails continually pushing beyond boundaries and resisting normalization. As my project entails defining Cather and Lewis's relationship at a particular moment in history, I have opted for "lesbian" as the most appropriate category.[12]

I also use the term "creative partnership" for their relationship because Lewis was a partner in the creation of Cather's fiction. At the beginning of the third section of an early typed draft of *The Professor's House* (Figure I.2), the narrator describes Godfrey St. Peter's ruminations on his life thusly: "The most disappointing thing about life, St. Peter thought, was the amazing part that blind chance played in it. After one had attributed as much as possible to indirect causation, there still remained so much, even in a quiet and sheltered existence, that was irreducible to any logic." In handwriting strikingly different from Cather's, Lewis boldly revised these two sentences: "All the most important things in his life had been determined by chance, St. Peter thought." After further slight revisions, this key sentence appeared in the published novel: "All the most important things in his life, St. Peter sometimes reflected, had been determined by chance." The working typed drafts of Cather's novels, short stories, and essays are key to my reconstruction of their shared life because, as this example reveals, Lewis served behind the scenes as Cather's editor (not, as she has improbably been called, Cather's "amanuensis"). As author and editor, the two women together produced Cather's mature stripped-down style theorized in her oft-quoted essay "The Novel Démeublé" (1922).[13]

In language echoing that in *The Professor's House*, Lewis mused in *Willa Cather Living* on the chance that led to their first meeting in Lincoln, Nebraska, in 1903: "If I had not met Willa Cather at this time, the chances

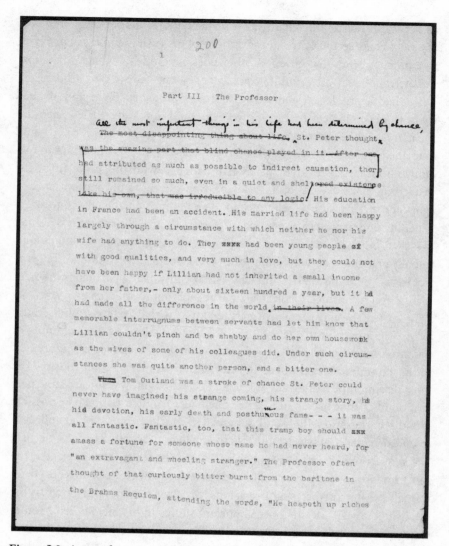

Figure I.2 A page from a typed draft of Willa Cather's *The Professor's House*, edited by Edith Lewis in pen. Courtesy Archives and Special Collections, University of Nebraska–Lincoln Libraries.

are that I would never have met her, and our long friendship and association, which lasted until her death, would never have happened." Those who suggest that Lewis was buried at Cather's feet also suggest that Lewis appropriated Cather's literary voice. Marilyn Arnold points to "unmistakable echoes of Willa Cather" in *Willa Cather Living*, calling the book "an unconscious symbol of the merging of one mind and life [Lewis's] into another [Cather's]." The edited drafts of Cather's fiction, however, suggest another scenario: that the fiction writer's public voice we identify as "Cather's" was always a product of her collaboration with Lewis as editor. In her memoir Lewis wondered what her life would have been like if she had not met Cather, but we may also wonder what the prose style of Cather's fiction would have been like if Cather had not met Lewis.[14]

Looked at in the broader context of the history of authorship, the fact that Cather had a regular editorial collaborator is quite ordinary. As literary historian Jack Stillinger has argued, drawing on a host of examples, solitary genius is a Romantic myth and collaboration an everyday reality. Nevertheless, Cather has long been portrayed precisely as a solitary genius who exerted control over every aspect of her fiction and resisted editorial intervention. She is also often characterized as shut off from the world and obsessed with privacy, as a backward-looking anti-modernist who scorned the tawdry commercialism of twentieth-century culture, and as a high literary artist who held herself apart from the marketplace. And yet Cather shared a home and a rich social life with Lewis, a woman who edited a popular cheap magazine and wrote advertising copy for mass-market consumer goods. I have come to see their diverging professional choices—Cather chose art and idealism, while Lewis made the pragmatic choice to abandon art for commerce—as a source of productive tension in the relationship. Neither irrevocably and absolutely chose one over the other, however. Cather issued aesthetic pronouncements against materialism and commercialism, and yet she cared deeply about the advertising of her books. Lewis edited a cheap magazine and wrote advertising copy for cheap soap, but she also had a keen aesthetic sense that she applied to her work as a magazine editor and advertising copywriter. Combining forces allowed each woman to commit herself to both art *and* commerce, to be both idealistic *and* pragmatic.[15]

This is a work of documented historical scholarship, not fiction, and finding documentation of the life of Lewis, who was not a public figure, was challenging. In recovering Lewis, I draw on a much wider range of documents than Cather biographers, who have relied on a very small group of documents and of scholars' accounts of their encounters with Lewis when she was old and acting as Cather's executor. Letters are often a crucial source for biography, and the number of known Cather letters has increased exponentially since the last book-length biography of Cather, Janis Stout's *Willa*

Cather: The Writer and Her World (2002). Some of these more recently discovered letters, especially those to Willa Cather's brother Roscoe and his wife,
Meta, make Lewis more visible. However, very few letters between Cather and
Lewis are currently known: only one letter and five postcards from Cather to
Lewis and none from Lewis to Cather. I have located nearly six hundred letters by Lewis, but less than 10 percent date from before Cather's death. In
order to locate Lewis and reconstruct the life she shared with Cather, I have
thus drawn on other sources, including many letters *to* Lewis from people
other than Cather, newspapers and magazines, census records, and a variety
of documents in college, corporate, and organizational archives. Indeed, the
shape of my book reflects the shapes of these archives: where I have found
enough documents to tell a story, I have done so. I sometimes consider
Cather's fiction in the context of her shared life with Lewis, but interpreting
Cather's fiction is not, as in the case of many queer analyses of Cather, my primary focus. Crucially, I do not seek evidence of Cather's life in her fiction: although Cather did not represent intimate, lifelong bonds between women in
her fiction, she did live in such a relationship with Lewis, and that is where
my primary focus lies. Because my focus differs fundamentally from that of
most published scholarship on Cather (and because of space constraints),
I cite this scholarship sparingly in the following chapters.[16]

From the documents I have found, Lewis emerges as a woman who combined a traditionally feminine reserve with a fierce determination to make
her way in the world on her own terms. I incorporate her voice into my narrative whenever I can, quoting liberally, for example, from the fiction she
published in a hometown paper as a precocious adolescent, her correspondence with contributors to *Every Week* magazine (of which she was the managing editor), her essays on the theory and practice of advertising, and the
advertising copy she wrote for beauty products. I also quote frequently from
Willa Cather Living, although I treat her recollections with the same caution
I do all other documents. Memories fade, and Lewis, like others, shaped her
text for her audience and purpose in ways that, by turns, reveal, obscure, and
romanticize.

In the chapters that follow, I seek to make "freely visible as itself" this
seemingly "impossible" shared life of Cather and Lewis. In my first chapter,
Cather is largely absent as I reconstruct Lewis's family history and early life
to provide the background to their first meeting in 1903. From there, I sit-
uate them both in Greenwich Village, where Lewis moved in 1903 and got
an entry-level job in publishing and where Cather moved in 1906 to work

at *McClure's Magazine* (Lewis soon joined her on the magazine's staff). In subsequent chapters I follow them through the decades, across various locations, and through a series of changes in both of their personal and professional lives. In the 1910s, Cather became a full-time author while Lewis continued magazine editorial work. The American Southwest was one of their favorite retreats from the pressure of New York City life, and I reconstruct their four southwestern trips together as the inspiration for both *The Professor's House* and *Death Comes for the Archbishop* (1927). I am concerned with Cather and Lewis's creative collaboration in the production of Cather's fiction throughout, but I give the most sustained treatment in the midst of my account of these travels because *The Professor's House* is the first Cather novel for which an edited typed draft survives. From the Southwest, I return to their evolving lives in New York in the 1920s, when Lewis became an advertising copywriter and Cather's reputation as a distinguished novelist was on the rise. In the 1920s, they first began vacationing together on Grand Manan, an island off the Atlantic coast of Canada. In New York City they did not belong to Heterodoxy, nor did they, to my knowledge, patronize the lesbian tearooms or mixed-gender gay bars that began appearing in Greenwich Village. On Grand Manan, however, they joined an all-women resort community encompassing same-sex couples like themselves, returning regularly through 1940. In my final chapter, I turn to their life together in the 1930s and 1940s in places other than Grand Manan, as well as to Cather's death, the early years of Lewis's life after Cather's death, and the circumstances of Lewis's death and burial in 1972.

The different shapes of these chapters reflect the strikingly different documents on which I built them. Furthermore, because this book is organized both thematically and chronologically, some periods of time and some events appear in more than one chapter. For example, my accounts of their southwestern travels, Lewis's advertising work, and their Grand Manan summers all encompass the 1920s. My final chapter, which overlaps chronologically with my account of their summers on Grand Manan, has, like my first chapter, a more conventionally biographical shape. This is a result of the comparatively rich quantity and quality of documentation about their day-to-day life together during the last fifteen years of Cather's life and the early years of Lewis's life alone.

In Lewis's early years as Cather's literary executor, she authorized E. K. Brown to write a biography of Cather and provided extensive assistance to him. In my epilogue, I shift from viewing Cather and Lewis's relationship from the inside to reconstructing how Brown and others viewed Lewis and understood (or misunderstood) her role in Cather's life. Brown died before completing his biography, and at this moment of crisis and uncertainty, the mythology about Lewis I contest throughout this book first began to form. Confronted with a powerful woman who was both Cather's executor and, in a very real sense, her widow, E. K. Brown's widow and a host of others with their own stakes in a nascent Cather industry sought both to undermine Lewis's authority and to establish Cather's reputation as a woman married to her art rather than to Edith Lewis. Cather and Lewis had lived openly together from 1908 to 1947 in a relationship valued and acknowledged by family and friends, but in the midst of the Cold War panic over homosexuality, this relationship that had fostered Cather's career as a novelist became, in the eyes of some, a threat to her postmortem reputation that needed to be contained.

As a college student with little research experience, I gave up on Edith Lewis. Confronted with the phrase "not for publication," I presumed that shame had caused Lewis to obliterate most traces of herself and her life with Cather. When I began the research for this book twenty years later, I was an English professor with research skills honed by doctoral study and by earlier work experiences in a rare book and manuscript library and as a paralegal. Because I had so often found that research into primary sources disproved what everyone was sure was true, I was willing to try again. I was still not sure, however, that I would find much. The record of what can be known about Lewis and her relationship with Cather turned out to be much richer than I thought possible, but perhaps this richness should not have surprised me. Willa Cather was no fool, and when she chose to live her life with Edith Lewis, she entered a partnership that enabled her to write some of the most loved and admired novels of the first half of the twentieth century.

1

Nebraska, New England, New York

Mapping the Foreground of Willa Cather and Edith Lewis's Creative Partnership

In *Willa Cather Living*, Edith Lewis briefly recounted the foreground to her first meeting with Willa Cather in August 1903 in Lincoln, Nebraska, in the home of their mutual friend, Sarah Harris, editor and publisher of the *Lincoln Courier* (Figure 1.1). At that time, Cather was working as a teacher in Pittsburgh, Pennsylvania, and she was stopping in Lincoln, where she had attended the University of Nebraska, on her return journey to Pittsburgh after visiting her family in Red Cloud, farther west. Teaching was not her vocation but merely a means to support herself as she sought to become established as an author. Lewis wrote little about herself before their meeting except that she admired Cather's published work and that after being introduced to Cather and being struck by her "eyes of genius," she admired her even more. The source of Cather's interest in Lewis seems less clear. Why did she talk to Lewis as if they "were fellow students, both pursuing the same vocation"? Why did Cather invite Lewis to stop over in Pittsburgh on her way east to New York City, where her plan was "to try and get [herself] a job there—any kind of job"?[1]

Lewis coyly mentioned that Harris had published "one or two of [her] college themes" in the *Courier*. She also briefly sketched the social world of Lincoln, where she was "born and brought up," describing Lincoln as "not more provincial than most college towns." There was, however, much more to the twenty-one-year-old Edith Lewis than seventy-one-year-old Edith Lewis let on. The young woman Cather met was determined to leave that provincial college town for New York City, the emerging center of American literary culture and publishing. This desire made her like many other young college graduates, then and today, but she was both better prepared than most and peculiarly suited to attracting Cather's attention.[2]

In Cather's essay "148 Charles Street," she recounted how in the parlor of the Boston home shared by Annie Adams Fields and Sarah Orne Jewett, "an

Figure 1.1 The Harris House, circa 1901. Sarah Harris introduced Willa Cather and Edith Lewis to one another here in August 1903. The woman pictured is likely Sarah Harris's mother, and the man one of her brothers. Courtesy History Nebraska.

American of the Apache period and territory [meaning herself] could come to inherit a Colonial past." Annie Fields was the widow of James T. Fields of Ticknor and Fields, the preeminent nineteenth-century American literary publishing house. When Cather first met Annie Fields in 1908, the meeting sparked a childhood memory of "little volumes of Longfellow and Hawthorne with that imprint" in "my father's bookcase" in Nebraska. Cather reeled off the names of nineteenth-century New England authors James Fields published ("Longfellow, Emerson, Whittier, Hawthorne, Lowell, Sumner, Norton, Oliver Wendell Holmes") who were "part of the very Charles Street scene." Meeting Annie Fields, Cather felt that she had met these dead authors and, by extension, their colonial New England ancestors.[3]

Even though Edith Lewis spent her childhood in Nebraska (in the Platte River valley as well as Lincoln), her family history and elite eastern college education made her a representative of that New England past as well. She was also driven to succeed as an author and had a plan to find literary work in New York. At the moment of their meeting, Cather found powerfully concentrated in Lewis two geographically located versions of the past she valued: the Nebraska of her own childhood, adolescence, and young adulthood and a New England–centered literary culture she encountered through reading. Cather also glimpsed in Lewis the future to which she herself aspired, the glittering promise of literary New York.

New England Comes to Nebraska

Edith Labaree Lewis was born in Lincoln on December 22, 1881. In July, her parents, Henry and Lillie Lewis, had moved from Illinois to the growing capital of Nebraska with their one-year-old son. Both Henry and Lillie came, however, from families with colonial-era New England roots only recently transplanted to the West. During their western years, their extended families were mobile urban people, creatures of the railroad, who maintained their New England connections through travel and chain migration and who recreated or created New England–based social networks in the West.[4]

Henry grew up as one of seven children on a modest farm outside the New Hampshire mill town where the Lewis clan had relocated from Massachusetts in the late seventeenth century. Henry's father was descended from an English Puritan physician who migrated to Massachusetts on the *Mayflower*, while his mother was descended from French Huguenots who sought refuge from religious persecution in seventeenth-century Massachusetts and relocated to New Hampshire in the eighteenth century. Henry and his four brothers graduated from the academy in a nearby town that their mother had attended. Graduating from Kimball Union Academy prepared them for admission to Dartmouth College, where, like many of their classmates, they taught during the winter terms to pay their way. All five brothers also joined the Psi Upsilon fraternity. Henry's three sisters had fewer educational opportunities. Two attended Kimball Union without graduating, and only one sister of the seven siblings who lived to adulthood seems not to have attended the academy. Nevertheless, all three sisters worked as teachers, although one gave up teaching to marry and raise a family on a Vermont farm.[5]

After his 1872 Dartmouth graduation, Henry taught in New Jersey and Vermont, but in 1876, he abandoned teaching and moved to Illinois to read law under his older brother Eugene, who had moved there from Boston in 1869. His brother Homer and sister Belle also went west in the early 1870s: Belle had moved to Moline, where she taught grammar school, while

Homer was teaching high school across the river in Davenport, Iowa. The Lewises had brought their children up in the Congregational Church, the denomination descending from the Puritan tradition, but Henry and Eugene converted to Unitarianism in college, and Davenport had a newly established Unitarian church.[6]

Edith's mother, Sarah Lydia Gould (always called Lillie), was born in Davenport in 1858. Her Rhode Island Quaker parents and their two daughters had arrived the year before as part of a wave of merchant and professional class migrants to the city after the Rock Island Railroad crossed the Mississippi. Lillie's father was a lineal descendant of Daniel Gould, an early English Puritan immigrant to Massachusetts who converted to Quakerism and moved to the more tolerant Rhode Island colony to escape persecution. In Davenport, Lillie's father established a furniture factory. Describing himself for a history of Davenport, he boasted of his descent from his Quaker martyr namesake, who was "scoffed and mocked by a rude mob" in Massachusetts, "received thirty stripes upon the naked back," and "was cast into prison and made to lie with his bleeding back upon bare boards." Lillie's mother was descended from the earliest English settlers on the island of Nantucket.[7]

The Goulds were reform-minded Quakers who supported abolition and temperance. Women in Daniel Gould's family had long taken prominent roles in radical reform circles. When Daniel's abolitionist cousin Rebecca Buffum Spring and her husband traveled to Europe in the late 1840s, they invited their friend Margaret Fuller (who had been part of Ralph Waldo Emerson's Transcendentalist circle in Massachusetts) to accompany them as a tutor for their young son. Daniel and Sarah Gould settled permanently in Davenport, but they sent their daughter Mary Elizabeth to live in New York City with one of Daniel's sisters so she could attend the Spingler Institute for Young Ladies. The Goulds sent Lillie, their youngest child, to school in Elmira, New York, where she completed her studies in 1878.[8]

As Hicksite Quakers, the Goulds focused on the inner light of the Gospel and social reform and were not in sympathy with the Orthodox Quakers, who more closely resembled mainstream evangelical Protestants and predominated in Iowa. In the absence of a Hicksite meeting, they helped to found, supported, and attended the Davenport Unitarian Church, but they signaled their continuing loyalty to their Quaker faith by not officially enrolling as members. For Daniel and Sarah Gould (and also for Henry Lewis and Lillie Gould, who married in the Davenport Unitarian Church on September 2, 1879), attending a Unitarian church in the Midwest was a marker of cultural and intellectual distinction and of New England heritage. In contrast, Lillie's sister Mary, who married a New England Quaker, joined the Congregational Church.[9]

Henry and Lillie Lewis traveled from Moline to Vermont and New Hampshire for their honeymoon so that Henry could introduce his new bride to family there. Rather than settle in Moline to practice law with his brother, however, Henry used the law as a stepping stone and a tool to create enterprises that drew New England capital westward. Eastern investors were anxious to invest in western mortgages, stocks, and bonds. In June 1881, Henry made a return visit to New England to secure funding commitments for Nebraska farm loans and to sell bonds for the Moline Plow Company (Lillie, who was pregnant with Edith, took their young son, Harold, to visit her family in Davenport while Henry was gone). From northern Vermont and New Hampshire, where Henry visited several bankers with Dartmouth or family connections, he traveled to Boston, where his brother Frank accompanied him on visits to banks. Frank and Henry then traveled to Worcester to visit Arthur, the only Lewis brother who never went west. Henry met up there with Homer, and together they traveled to New York City before Henry finally returned home to Illinois.[10]

Soon thereafter, Henry and Lillie moved to Lincoln, Nebraska's up-and-coming capital city. In July 1881, about thirteen thousand people lived there, but conditions were still primitive. The city lacked paved roads, sidewalks, gas lines to supply homes or streetlights, and municipal water and sewer service. However, Lincoln was well connected to both coasts by rail. Henry rented an office downtown and by early August was advertising "money to loan on improved farms at lowest current rates." He and Lillie rented a house close to downtown at 1335 G Street, where Edith was born in December. Henry's loan brokering required regular travel. He made another trip to New England in 1882, again seeking funds for farm loans and this time selling Moline Plow Company stock. He also traveled frequently within Nebraska to judge the value of collateral for loans.[11]

There was no Unitarian congregation for Henry and Lillie to join in Lincoln. There was, however, a Universalist chapel around the corner. The Universalists were fractious and underfunded and had not managed to support a minister or hold regular services for nearly a decade. Henry scoffed at the "spiritualist" preaching he heard in Universalist churches back in New England. He favored the intellectualism of Unitarianism, with its focus on reason and moral action in the world, rather than the doctrine of universal salvation and concomitant focus on the afterlife. In Nebraska, however, he aspired to "unite together" Unitarians and Universalists in "a common liberal movement." In November 1882, he and George E. Church attended a "joint conference of Unitarians and other liberal religionists" in Omaha convened by the Nebraska State Missionary of the American Unitarian Association. Professor Church was the only faculty member appointed at the University of Nebraska's founding who was not an ordained Protestant minister, but he had been dismissed by the regents in January 1882 and was staying in Lincoln while appealing his dismissal. Unlike Henry Lewis, Professor Church aimed for a Unitarian takeover of the Universalist Society. By the end of 1882, however, Church had given up on his prospects of being reinstated at the university and had decided to leave. Henry subsequently wrote to Lillie when she and the children were again visiting her parents, "I asked Church . . . whether he was going to rent his place if he did not sell: he said yes & that he would give me the first choice at it, if I wanted to try it. He says if we rent it he knows we will buy it.—What would you think of renting it?"[12]

Church's planned takeover of the Universalist Society fizzled with his departure from Lincoln, and Henry and Lillie joined the Universalist Society. In March 1883, with the support of the Universalist General Convention, they called the Reverend Eben H. Chapin. Illinois-born with a degree from Tufts Divinity School, Chapin brought his Massachusetts-born wife with him. For a time Henry served as secretary of the society, and Lillie was active in the Ladies Aid.[13]

Also in March 1883, when Professor Church departed the Lewises moved into the large, two-story home he had built on the edge of town. In 1867, the city had platted for development only to Sixteenth Street. Church's unplatted double lot was a mile east of this original plat, on a ridge above the Antelope Creek with a commanding view of Lincoln on what became the northwest corner of Twenty-Seventh and N Streets. In October 1883, the Lewises purchased the property from Church for $5,000 and would occupy it for more than thirty years. Even in the center of Lincoln in the 1880s people kept pigs, but Henry and Lillie now had more land and a small barn, where they kept a cow, hogs, chickens, and a horse. The house was not a farmhouse, however, but an elegant Victorian home with features such as "Gothic shaped windows" with "sparkling panes of glass" in the dining room. In later years, as Twenty-Seventh Street became a major thoroughfare, Henry fiercely defended his land and house from encroachment as suburban and then urban development surrounded it: he protested against a planned at grade crossing of the Rock Island Railway a block north, and he appealed his dispute with the city about the boundary between his front yard and Twenty-Seventh Street all the way to the Nebraska Supreme Court.[14]

Once the Lewises were settled in their large house and integrated into Lincoln through church membership, they triggered more westward chain migrations in their families. In 1883, Homer Lewis left Davenport to become principal of the Omaha High School, and Belle Lewis followed, teaching in the grammar school that shared a building with the high school. In the spring of 1884, Lillie's sister Mary Wing moved with her family—her husband, two daughters, and two sons—to an orchard property south of Lincoln. By June 1885, Frank Lewis had moved his family from Massachusetts and joined his brother in his law practice. Frank, his wife, and their three children first lived with Henry and Lillie and their children and then bought their own house nearby. In November 1885, Lillie gave birth to her second daughter, and in October 1889, she gave birth to her second son. As a young girl in Lincoln in the 1880s, then, Edith was surrounded by family, including siblings, cousins, aunts, and uncles.[15]

Bank, Church, Club, School: Lewis Family Networks in Late-Nineteenth-Century Lincoln

Most who migrated to Nebraska after it was opened for settlement came from the mid-Atlantic states, the upper South, and states settled earlier by westward migrants from those areas. The Lewises, however, formed bonds with others from New England or with New England roots, and with them they attended church, formed clubs, founded institutions, and created business enterprises. Silas Burnham and Henry Lewis and their families were close. Burnham, who was from Maine, graduated from Dartmouth the same year as Homer Lewis and was a Psi Upsilon member. He first moved to Lincoln in 1880 and practiced law for a year before he began commuting between the capital city and ranching country farther west, where he established several banks. In 1888, he founded the American Exchange National Bank in Lincoln and remained active in banking in the capital city for the rest of his life. The Harrises were also part of the Lewis's New England–connected network in Lincoln. George Samuel Harris, land agent for the Burlington & Missouri Railroad, arrived in Lincoln in 1872 with his wife, Sarah Fisk Bacon Harris, whose family background closely matched Henry's—Puritans on her father's side, Huguenots on her mother's. At the time of George's death in 1874, one of their daughters was studying at the Boston Medical College and one of their sons at the Massachusetts Institute of Technology. Sarah's young adult sons persuaded her to remain in Lincoln after George's death, and Celia, her physician daughter, moved there to practice medicine. Sarah Harris's other daughter, Sarah Butler Harris, eventually became editor and publisher of the *Lincoln Courier* and lived with her mother in the house near the state capital where Edith Lewis and Willa Cather would meet in 1903.[16]

In 1886, Henry Lewis became vice president and board member of the newly founded Union Savings Bank, adding bank officer to lawyer and farm loan broker to his professional repertoire (farm loans took place largely outside the banking system in the 1880s). In 1889, he became president, manager, and director of the Lincoln Savings and Safe Deposit Company (New England family members predominated as the bank's capital stockholders). As a teenager, Henry and Lillie's nephew Dan Wing began his banking career as a clerk and then a bookkeeper at the State National Bank, located under Henry's law office. When Silas Burnham became cashier of the American Exchange Bank (cashiers were high-level on-site bank managers), he hired Dan as his assistant cashier. Nathan Harwood, president of the Lincoln National Bank and another of Henry's close associates, was born in Michigan to Vermont emigrant parents, and after his first wife died he married Celia Harris. In the late 1880s, then, three men with New England roots, two of them Dartmouth graduates and all of them closely connected friends, held responsible positions at three Lincoln banks at the intersection of Eleventh and O Streets.[17]

The Lewises, like other genteel middle-class residents of the capital city, defined themselves socially and culturally by joining clubs and associations. In 1888, Henry Lewis, Mary Wing, Nathan Harwood, Sarah Harris, and Charles Gere (publisher of the *Nebraska State Journal*) organized the Haydon Art Club, which arranged for the exhibition and purchase of artwork. The Lewises, Harrises, and Burnhams were also active in the Patriarchs, a club that organized social dances and provided dance instruction.[18]

In addition, Henry and Lillie each joined a gender-segregated study and discussion club. The young lawyer William Jennings Bryan arrived in Lincoln in 1887 and, in 1888, founded the Round Table, a club that became central to Henry Lewis's social and business networks. Lincoln was a Republican-dominated railroad town, but Democrats like Henry Lewis initially predominated in the Round Table—the only Republicans were Eben Chapin, Nathan Harwood, and Bryan's law partner, Adolphus Talbot. The club later further diversified politically, adding, among Republican members, Charles Gere and lawyer Charles Gates Dawes. At each meeting, one member read prepared remarks on an announced topic and then moderated the discussion. Topics ranged widely across philosophy, culture, and politics. Dawes, whose office was in the same building as Bryan's, had "a pleasant time" at his first Round Table meeting at Talbot's house in February 1890, at which Bryan led a discussion on "the proper sphere of state and individual activity." Sometimes the members' varied political and business commitments produced more heated discussions, especially when the club discussed monetary policy. Bryan was elected to Congress in 1891, and in January 1893, while he was in Washington, Nathan Harwood led a discussion at Dawes's house on the silver question—"the discussion waxed quite warm," Dawes observed in his diary, and they "all enjoyed it." In February 1893 at the Lewis house, Dawes "spoke very decidedly against the present outrageous and iniquitous system" of railroad freight. At a meeting in the "little dining room" of the Universalist parsonage, "W. J. Bryan introduced his startling 16 to 1 silver plan," the policy that would become central to his 1896 and 1900 presidential campaigns. He "was immediately attacked by every one present," the Reverend Chapin's wife recalled. "It was a lively meeting."[19]

Lillie Lewis devoted herself to the Lotos Club. Organized in 1880 as a Shakespeare study club, by the time Lillie and her sister Mary joined, the club had moved on to other topics. When they were studying ancient Egypt in 1890, Lillie read aloud from Lubke's account of the Temple of Luxor, and they decided to change their name from the Avon Club to the Lotos Club, retaining the name as they moved on to ancient Greece and beyond. With the exception of Sarah Butler Harris, the members of the Lotos Club in the 1890s were married women, the wives of business, professional, and university men. Many Lotos Club members, like Lillie Lewis, were married to Round Table men: Elizabeth Burnham (wife of Silas Burnham), Celia Harris Harwood, and Mariel Clapham Gere (wife of Charles Gere) all belonged to the Lotos Club. Flavia Canfield, wife of James Hulme Canfield, the university chancellor and a Round Table man, never joined the Lotos Club, but she frequently attended meetings as a guest.[20]

When the Lotos Club president addressed the assembled members in January 1893, she reflected on the "harvest of intellectual culture, unfaltering friendships and golden memories" the club fostered but also the "many changes and varied experiences in life, some sweet & some bitter" that had come "within [the club's] the charmed circle." For Lillie Lewis, the bitter included the death of her four-year-old son in April 1892 and the sweet the birth of two more daughters, one in 1893 and the other in 1894. Noting Lillie's absence in December 1894, the club secretary suggested Lillie was "no doubt instructing the baby girl whose arrival was on Thanksgiving day, in the duties and responsibilities of the Advanced Woman."[21]

Through the 1880s, the Universalist Society had continued to hold together a broad variety of Lincoln's religious misfits, including Unitarians, Christian Scientists, Ethical Culturalists, "advanced thinkers," and Theosophists. However, in 1891, the New England Unitarians, including the Lewises, departed. Sarah Curtis Thayer Weeks, married to the engineer for all Burlington lines west of the Missouri River, led the charge. Sarah (a Lotos Club member) criticized Reverend Chapin for using "the word 'God' instead of 'Good' & reading selections from the Bible instead of poems." The new Unitarian Society's constitution reflected this anti-theist position, proclaiming, "Our object is to study and practice religion as the law of love and duty for all mankind." Members were not required to subscribe to any "articles of faith or creed," but the constitution specified that three of the society's nine trustees must be "ladies." In 1892, the new society elected Henry Lewis its president. Lillie served on the executive committee of the society's discussion club, the Unity Club, of which Nathan Harwood was president. The Lewises' affiliation with this short-lived congregation testifies to how Unitarianism tied them to their New England roots and marked them as intellectual and cultural progressives.[22]

Henry also took great pride in his Dartmouth education and was self-consciously literary. He sprinkled his letters with Latin phrases and delighted in listening to his nephew Dan Wing's Latin and Greek recitations. He read both classics in the English-language tradition (for example, leading a discussion of Nathaniel Hawthorne's *The Marble Faun* at his church) and kept up with modern literature: when he and Homer took a steamboat trip to New Orleans in 1885 to cure their persistent cases of bronchitis, he reported regularly to his wife on his reading in national literary magazines, including the *Century*. Henry also read aloud to his children every night from an anthology of poems and songs edited by William Cullen Bryant and used a primer to teach his daughter Edith to read when she was four years old. She long remembered his "musical voice" when he read aloud and felt "so grateful" to him "for having encouraged [her] in the taste for reading while [she] was quite little."[23]

Even before Henry and Lillie's children were old enough to enroll at the state university, it was central to their family life. The university-associated School of Fine Arts drew middle-aged women seeking culture. Lillie Lewis and Sarah Harris studied art history together there in 1888–89, and in the early 1890s, Lillie also enrolled as a "special student" in classes at the university proper. At its founding the university opened a Latin School, where rural students made up courses necessary for university admission—Willa Cather was required to study there during the 1890–91 academic year before being admitted to the university course. Many in Lincoln opted to enroll their children there as well rather than at Lincoln High. In the late 1880s and early 1890s, Edith Lewis's cousins Alice and Bessie Wing and Gilbert Lewis were enrolled there. Alice and Bessie progressed to the university course, but Gilbert, placed in the same Latin School class as Willa Cather, instead went east to enroll at MIT after only a short time in the university course.[24]

As a young girl, Edith Lewis was deeply embedded in the educational and social networks of her extended family. She began studying violin at the School of Fine Arts at age seven, adding drawing to her studies at eleven. Mirroring the club-centered and public-minded activities of her parents, she was among a group of "little girls in East Lincoln" who founded the Dorcas Club in the fall of 1893. They made pen wipers, needle cushions, and doilies, which they sold to raise money for charity. Her parents were prominent society hosts. "As entertainers Mr. and Mrs. Henry E. Lewis have but few equals" the *Lincoln Courier* reported when her father brought the national Psi Upsilon alumni meeting to Lincoln in 1891; the Lewises hosted a "most elegant" reception "at their hospitable home on Twenty-seventh street." The *Courier* accorded the same prominence to children's parties, reporting later in 1891 that the "beautiful home of Mrs. H. E. Lewis at Twenty-seventh and N streets was thrown open . . . to a large and merry gathering of children." "Edith, Margaret, Harold and Frederick Lewis proved delightful entertainers," providing a "delightful evening" for nearly sixty guests, including their Lewis cousins, the Weeks and Burnham children, and Dorothy Canfield (James and Flavia Canfield's daughter and Edith's fellow violin student at the School of Fine Arts). Henry Lewis began serving on the school board in 1892, and in 1894, Edith graduated from the sizable and recently built Elliott Elementary School around the corner from their house. She performed a violin solo at her graduation, "indicative of much musical talent for a performer so young."[25]

Panic, Drought, and Grand Schemes: Henry Lewis Looks West

The year before Edith Lewis graduated from elementary school marked a crucial turning point for her family. On January 23, 1893, Dan Wing roused Charles Dawes from his sleep at 6 a.m. to inform him that the Capital National Bank had failed. This failure, which sent shock waves through Lincoln and resulted in criminal prosecution of its officers, preceded and was unrelated to the national financial panic that erupted soon after. In December 1893, Henry Lewis resigned as president of Lincoln Savings Bank to focus on the newly formed Merchants Trust Company, yet another enterprise designed to draw eastern investment dollars to Nebraska. As secretary, treasurer, and "western manager," Henry hired Tom Wing, then studying law at the university, as his clerk, while Frank Lewis moved his family to Massachusetts to serve there as president of the company and its "eastern manager." The Merchants Trust Company limped along for a few years, but Henry's timing was bad—1893 was the worst possible time to start such a company. The extreme drought that gripped the state in 1894 intensified the effects of the national panic, halting growth and feeding the populist revolt that launched Henry's friend William Jennings Bryan into national prominence. In October 1894, Henry accepted an appointment as receiver for the First National Bank of Kearney and soon accepted a second receiver appointment when another Kearney bank failed. These receiverships were plum political appointments during difficult times, facilitated, perhaps, by Bryan or Dawes, then both in Washington.[26]

In the early 1880s, Kearney's residents had great hopes for their small city, which was 140 miles west of Lincoln and halfway between Boston and San Francisco on major rail lines. Water diverted from the nearby Platte River to the Kearney Canal generated electric power and was supposed to transform the city into an industrial powerhouse after the fashion of New England mill towns. Investment capital poured in, and new residents built grand houses and spent lavishly. The "Kearney Bubble" burst in the late 1880s, leaving whole swaths of houses standing empty, and the national financial panic only intensified the effects of this earlier crash.[27]

At first Henry traveled alone back and forth to Kearney by train, leaving Lillie and the children in Lincoln. In February 1895, however, after Lillie gave birth to their last child (a daughter), Henry brought Lillie to visit Kearney, and she and the children soon joined him there. The Lewises did not sell their house in Lincoln—they could rent in Kearney for very little—but they withdrew Harold and Edith from the Latin School and enrolled them in Kearney High, while they enrolled Margaret in elementary school in Kearney. "Little Edith Lewis" took her violin with her, performing solos at the 1895 Kearney High School Arbor Day observance and at a music recital in the Masonic Hall in January 1896, where her performance of Robert Schumann's "Traumerei" "got a hearty encore."[28]

In the fall of 1896, even though the affairs of the two Kearney banks had not yet been brought to a close, the Lewis family and their household goods returned to Lincoln. Edith resumed her studies at the Fine Arts and the Latin schools, and Harold enrolled in the university course. Lillie's sister Mary Wing had died the year before in Lincoln. During her final days, Lillie came in from Kearney and Ellen, their unmarried sister, came in from Davenport to be at her side. Widower George Wing and the Wing children remained in Lincoln—Alice and Bessie were teachers, Tom was nearly done with law school, and Dan was still an assistant cashier at Silas Burnham's bank, where George was a bookkeeper.[29]

While Lillie and her children reimmersed themselves in the educational and social worlds of Lincoln, Henry was developing a new business in central Nebraska. The 1894 drought made a mockery of the theory that rain would follow the plow when farmers broke up the prairie sod, and drought had also made Nebraska farm mortgages less appealing to eastern investors. Raised on a farm, Henry saw the business potential of irrigation as a strategy for surmounting the challenges of farming in Nebraska's semi-arid climate. In February 1896, before the family left Kearney, he filed articles of incorporation for the Farmers Union Ditch Company, its stated purpose "the purchase, construction and operation of canals and other works for irrigation and water power purposes in Buffalo and Dawson counties." It was a capitalized private corporation, not the cooperative enterprise its name implied, and three men Henry met in Kearney, including the man who had been president of the failed Kearney Canal Company and an original stockholder of one of the failed banks of which Henry was receiver, joined him as officers. After Henry's wife and children moved back to Lincoln, he traveled regularly to Kearney to attend to his bank receiver duties and farther west to Elm

Creek, in Dawson County near the border with Buffalo County, where his new company acquired and began making improvements to an existing irrigation canal.[30]

Henry kept up a convincing show of prosperity for his friends and former, current, or future business partners and investors. For example, he threw a series of whist parties in Lincoln to introduce one of his Kearney business partners and his wife to his Lincoln social and business connections. In actuality, however, Henry and his family were living on borrowed money. In 1895, Henry and Lillie subdivided their large Twenty-Seventh Street lot and sold the undeveloped half, and around the same time they stopped paying their county real estate taxes on the property. Lancaster County advertised the house and lot for sale, but no bids were received and the county sold the tax indebtedness to investors. By early 1898, Henry had "nearly cleared up the bank properties" in Kearney, but he traveled so frequently between Lincoln, Kearney, and Elm Creek that he spent most of his time on trains and in hotels. After the Elm Creek irrigation canal finally began operating in 1898, he spent most of the growing season there. Nevertheless, he continued to appear regularly in Lincoln to meet his social and philanthropic obligations.[31]

The Unitarian Society the Lewises helped establish in 1891 quietly disappeared by the end of 1892, and its members, including the Lewises, rejoined the Universalists, who dedicated a substantial new building in January 1893. In 1896, when the economy was still weak and the church was tottering under construction debt, Reverend Chapin left to teach at a seminary in Illinois. In 1898, after the congregation had limped along for two years and the national Universalist Association failed to provide the financial assistance needed to prevent foreclosure, the American Unitarian Association stepped in, and All Souls Unitarian Church of Lincoln was born. Although the church's constitution required no "articles of faith or creed as a test of fellowship," it accommodated the remaining Universalists by hewing closer to the middle theologically: All Souls both "accept[ed] the religion of Jesus" and defined "Our Faith" as "The Fatherhood of God. The Brotherhood of Man. The Leadership of Jesus. Salvation by Character. Progress of Man Onward and Upward Forever." Lillie Lewis took charge of the church's Post Office Mission and oversaw many of its social events, but Henry, broke and traveling constantly, assumed no leadership role.[32]

Lillie had resigned from the Lotos Club when she moved to Kearney, but in 1897, she was reappointed as a member. The club increasingly focused on social issues. Lillie invited a non-club member to present a talk titled "Ventilation and Sanitation in the Public Schools," and she reviewed and led a discussion of Charlotte Perkins Gilman's *The Home, Its Work and Its Influence* (in which Gilman advocated for the collectivization of housework). Lillie also led the club in its response to the YWCA's request for support in outfitting a room for "poorer girls" who might reside temporarily at the Y. The Lotos Club proclaimed itself to be in sympathy with this particular project but objected to the YWCA's Evangelical Test for full membership. Although local Ys had considerable autonomy in interpreting the meaning of "evangelical" in vetting members, Unitarians (along with Jews) were clear targets for exclusion. Lillie was a member of the Lotos Club committee that drafted a resolution criticizing the Evangelical Test as "unChristlike in its spirit of limit[ing] the scope of the work, which might be done in this city." Like her female Quaker ancestors, Lillie Lewis was a force to be reckoned with.[33]

Edith Lewis: Adolescent Voice and Agency in a Midwestern City

On the family's return from Kearney, Edith Lewis's voice and agency as a privileged adolescent emerged; she was able to enjoy this sense of privilege, it seems, because her parents shielded their children from knowledge of the family's financial precarity. Like many teenagers, she both embraced and rebelled against her family, particularly her oft-absent father. At age fifteen she sought to impress him by memorizing the choruses of his favorite poem, Algernon Charles Swinburne's verse drama *Atalanta in Calydon*. Also at fifteen she was founding president of the Lincoln chapter of the Children of the Revolution, commemorating her father's descent from a Revolutionary War veteran (her mother's Quaker ancestors did not fight). In the spring of 1898, Edith added college-level classes to her prep classes and was initiated into the Delta Gamma sorority (Figure 1.2), which her cousins Alice and Bessie Wing had helped found. By doing so, she was following in her mother's clubwoman footsteps. The sorority swept her up into a whirl of Valentine, chafing dish, and lawn parties, and "at homes," trolley rides, and chartered train journeys. Some events were only for Delta Gammas but many were joint with fraternities.[34]

One of her 1898 college-level courses was theme-writing. In the late nineteenth century, such courses covered a range of modes and genres, not just

Figure 1.2 The Delta Gamma Sorority from the 1899 University of Nebraska yearbook. Edith Lewis is in the front row, far right. Courtesy Archives and Special Collections, University of Nebraska–Lincoln Libraries.

persuasive or expository essays, and by writing fiction, Edith rebelled against the values of the insulated, privileged world her parents created for her. From June through December 1898, when she was sixteen, she published a dozen stories and sketches in the *Lincoln Courier*, of which Sarah Harris had taken control in 1895. She precociously ranged across subject matter within and beyond her experience, and these stories reveal her literary ambition and her desire to escape her conventional midwestern life.[35]

Lewis initially focused on her home region, the Great Plains. In "Sunflower," her first story, she adapted the legend of a Plains Indian girl betrothed to the sun. "Anne," her second story, is a grim regional tale in the manner of Hamlin Garland. In it, "Miss Selina North" meets the seventeen-year-old title character on the train and urges her to return to her family's farm rather than seek her fortune in the city. Anne refutes Selina's romantic notion that leaving the farm is a loss. "That's not my West," she explains. "It's the West you rich people, you educated people h'v found. My West has been ignorance and misery. I'm only leaving it until our West c'n be th' same. Then I'll come back." Lewis then shifted her focus to city life. In "The Story of Pansy," her protagonist is a tenement-dwelling criminal waif. In "A Sacrifice," Sara Brenner is the daughter of a millionaire father who has chosen to live in a tenement apartment and write for a small labor newspaper. Sara's brother, repulsed by her socialism, pleads with her to return to the family. He concedes that her writing is good and asks whether she might write for the "capitalist papers," a suggestion to which she responds "passionately," "Not as long as anybody's starving. Not as long as people work twelve hours in sweat shops, and the little children grow up ignorant."[36]

Sarah Harris paid for some of Lewis's contributions with railroad passes from her brother, who was president of the Burlington Railroad. In late July 1898, Lewis traveled by train to the resort town of Evergreen, Colorado, west of Denver, and on her return the *Courier* published "Mountain Echoes," a two-part travel sketch in a starkly different regional mode than "Anne." In part 1, the genteel tourist narrator and her friend take a stage coach to "Clearmount," where they enjoy a country dance with quaint locals. In part 2, they awake early to see a Rocky Mountain sunrise and get caught in a mountain storm. Lewis's next three stories were brief vignettes. In "Virginia" the narrator recounts a night when the alluring title character draws him—or her (the narrator's gender is not specified)—out on a rainy spring night. In "The Runaways" young Dick lures his little sister Meggie out on a moonlit ramble, which ends with their father finding them asleep, "curled up like kittens." In "A Sketch," "the Philosopher," who is rambling along rainy city streets at night, looks through a window at a large happy family eating dinner until the mother turns off the gaslights and the scene vanishes.[37]

Edith Lewis's desire for escape from her tame conventional life is especially clear in her last three stories published in 1898, all of which focus on art and artists and Bohemian life. French author Henri Murger popularized the ideal of *la vie bohème* in 1840s Paris, and Bohemianism became the subject of countless poems and works of fiction in the late-nineteenth-century United States. As Joanna Levin explains in *Bohemia in America*, the American embrace of Bohemianism was sometimes paradoxical. All things "Bohemian" were "the obverse of the disciplined, well-regulated bourgeois," and yet in "even the most decorous bourgeois drawing rooms" one heard recitations of a John Boyle O'Reilly poem that celebrated the pure and oppositional character of Bohemianism. The poem begins with the line "I'd rather live in Bohemia than any other land." That Lewis published her Bohemian tales in a weekly Lincoln society paper edited by a friend of her parents epitomizes this paradox.[38]

Her first Bohemian story, "The Portrait She Painted," resembles artist tales by Nathaniel Hawthorne and Henry James, although Lewis shifted the fictional dynamics by making a female portrait painter her protagonist. Mr. Phillips sends the actress Evalyn Pennington to the dirty, dreary Paris studio of Selina Rathe, his childhood friend from Illinois. In the portrait Selina paints of Evalyn, she "contrived to make a face at once so beautiful and so unattractive," revealing "every plebeian tendency, and every ignoble possibility, and every unlovely trait of the other's nature" in "glowing color." When Evalyn protests that she doesn't "quite like the expression," Selina responds, "But it isn't for you—it's for him." "Rhoda Inconsistent" presents "two girls of limited means, who, while comfortable enough, found themselves constantly subjected to such trials as the necessity of hard work, of shabby clothes, of few luxuries, of many annoyances." In the story's opening vignette, Rhoda wishes to "be rich," but Winnie argues that as "imaginative people" it is more interesting for them to be poor. Rhoda then changes her position, saying she would be "perfectly happy" if she had "a pair of bronze boots, and a lace shawl, and a large box of macaroons, and a book called Leaves From the Life of Good for Nothing, translated from the German." In the second half of the story, Winnie returns with everything Rhoda asked for, having sold her ruby ring to finance the purchases. Rhoda sighs as she looks up from the book she asked for (a fictional memoir of the protagonist's loves and wanderings by the German Romantic author Joseph von Eichendorff), saying she now wants "Nothing" and "feel[s] stupid." The story closes with Winnie murmuring under her breath, "Nous somes [sic] comme tous le autres" (we are like all the others).[39]

In December 1898, as Lewis's seventeenth birthday approached, her story "Bohemia," in which she embraced all of the standard tropes of Bohemian fiction, appeared in the Courier. In this story, a mixed-gender group of American artists in Paris drink and sing to Louis's mandolin in the alcove of one of their studios. Because "Precious" (in quotation marks) is about to return to America to become a lawyer, Viola declares they will "have a trial" of "Precious's" life. They contrast their lives in Paris ("We make the most of life. We paint when the sun shines, and sing when it rain falls, and if we're poor, we're free. . . . We're a shabby, out-at-the-elbows lot, but we know the beautiful!") to the stultifying life he will lead back home as a "white sheep" pining for the artist's life he abandoned. After each of his friends proclaims her or his determination to remain in Paris, "Precious" abandons his plan to abandon Bohemia. The story affirms the group's choice of joyful poverty and a commitment to art over bourgeois (and pointedly midwestern) respectability.[40]

Nebraska Moves to New England: Edith Lewis
at Smith College

In the late 1890s, Willa Cather lived in Pittsburgh but was nevertheless a regular contributor to the *Lincoln Courier*. During most of the seven months Lewis's stories appeared in the *Courier*, Cather was on hiatus from writing her "Passing Show" column, but she resumed the week before Lewis's "Bohemia" appeared. Cather probably read Lewis's story, but even if she did not, the two women were publishing in the same venue, and both were writing stories about the West and the lives of artists. The stage was almost set for their 1903 meeting in Sarah Harris's living room. But first, Edith Lewis would complete one more semester (spring 1899) at the University of Nebraska before going east to finish her degree.

Like most western land grant universities founded after the Civil War, the University of Nebraska was coeducational from the start. However, private colleges in the East founded before the war, including Dartmouth, alma mater of Edith Lewis's father and uncles, remained closed to women. Smith College was founded in Northampton, Massachusetts, in 1871 in order to offer a rigorous college course to women. Leaving the University of Nebraska for Smith in 1899 both decisively changed Lewis's life and confirmed her already-deep New England connections.[41]

Edith had been to New England at least once before enrolling at Smith. In the summer of 1890, Henry had taken the children to Maine on holiday, while Lillie went to a resort town in Michigan with Sarah Harris. New England friends and family also often visited the Lewises in Lincoln. Most notably, Mary Delia Lewis, daughter of Henry's brother Arthur, visited Lincoln and Kearney in 1896. Raised in Worcester, Mary graduated from Smith in 1894 and at the time of her visit was on holiday from teaching English in Connecticut. In addition to meeting this one Smith graduate from her own family and another who was a member of her mother's Lotos Club, Edith likely encountered the "Smith College girl" in popular culture. For example, "Three Freshman" began appearing serially in the *St. Nicholas* children's magazine when Edith was enrolled at Kearney High. Even without the New England family connections, Lewis was not an anomaly as a "western" student at Smith. At its founding the college drew students mostly from New England, but by 1898, it had enrolled 1,104 students from thirty states and four foreign countries. Jessie Anderson, the Smith College graduate who wrote "The Free Freshman," made the geographic range of incoming students her organizing conceit: the titular characters are from Boston, Chicago, and a Virginia plantation.[42]

Sending a daughter east to college was an expensive status symbol for Henry and Lillie Lewis, as it was for the fictional Chicago family that sends a daughter to Smith in "Three Freshman." Students at the University of Nebraska paid a $5 matriculation fee when they enrolled and a $5 diploma fee when they graduated but no tuition in between. The university offered no campus housing to students but advised them that the average cost of room and board in town was $175 a year. When Edith was studying there, her parents thus incurred only the nominal expense of having her continue to live at home. In contrast, tuition at Smith for 1899–1900 was $100 a year, and room and board in a college house was $300. Edith's attendance accrued to Henry and Lillie's social status, but Smith was also an attractive target for Edith as an aspiring young author. As widely reported in 1898 and noted in the University of Nebraska student newspaper, the *Century Magazine* awarded all three of its prizes for the best works by 1897 college graduates to eastern women's college graduates: the essay and story prizes went to Vassar graduates and the poetry prize to Anna Hempstead Branch, a Smith graduate.[43]

In April 1899, thirteen-year-old Margaret, Edith's sister closest to her in age, died of meningitis. If Henry and Lillie had any anxiety about sending seventeen-year-old Edith to college so far away, Margaret's death would have increased it. Nevertheless, in June 1899, Henry and Lillie took their two younger daughters to Kearney and then to Elm Creek so Henry could attend to the Farmers Union Ditch (Harold soon joined them to help his father), but they left Edith behind in Lincoln to prepare for her journey east. Edith's cousin Tom Wing was established as a Wall Street lawyer, and later that summer he was enlisted to escort Edith on her eastward journey. "Miss Lewis will enter Smith College this fall," Sarah Harris's *Courier* explained in a report of her early August departure, "and will not return to her home for a year."[44]

Because the academic year did not begin until September 21, Edith had time to explore New York and New England before settling in at Smith. She probably did so only under family supervision, but there were many Lewis and Gould family members who could step in. Some relatives of her parents' generation and older had never left New England, and Lincoln cousins other than Tom Wing had also migrated east. Through his friendship with Charles Dawes and his work for the Republican Party, Tom's brother Dan had secured a plum political appointment as receiver of two failed Boston banks and would soon be a bank president there. Two of Frank Lewis's children were also in the Boston area: MIT-educated Gilbert was doing postgraduate work at Harvard, where he had earned his Ph.D., while Roger was still living at home and attending high school in suburban Boston.[45]

Once Edith arrived on the Smith campus, the college's architecture invited her to think of herself as surrounded by family. Rather than constructing a central seminary-style building or large dormitories, the college had opted to build smaller "houses." As the college circular advertised:

> It is the wish of the Trustees to combine, as far as possible, the advantages of a literary community, in which young women may have the best intellectual discipline, with the culture of refined and well-ordered homes. To this end twelve dwelling houses have already been provided. Each household is organized, as far as possible, like a private family with its own parlors, dining-room and kitchen, and is presided over by a lady who directs its social and domestic life.

Rapid enrollment growth made this vision a fantasy for many students, however. In 1899, fewer than half of enrolled students were accommodated in the houses, and even those whose families paid a deposit several years in advance to secure a room in a preferred house had to board in town the first year. Notably, Edith was immediately accommodated in Hatfield House, where her cousin Mary Delia had lived (Figure 1.3). Clearly, Henry and Lillie had entered her for enrollment years before, and the University of Nebraska had merely kept her occupied until she was old enough to travel so far from home.[46]

Hatfield, one of the smaller houses, was situated at the center of campus. Built in 1877 and expanded in 1894, it accommodated twenty-five students in the fall of 1899. Like the other college houses, it had its own dining room, where students took their meals under the watchful eyes both of the "lady" assigned to the house and of a female faculty member in residence. Jeanette Shew Garrison, a widow whose son had recently graduated from Yale, was the "lady" at Hatfield. Born in New York State, in Michigan she married a Civil War veteran and followed him to Ohio and then to ranches in Colorado and Texas. If Edith Lewis experienced homesickness, she may have found comfort in having a western woman in charge.[47]

Figure 1.3 Hatfield House, the Smith College student residence where Edith Lewis lived from 1899 to 1902. Photograph circa 1891. Courtesy Smith College Archives.

Like her cousin Mary, Edith would come strongly under the influence of English professor Mary Augusta Jordan, who was the Hatfield faculty resident. Smith president L. Clark Seelye had recruited Jordan away from Vassar, where she earned her B.A. and M.A. Like Smith as an institution, Jordan mixed conservatism and progressivism. In an 1892 *Atlantic Monthly* essay, she proclaimed that "the student's mind is a republic of powers, not a receiving vault," and she credited women's colleges with having "revolutionized the intellectual training of women without making them invalids or bluestockings. It has made them wiser and happier." When she retired in 1921, she contrasted her own vision of the classroom to that propounded in novels like *Tom Brown's School Days*: "The classroom was not a morgue or a machine shop nor a factory. The students were not enemies nor cases, but very much alive and observing." She enacted this philosophy in her rhetoric and writing classes by urging her students to take stances on public questions, but she also actively opposed women's suffrage. Jordan inspired deep respect and passionate devotion from generations of Smith students, especially those who aspired to write. Jordan had a particular reputation for

drawing out reserved students. "She was the friend of all outstanding personalities," wrote Edith Kellogg Dunton (class of 1897 and an author of children's
and young adult fiction), "but she meant even more, perhaps, to the shy,
aloof, undeveloped girls, whose ambitions she shrewdly guessed, whose ti-
midity she infused with confidence, and whose share in the pleasures and
honors of student life came wholly in many cases from the influence of Miss
Jordan's suggestions."[48]

Lewis was assigned a sophomore student, Achsah Leona Barlow of New
Haven, Connecticut, as a roommate (Figure 1.4). Their New England and

Figure 1.4 Achsah Barlow, Edith Lewis's 1899–1900 roommate and then
lifelong friend. Courtesy Smith College Archives.

western pairing replicated the Chicago-Boston roommate assignment in "Three Freshman," which was set in Hatfield House. Barlow had already lived in Hatfield for a year and would become Lewis's lifelong friend. Through her mother, who died when she was a child, Barlow was descended from the Pilgrims. In contrast, her father had immigrated to the U.S. from England as a small child and began his working life as a laborer in a gun factory. He ultimately achieved sufficient prosperity as a hardware manufacturer to send all three of his daughters to Smith: Alpha had graduated in 1896 and Lola in 1899.[49]

Of the twenty-five young women living in Hatfield in 1899–1900, most were from New England and New York State, reflecting the overall makeup of the student body; however, one first-year student was from Chicago, two juniors were from San Francisco, and one junior was from Florida. In Lewis's remaining two years in Hatfield, students from Indiana, Wisconsin, Minnesota, Oregon, Colorado, California, Ohio, Kansas, and Illinois would also live there. Even as a "western girl" Lewis was connected to New Englanders in Hatfield House. Senior Harriet Goodwin was from the same town in Vermont where Henry Lewis's sister Ellen and her husband farmed, and sophomore Susan Dow Smith's father graduated from Dartmouth the same year as Henry. Other students also came from mobile region-crossing families. For example, Lucy Southworth Wicker, who moved into Hatfield in January 1900, was born in Chicago to a Vermonter father who went west with the railroad and married the daughter of the governor of Illinois. By the late 1890s, Lucy's mother had died and her father was a railroad executive in New York City.[50]

The Smith College administration was intent on shaping students into "intelligent gentlewomen," and faculty members were preoccupied with curricular matters. On their part, Smith students wrested control from authority and created something they called "college life" and identified themselves as "college girls." At Smith, Edith Lewis became a significantly different kind of college girl than she had been during her last year in Lincoln. There, she lived at home with her parents and four siblings (until Margaret's death reduced the number to three), commuted to the University of Nebraska's nonresidential campus, and participated in a nonresidential sorority that often paired itself for social activities (like a Valentine's dance) with a fraternity. At Smith she lived in a college house with twenty-four other female students and two adult women and became part of a social world centered almost entirely on women.[51]

As Ada Comstock, an 1897 graduate who entered Smith after studying for two years at the University of Minnesota in her home state, later recalled:

> The thing that impressed me at Smith when I went there was the fact that there were so many girls gathered together in the dormitories, all accessible. I had this great sense of richness of girl companions at Smith as compared with the University where we were scattered about. I remember when I was in my first year at Smith, I used to think sometimes at night when I was opening my window, "Now there are all these hundreds of girls here, so many that one would like to make intimate friends of and could by a little effort." There seemed to me a great richness in female companionship.

Smith students fostered this intimacy and companionship through formal and informal student-directed activities. Sophomores staged a "freshman frolic" for new students—as with all dances on the Smith campus save the Junior Promenade, only women attended, taking each other as dance partners. Nearly all students took part in some form of dramatics, from brief farces performed in the houses after dinner and at club meetings to fully staged performances in the gymnasium sponsored by houses and the senior Shakespeare play performed during commencement weekend. Women performed all roles, cross-dressing to play men. "Spreads" of food in student rooms, whether shared boxes of treats from home or food cooked over spirit lamps and in chafing dishes, were the most popular focus of informal socializing. In this all-female social world, students formed crushes on other students, called "smashes." Some were beginning to find these intense emotional relationships between young women concerning in light of changing social mores and understandings of female sexuality, but they were still common during Lewis's Smith years.[52]

Before Lewis could enter into this social whirl, college authorities had to certify her academically and physically. In the *Smith College Circular* published before her arrival, she was listed as a first-year student. However, through her coursework at the University of Nebraska and its Latin School, she had met all of the entrance requirements and was awarded transfer credit for required courses in English literature, theme-writing, the theory of rhetoric, Latin, and French. As a result, she was placed in the sophomore class. In 1899, Smith students could choose between three courses of study: the classical course (the B.A. degree), which required competency in Greek and Latin; the letters course (B.L.), which substituted a modern language for classical languages; or the scientific course (B.S.). Lewis chose the challenging classical course, the original plan designed to emulate the curricula of the men's colleges.[53]

Women's colleges felt intense pressure to prove that higher education did not harm the health and reproductive potential of their students. To make the case that college study didn't harm them, Smith College required two physical exams, one on entry and the other junior year, the data from which was subjected to anthropometric analysis. Lewis would have been asked to strip down to the skin and don something akin to a hospital gown so that her height, weight, girth, chest, length of waist, arm span, capacity and strength of lungs, eyesight, hearing, and eye and hair color could be charted. The report from Lewis's exam did not survive, but her new roommate described her eyes as "hazel-brown" and her hair as "brown curls." The examiner also judged each student's temperament and asked her to report the nationality of her parents and grandparents, her father's occupation, and hereditary diseases in her family. On the basis of this examination, Lewis would have been assigned to regular or remedial physical education. All students took two years of physical training and needed a regulation gym suit, consisting of a loose blouse and bloomer-style trousers. Provided instructions for its manufacture, Lewis would have either sent them home to her mother or sought a dressmaker in town. Smith students found gym suits liberating but were not permitted to wear them off campus. Posed for formal pictures, they wore dresses, but they normally fashioned themselves as Gibson girls, wearing shirtwaists with ties and skirts shortened several inches from the floor to allow them to stride freely across campus.[54]

In her first year at Smith, Lewis merged what would normally have been required first- and second-year coursework. Smith had affiliated schools of art and music, but violin instruction was not offered. Lewis thus passed up elective music study to focus entirely on required academic courses. In her first semester she began required yearlong courses in mathematics, science (she chose chemistry, offered in a brand-new "nearly fireproof" building equipped with the most modern scientific apparatus), Greek (given credit for one semester of Latin, she needed only the second required semester of Latin), and biblical literature, a course that she and Barlow delighted in skipping together. Lewis also took a required semester-long course in "fortnightly themes" ("papers written by the students, discussed and criticized by class and teacher") taught by a newly hired assistant in English.[55]

None of Lewis's letters home to Nebraska survive, but she sent home one of her first-semester themes, which the *Courier* published in December 1899. In "The Friend in Letters," Lewis dissected the personal character of John Keats and Robert Louis Stevenson based on a reading of their published letters. Finding in Keats's letters both "extraordinary personal attractions" and "weaknesses, sublimities, extravagancies and unworldliness" of character, in Stevenson she found "the flawless expression of that warmth, that affectionate kindliness and fearless gayety which were his birthright." Lewis's analysis of Keats and Stevenson, two of Cather's favorite authors, appeared in the same issue of the *Courier* as Willa Cather's "Passing Show" column about opera singer Lillian Nordica. Lewis's first publication in the *Smith College Monthly*, a student-edited magazine, also appeared in December 1899. "Light o' Life," like some of Lewis's earlier *Courier* stories, suggests that she longed for the freedom of urban life. Her protagonist, Sara Cornish, has "left home, friends,—at any rate relations" to come to a "vast city," where she plans to find work and be "happy and free." She arrives in a hansom cab at what she thinks is her brother David's New York City studio, but it is the lodging of another man. Puzzled to find a beautiful young woman in his apartment, he seeks to rectify the mistake without frightening or embarrassing her.[56]

The second semester of her first year, Lewis finished her Latin requirement, took a required one-credit course in elocution (The Intellectual Element in Expression: Emphasis, Inflection, Phrasing), and, for the first time, took Mary Jordan's legendary English 13 class, which allowed for either "daily themes" or "topics requiring consecutive treatment." For generations, Smith students found Jordan's English 13 both challenging and exhilarating. "Her class-room conversation implied that she thought she was dealing with educated women," an 1894 graduate explained, "so that if we found ourselves falling short of her expectations, we felt impelled to make good immediately." Novelist Grace Kellogg (class of 1908) vividly recalled "Miss Jordan, standing, holding aloft in one hand, somebody's brain-child, scissoring the air with two fingers of the other hand, like Solomon waving his sword, the while a mysterious smile wreathes her lips and her delighted eyes dance impishly to and fro across our uneasy upturned faces." Jordan's pithy written comments both challenged and praised. She wrote on student themes "not merely 'Good,' nor merely 'Bad' . . . but 'Good enough to be better.'" She drew on the principles of classical rhetoric in English 13, but "everything" went into student writing for her, "[b]eauty in Crito and Horace, the discovery of Walter Pater, the Russian of 'War and Peace,' trips to Mt. Tom, music, college friendships." "Everything" also included every genre. In the 1970s, a 1901 graduate characterized English 13 in more modern terms as a "creative writing class" and recalled being "in seventh heaven" when Jordan wrote "Very nearly perfect" on blank verse she had submitted. "Above all," recalled Anna Hempstead Branch, Jordan "desired for us the privilege of growing in freedom" and had a "rare ability to discover, protect and inspire the creative instinct." Honing her craft as a fiction writer in English 13, Lewis thoroughly revised, expanded, and transformed "The Runaways," which had appeared in the *Lincoln Courier* in 1898, for publication in the *Smith College Monthly* in March 1900. She sent "The Proposal" back to Lincoln, where it appeared in the *Courier* in June. In this new story, a wealthy Englishman in San Francisco meets a nineteen-year-old widow with a son and proposes to adopt her to make her life comfortable.[57]

Lewis's academic performance her first year at Smith was solid but mostly undistinguished. In order to protect the delicate psyches of students and avoid unfeminine academic competition, students were not notified of their final course grades unless they were in danger of failing. The letter scale also inverted what we now think of as the norm: the highest grade was D ("peculiarly excellent"), the next C ("good"), then B ("fair"), and finally A ("merely passed"). Lewis received mostly Bs, although she "merely passed" her second semester of math and was "good" in her second semester of Bible. The notable exception was her one elective, English 13, in which Jordan judged her work "peculiarly excellent."[58]

Although Lewis left no visible traces of her first year at Smith beyond her transcript and short stories, she was doubtless a spectator at the greatest semi-public ritual of Smith student life, the freshman-sophomore basketball game. Senda Berenson, the director of physical training, had adapted the recently invented game for her female students, and the entire student body crammed into the gymnasium for the contest. The president, male faculty members, and visiting male family members were permitted to attend, but members of the general public were excluded because student athletes played in their gym costumes and student spectators filled the gym literally to the rafters, dangling their legs over the edge of the suspended running track. Berenson tolerated student chanting and singing before and after the game but repeatedly warned the students against unladylike cheering during play. As Josephine Dodge Daskam (class of 1898) described the atmosphere in *Smith College Stories* (1900), when the freshman team made a basket "the roar of delight from the freshman was literally deafening" and "it seemed . . . that the roof would surely drop." In Lewis's first year, Berenson added a competitive display of Swedish gymnastics and running by student teams from all four classes, and this competition attracted nearly the same level of spectatorship as the freshman-sophomore game. Lucy Wicker, Lewis's Hatfield housemate and a member of the 1902 basketball team, wrote her father with great enthusiasm about her class's "grand success" in the competitive gymnastics exhibition, for which her class "won the cup! You ought to have seen the rejoicing afterwards! Our girls carried . . . their captain, around the room on their shoulders, waving the cup wildly in the air, and everybody simply yelled herself hoarse."[59]

Around the time that the members of the class of 1902 were cheering loudly for their class captain at the gymnastics meet, Professor Jordan invoked the name of William Jennings Bryan, a western friend of Edith Lewis's father, in remarks at morning chapel. Chapel included prayers but was not strictly religious, and Jordan felt compelled in February 1900 to speak about U.S. policy in the Philippines, which Spain had ceded to the U.S. by the 1898 treaty ending the Spanish-American War. In early 1900, the U.S. was engaged in military conflict with Filipinos who opposed American rule. Jordan's remarks were prompted by an announcement that John Barrett, former U.S. minister to Siam (now Thailand) and staunch advocate of President McKinley's Philippine policy, would be the featured speaker at "Rally Day," a daylong celebration of George Washington's birthday. The Democratic National Convention was not until July 1900, but by February, Bryan was considered the presumptive Democratic presidential nominee, and the pillars of his political program were "'an unceasing warfare against all trusts,' the restoration of silver coinage at 16 to 1, and opposition to imperialism and militarism." Bryan and his supporters thus objected to the then-current U.S. policy in the Philippines. A dismayed Lucy Wicker wrote home to her father that "Miss Jordan gave us an informal address this morning after prayers, on the subject of the Philippines." Jordan told students that the U.S. war with Spain resulting in the acquisition of the Philippines was "begun by the trusts" and that "if Bryan is elected, as Miss Jordan hopes he will be, he will drop the free silver tactics and devote himself chiefly to putting down the trusts." After she "let off all the feelings" at chapel, Jordan had "kept [them] suppressed." Wicker, however, sought factual and rhetorical ammunition from her railroad executive father so she might argue against Jordan's position in a theme she planned to submit for Jordan's class.[60]

Having flourished in English 13 and having published two stories in the *Smith College Monthly*, Edith Lewis came to the attention the Phi Kappa Psi literary society toward the end of her second semester. Phi Kappa Psi and its rival, Alpha, were the only mutually exclusive clubs on campus—a student could belong to only one of the two. Through its regular member-only meetings, Phi Kappa Psi aimed to "help maintain a high grade of scholarship, especially along literary lines" among its members. Its annual "open-closed" meeting featured an invited speaker, and nonmembers could attend by invitation, giving the society a means to contribute "in a general way to the literary interests" of the college. Because Phi Kappa Psi was highly selective and aimed "to bring into more intimate and friendly relations girls who are congenial in aims and interests," it also functioned, in some respects, like a sorority on a campus that had none.[61]

Both of the literary societies elected members only after they had studied at Smith for two semesters, meaning all freshman were excluded, as was Lewis as a sophomore transfer student. In May of her first year at Smith, however, she was put forward for membership for the next year. Like other nominees, she was evaluated on general scholarship, literary ability, and general desirability; she was awarded a near-perfect score of 3.97 out of 4 points in literary ability. Phi Kappa Psi and Alpha alternated yearly as to which society made bids first, leading to intense strategizing behind the bidding process. Because this process went on in secret, Lewis finished her second semester not knowing, however, that she would be elected in the fall to this organization that would define her for her remaining two years at Smith.[62]

Perhaps Lewis went home to Nebraska in the summer of 1899, perhaps she did not. In any event, when she returned for her second year at Smith, she came into her own intellectually and socially. On September 29, 1900, the secretary and members of Phi Kappa Psi left their meeting with a list of newly elected members to deliver invitations in person. As Alice Fallows (class of 1897) described the "pretty ceremony" in an article in *Scribner's* magazine, the secretary knocked on the invitee's door, and "[s]uddenly the [student's] room is full of girls crowding about her with congratulations; an envelope is thrust into her hand, a society pin fastened on, and the vantage of one of her greatest desires is gained." Friends then deluged the new member with floral tributes, and she enjoyed a week of the "joys of fame and popularity," including recognition at morning chapel. Lewis's election to Phi Kappa Psi yet again testified to her New England ties: the society's secretary, who delivered the invitation to her room, was Ruth Hawthorne French, daughter of a New Hampshire lawyer who was Henry Lewis's Dartmouth classmate.[63]

A breathless report of Edith's election to Phi Kappa Psi soon appeared in the *Lincoln Courier*: "Miss Edith Lewis, now an undergraduate of Smith college has been elected to one of the two literary societies. She was one of the first three chosen and as very few out of the twelve hundred or more students can be chosen annually, Miss Lewis' selection is a very great tribute to her ability, scholarship and talent as well as to her capacity for making friends." When Lewis took the pledge at her first triweekly meeting on October 29, 1900, she claimed two prized tickets, one for herself and one for a nonmember friend, to the November 10 open-closed meeting, at which Dr. Edward Waldo Emerson lectured titled "Life and Character of Henry David Thoreau." Dr. Emerson was Ralph Waldo Emerson's son, and Thoreau had been his tutor and companion for a year. Ellen Tucker Emerson, a member of Phi Kappa Psi and president of the class of 1901, was Dr. Emerson's daughter.[64]

Not all of Lewis's social connections came through Phi Kappa Psi. Her second year she also acquired an important new friend with similar class and regional origins, Laura Jerauld Paxton, daughter of a Harvard-trained Indiana lawyer, who moved into Hatfield House in September 1900. Even though Lewis was no longer studying the violin, with Paxton she took the opportunity to hear the Kreisel Quartet play in College Hall, and they were delighted when the group played Dvorak's American Quartet. The two also enjoyed long walks together through the New England countryside. In 1899, Senda Berenson had instituted a new system of exercise cards designed to encourage outdoor recreation by junior and senior students after they completed their two years of Swedish gymnastics, but students needed little encouragement to ramble: they tramped not just on Mountain Day but year-round in all kinds of weather. A favorite walk was the six miles from Northampton to Hadley and back, which required crossing the Connecticut River. As Alice Fallows explained, when Smith student ramblers returned to Northampton from Hadley over the "beautiful Connecticut," "the purple 'meadows' lie spread out before them, with the river in the far distance, and the mountains rising sheer and straight from the level, they feel the fascination that will draw them again and again to those strange lowlands, till 'the meadows' have a personality of their own, and an inspiration for them that cannot fail while memory lasts." How different this landscape was (and is) from those of Indiana and Nebraska. Reading Lewis's *Willa Cather Living* half a century later elicited from Paxton an intense memory of place and companionship, of her many long rambles "over the meadows to Hadley" with Lewis.[65]

After completing their two years of required courses (which Lewis had done by the end of her first year at Smith), students were free to take electives. The college loosely directed them to elect a "connected" course of study, but there were no majors in the modern sense, and few disciplines required sequencing of courses. Little wonder, then, that Lewis did what others before her did and after her would do, "elect[] anything . . . that the Head of the English department [Mary Jordan] offered." In the first semester of her second year, Lewis elected two courses with Mary Jordan, English 9, Exposition in Oratory, Science, Philosophy, again earning the highest grade, and enrolled a second time in English 13, earning just below the highest grade. She also elected Principles of Sociology, taught by Charles Emerick of the Department of Economics and Sociology. Emerick "pushed students" in his classes "to consider capitalism as a cause of poverty and to seek solutions that included suffrage, eight-hour days, equal pay for equal work, and more equitable distribution of wealth." He judged Lewis's work "good." Students were required to take philosophy but in their junior year rather than in the first two years. Lewis thus enrolled in Philosophy 1 (Logic) in September 1900 and earned the highest grade.[66]

American women did not yet have the right to vote, so Smith students could not vote in the U.S. presidential election in the middle of the fall 1900 semester. The college nevertheless conducted a mock presidential election, in which William Jennings Bryan failed to oust the incumbent, William McKinley. Mary Jordan's outburst at chapel the previous semester had not been effective. Shortly after Bryan lost both the real and mock presidential elections, Lewis was elected to the Phi Kappa Psi Recommendations Committee, a position that made her a gatekeeper for society membership. Like other members, she attended triweekly closed meetings at which members read papers on selected subjects and staged brief plays. During her first semester as a member, German literature was their subject of study, and during her second, they studied the Turk's Head Club (a dining and literary society organized by eighteenth-century British author Samuel Johnson). Yet another artist story, which Lewis certainly wrote for Jordan in English 13 in the fall 1900 semester, appeared in the January 1901 Smith College Monthly. In "The Interloper," a wealthy young man has married "a concert-singer, a girl of the music-halls" (the interloper of the title) over the objections of his family. By the story's conclusion the child of his first marriage, which ended in divorce, has begun reconciling the music hall singer to motherhood and her father's family to his second wife.[67]

In Lewis's remaining three semesters, she consistently elected courses taught by Emerick and courses offered by the Philosophy Department. Second semester of her junior year, she took both Socialism and Social Reform and Some Sociological Problems: Causes of Degeneracy, the Treatment of Dependents and Delinquents, in which "particular attention" was given to the study of "organized charities." Emerick judged her work in these courses "peculiarly excellent." She earned the highest grade in Psychology, a course offered by the Philosophy Department covering "facts and principles of general psychology" (William James's *Principles of Psychology* was a central text). That semester the philosophy faculty recommended both her and Achsah Barlow for the departmental Philosophy Club, a "much-prized distinction" touted in the *Lincoln Courier* back in Nebraska. The spring semester of her junior year, Lewis again elected two courses with Mary Jordan, English 13 (for the third time) and English 9a, a course in debate, argument, and parliamentary procedure. She shared the classroom in English 9a with Helen and Ethel Chesnutt, daughters of fiction writer and legal stenographer Charles Chesnutt and the first self-identified black students enrolled at Smith.[68]

Between her junior and senior years, Lewis spent the summer at home in Lincoln. As usual, her father and her brother spent much of the summer in Elm Creek and Kearney attending to the Farmers Union Ditch, leaving Edith immersed in an urban social world run by women. She made an appearance at a Delta Gamma picnic and informal dance on July 1, and on July 31, her mother gave a farewell supper for Bessie Wing, who had been visiting and was about to return home to Massachusetts. On August 23, Henry and Lillie entertained sixty neighbors at a lawn party, their yard decorated and the tables placed under their shade trees in the Nebraska summer heat. Several days later, Lillie threw a five o'clock tea party for Edith, with the "table . . . set on the lawn" and enclosed in canvas to screen it from the street.[69]

Precisely how Henry and Lillie were paying for these lavish entertainments and their daughter's education is unclear. Very limited forms of scholarship aid were available to Smith students: the college made grants of $50 or $100 and the Student Aid Society made small interest-free loans. Henry and Lillie still weren't paying the property taxes on their house in Lincoln, and Henry was in default on several loans, including an April 1900 unsecured personal loan for $585 from an Omaha businessman. Perhaps he had taken out the loan to pay Edith's tuition, room, and board—in any event, he did not pay back the loan by October 1900 as promised.[70]

Nevertheless, Edith Lewis somehow returned to Northampton in September 1901 for her final year at Smith, where she again immersed herself in coursework offered by the English, Economics and Sociology, and Philosophy Departments, and in her literary society work. In the fall she took Principles of Economics with Charles Emerick, English 13 with Mary Jordan for the fourth time, Greek Philosophy with Norman Gardiner, and the first halves of two yearlong courses, American History from the Revolution through the Civil War with Charles Hazen and English 13a, Lectures on the Principles of Criticism.

Jordan normally taught the criticism course, but committee work had overwhelmed her and impaired her health, so Jennette Barbour Perry Lee took her place. Jennette Perry graduated from Smith in 1886 and immediately married Gerald Stanley Lee, then a student at Yale Divinity School. She taught at the secondary and college levels for several years before leaving teaching to pursue writing as a profession. She had no desire to return to teaching, but her husband's work had brought them to Northampton, the English Department was shorthanded due to faculty turnover, and in 1901, she was persuaded to step in, becoming the only married woman faculty member. While Lewis was studying criticism with her, Lee was associate editor of *The Critic* and a member of the *Atlantic Monthly*'s Contributors' Club, and Houghton Mifflin had just published her novel *The Pillar of Salt* and was about to publish her short story collection *Son of a Fiddler*.[71]

Certainly Lee's success as an author and critic would have attracted the attention of Lewis as an aspiring author. Lee, like Jordan, became a memorable teacher. A member of the class of 1908, who later trained as a painter and became an art critic, remembered Lee as

one of Smith's greatest teachers of all times. She had a curious way of germinating things in you. You never forgot all your life what she made us do. "Always look for quality." Sometimes she would give us two pieces of prose and say, "Now, which of these do you think has any enduring qualities?" It was that sort of stunt, but it was a great inspiration to me. . . . [S]he showed us how to search for the fundamental values and the creative essence in any work of art. It implies a standard . . . it also implies you have to have a sense of balance, a feeling that something works.

Prized positions on the editorial staff of the *Smith College Monthly* were reserved for seniors, and as an editor Lewis could have applied what she was
learning in Lee's class to vetting submissions from her classmates. She did
not, however, secure one of these plums. She did publish her first poem in
the *Monthly* in October 1901. In her Shakespearean sonnet, the speaker
juxtaposes the false and fatuous public fame and adulation she has received
with "the verdict" she sees in her beloved's eyes.[72]

Reelected her senior year to the Recommendations Committee of Phi
Kappa Psi, Lewis contributed to a noticeable shift in the society's membership
(Figure 1.5). In 1901, five of the twenty-three graduating senior members
were from "western" states (22 percent), while in 1902, nine of twenty-two
(40 percent) were: four were from St. Louis, two were from Nebraska, and
one each was from Kalamazoo, Michigan, suburban Chicago, Minneapolis,
and San Jose, California. Lewis herself was, of course, one of the Nebraska
graduating seniors, and the other was a graduate of Omaha High School, of
which Edith's Uncle Homer had been principal. Even a graduating senior

Figure 1.5 The Phi Kappa Psi literary society in the 1902 Smith College
yearbook. Edith Lewis is in the back row, fifth from the right (square nautical
collar and tie). Courtesy Smith College Archives.

from Passaic, New Jersey, was a Nebraskan in disguise: Amy Young and Faith Potter graduated from Omaha High together before Young's family moved east.[73]

Ruth French was elected Phi Kappa Psi president for the fall 1901 semester, and "some modern authors" was chosen as the study topic. The open-closed meeting for the academic year was supposed to feature Walter Wyckoff, a Princeton sociology professor known for his books about working his way across the country as a laborer after he graduated from Princeton. Canadian poet Bliss Carman stepped in when Wyckoff canceled, "read[ing] from his poems, some of which have been published in books and magazines, while others have never been given to the public. The latter fact at once established an intimacy between the poet and his hearers." A reception after the reading allowed faculty and members of Phi Kappa Psi to "meet[] Mr. Carman in a more personal way." Edith Grace Platt of Lake Forest, Illinois, was elected president for the spring semester, and Lewis replaced a member of the large St. Louis contingent as the "editor." Individual members read their own serious papers on the new topic of "commercialism in modern literature." In contrast, Lewis's job as editor was to assemble and read "a 'paper' . . . composed exclusively of original prose and verse by the members of the society— in a lighter vein than the critical papers on assigned subjects."[74]

In Lewis's final semester of academic work, she took the second semester of Lee's and Hazen's yearlong courses, theme-writing with Jordan for the fifth and last time, her fourth class with Charles Emerick (Economic Problems: The Tariff; Transportation; Money; Credit), and Modern Philosophy with Norman Gardiner ("the main lines of the development of modern philosophy, including detailed study of Kant's Prolegomena to any Future Metaphysics"). Regular meetings and distinguished public lectures sponsored by the Philosophy Club supplemented her philosophical studies. In the fall, J. E. Creighton of Cornell University had lectured on "Eighteenth and Nineteenth Century Modes of Thought," while in the spring, Josiah Royce of Harvard gave a lecture titled "Recent Discussions Concerning the Concept of the Infinite."[75]

Lewis's work in three different genres appeared in the Monthly during her final semester. First, in February 1902, her essay "College Independence" launched a stinging critique of her fellow students. Smith had recently established a college council made up of students, but it was merely advisory rather than allowing for true self-government. Lewis chided her fellow students who were calling for self-government because, in her estimation, their conduct demonstrated that they were not fit for it. She argued, "Governments, like individuals, are subject to the laws of evolution and natural selection, and when a community becomes so equipped, mentally and morally, as to merit and demand self-government, self-governed it will of necessity become." As evidence for her claim that Smith students were not yet "mentally and morally" equipped, she cited their reaction to Smith's literary societies:

> What is indicated by that "left-out feeling," so much discussed in reference to our literary societies, but a perverted and inefficient public sentiment? That most effective of all our weapons—healthy adverse criticism—is so far captive to a general timidity and suspicion that it forms not even a respectable opposition. It is safe to predict that if, for a single day, every student in college were to speak the truth, as she sees it, a social revolution would be accomplished.

She brought all of her curricular and extracurricular experiences at Smith to bear in this essay: Jordan's training in rhetoric, her study of history and sociology, and her authority as a member of the selection committee for Phi Kappa Psi.[76]

Lewis had not abandoned belles letters. In May 1902, she published a second Shakespearean sonnet in the *Monthly*, which tackles a theme similar to that of her first and typical of the genre: the despairing speaker's mind has been thrown into turmoil by the loss of public acclaim, but in the final couplet she finds "heaven" when her mind turns to rest on "thee." Her last story published in the *Monthly*, "Where Are You Going, Pretty Maid?," was her longest and most fully developed yet. In it, two wealthy young people deceive each other: a young London lawyer who has come over to America pretends to be a Bohemian artist, and Miss Crittendon, his American cousin and the lady of the manor, pretends to be Miss Crittendon's milkmaid. In the end, they are unmasked and their destined marriage is on the horizon.[77]

One final unpublished piece of writing, a mock lawsuit against classmate Rachel Berenson, gives a glimpse of Lewis's sharpness and wit and her participation in college life outside Phi Kappa Psi. The document is in Lewis's handwriting and was signed by all eight graduating seniors in Hatfield House. In it, Lewis demanded the return of the May 1902 issue of the *Century Magazine* that Berenson had removed from her Hatfield House room. Berenson, who lived in Lawrence House, was the youngest child of a remarkable Lithuanian Jewish immigrant family from Boston. Her sister

Senda, director of physical training at Smith, was a graduate of the Boston Normal School for Gymnastics, as was Bessie Berenson, who worked as one of Senda's assistants. Their brother Bernard, a Harvard-educated art critic and connoisseur, lived abroad and was advising his patron, Isabella Stewart Gardner, on purchases for her grand house in Boston. Rachel was a brilliant student of classical languages, who would go on to study classical Greek and archaeology at the American School of Classical Studies and earn an M.A. in classics from Harvard.[78]

In her mock lawsuit against Rachel Berenson, Edith Lewis, the daughter of a lawyer, commanded and parodically subverted the conventions of legal writing. She addressed Berenson as "a resident of the Rough House Alley, of the House of Lawrence" and playfully suggested that Berenson was the "proprietor of a certain notorious resort, called, in vulgar parlance, Rahar's Inn" (a Northampton dive bar with a dance floor still in operation in the late twentieth century). Lewis described herself as "a refined inmate of the House of Hatfield of eminent fame" and cited "conclusive testimony" that Berenson "did thence seize, convey away, and abscond with" the *Century Magazine* by "enter[ing] the abode" of Lewis "under false pretences" to take one of "their choicest possessions," which the "Seniors of the said Hatfield House" had purchased through "strenuous and long continued effort, and by means of conscriptions levied upon their by no means well-filled purses." Characterizing the theft as "abhorrent in the eyes of all right minded and respectable persons, and conducive to a general overturning of those fundamental principles which constitute the fabric of society," Lewis conveyed "unmitigated censure" on Berenson and demanded she return the magazine to her room, along with a "fine of <u>five cents</u> in the national currency of the realm."[79]

This feud was all in fun, but the *Century Magazine*, which represented the zenith of late-nineteenth-century literary culture and the return of which the Hatfield seniors demanded, hints at the serious literary ambitions of Lewis and her classmates. As mentioned earlier, for four years the magazine ran a contest seeking the best poem, story, and essay submitted by recent college graduates. The contest began with 1897 graduates and concluded with 1900 graduates. As mentioned earlier, in 1898, Anna Hempstead Branch had won the poetry prize for an 1897 graduate, and in January 1902, the magazine had published the works of winners who graduated in 1900. Because the contest had concluded, Lewis herself could not enter it, but the *Century* remained the sort of national magazine to which an ambitious college graduate might submit a poem or story. And unlike the *Atlantic Monthly*, which was published in staid old Boston, the *Century* was published in rising New York City.[80]

"The College Girl at Home": Edith Lewis Returns (Briefly) to Nebraska

When the Hatfield House seniors sued for the return of the *Century Magazine*, they were about to transition to postcollege life. In an informal talk subsequently reported in the May *Smith College Monthly* titled "The College Girl at Home," Julia Caverno, a Smith graduate and classics professor, counseled graduating students not to think it "a crime for a girl to be depending upon her parents" as long as she was not a burden. "The college girl will find enough to do at home," especially in "small towns," where she could engage in "philanthropic work outside of the settlement work" of larger cities. Caverno recognized potential friction between college girls and their mothers but advised returning students to submit to maternal authority even though in college they had been "independent" and "accustomed to directing affairs." She similarly cautioned them not to attempt to revolutionize their churches but rather to "consent to work according to the methods" already established.[81]

Edith Lewis's Smith College career culminated in June 1902 with several days of events and ceremonies—the senior Shakespeare play on Friday, the Ivy Day procession on Saturday, the baccalaureate service on Sunday, and the commencement ceremony on Monday (Figure 1.6). Lewis served on the committee that selected Edward Everett Hale, the distinguished Boston Unitarian minister and author, as commencement speaker. Her parents may have come from Nebraska, or perhaps closer-by aunts or uncles acted as substitutes. In any event, after commencement she returned to Nebraska and, like her classmates, faced down precisely the prospect Julia Caverno described: living "at home" without any particular occupation.[82]

Some of Lewis's fellow 1902 graduates from Hatfield went to work, while others did not. Lucy Wicker returned to her widowed father's New York City home to "take charge of the housekeeping." Anna McClintock, who was from Denver, planned to accompany her family to New York City for the winter and to study music while they were there. Alice Duryee, a minister's daughter from New Jersey, went all the way to China to teach at a Christian girls school established by her two older sisters as a memorial

Figure 1.6 Edith Lewis's 1902 Smith College yearbook photo. Courtesy Smith College Archives.

to their dead mother. Susan Smith immediately went to teach at a private school in Massachusetts, but it took Ethel Eddy Treat a year to find her teaching position in New Hampshire. Achsah Barlow was perhaps the most intrepid, moving to New York City on her own to study painting at the New York School of Art and the Art Students League, although New Haven and her family were a short train ride away.[83]

Edith Lewis returned to her family's home in Lincoln to live, but she soon went to work as a teacher at Whittier Elementary, a small public elementary school occupying two houses at Twenty-Seventh and Vine Streets, a half mile north. She also dutifully taught a Sunday school class at All Souls Unitarian Church, began making regular appearances as her mother's guest at Lotos Club meetings, and reestablished ties with Delta Gamma, becoming active in the sorority's local alumnae chapter. Her sisters, Helen and Ruth, were still at home, while her brother, Harold, had enrolled in the electrical engineering course at Columbia University.[84]

Even though Henry was still spending much of his time in Kearney and Elm Creek looking after his interests there, he made regular appearances in Lincoln. In 1898, Henry and his friend Silas Burnham had established the Dartmouth Alumni Association of the Plain [sic], which alternated holding its annual banquet in Lincoln and Omaha. For the January 1903 banquet in Lincoln, Edith wrote a sentimental ballad about her alma mater and New Hampshire landscapes, which her parents proudly submitted to the newspapers for publication. Burnham, as she later recalled, "had a very good tenor voice, but could sing only one tune, 'The Bendemeer's Stream,'" so she had to compose lyrics to fit this tune. In the first of the ballad's four stanzas, the speaker returns in memory to "the heart of the hills," the "spot that once sheltered my youth's golden dream." In the second stanza, he cries out to "Thou Fostering Mother," asking her to "Be with" him until "the charm of thy memory" and the "dreams and desires of the days that are gone" obscure the "cares of the present." Such nostalgia seems out of key for a twenty-year-old recent college graduate, but perhaps teaching elementary school in Nebraska did not fulfill the "dreams and desires" of Edith's own college years.[85]

She was also, however, seeking experiences that would set the stage for the "literary work" in New York she would soon successfully pursue. Sarah Harris enlisted her as a judge for a *Lincoln Courier* story prize competition. When Harris published the winning entries, she boasted that the stories (with the names of their authors removed) had been "sent to Miss Edith Lewis of this city, a young woman who was graduated from Smith college last year with high honors, especially in the department of literature." Lewis also became a contributing editor to her sorority's national magazine, the *Anchora of Delta Gamma*. In an essay on sorority rush season, she observed ironically, "Those of our fathers who advocate *laissez faire* and free competition in the economic world should look with pleased approbation upon our application of their hobby in the 'rushing' system." With dry wit and drawing on the language and concepts she had learned studying with Charles Emerick at Smith College, she described the rush season as "a beautiful spectacle of Darwinian evolution at its purest and best." Becoming serious, she criticized "the deplorable waste" of the rush season, "waste of time, waste of money, waste of energy and nervous fibre, and moral expenditure." She first proposed a radical solution, an "utterly impartial board" to place students with sororities, but recognizing that "nobody would believe it is impartial," she proposed "truces, armistices, ameliorated conditions" of the "warfare" of rush season imposed through "Pan-Hellenic associations, or tacit contracts."[86]

Lewis hosted the annual alumnae chapter dinner at her family's home, which had been engulfed by eastward development of the city. The larger combined annual banquet of the alumnae and current members took place in the grander surroundings of the Fairview, William Jennings Bryan's gentleman's farm, then well outside the city (Bryan's daughter Ruth was a University of Nebraska student and Delta Gamma member). Bryan had designed his newly completed house to be large enough that public functions could take place on the elevated first floor while everyday family living took place undisturbed on the ground floor. Nevertheless, as Lewis reported in the *Anchora*, the fifty Delta Gamma students and alumnae members were "served down stairs in the large dining room and ordinary, which were embowered in spring flowers." As the *Courier* reported, the tables were decorated "with bride roses and ferns, and lighted by green candles in silver candelabra" and the place cards "prettily decorated with flowers in water colors." The menus were particularly "artistic," made of "green burlap with rough edges . . . tied with pink and green cords." A "blue-print" of the newly built Fairview was on the cover, "thus combining the Delta Gamma colors, pink, blue and green." Lewis served as the toastmistress. "After the toasts and songs," Lewis reported, "hand bills were circulated on which were printed the announcements of a play, 'Mr. Bob.'" She praised "the triumph of interpretation and nearly extemporaneous effect, the male parts being taken with exceptional brilliance and realism by the undergraduate chapter. Before the crowd broke up hearty cheers were given to our hostesses for the generosity and hospitality with which we had been entertained."[87]

Lewis's reports in her sorority's magazine seemingly waver between earnest enthusiasm and enthusiasm so great it crosses over to parody. "A joyous event has taken place of late in our midst," she wrote in the spring of 1903, "the birth of a son to Dr. and Mrs. (Elizabeth Wing) Brace"—her joy over the birth of the first child of her cousin Bessie and her husband, a physics professor, seems genuine. One wonders, however, about her report in the same article about how the "atmosphere" of the sorority's alumnae chapter "has vibrated of late to the music of numerous wedding marches." Of the marriage of one alumna, she claimed, "There is not a member . . . active or alumnae—who does not count the bride among her dear personal friends—or who did not cherish some slight resentment toward the unkind fate that sent her out of our sight—not of our hearts." Of the marriage of another member, she noted it is "a career for which her late domestic science training has no doubt brilliantly prepared her."[88]

Marriage conventionally defined the lives of middle-class white women, but graduates of women's colleges in the late nineteenth century and into the prewar twentieth century married at significantly lower rates than women in the general population, about 50 percent as opposed to about 90 percent. This led some to lament that higher education for women made them unfit for marriage and motherhood, and there was a particular concern that the elite eastern women's colleges were leading to "race suicide." Lewis's fellow Hatfield House residents who graduated in 1902 were an even more extreme example. Of the eight, only Achsah Barlow married, and her marriage, which produced only one child, was hardly conventional. Charles Emerick, writing from a sociological perspective, defended his students at Smith against these charges, arguing that women who sought out a college education were probably less inclined to marry in the first place.[89]

Lewis's articles in the *Anchora*, like her short stories of urban and Bohemian life, offer a glimpse of her desire to escape a conventional life in the midwestern city of her birth. As a reader rather than a contributor to her sorority magazine, she may have also sighted her desired future in New York City. The chapter secretary of the newly formed New York City Delta Gamma alumnae chapter reported in April 1903, "We meet the first Saturday of each month at the houses of different girls." In March, when the Lincoln Delta Gamma chapter was banqueting at Fairview, the New York Delta Gammas were meeting at the Christodora settlement house on the Lower East Side. Edith Lewis would not be reporting on the marriages of her sorority sisters in Nebraska for much longer. Instead, in September 1903, shortly after she and Willa Cather met in Sarah Harris's living room, she boarded a train to New York City, her sights set on the emerging Bohemia of Greenwich Village.[90]

2

Office Bohemia

At Home in Greenwich Village, At Work
in the Magazines

In December 1908, author Sarah Orne Jewett, whom Willa Cather met in Boston on *McClure's Magazine* business and who became an important mentor to her, wrote Cather a famous letter of advice, telling her to give up her work as a magazine editor to focus on writing fiction. Jewett praised "what we are pleased to call the 'Bohemia' of newspaper and magazine office life" as "background[]" for fiction writing. She was worried, however, that because Cather was "stand[ing] right in the middle" of the office and making it her audience, she would fail to progress as an artist. "[Y]our vivid exciting companionship in the office," she advised, "must not be your audience, you must find your own quiet centre of life, and write from that to the world that holds offices, and all society, all Bohemia."[1]

Critics and biographers have generally agreed with Jewett that magazine work presented an obstacle to Cather's full emergence as a writer of fiction. However, she took her time in taking Jewett's advice. Jewett died in 1909, after Cather had known her only a year, and Cather did not fully break with *McClure's* until 1912. Instead Cather continued to embrace two quintessentially modern spaces of the early twentieth century, the office as a workplace and Greenwich Village as the emerging capital of American Bohemia. Notably Edith Lewis, who had moved to New York in 1903, began working at *McClure's* a few months after Cather did in 1906, and the collaborative nature of magazine work fostered their later editorial collaboration. Lewis continued working at *McClure's* after Cather finally departed, and then at *Every Week* magazine after she herself left *McClure's*. By continuing her editorial work in magazine offices, Lewis provided financial stability as Cather took career risks, but Lewis also acted as Cather's editor when Cather contributed to *McClure's* and *Every Week*.

Even though, for a time, Cather put aside Jewett's letter of advice about her writerly life, she immediately followed Jewett's example in her personal life. For a significant portion of every year from 1881 until her death, Jewett shared a home in Boston with Annie Adams Fields, widow of publisher James T. Fields, and starting in late 1908, Cather made a home in New York City with Lewis in the first of a series of shared apartments. Cather and Lewis thus transplanted the Boston marriage tradition that Jewett and Fields exemplified to the soil (or concrete sidewalks) of Greenwich Village, modernizing it and adapting it to their own needs and circumstances. Cather's career as a novelist emerged out of both the magazine office and domestic Greenwich Village spaces she shared with Lewis.[2]

When Cather and Lewis first met in 1903, Cather was nearly thirty years old and was making her way to New York City more slowly than Lewis. Cather had spent nine years in rural Virginia and thirteen years in Nebraska (with her family first on a Webster County ranch and then in Red Cloud, and next on her own in Lincoln studying at the university). In 1903, she was seven years into what would become a decade in Pittsburgh, where she worked in succession as a magazine editor, newspaper reporter, and high school teacher. Three years passed between Cather and Lewis's first meeting on the eve of Lewis's departure for New York and Cather's own move there. During those three years, Lewis established herself in Bohemian Greenwich Village, in publishing, and in the broader city. As a pilot and an anchor, Lewis made Cather's New York–centered personal and professional life possible. Even as both women acculturated to New York, they retained their shared identity as Nebraskans. Indeed, both Greenwich Village and the magazine offices where they worked were full of people from various parts of the American West.

No letters between the two women documenting the growth of their relationship are currently known, but Cather's letters to other people during this period (including letters to Jewett and Fields) often mention Lewis. Furthermore, Cather and Lewis left a different sort of correspondence, a series of books exchanged as gifts that document not only their growing relationship but their shared commitment to aesthetic ideals. They eventually chose different paths, Cather committing herself to art and Lewis to the commercial craft of editing, but behind the scenes they continued to think and work together.

"Discoveries in Local Color": Edith Lewis on Washington Square

On August 27 or 28, 1903, Willa Cather and Edith Lewis met in Sarah Harris's living room. A few days later, Cather boarded a train for Pittsburgh.

On September 7, Lewis left for New York City, where, the Lincoln papers reported, she was making an "extended visit." In 1903, she had family to visit there. Her brother Harold was still enrolled at Columbia University and living in midtown, her cousin Tom Wing was still practicing law on Wall Street, and her cousin May Lewis had just begun teaching third grade at the Horace Mann School, affiliated with the Teachers College at Columbia. Edith Lewis also had Lincoln connections in New York City through her sorority. Helen Gregory, an 1895 University of Nebraska graduate and daughter of Reverend Lewis Gregory, Henry Lewis's friend from the Round Table, lived in Manhattan. She had spent her 1903 summer holiday visiting her family in Lincoln, and as reported in the Delta Gamma magazine, she was "very enthusiastic over the future of the [the sorority's] New York Alumnae Chapter." Once Edith Lewis got to New York, she announced to her sorority sisters that she was doing "journalistic work" there.[3]

Perhaps one "journalistic" piece she wrote at this time was a "Special Correspondence" report on the "Lincoln Colony" in New York City, published in the *Nebraska State Journal* (Charles Gere, her father's friend from the Round Table, owned the paper). The special correspondent began her report by puffing James Canfield, former chancellor of the University of Nebraska (and former member of the Round Table), who was then librarian of Columbia University. The correspondent segued to "Miss Dorothy Canfield," his daughter and Edith Lewis's fellow violinist in the University of Nebraska School of Fine Arts orchestra. Dorothy Canfield had "just begun her secretarial duties at the Horace Mann school" and had already achieved what Edith Lewis was aiming for—she had published an article in *Collier's Weekly* and "two clever stories" in *Metropolitan* magazine and *Harper's Bazar*. The correspondent devoted the most space, however, to Elmer Scipio ("Skip") Dundy, Jr., and his Luna Park attraction at Coney Island. The amusement park opened in the spring of 1903 and had just completed its wildly successful first season. After carefully reporting admissions and entrance fees, the correspondent lapsed into wonder at the spectacle: "The aggregation of shows and fun-making devices was really wonderful and beautiful to behold, and was on a scale never before seen about New York." Nevertheless, the management had great plans for expansion—doubling the twenty acres to forty and adding several attractions. Making an observation perhaps characteristic of the daughter of a Lincoln lawyer, the correspondent observed, "Mr. Dundy looks a little queer giving personal attentions to the details of the gay place, when one has previously seen him chiefly as clerk of the United States court at Lincoln, but the new work seems to agree with him."[4]

For at least a year, Lewis "furnished numerous sketches of New York life to the daily papers," but she needed a steady income to stay in New York, so following the established Bohemian pattern of taking paying jobs adjacent to the literary, within weeks of her arrival she took an entry-level position as an editorial proofreader for the *Century Dictionary*. This massive encyclopedic dictionary had been published in the late nineteenth century, and a two-volume supplement was being compiled in the early twentieth century. Lewis's work was only marginally literary, but she was working at the Century publishing company, in the same offices as the editorial staff of the *Century Magazine*, the target of her literary aspirations. It seems that her parents were no longer hiding their financial problems from her, and she was supporting herself. She later recalled wearing rubbers over her stockinged feet to work for three weeks because she had no money to buy shoes. However, she was in New York, doing "literary work," and experiencing the inexpensive pleasures of Bohemian life, including those she shared with her Delta Gamma sisters. The alumnae chapter aimed to "meet once a month at some point and proceed to 'do' New York." In November 1903, they met for lunch at the Martha Washington Hotel, a residential hotel for women, and then "went up to Miss Gregory's room," which was just like "a cozy college girl's room." In December, a member led an "expedition" to Chinatown, where they had the novel experience of eating with chopsticks and where they toured the Joss House.[5]

By 1904, Lewis had rented a room at 60 Washington Square South (Figure 2.1). Greenwich Village had not yet become the capital of New York and American Bohemian life—indeed, the neighborhood was still referred to as Washington Square rather than Greenwich Village. However, the southern side of the square was *a* Bohemian district and had been since the early 1860s, when the first Americans to embrace the ideal of *la vie bohème* began meeting at Pfaff's saloon on Broadway, a block from the southeast corner of Washington Square. Large houses occupied by wealthy families (and their servants) still predominated on the north side, but by the late nineteenth century similar houses on the opposite side of the square had become boarding and lodging houses catering to artistic types of modest means. 60 Washington Square was a four-story building near the intersection of Fourth (the southern boundary of the square) and Thompson Streets (perpendicular to Fourth). Lewis's building was part of a group of houses later christened

Figure 2.1 The intersection of Fourth and Thompson Streets on South Washington Square, circa 1905. The four-story building with an arched lintel over the entrance is 60 Washington Square. Courtesy New York University Special Collections.

"Genius Row" because many painters and writers lived and worked in them. On the corner were stores in ramshackle two-story wooden buildings, rare survivals of an earlier era, and horsecars ran on tracks on both Fourth and Thompson. Occupants of the cheap lodging houses on the south side of the square could hear the clanging of the cinder-spewing elevated train running on Amity Street behind them.[6]

In her adolescent short story "Bohemia," Lewis portrayed artists living with wild abandon in Paris, but in *Willa Cather Living* she described South Washington Square as "a very sedate Bohemia," where "most of the artists were poor and hard-working." Lewis did not meet Earl Brewster, the future husband of her Smith College roommate, Achsah Barlow, until 1910, but in 1905, he was a poor and hardworking artist sharing a studio at 42 Washington Square South with fellow painter Fred Shaler. Barlow was living in midtown, near the American Fine Arts Building, home to the Art Students League, where she was studying painting. Lewis had other college friends closer by, including two living at 60 Washington Square. Margaret Hamilton

Wagenhals (class of 1903), a minister's daughter from Muncie, Indiana, had lived in Hatfield House with Lewis and Barlow and was Lewis's fellow Phi Kappa Psi member; she was doing "magazine work" in the city, while her sister Katherine, a 1905 Smith graduate, came to New York periodically to take classes at the Art Students League. Abby Shute Merchant (class of 1904), a native of Gloucester, Massachusetts, worked for *Munsey's*, a pioneering mass-circulation magazine. Edith Wheeler Vanderbilt (class of 1902), who was doing settlement work uptown, lived with her family in the Judson, a modest residential hotel at 53 Washington Square, across Thompson Street from 60.[7]

Willa Cather had been to New York City only twice before she met Lewis: she spent a week in Manhattan in February 1898, taking in the theater, and in April 1903, S. S. McClure summoned her to the city to talk about short stories she had submitted to his magazine. At their meeting McClure had promised to publish *The Troll Garden*, her collection of short stories about art and artists, and to place the stories in magazines before the book came out. In the spring of 1904, however, when Cather was trying to finish *The Troll Garden* and was working on "Fanny" (a never-published Pittsburgh novel), she complained to Dorothy Canfield (whom she had befriended when she was a student at the University of Nebraska and Canfield's father was the university chancellor) that her teaching duties were interfering with her writing and she needed a break. "[M]y present plan," she explained to Canfield, "is to spend the summer in New York, down near or with Edith Lewis, in Washington Square. She has been a regular trump about looking up rooms for me and such things. I want to get off somewhere and make a final struggle with this accursed and underdone novel, and New York seems a good place to do it." Describing herself as having gotten into a "rut," she wrote, "I think Miss Lewis would be a good pilot for me, she's all wrapped up in her discoveries in local color."[8]

When Cather visited Lewis on Washington Square in July and August 1904, she entered her young friend's world and was observed critically. Barlow and Lewis alternated Sunday visits to one another's lodgings, and Barlow later recalled the two of them hanging over the banister at 60 Washington Square to watch Cather depart for a dinner party wearing a satin gown and an opera cloak. Abby Merchant, reading *Willa Cather Living* half a century later, praised Lewis's "beautiful, clear warm picture of [Cather] as I knew her," which awakened "an almost physically painful nostalgia for the Washington Square days."[9]

Cather and Lewis certainly took in the city together, but both were also working, Lewis daily at the Century Co. offices and Cather at 60 Washington Square. *The Troll Garden* was scheduled for publication by McClure, Phillips & Co. in late 1904 or early 1905. In Lewis's "Bohemia" story, artists are happy and carefree, but Cather's artists' tales were dark and grim. Two that she had written by 1904 but which had not yet been published typify the whole: in "The Sculptor's Funeral," the body of an internationally known sculptor arrives by train in his Kansas hometown, where the greedy, hypocritical townspeople do not recognize his genius, and in "Paul's Case," a Pittsburgh teenager with a rich fantasy life fueled by the theater and paintings steals money from his employer and flees to New York, where he briefly lives his dreams before throwing himself in front of a train. Lewis read Cather's work-in-progress and took one of these stories to the office "to show an officer of the company whom I knew; but he regretfully though kindly declined it, saying that for the *Century Magazine* they preferred stories 'about equally combining humour and pathos.'" Cather returned to Pittsburgh in August, and grateful for Lewis's hospitality, she gave her an 1895 translation of Ivan Turgenev's 1860 novel *On the Eve*, one of the first in a long line of literary gift exchanges that marked the growth of their relationship.[10]

That this friendship between two women separated in age by eight years and living hundreds of miles apart flourished so rapidly may seem strange, but they both cared deeply about art and were ambitious for themselves as authors. Indeed, Lewis was also writing and submitting poetry and fiction to national magazines and would soon succeed. They also had many Lincoln friends in common. Both Cather's and Lewis's fathers had worked for Lincoln financier Charles Emmett Moore. The entire Gere family had been important to Cather during her Lincoln years: Frances, Ellen, and Mariel were her contemporaries and classmates, their mother (also Mariel) welcomed the young Cather into their family home, and Charles Gere, editor and publisher of the *Nebraska State Journal*, gave her a job on his paper. Charles and Mariel Gere were "warm friends" of Edith Lewis's parents: Charles was a member of Henry's Round Table and Mariel a member of Lillie's Lotos Club. Edith's older cousins were Cather's university classmates when the university was quite small. And, of course, there was Sarah Harris, editor and publisher of the *Lincoln Courier*, who was deeply connected to both the Lewis family and to Willa Cather, who had published both Cather and Lewis in her paper and who had introduced them to each other.[11]

The Canfield family also tied them together and, inadvertently, led to a crisis in Cather's developing career as a writer. In late 1904, when Cather was back teaching in Pittsburgh, Dorothy Canfield invited Lewis out for dinner. Over dinner Lewis relayed her enthusiasm for the stories in the forthcoming *Troll Garden*, singling out for praise "The Profile." Cather derived the central conceit of the story—the protagonist with a disfiguring scar on one side of her face who will allow herself to be painted only in profile—from one of Canfield's graduate school friends whom Cather had met in France in 1902. When Canfield expressed shock and dismay about the story to Lewis, Lewis defended Cather, explaining that "as far as she knew Miss Cather had only met the person once or twice and that the character in the story was wholly unlike the real person and therefore the original could not be offended." Canfield was not convinced. She argued vigorously with Cather against the publication of "The Profile," and when Cather herself refused to withdraw it, she successfully campaigned to have the publisher remove it from the volume. Their argument nearly destroyed their long-established friendship.[12]

Art and the Market in Greenwich Village: Willa Cather's "Coming, Aphrodite!" and Edith Lewis's "Chains of Darkness"

These events had the opposite effect on Cather and Lewis's newly established friendship, intensifying the bond between two women whose literary careers were both ascending. Literary gift exchanges and more visits by Cather to New York tied together Cather and Lewis's shared commitment to aesthetics and their personal relationship. In December 1904, in the midst of Cather and Canfield's dispute, Lewis gave Cather *The Golden Bowl*, Henry James's new novel. Through this gift Lewis communicated her understanding of Cather's current aesthetic preoccupation (Cather admired and was emulating James in her fiction). The volume, priced at $2.50, represented a substantial financial commitment for Lewis, who was making only $25 a week. Also in December 1904, Lewis learned that her poem "Aliens" had been accepted by *Scribner's Magazine*, where Cather's story "A Death in the Desert" had appeared in January 1903. It was Lewis's enthusiasm for that story that led Sarah Harris to introduce her to Cather. Lewis's poem appeared in March 1905, just as McClure, Phillips was announcing the April publication of *The Troll Garden* (minus "The Profile"). In the four rhymed octaves of Lewis's

"Aliens," the speaker, who is on a moonlit urban rooftop, watches "lads" go "up and down the pavements" from "eve till morn" because their dreams and desires, like hers, are unfulfilled.[13]

Cather stayed with Lewis on Washington Square again for a week in the late summer of 1905. Likely before Cather arrived, Lewis submitted another poem, "At Morning," to *Harper's*, which published it in December. In two rhymed octaves, the speaker juxtaposes "Young lovers [giving] their hearts away" in a fresh spring landscape with another urban scene of "streets of breathless stone" on which "A thousand weary travellers fare." Fortuitously, a seventieth-birthday dinner for Mark Twain organized by Twain's publisher, Harper & Brothers (publisher of *Harper's* magazine), brought Cather to New York in early December 1905. Grateful to Lewis for hosting her again, Cather sent her as a Christmas present Israel Zangwill's influential realist fiction *Children of the Ghetto* (1892), while Lewis sent Cather *Modern Painting* (1893) by Irish novelist George Moore as a New Year's gift.[14]

In Lewis's poems, with their urban settings, and her short story published in November 1905, "Chains of Darkness: A College Graduate and the Cold, Cold World," we can glimpse Lewis's urban experiences of "local color" that allowed her to "pilot" Cather through Bohemian New York City. They also provide insight into her own struggles to pursue art in the city. Although *Collier's Weekly* published "Chains of Darkness" in 1905, Lewis had submitted it to the magazine's short story contest before Cather visited her in New York in the summer of 1904 (the contest deadline was June 1, 1904). In order to allow the judges (Henry Cabot Lodge, William Allen White, and Walter Hines Page) to focus on quality rather than established reputation, contest rules required anonymous submission. Lewis was not among the top three who were declared the contest winners, but the contest was designed "to secure as many good short stories as possible" for *Collier's*, and when the combined list of sixty-nine prizewinning and purchased stories appeared in May 1905, she was in impressive company. Cather's friend Margaret Deland won the $3,000 second prize for "Many Waters," and other established authors, including Edith Wharton, James Branch Cabell, and Rex Beach, had non-prizewinning stories purchased. Competition rules allowed for unlimited submissions, and Lewis's senior-year English professor, Jennette Lee, had three stories purchased. Notably, *Collier's* also purchased stories submitted by several staff members of *McClure's Magazine* (Samuel Hopkins Adams, Ray Stannard Baker, Viola Roseboro', and Lincoln Steffens).[15]

Lewis could not have read Cather's *Troll Garden* manuscript before submitting "Chains of Darkness," but in the summer of 1904, Cather might have read Lewis's retained copy of the story while she was working on her own stories. Indeed, Cather's 1904 Christmas gift of Zangwill's book suggests that she had read Lewis's story. In any event, the two women were converging on the same themes: the perils of pursuing an artistic vocation and the conflict between art and the market. Cather derived her volume title from Charles Kingsley's *The Roman and the Teuton*, a quotation from which appeared on the title page: "A fairy palace, with a fairy garden; . . . Inside the trolls dwell, . . . working at their magic forges, making and making always things rare and strange." Cather's other epigraph is from Christina Rossetti's long poem "Goblin Market": "We must not look at Goblin men, / We must not buy their fruits; / Who knows upon what soil they fed / Their hungry thirsty roots?" In all of the *Troll Garden* stories, characters enter or want to enter this seductive and yet dangerous and destructive realm of art. Lewis took the opening epigraph of her short story from her father's favorite poem, Swinburne's *Atalanta in Calydon*: "Behold, thou art over fair, thou art over wise; / The sweetness of spring in thine hair, and the light in thine eyes. / The light of the spring in thine eyes, and the sound in thine ears; / Yet thine heart shall wax heavy with sighs, and thine eyelids with tears." In both *The Troll Garden* and "Chains of Darkness," tears, struggle, and danger await those who attempt to enter the walled garden of art.[16]

Lewis's protagonist, Geoffrey Landis, was the "Lion Rampant" in college, effortlessly taking all of the honors. Sure of his gifts as a writer, he moves to New York City after graduation, where he

> rented an inexpensive room in the downtown quarter of the city, paid for a month's board in advance, and for a while did nothing but loaf about the streets, the parks, the wharves, staring, smoking, meditating in silence, drinking it in, little by little—this mighty brew of the affairs of men, lingering, smacking his lips over the matchless flavor of it all.

Finally, he returns to his room to write like the devil. Emerging with a manuscript under his arm, he takes it to the office of Kempton Thomas, one of the city's premiere publishers, where it is rejected. After several more publishers reject his manuscript, Landis writes another story, but because he is running low on money, he takes "a cheaper lodging" and starts eating at "twenty and fifteen-cent tables d'hôte, dirty basement holes where the linen was soiled and the food oddly flavored, where the waiters dropped dishes of food upon the floor, and the proprietor smoked a pipe behind the counter"—in short, he eats like a New York Bohemian.[17]

None of Cather's artist tales in *The Troll Garden* are set in Greenwich Village, but a much later story, "Coming, Aphrodite!" (1920), takes place at 60 Washington Square around the time of her visits with Lewis, in 1904 when "Chains of Darkness" was under consideration at *Collier's* and in 1905 in the wake of the good news that the magazine had purchased it. Cather locates her protagonist, Don Hedger, in a rented room "on the top floor of an old house on the south side of Washington Square," where he has a sink and two gas burners but no bathroom or proper kitchen. Although he sometimes cooks on his gas burners, he delights in a basement oyster house in the immigrant neighborhood south of Washington Square, where "there were no table-cloths on the tables and no handles on the coffee cups, and the floor was covered with sawdust." When he befriends Eden Bower, the aspiring opera singer in the adjacent two-room apartment, he takes her to Coney Island (where Lewis, in her first weeks in New York in 1903, had perhaps gone to interview Skip Dundy about his Luna Park). Don and Eden eat a "shore dinner" at Coney Island and watch a balloon ascent by a woman who is also Don's model. Eden then infuriates him by surreptitiously switching places with the model so that she herself, clad in tights, can hang from a trapeze under the balloon. After they return to Manhattan, he takes her to a café at "a little French hotel on Ninth Street [in the Village], long since passed away."[18]

In both "Chains of Darkness" and "Coming, Aphrodite!" the plot turns on a conflict between the values of art and the marketplace. In Cather's story, an argument about this conflict ends Eden's and Don's romance. Eden believes he should want an audience for his art, should want to sell his paintings and gain popular recognition. Conversely, although Don occasionally does commercial work to bring in cash, he proclaims to Eden that he paints not for "the public" but "for painters,—who haven't been born." In "Chains of Darkness," Geoffrey Landis knows that his fiction is "good; it's as good as they make 'em,' but he curses "the people" who don't recognize the value of his work. When his money runs out, he lives for a time on the street "with tramps and vagabonds." He finally pulls himself off the street by taking a job waiting on tables at a "cheap 'Hungarian' restaurant" on Grand Street in the largely Jewish immigrant Lower East Side, where, donning a "soiled apron," he "hurr[ies] out orders to the noisy Hebrew crowd that filled the place." When he loses this job, he sits in his cheap room, "aching with passionate weariness and regret." As he sighs over his fate and the failed dreams of authorship that brought him to the city, "suddenly there came welling up in his memory a little song he had read long since and forgotten." The "little song" is actually a verse from A .E. Housman's *A Shropshire Lad*, in which the poet adapted Jesus's words in the book of Matthew in the Bible about how to achieve salvation ("if thy right eye offend thee, pluck it out, and cast it from thee"). The emergence of the Housman stanza from Landis's consciousness marks his recognition that he has failed to enter the seductive troll garden of art: "If your hand or foot offend you, / Cut it off, lad, and be whole; / But play the man, stand up and end you, / When your sickness is your soul."[19]

At this crucial moment of suicidal despair, Lewis provided a deus ex machina for her hero. An angelic young neighbor sees Landis on the day he is fired and asks him to come sit by her fire, where she tells him to "believe" that his "gift" will return; she also asks him to bring his manuscripts to her. The next day, he pulls himself together and manages to find a low-status office job. That evening, the neighbor reveals to him that she took his manuscripts to Kempton Thomas, for whom she works as a clerk, and Thomas has accepted all of his stories and vows to continue to publish his work. Thomas relays a message through his clerk: "Tell that young man . . . that nine publishers out of ten were right in refusing his tales. They acted according to their lights. But tell him that I'm the tenth, and that I'll take all the stuff he cares to send me, and make his fortune besides."[20]

Lewis's story intricately reconfigured her own experiences in New York and perhaps Cather's as well. She, like her male protagonist, came to New York City to write, but unlike him, she didn't retreat to a garret to write until her money ran out. Rather, she immediately got an editorial job *and* she wrote newspaper sketches, stories, and poems for publication (indeed, she likely wrote and had many more rejected than ever saw print). When Landis's angelic neighbor tells him that her boss has accepted his stories, he is astonished. "I thought I told you," he explains, "I took them there first of all. But . . . they came back directly." She explains that his manuscripts "never went beyond the readers" but he "must not blame them—poor routine workers, fitted to the groove." When Cather and Lewis met in Lincoln in 1903, or in their subsequent correspondence or in-person meetings, perhaps Cather told Lewis her own story about being called to New York in the spring of 1903 by S. S. McClure to confer about her stories. They "had been sent back to me by Mr. McClure's readers without having ever reached him at all," she wrote in May 1903 to Will Owen Jones, her journalist friend in Lincoln.

While Cather was in McClure's office, he had "the two readers sent in and asked them to give an account of their stewardship. Surely I sat and held my chin high and thought my hour had struck." And McClure promised "to take everything I do and place it for me if he cannot use it himself." When Cather stayed with Lewis in the summer of 1904, Lewis herself had attempted to enact the role of the angelic publisher's clerk by taking one of Cather's stories to an officer of the Century Co.[21]

Collier's purchase of her 5,600-word story at the advertised rate of five cents per word produced a significant financial windfall of $280 for Lewis, nearly three months of her salary at the Century Co., and she likely used this windfall to pay for an expensive cross-country train trip in 1906 to visit her cash-strapped family in Nebraska. After 1905, however, no new poems or stories (about angelic publisher's clerks or otherwise) appeared in print under Lewis's name. Certainly anonymous or pseudonymous publication or additional failed attempts to publish cannot be discounted, but it seems that Lewis stopped writing poems and stories, at least with an intention to publish.[22]

Her withdrawal from authorship has been claimed as evidence that she subordinated herself to Cather. All relationships require negotiation and compromise, but there is no reason to presume that Lewis made all of the compromises while Cather forged ahead, paying no attention to Lewis's needs. Their partnership was not static but dynamic as they shifted positions and allegiances over time and in response to circumstances internal and external to their relationship. If in the summer of 1905 Cather and Lewis argued, like Don and Eden, about art and the market, the argument did not end their relationship. Instead, Lewis turned to behind-the-scenes work in magazines and advertising, while Cather eventually claimed a high place as an author in American literary culture. Together, they would form a partnership between pragmatism and idealism, between the market and aesthetics. If Lewis sacrificed her literary ambitions in favor of Cather's, her choice did not make her subordinate to Cather in all aspects of their relationship. Indeed, in later years Cather would express resentment at the heavy demands Lewis's job and family made on her. Lewis was not willing, however, to give them up in order to focus all of her energy on Cather, much as Cather seemed to wish she would.[23]

But first, in 1906, both of them would assume behind-the-scenes roles at *McClure's Magazine. McClure's* was a key player in the revolution in magazine publishing in the late nineteenth century as magazines shifted from relying on subscription payments from readers to relying on advertising revenues. In the early years of the twentieth century, *McClure's* also pioneered investigative long-form journalism with a progressive political bent, denigrated by its critics as "muckraking." Because magazine editorial work was collaborative and mostly meant to be invisible, it is difficult to recover the nature and scope of one person's work. An identified editor in chief (in this case, S. S. McClure) and the collective editorial "we" can encompass an entire office full of people working together. Furthermore, no complete editorial office archive survives for *McClure's* (or for *Every Week* magazine, for which Lewis later served as managing editor). Nevertheless, through scattered pieces of evidence we can observe both Cather's and Lewis's magazine editorial work and locate the genesis of Lewis's role as Cather's editorial collaborator in their shared work at *McClure's*.[24]

Entering the Cyclone: Cather and Lewis Go to Work for *McClure's Magazine*

In early April 1906, Cather left Pittsburgh for New York to join the editorial staff of S. S. McClure's magazine. At that time McClure was engaged in protracted negotiations with his business partner, John Phillips, and staff writers and editors who also had an ownership stake in the magazine. On May 10, the group departed, having purchased *Leslie's Monthly Magazine* with a plan to relaunch it as the *American Magazine*. In April, however, when McClure hired Cather, it was already clear that most of his editorial staff would depart, with only Witter Bynner, Viola Roseboro', and the recently hired Burton Hendrick remaining. In April, McClure was also negotiating with Will Irwin, who would start as managing editor in June, replacing the departed Ray Stannard Baker. Irwin was a young Stanford-educated journalist, then reporting for the *New York Sun*, who grew up in the rough mining towns of Colorado and had a chip on his shoulder about his modest Western origins.[25]

When Cather arrived in New York, she checked into the French-owned Griffou Hotel, north of Washington Square, with May Willard, a librarian friend from Pittsburgh. Lewis had recently returned from a monthlong Nebraska visit and may have given up her room at 60 Washington Square while she was away—perhaps Cather did not stay with her as she had before because of this. In Lincoln, Lewis was briefly immersed in the world she had left three years earlier. Ella Andrews, a member of the Lotos Club and wife of the university chancellor, gave a "chafing dish party" for "a few young ladies" in honor of her. Edna McDowell Barkley, the dean of women at the university (and years before, Lewis's eighth grade teacher) gave a "violet tea" for the Delta Gamma sorority in her honor as well (Edna and her banker husband were members of All Souls Unitarian Church with the Lewises and lived around the corner from them).[26]

Henry Lewis was still making his living (or trying to make his living) through business enterprises in central Nebraska. In 1901, he had purchased a section of land in Dawson County, near his Farmers Union Ditch Company in Elm Creek, financing the purchase through an installment agreement with the seller, Charles E. Perkins, president of the Burlington Railroad (Burlington tracks ran across a corner of the property). In November 1905, Henry had created the Midland Alfalfa Company, a capital stock corporation; its stated purpose was to "acquire farm lands by sale or least to cultivate such lands and feed and raise live stock, and construct irrigation reservoirs and ditches and borrow money and issue bonds." Two of his friends from the Round Table joined him as incorporators: an engineer who had turned lawyer and judge, Addison S. Tibbets, and a lawyer and the former Democratic mayor of Lincoln, Andrew Sawyer. Also incorporators were W. E. Barkley and Henry's lawyer, E. F. Pettis, who represented him in his many lawsuits and was a law partner of Henry's longtime friend and fellow Round Table member Nathan Harwood. Alfalfa was a relatively new crop in central Nebraska. It had been promoted by H. D. Watson, who came from Massachusetts early in the Kearney boom and who later discovered that alfalfa survived the 1893 drought on unirrigated land. As the Elm Creek newspaper touted in 1898, "All that is lacking in this locality to make a good feeding point for cattle and sheep is hay," and the editor recommended alfalfa as a "prolific" hay crop. It seems that the only land the Midland Alfalfa Co. leased and on which it cultivated alfalfa and fed livestock (hogs) was Henry Lewis's section in Dawson County. In 1906, shortly before Edith arrived for her visit, Henry began a series of transactions that transferred the property to his wife (in a seeming attempt to protect it from claims by his other debtors) and remortgaged it. He was buying himself time, but his financial house of cards was long overdue for collapse.[27]

On Edith's return to New York, she moved back to 60 Washington Square. Her tenure as a proofreader for the *Century Dictionary* supplement had run its course, and she had a job with the educational publisher Barnes Co. In early summer, her mother visited her and "found her showing the effects of over-work." Meanwhile, Cather was immersed in her new and demanding job at *McClure's*. In mid-May, after Will Irwin signed his contract but before he officially started as managing editor, he first met Cather, whom he found "efficient, a little masculine" and "steel blue in the eye, firm in the jaw." Neither had much taste for the muckraking then characterizing *McClure's*. When Irwin took the editorial chair in June, he "had an hour with Miss Cather trading our ideas" about the editorial program, which were "very much alike." Although Irwin was fond of Viola Roseboro', their ideas about the magazine "turned out to be very much unlike" because she "*will* believe in muckraking—says we owe the country a moral debt."[28]

Ellery Sedgwick, formerly editor of *Leslie's*, was brought on to manage the McClure Newspaper Syndicate, which shared offices with the magazine. He recalled working "under some natural law of desperation" because whenever the "chief" was in the office, he was "forever interrupting, cutting every sequence into a dozen parts" and producing chaos in the working lives of his staff. Mark Sullivan, who had worked at *McClure's* in 1905, called McClure a "very queer bird" but "a great editor." McClure did not sit patiently reading manuscripts but was instead "a geyser of ideas." The job of his staff, then, was "screening the one most practicable idea out of a hundred of McClure's suggestions, and seeing that the chosen idea was well and thoroughly developed and written." Lewis recalled that "[w]orking on *McClure's* was like working in a high wind, sometimes of cyclone magnitude, and of course S. S. McClure was the storm center." She also noted that McClure was "often criticized, and sometimes ridiculed by people in the office who could not understand how a man of genius could so outrage their common sense." In the vague category of "people," Lewis perhaps discreetly included Will Irwin, who repeatedly characterized McClure as crazy, insane, and a maniac.[29]

By late June, McClure's demands, both professional and personal, had exhausted Cather, so she took a week's vacation. In July, McClure departed for Europe, giving his staff a chance to focus on their work. McClure had retained control of the magazine bearing his name, but it was saddled with nearly insupportable debt—indeed, his precarious financial situation resembled that of Henry Lewis. Will Irwin felt that the magazine's success or failure rested on a planned series on Mary Baker Eddy and Christian Science. McClure had acquired the material from journalist Georgine Milmine, but it required more research and extensive rewriting. After McClure's departure, Irwin had great "trouble" with Milmine, who felt disrespected and threatened to withdraw her articles. Irwin entered into a new contract with her, paying her an additional $1,000 and averting a crisis. For her part, Cather encouraged Lewis to apply for an open position as an editorial proofreader, and Lewis was on the job by August 1906. Cather scarcely needed to exercise influence on Lewis's behalf. She had three years of experience in New York as a proofreader, her college coursework made her well versed in the progressive social science theories behind the magazine's muckraking, and she had recently had poems published in *Harper's* and *Scribner's* and a story published in *Collier's* as the result of a contest entered by several staff members of *McClure's*. If anything, she was overqualified.[30]

In August 1906, the magazine began running Christopher P. Connolly's serial exposé about the corrupting influence of mining interests on Montana politics. Before McClure left for Europe, he proposed that Irwin both rewrite Connolly and go to Colorado and Idaho to research the confession of Harry Orchard, assassin of former Idaho governor Frank Steunenberg, which McClure had acquired for the magazine. Irwin's childhood in Colorado's mining camps made him unusually well qualified for this task, but Viola Roseboro' believed him not to be of sufficient "calibre" for the task, and in the end, Irwin did not go. In any event, at the moment Lewis joined the staff of *McClure's* in August, western subject matter was central. The magazine also prominently featured fiction, and two western tales, "Archie's Baby" by Roseboro' and "The Lady Peddler and the Diplomats" by Mrs. Woodrow Wilson, appeared in August. On November 1, 1906, after returning from a visit to Pittsburgh, Cather left the Griffou and rented a room at 60 Washington Square. As two women from Nebraska, Cather and Lewis lived in the same Greenwich Village rooming house and walked together the mile from Washington Square to the *McClure's* offices on Union Square.[31]

Irwin was estranged from his wife and was carrying on an affair with author and feminist Inez Haynes Gillmore, who lived in Boston and to whom he wrote long, hyperbolic letters about his sufferings as the managing editor of *McClure's*. Rather than travel to the West to fact-check Harry Orchard, Irwin traveled several times in the fall of 1906 to Boston for research on the Christian Science articles. Even though S. S. McClure was in Europe, he continued to exercise force from a distance, and his wife, Hattie McClure, was often in the office. The magazine's directors were trying to keep McClure on a tight leash, but he was determined to prove that *McClure's* was still his magazine, so against everyone's advice and counsel, in September he paid British actress Ellen Terry a large sum to serialize her memoirs. When he was negotiating with Terry, he failed to send his wife a telegram when her father died.

Hattie McClure "wept on the shoulder of Miss Cather," whom she barely knew, and Cather and Roseboro' both "went off like . . . a string[] of giant [fire] crackers" in reaction to Hattie McClure's demands. "When anything comes into that office it is taken," Irwin complained to Gillmore, "not exactly into the family, but into the retinue of family servants." Having job offers in hand from two competing magazines, Irwin planned to put his resignation on the table when S. S. McClure returned from Europe in early October, but the crisis was averted. Irwin withdrew his resignation, and as McClure explained in a letter to his former business partner John Phillips, with the advice and support of his directors, he promised to give Irwin "very general business and editorial authority." McClure also trusted Cather's judgment. "Miss Cather," he wrote to Phillips, "has proved to be very able in the matter of looking after the immediate operation of articles for the magazine."[32]

Reading literary manuscripts and making judgments about whether to publish them was a collective activity at McClure's, and by November 1906, Lewis was pitching in. As her parents boasted back in Lincoln, she had "already won recognition among literary people for the intelligence and sympathy displayed" in this work. Cather reported back to Lincoln that she had "for the present been assigned to the task of looking after literary lions when they come to New York to consult with Mr. McClure. She takes them out to dinner and to the theater and gives them a good time generally. It is supposed to be a wearing occupation, but it gives one a great opportunity to become acquainted with literary folk." The staff did not always agree about which submissions to publish. Irwin styled himself a "lowbrow" struggling against the "highbrows," including Cather. He was proud of winning an office argument in favor of publishing Mary Stewart Cutting's serial novel The Wayfarers, claiming that Cather opposed it because it wasn't "decadent" enough (Roseboro' championed it as "subtle"). Irwin implicitly associated Cather's aesthetic preferences with her sexuality, writing Gillmore that "Miss Cather has the Lesbian in her which repels me, so that I am ill at ease with her." Witter Bynner, who had been disappointed that McClure appointed Irwin rather than himself as managing editor, also read literary manuscripts for the magazine. In mid-October, Irwin discovered that Bynner had been using the office letterhead and a staff stenographer to write authors in the McClure's "stable" informing them that he was leaving the magazine to go into the publishing business. Nobody was sorry to see Bynner go.[33]

Responsibility for the Christian Science articles was repeatedly a point of contention in late 1906 and early 1907. Burton Hendrick was assigned responsibility for the first installment, but McClure was displeased with his attitude toward Mary Baker Eddy, the founder of the church, and assigned Irwin the task of rewriting Hendrick's rewrite of Milmine. Viola Roseboro' pitched in on the rewriting, too. As the fall progressed, more than once McClure was inclined to take Irwin away from his editorial responsibilities to have him rewrite the entire thing, but by mid-December, McClure had assigned primary responsibility to Cather (although the series remained a collaborative enterprise). Stuck in town for Christmas because of this collective effort, Cather, Roseboro' and Irwin awkwardly spent Christmas Eve together after Cather protested that she was "mourning because she would have a lonely and stupid Christmas" (Lewis seems to have left town for the holiday, perhaps to visit the Barlows in New Haven or family in Massachusetts). The three *McClure's* staffers gathered at Cather's room at 60 Washington Square, dined and drank at Martin's Café on Madison Square, and then continued their drinking back at Cather's room. "Miss Cather and I are never quite at ease alone in the company of one another," Irwin complained to Gillmore. Finding a fundamental conflict between "the somewhat padded decadent philosophy of Willa Cather" and "the bald primitive philosophy of Will Irwin," he found that Roseboro', who was "at home with both" of them, served as "something of a bridge."[34]

In mid-January, after being housebound with a cold, Cather finally departed for Boston to work on the Christian Science articles, giving up her rented room on Washington Square. For the first few months, she stayed at the Parker House hotel, but by the spring, she had taken a small flat on Chestnut Street in the Back Bay neighborhood. In early February, when Cather had been in Boston for just a few weeks, Irwin became convinced that she was in league with McClure to wrest the managing editor position away from him. He threatened to resign yet again, but the directors and Cameron Mackenzie (S. S. McClure's son-in-law, who had recently been brought on to the magazine) implored him to stay, at least until he had finished rewriting the Connolly serial.[35]

His nerves shot, Irwin sailed off to Bermuda in late February to recuperate. He wrote to Gillmore that there was "a love affair between Miss Cather and the Chief, which, with his customary chivalry, he has given away to Mrs. McClure. Mrs. McClure is on the warpath, and it comes just at the time when the duplicity of Miss Cather (who is only shadowing the Chief in this) has opened a campaign to get me out of the place." Irwin "pitied" himself for getting caught in "the tangles of this queer affair," but even as he sought Gillmore's pity, he acknowledged the incoherence of his theory. He found it "puzzling" that Cather was, as he thought, seeking to become managing editor when "the whole Christian Science thing" was "in her grasp" and would keep her in Boston "at least for six months." In early February, Irwin had lost both Connolly's manuscript for the Montana serial (still in progress) and his own extensive revisions to it. He knew this was grounds for termination, and only the fact that Connolly had retained a copy of the unrevised manuscript saved him. Earlier, Irwin had accurately perceived Cather's sexuality, and he knew she couldn't be managing editor while she was in Boston. However, he was incapable of holding himself responsible for his own professional failure, so he concocted a manifestly illogical theory to justify himself. As he rationalized the situation to Gillmore, McClure could want to force him out only because he had a sexual interest in Cather, and only romantic love could make Cather loyal to McClure.[36]

Meanwhile, Cameron Mackenzie—not Willa Cather—became managing editor when Irwin departed, and Edith Lewis continued to sit quietly at her proofreader's desk, watching the office chaos swirl around her. The eminent novelist, editor, and critic William Dean Howells stopped by and asked her what she was doing. When she explained that she was proofreading, he "said in his beautiful voice: 'I was a proof-reader, too.'" Although Lewis had lost Cather's daily companionship at 60 Washington Square, each month as Cather completed an installment of the Christian Science series, Lewis was sent to Boston to read proofs with her. "This," Lewis later recalled, "was the beginning of our working together." The Christian Science exposé was not the only McClure's work on which they collaborated. In 1907, Cather was involved in the serialization of the Ellen Terry memoir McClure had acquired in 1906, and she dispatched Lewis to the New York apartment of a friend of Terry's to find photographs to accompany her memoirs. Lewis also began copyediting as well as proofreading—she was one of several copyeditors who worked over a follow-along to the Christian Science series, Richard Cabot's "One Hundred Christian Science Cures" (published September 1908).[37]

The McClure's Christian Science exposé was a great success in 1907 and 1908, keeping the magazine afloat. However, the fortunes of Edith Lewis's family back in Nebraska began to collapse. In 1904, Henry and Lillie Lewis had subdivided their large residential lot in Lincoln, retaining the portion on which their house was situated but selling the undeveloped portion to William Shinn, who immediately built a house on it. Their attempt to raise cash soon backfired, however. Shinn claimed the Lewises' title was defective and stopped making installment payments. In January 1906, a judge compelled Shinn to pay what he owed, but the delay in receiving the benefit of the sale further strained Henry and Lillie's finances. Henry owed more than $1,200 in taxes and interest to Allison Cope, an investor who had bought the tax indebtedness on their house years earlier, and in January 1907, Cope filed for foreclosure. In April, Cope agreed not to issue an order for sale for two years, but Henry Lewis's level of debt made recovering his fortunes nearly impossible. Henry told the court that the market value of his house, by then on a smaller lot, was $2,000. However, as his cousin who was an officer of a New Hampshire bank disclosed, his bank held $10,000 of mortgage loans against it.[38]

Henry's fortunes further unraveled in June 1907 when Dawson County road crews ruined his irrigation ditch. With no functioning ditch, payments from farmers ceased. Henry and Lillie and their two daughters still at home, Ruth and Helen, moved out to their Dawson County ranch for the summer. They returned briefly to Lincoln in October, but they opted to rent in Kearney in the fall so Henry could more easily pursue his lawsuit against Dawson County and look after his ranch and operations of the Midland Alfalfa Company. The family returned occasionally to Lincoln, allowing Henry and Lillie to maintain connections to their clubs, but their quarter century in Lincoln was drawing to a close, even as their oldest daughter was more firmly establishing herself in New York City.[39]

The timing of this long-delayed, yet inevitable collapse provides a crucial context for Edith Lewis's decision to stop pursuing authorship and buckle down to magazine work. Perhaps she felt compelled to be practical. In contrast, the economic circumstances of Willa Cather's family improved after she left Nebraska. During her Red Cloud childhood, her parents rented a small house that could barely contain their growing family. In 1903, however, Charles Cather bought a much larger house that gave the younger Cather children more space than their older siblings had had. Willa Cather still felt the need to support herself—she delayed her exit from magazine editing until she had saved enough money to write full time—but she was experiencing nothing like the family financial catastrophe Lewis was facing.

148 Charles Street and 82 Washington Place: Following the Example of Sarah Orne Jewett and Annie Adams Fields

In December 1907, Cather traveled to Pittsburgh to take care of Isabelle McClung, who was ill. At Christmastime she returned to Washington

Square long enough to give Edith Lewis a fine press edition of Edgar Allan Poe's poems before she set out for Boston to finish work on the Christian Science articles. After two weeks staying with Margaret Deland in suburban Boston, Cather checked back into the Parker House. The year before, S. S. McClure had promised to come up from New York to introduce her to Sarah Orne Jewett, an author Cather had long admired, and to Annie Adams Fields (Figure 2.2). Although Jewett was strongly associated with the elite Boston magazine the *Atlantic Monthly*, she had also published fiction through McClure's Newspaper Syndicate and in *McClure's Magazine*. McClure failed to carry out his plan in 1907, but in March 1908, Alice Goldmark Brandeis, wife of Harvard Law School professor Louis Brandeis, whom Cather had befriended the year before, provided the fateful introduction. At the end of the month, after Cather had visited Jewett and Fields at 148 Charles Street as many times as she could, Jewett inscribed a copy of her book *A White Heron and Other Stories* (1886) to her new friend and fellow fiction writer. When Jewett penciled a note on the first page of her story "A Business Man"—"This was one of the first stories for

Figure 2.2 Sarah Orne Jewett (*left*) and Annie Adams Fields (*right*) at 148 Charles Street in Boston. Courtesy Historic New England.

Mr. McClure's Syndicate"—she acknowledged their common tie to the demanding McClure.[40]

At the end of March, Cather boasted to Alice Goudy, her high school English and Latin teacher, that she had seen "a great deal of Miss Jewett and Atlantic Monthly and Harvard people." Buoyed by this experience, she felt "as if [she] had really got a start at last" and had "a long happy period of happy work and happiest human companionship in the world before" her. But who was her "happiest" human companion, Isabelle McClung or Edith Lewis? Or did she need to choose? Cather continued to maintain ties to both, making long visits to Pittsburgh to write in the sewing room of the McClung family house, where she still kept much of her library, and when McClure granted her a long holiday as a reward for completing the trying work on the Christian Science articles, she traveled to Italy with McClung, not Lewis (although Lewis probably could not have afforded the trip).[41]

Even though Cather continued to write in Pittsburgh and travel with McClung, she was about to begin in earnest her work as managing editor of a national magazine, and she chose to make a home in New York City with her fellow magazine worker. Cather officially assumed her post in September 1908. The magazine's finances were still shaky. McClure considered Cather and staff writer George Kibbe Turner essential, and he urged a director of the magazine to offer them yearlong contracts starting October 1 so that they could sign apartment leases. With Cather's employment secure for a year, she and Lewis began a new chapter in their relationship, signing a lease for an apartment at 82 Washington Place, a modern six-story apartment building just off Washington Square (Figure 2.3).[42]

Shortly after the two women signed their lease, Cather returned to Boston on magazine business (complex negotiations concerning the publication of letters of the deceased sculptor Augustus Saint-Gaudens). Her trip also allowed her to spend two beautiful "blue-and-gold days" with Fields and Jewett at Thunderbolt Hill, Fields's house at Manchester-by-the-Sea. A telegram called Cather back to New York, where the office was "a good deal too tense and strained . . . just now to be agreeable," making it "hard to do one's work well with this kind of uncertainty." Cather longed to return to Thunderbolt Hill, but she also pointedly described herself to Fields as writing while sitting "in the little apartment in which you took such a kindly interest." No longer renting a room in a shabby rooming house, Cather was sharing a furnished apartment with Lewis. "Some of the wall paper is too bright and some of it to[o] dark,"

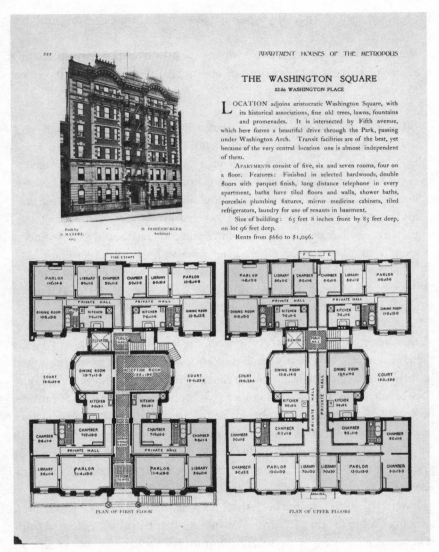

Figure 2.3 82–84 Washington Place from *Apartment Houses of the Metropolis* (1908), advertising five- to eight-room apartments renting for $660 to $1,096 a year.

Cather wrote to Fields, "but it is all bran[d] new and clean." Implicitly placing herself and Lewis together both at the office and at their apartment, Cather further complained that "[s]ome of the furniture" was "distinctly ludicrous—but then it is well enough to have certain pretexts for dull wit about, especially when the days at the office are long and discouraging as they are now."[43]

Writing to Jewett later in October, Cather described her increasing pleasure in the shared adventure of apartment life and days at the office with Lewis:

> Miss Lewis and I are enjoying our apartment more every day, although we lead no dreamy, idle lives in it. Mrs. Fields, I know, will exclaim when you tell her that so far we have largely fended for ourselves and have managed to get our own breakfast and luncheon and, about three days a week, our dinner. We dine at the Brevoort on other nights and have a maid come in to clean two days a week. There are good reasons why we should each of us practice reasonable economy this winter, and cooking does take one's mind away from office troubles. These latter cares will, we hope, be somewhat lighter after the middle of November. Meanwhile, we shall have a pretty thorny path to tread until then. The sales for October were 10,000 more copies than last October, and November has started well.

Cather insistently drew parallels between the long-established Jewett-Fields ménage and her own newly established one with Lewis. She also dropped into the first person plural, making herself and Lewis a unit both at home ("we" cook) and at the *McClure's* office ("we" cook together to keep our minds off troubles at the office). Cather expected Jewett to report to *her* partner in Boston about Cather's economical apartment living with her partner in New York, so different from Fields's large townhouse on Charles Street or grand summer "cottage" at Manchester-by-the-Sea, both staffed by many servants.[44]

Jewett had not yet written her letter, quoted at the beginning of this chapter, advising Cather to quit *McClure's*. However, Cather had already learned from Jewett and Fields's example that, in the words of Cather biographer Sharon O'Brien, "love and work might coexist." In 1908, the work both Cather and Lewis chose was magazine editing rather than authorship, although Cather did publish a few new stories and poems. They continued to do their magazine work *together*, as they had the two previous years, and as managing editor, Cather was Lewis's direct supervisor. Cather soon promoted Lewis to makeup editor, the person who laid out and pasted up the magazine's verbal and visual content. In 1908 and 1909, when a few new short stories by Cather and poems reprinted from her *April Twilights* collection (1903) appeared in the pages of *McClure's*, Lewis played a crucial role in how they were presented to the magazine's readers.[45]

Even as Lewis was establishing her new life with Cather in New York City, the collapse of her family's fortunes in Nebraska accelerated. In September 1908, the woman holding the mortgage on the Dawson County ranch obtained a judgment against the Lewises, who owed her more than $9,000. The family rented another house in Kearney in October, and in November, Addison Tibbets, Henry's old friend and Midland Alfalfa officer, filed suit against the company and the Lewises personally for failure to make payment on bonds. The hogs being fed on the ranch secured Tibbets's debt, and because Henry Lewis had no money to pay for their feed, Tibbets got an emergency court order allowing him to feed the hogs.[46]

Ironically, Edith Lewis was helping to disseminate romanticized versions of life on the western plains through *McClure's* just as her family's western phase was coming to a messy end. In November 1908, *McClure's* published "Loving's Bend" by Edgar Beecher Bronson, whose autobiographical *Reminiscences of a Ranchman* had just appeared. During the 1870s cattle boom, Bronson had owned a ranch in Sioux County, Nebraska, and trailed cattle up to Wyoming and Montana. His memoir presents a glorified, highly inaccurate account of his exploits, and "Loving's Bend" was part of a new series treating the western exploits of others, later collected as *Red-Blooded Heroes of the Frontier* (1910). In *McClure's*, Bronson's account of a Comanche attack on Texas cattleman Joe Loving on the Pecos River appeared with lavish illustrations by Maynard Dixon: cowboys on horseback with lariats guide a long stream of cattle, a Comanche spies on the cowboys, Comanches in war bonnets try to dislodge the cornered title character and his companion, and a Mexican trader on horseback finds the body of Loving out in the open, where he died trying to seek help for his friend. This version of the cowboys-and-Indians and cattle-drive West of the open range era was much more romantic than legal disputes about Henry Lewis's alfalfa "ranch" and hog-feeding operation.[47]

By early 1909, Henry's fortunes were in total collapse. The Farmers Union Ditch was a dead letter, he had lost the ranch to foreclosure, and Midland Alfalfa was in receivership. Because he was unable to pay the back taxes, he was also about to lose the house in Lincoln. By the spring, Henry had lost everything in Nebraska, retaining only substantial debts he could not pay. Furthermore, his pattern of mixing his business and social networks would have made staying in Nebraska socially awkward, even impossible. More than one longtime friend was suing him as a result of his business failures—even the judge in one lawsuit was an old friend from the Round Table. The wives of these men were also members of Lillie Lewis's Lotos Club, and because Henry had transferred property into Lillie's name, she became a named defendant.

In April, Henry traveled to New England to scout for employment and a place to live. While visiting his brother Frank (formerly his neighbor and law partner in Lincoln) in New Hampshire, he wrote his daughter Ruth in Kearney, making the trip sound exciting. However, it was surely discouraging to be starting over at age sixty, with two teenage daughters to support. His oldest daughter's success in New York was one bright spot. "Do you know," he queried Ruth, "that Miss Viola Roseboro has invited Edith to go with her to her country place in May?" In Boston, Henry executed a deed in lieu of foreclosure on the family house in Lincoln, and Lillie, Ruth, and Helen soon joined him in Winchester, a Boston suburb.[48]

Poet Ridgely Torrence later recalled that around this time he often saw Cather and Lewis dining together at the café at the Judson Hotel, and "Miss Lewis always cried straight through meals." Certainly, the total collapse of her family's fortunes in Nebraska was an occasion for tears. Her future, however, was in New York City with Cather. Cather's 1908 Christmas present communicated to Lewis that their newly established life together paralleled that of Jewett and Fields, that they were, in a sense, heirs to an established tradition (Jewett and Fields began sharing a home in 1881, the year Lewis was born). Cather had already shared her enthusiasm for Jewett's work with Lewis earlier in the year: in June 1908, while Cather was in Europe with Isabelle McClung, Lewis bought herself a copy of Jewett's masterwork, *The Country of the Pointed Firs* (1896). Cather, echoing Jewett's gift of *A White Heron* to her in March, gave Lewis two of Jewett's books as Christmas presents, *The Mate of the Daylight and Friends Ashore* (1883) and *Strangers and Wayfarers* (1890). *Strangers and Wayfarers* included one of Cather's favorite Jewett stories, "Going to Shrewsbury," which she would later select for *The Best Stories of Sarah Orne Jewett* (1925). *The Mate of the Daylight* had an important place in the development of Fields and Jewett's relationship. This volume encompassed stories Jewett published in the *Atlantic Monthly* in 1882 and 1883 and two previously unpublished stories. It thus collected the first stories Jewett wrote and published after beginning her partnership with Fields, and Jewett commemorated this by dedicating the volume in print "To A.F."[49]

In one of the stories collected in *Mate of the Daylight*, "Tom's Husband," Jewett used a story of gender role reversal in marriage to comment playfully and obliquely on the beginning of her partnership with Fields. Protagonists Mary and Tom Wilson, married relatively late in life, are not well suited to conventional marriage. Because Tom has lived off his family's wealth rather than enter business, he has become "very old-womanish" in his devotion to managing the affairs of his house, while Mary has great "executive ability" wasted in a wife. In her father's opinion, "she needed a wife herself more than she needed a husband." They try to be a conventional husband and wife, but Mary decides to revive the shuttered Wilson family mill, leaving Tom to manage the house. This arrangement satisfies them both until they lose two well-trained servants, and Tom comes to feel like the woeful "wife," ignored by his "husband" (thus the story's title). In her youth, before she met Fields, Jewett herself is reputed to have said that she "had more need of a wife than a husband."[50]

When Jewett and Fields established their partnership in 1881, neither woman became a wife *or* a husband. They formed a deep, lasting, and intimate bond while maintaining their own lives and careers. While they lived together for a portion of every year, their partnership was open and flexible enough that they spent months apart: Jewett continued to spend part of every year in the family home in Maine she shared with her mother and sister Mary and did much of her writing there. Inscribing *The Mate of the Daylight* and *Strangers and Wayfarers* to Lewis, Cather both shared with Lewis her pleasure in her new friendship with Jewett and Fields and invited Lewis to see the parallel—Cather aligned herself with Jewett and Lewis with Fields—and communicated her hopes for the future of their relationship.

Even though Lewis embraced their new shared domestic life, she remembered their Washington Place apartment as "unsettled and uncomfortable . . . very small, and not a very good place to work in." Cather thus continued to write in Pittsburgh and to retreat there when magazine work and S. S. McClure exhausted her. When an ill Cather retreated to Pittsburgh in March 1909, McClure wrote her that he was "anxious all day Sunday about you and I hoped Miss Lewis would have some word on Monday morning, but she had none." He was reassured by Cather's own letter from Pittsburgh and assured her that she could take time to recuperate. Nevertheless, he bombarded her with information about the magazine, and after she returned from Pittsburgh, he sent her to London on magazine business. McClure was not the only person at *McClure's* who recognized Cather and Lewis as a team both at Washington Place and at the magazine office. When Viola Roseboro' set sail for a European spa vacation in the fall of 1909, Cather and Lewis came to the docks together to see her off. "My love to Miss Cather and Miss Lewis," she wrote to McClure. "It was good of them to see me off." Around this time, Cather promoted Lewis from makeup editor to art editor, in which capacity she worked with artists to develop illustrations for *McClure's* content. For example, Lewis commissioned John Sloan, whose studio was near their old digs on South Washington Square, to develop illustrations for a story that ultimately appeared without them.[51]

Lewis also became visible to Cather's family. To her sister Jessica, who was married to a local banker back in Red Cloud, Willa Cather described "Miss Lewis" as "the girl who is in partnership-housekeeping in a flat with me." Willa's sister Elsie would soon meet Lewis in person. Elsie had begun her post-secondary education at the University of Nebraska in 1908, but after Willa had shared an apartment with Lewis for two years, she decided to send her baby sister to Lewis's alma mater. Elsie spent the Christmas holiday in 1910 with them in New York rather than travel from Smith College to Red Cloud.[52]

Shortly before that Christmas, Lewis participated in the festivities surrounding the marriage of Achsah Barlow to fellow painter Earl Brewster. Brewster and his friend Fred Shaler had been painting pictures of Central Park for an imagined book about the park, and, excited about being introduced to the art editor of *McClure's*, he brought along to his first meeting with her "one of the paintings for the book hoping it might be used as a cover for *McClure's*." Lewis did not acquire the painting for the magazine, but she was nevertheless "kindly, considerate, and very attentive." Lewis also met Shaler and another of Brewster's art school classmates, Rudolph Ruzicka, a Czech immigrant and wood engraver; both men became Lewis's friends when she met them again in Europe. Lewis gave Achsah and Earl "several volumes of Gilbert Murray's translations of Euripides" as a wedding present. The newly married couple sailed for Europe, where they planned to live, and on the voyage over they read Euripides aloud to one another.[53]

By 1911, Cather and Lewis had spent three years working and living together, a team both at home and at the office. Cather took her work seriously. After she "had charge" of the magazine as managing editor for a year, she boasted to her brother Roscoe that "we made sixty thousand dollars more than the year before." She also made important friends through her editorial work—she met Elizabeth Shepley Sergeant and Zoë Akins because they submitted work to the magazine, for example. She also complained about the work—to Roscoe she compared *McClure's* to "a sick baby—you've always got to be stuffing something into its blessed insides or it dies." Cather also remained ambivalent about the muckraking character of the magazine. Sergeant was strongly committed to progressive politics, but Cather wrote to her criticizing another contributor (Edith Wyatt), complaining that she "has given herself over [so] wholly to the cause of the White Slave" (efforts to end the recruiting of women into prostitution) that she seemed "to be maddened by having lived to[o] long in the company of a horrible idea—like Electra." Cather was ready to step away from her editorial responsibilities. By so doing, she changed part of her relationship with Lewis, but rather than cease to work together, they would begin to collaborate in a new way.[54]

O Pioneers! Cather and Lewis as Author and Editor

Sharing expenses with Lewis, by the late summer of 1911, Cather had finally saved enough to take a leave of absence from *McClure's* to write fiction full time. At this transitional moment, when Cather was poised between editorial staff and freelance contributor status, Lewis was identified as either literary editor or assistant managing editor of the magazine. Office protocol required that staff members submitting original short stories and poems use an assumed name, and Cather had submitted her poem "The Swedish Mother" without her name attached to it before she began her leave in the fall. This typed copy, which was used to typeset the poem for publication in the September 1911 *McClure's*, provides the first evidence of Lewis acting as Cather's editor (Figure 2.4). The poem was a last-minute substitution for some other poem, and Lewis wrote "Willa Sibert Cather" under the poem's title.

The poem has two speakers. The speaker of the opening three stanzas (which appeared in italics in the magazine) sets the scene for an immigrant woman to tell a story to her "red-haired daughter" about events that transpired many years before in Sweden. The central section of the poem, which appears in quotation marks, is in the voice of the title character, who tells a story about her father (grandfather of the red-haired child) caring for a sick lamb. The first speaker returns to close out the poem in the final three stanzas (also italicized). Cather had presented the title character's words in eye dialect (spelling "country" as "countree," for example), but Lewis, acting as

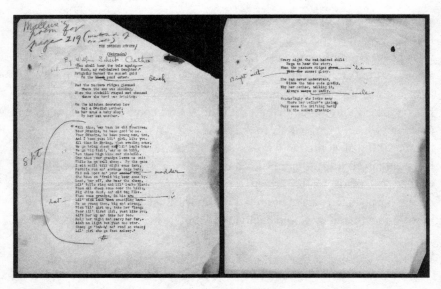

Figure 2.4 The typesetting copy for *McClure's Magazine* of Willa Cather's poem "The Swedish Mother," edited by Edith Lewis. Courtesy the Lilly Library, Indiana University, Bloomington.

Cather's editor at *McClure's*, made her speech more consistent by substituting "dat" for "that" and "mudder" for "mother," thus intensifying the contrast between the speech of the first speaker (presented in standard English) and that of the Swedish grandmother. Lewis also subtly shifted the diction and prosody in the opening and closing stanzas, changing the "bleak pond water" to "black pond water" and the "pasture ridges" that "gleam / With the sunset glory" into "pasture ridges" that "lie / Bright with sunset glory." Lewis also transformed the Swedish mother herself into someone who "always smiles so sadly" rather than "always weeps so sadly."[55]

Although Willa Cather placed the story of "Grandpa" and the sick lamb in Sweden, when her sister Elsie read the poem in *McClure's* she recognized that Willa had derived the incident from her Virginia childhood. Willa encouraged Elsie to come visit on her way to her final year at Smith College to see "the last of the apartment." She and Lewis were about to "tear [it] up" in preparation for Willa's retreat to a rented house in Cherry Valley with Isabelle McClung. Lewis took a room at 60 Washington Square again and kept soldiering on at the office until Cather was ready to come back to New York.[56]

During this transitional period, Cather delicately balanced both her relationships with McClung and Lewis and her identities as a novelist and a *McClure's* staff member. Cather's leave was designed to give her time to revise her novel *Alexander's Masquerade* (soon to be titled *Alexander's Bridge* for book publication), which, following office protocol, she had submitted to *McClure's* pseudonymously earlier in 1911. Once she was on leave, she dropped the masquerade, sending the revised first installment of the novel from Cherry Valley through Lewis (McClung had earlier gone down to the city to talk with Cameron Mackenzie about some "misunderstanding" concerning its serialization). In any event, Mackenzie was managing editor during Cather's leave, so the revised novel was accepted on his authority.[57]

In early 1912, Cather traveled frantically around the northeastern U.S. From Cherry Valley she went to Boston, where her book publisher, Houghton Mifflin, was located, to read the proofs of *Alexander's Bridge*. After emergency surgery there, she read the proofs while flat on her back at Margaret Deland's house. From Boston, she returned to New York and 60 Washington Square. As long as she was not actively involved in the office, she could interact with *McClure's* staff like an ordinary author. Over lunch in late February 1912, Mackenzie asked her whether she had "nothing to show for [her] stay in the country," and in response she offered her story "The Bohemian Girl." Mackenzie paid her $750 for it and wheedled out of her the plot of a potential story about an opera singer. Soon, someone at the office was asking Lewis "which character she thought more interesting" in a story Cather had not even begun writing. Cather was in New York only two weeks, however, before the illness of McClung's mother called her to Pittsburgh. In April, Cather finally departed for Winslow, Arizona, to visit her brother Douglass, who worked for the railroad, and to explore southwestern attractions. In June, on her way back east, Cather made a long visit to Red Cloud.[58]

Lewis remained anchored at the *McClure's* office and made do with her temporary quarters at 60 Washington Square, although while Cather was in Red Cloud, Lewis was with her mother on Cape Cod. Her parents were struggling with their new lives in Massachusetts. Henry Lewis was sixty-four, in poor health, and not very successful at selling real estate. He "greatly approve[d]" of Edith's taking Lillie to the Cape as a "Godsend to her to get away for a little!" Edith's sisters Helen and Ruth were thriving, at least, keeping up a voluminous correspondence with their friends in Lincoln and Kearney and being star players on their high school basketball team.[59]

Precisely when Cather officially resigned from her position at *McClure's* is not clear, although S. S. McClure's ouster from the magazine reinforced her slow drift away. McClure's control of the magazine was already in peril when she went to Cherry Valley in 1911, but in February 1912, his ouster was complete. To promote the illusion that McClure was still in control, Mackenzie and Frederick Collins commissioned McClure to write his autobiography for serialization in the magazine still bearing his name. When McClure wrote Cather asking for help, she was in Red Cloud, and she assured him that she would not expect payment from him, that her "interest in the work would be in an interest of friendship, a purely personal interest."[60]

When Cather returned to New York in August 1912, she spent "two very busy weeks" making "satisfactory arrangements" for paid writing commissions (Mackenzie had promised to pay her $300 apiece for a series of nonfiction articles on theater, opera, and dance). From New York, she went to Pittsburgh to work on her new "Swedish story," which would become part of her second published novel, *O Pioneers!* Continuing her frantic movement, she traveled to New York twice from Pittsburgh in late September, first to sign the lease for the apartment Lewis had found for them and then to move her effects into it.[61]

Cather boasted to Elizabeth Sergeant that it was "the perfect apartment, large, old-fashioned, roomy, one flight up; good fireplace, good windows, good woodwork, wide stairs up." Lewis was relieved by the change from the "box-like" Washington Place apartment, and the rent was even cheaper— only $42 a month. However, they had to do without modern comforts they had enjoyed at Washington Place to get so much space for so little: the apartment had gas rather than electric lights and was heated primarily by coal. Although far enough from Washington Square to be quiet, 5 Bank Street was still in Bohemian Greenwich Village, and Lewis could still walk to work on Union Square. Honoring their new home, Cather gave Lewis a translation of *The Journal of Françoise Krasinska, Great Grandmother of Victor Emmanuel.* Cather was not yet ready, however, to commit to writing in their new apartment, so she quickly returned to Pittsburgh to work.[62]

Meanwhile, Lewis continued to work under the people who had ousted McClure (Mackenzie, McClure's son-in-law, was part of the coup). She remembered those who took charge as "hard-headed business men," and Collins as talking "exultantly" of "having got rid of Mr. McClure" and treating him "contemptuously . . . when he occasionally came into the office." In contrast, she remembered the "kindness and genius" of her former boss and tried to help him when she could. She discreetly handled mail still coming into the office for him, and for a time she became deeply involved in his new project, the promotion of Maria Montessori's educational ideas in the U.S.[63]

Together, Cather and Lewis also coached McClure through the serialization of the autobiography Cather had ghostwritten for him (its installments appeared from October 1913 through May 1914) and the transition from serial to book. Mackenzie was managing editor, but it was certainly Lewis, not he, who wrote the August 1913 editorial announcement of the imminent publication of McClure's autobiography as part of the "celebration of the twentieth anniversary year of MCCLURE'S MAGAZINE." Describing it as a "most romantic and typically American" story of the success of someone who arrived in the U.S. as a "penniless immigrant," the announcement celebrated "the founding of the magazine" as "a thrilling and inspiring chapter in the ever wonderful adventure of American business." In December, Cather suggested that McClure contact William Morrow at Frederick Stokes and Company to discuss book publication of his autobiography, telling McClure that she was sure Morrow would "meet [his] wishes in every respect." In the same letter, she let him know that "Miss Lewis says the material you sent in for illustration is excellent." Then in 1914, Lewis became Morrow's point of contact for transferring the illustrations from the magazine office to the book publisher. *McClure's* swelled the length of the serialization of the autobiography by publishing reader's letters responding to it, which Lewis and Edith Wyatt (another McClure loyalist) edited for publication after securing permission to publish them.[64]

Cather and Lewis could not live on S. S. McClure's gratitude, however. Lewis's salary was less than $60 a week, and Cather was drawing down her savings as she waited for royalties from *O Pioneers!* to come in. Cather needed to write the article Mackenzie had commissioned in order to keep their household finances in the black. When Cather wrote to McClure in December 1913 that she was "under pressure to finish an article by Saturday," that pressure likely came from Lewis both as assistant managing editor of *McClure's* and as Cather's partner in housekeeping. On the one hand, Lewis needed Cather's "New Types of Acting: The Character Actor Displaces the Star" to fill the pages of the February 1914 issue of *McClure's*, soon to go to press. On the other hand, she needed Cather to finish the article so that she could pay her share of the rent. No prepublication versions of Cather's *McClure's* articles have surfaced, but doubtless Lewis edited them just as she had edited "The Swedish Mother."[65]

Although Cather and Lewis had been leasing apartments together for five years, Cather did not slow down her constant movement between Pittsburgh and New York and truly settle into life with Lewis at 5 Bank Street until late 1913. On Christmas Eve, the two women went to see Cather's new friend, Olive Fremstad, perform as Isolde in Richard Wagner's *Tristan and Isolde* at the Metropolitan Opera. They had seen Fremstad perform many times before, but researching her essay "Three American Singers: Louise Homer, Geraldine Farrar, Olive Fremstad," just out in *McClure's*, had given Cather the opportunity to get to know the diva personally. Cather had finally had most of her books shipped from the McClung house in Pittsburgh to 5 Bank Street "to swell the glory of this apartment—which I like better and better," as she explained to her sister Elsie. She rebuffed, however, her sister's suggestion that she might find a teaching position in New York and share in that swollen glory, explaining, "I'm afraid our apartment is not built for three." The boxes of books "had been piled mountain high in the dining room, in their boxes, for a week" when, on Christmas day, she and Lewis "tackled them" like soldiers in battle, not stopping until they were done at nightfall. Dressed in their "oldest clothes," they went at 5:30 to Guffanti's Table d'Hote, an Italian restaurant in midtown, hoping that no one would see them, and then went to bed early after getting soaked in a rainstorm. On New Year's Eve, they boarded a train for Boston together, Lewis to visit her family for a few weeks and Cather to visit Margaret Deland and Annie Fields.[66]

Cather and Lewis's relationship continued to allow them the freedom to spend time apart, just as Fields and Jewett's had. Later in 1914, Cather spent two weeks at Olive Fremstad's camp in Maine before she headed west, first to Red Cloud and then to Colorado and New Mexico. Concurrent with Cather's travels, Lewis had a long and magical visit with Earl and Achsah Brewster in Italy (Figure 2.5). The Brewsters were renting a villa on the Amalfi Coast in Ravello, and Achsah had given birth in 1912 to a daughter, Harwood. Earl's art school friend Fred Shaler was living with them, and Rudolph Ruzicka was making a long visit. Achsah remembered Lewis as "slender as a willow-wand" and "still . . . lisp[ing] if embarrassed." Achsah also attributed to her the "charm and detached wisdom" of Aspasia, the Greek goddess of philosophy, which allowed her to "forget all about herself in enjoying everyone and everything else, and seeing it with humour and philosophy." During Lewis's visit, the two women took an overnight steamer together to Capri (Figure 2.5). The new mother was anxious about leaving her toddler for the first time, but she and Lewis laughed over her anxiety and "drove, walked, visited historical sites,

Figure 2.5 Edith Lewis (*right*) and Achsah Barlow-Brewster (*left*) on their excursion to Capri in 1914. Courtesy Archives and Special Collections, University of Nebraska–Lincoln Libraries.

read learned discourses and talked over all the girls in our class at Smith, and why they did as they did, and admired everything altogether, and loved it all tremendously." Back at their villa, Lewis spent much of her time outdoors. Achsah recalled that Lewis "took to the water like a duck" (Figure 2.6). The villa had, Lewis recalled, "a little bathing beach at the foot of the garden," where she and her friends "bathed every day, and the maids brought great trays of wine and spaghetti down to the beach for our luncheon." When they weren't bathing, they "drove all over the chestnut-covered hills, in little horse-carriages with red tassels." They ate dinner on the terrace of the villa, wearing crowns of flowers and ivy and entertaining themselves by blowing soap bubbles with reeds. When it got dark, they lit Japanese lanterns. The group had been pooling money to buy lottery tickets every week, and over dinner they all wove elaborate tales about how they would spend their winnings if they won (traveling to Greece was a favorite fantasy). By moonlight, Lewis told "fabulous tales to match the fabulous unreality of the silver night," and each in turn picked up the thread and "embellish[ed] the yarn."[67]

In a sense this vacation in Italy allowed Lewis to live the Bohemian fantasy depicted in her short stories published more than a decade earlier, but the magic and whimsy dissipated like their soap bubbles when she returned

Figure 2.6 Edith Lewis (*far left*), Achsah Barlow-Brewster, and Earl Brewster in Ravello in 1914 on the bathing beach below the Brewster's rented villa. The man buried in the sand may be Fred Shaler or Rudolph Ruzicka. Courtesy Archives and Special Collections, University of Nebraska–Lincoln Libraries.

to the *McClure's* office. By late 1914, she had been at *McClure's* for more than eight years and was serving as its acting managing editor. She had finally had enough, however, of the magazine's ever-shifting editorial policies (by this time, muckraking articles were no longer appearing) and internal power struggles. She later identified "fundamental changes (for the worse) in the policy and organization" as her reason for leaving. Cather was finishing up her third novel, *The Song of the Lark*, inspired both by the life of Olive Fremstad and by Cather's own southwestern travels, and the time was ripe for Lewis to make a change. Neither Cather nor Lewis, however, was interested in leaving their shared Greenwich Village home.[68]

"The Best Boss Ever" and "One of the Best Judges of Fiction": Edith Lewis as Managing Editor of *Every Week* Magazine

Lewis applied for and was offered a position as an advertising copywriter at the J. Walter Thompson Co., but she wasn't ready to leave magazine editing behind. Instead she accepted an offer from the Associated Sunday Magazines (ASM). ASM had long been established as a provider of a Sunday supplement magazine for newspapers not controlled by Hearst or Pulitzer. Because it was losing affiliates, ASM decided to launch a new standalone three-cent weekly, *Every Week*, which would circulate through subscription and on newsstands in markets not served by ASM's remaining affiliates. Stanley Knapp, the owner of ASM, had hired Bruce Barton, a brash young Amherst College graduate with a genius for promotion, as editor in chief. Barton, who had little magazine experience, wisely hired Lewis, a seasoned magazine professional, as his managing editor.[69]

Every Week was published in a large format with colorful pictures of pretty girls by top illustrators on its front cover, while an evolving mix of fiction, advice, commentary, news items, and photographs with a human-interest focus appeared inside. Barton's provocative editorials promoting Christian morals, capitalism, and self-improvement featured prominently in each issue, and when he began signing them in 1916, he became the identifiable public face of the magazine. Even though Lewis's name appears nowhere in *Every Week*, she was largely responsible for hiring and managing the junior editorial staff and for the magazine's content, a substantial portion of which consisted of anonymous text written by the magazine's staff.[70]

Just as her relationship with Cather crossed over to her work at *McClure's*, it crossed over to her work at *Every Week*, although in new ways. As Lewis recalled in her memoir, "From the time that [Cather] wrote *The Song of the Lark*, we read together the copy and proofs of all her books. It was one of our greatest pleasures." They read the proofs of *The Song of the Lark*, a novel based in part on Olive Fremstad's life, in May and June 1915, shortly after *Every Week* published its first issue, and Lewis mined Fremstad's life for material for anonymous short articles. In late June, Fremstad was featured in an *Every Week* article titled "Two Women Wood-Choppers." The other woman was a New Hampshire widow who supported her family by chopping wood, but Fremstad was, as Lewis explained, "only what might be called a half-time worker." In the summers she engaged in the "business" of woodchopping "out in her Maine back lot" (where Cather had visited her the summer before while Lewis was in Italy), but in the fall "she goes off on a concert tour." Although Fremstad made large sums from touring, woodchopping allowed her to be "out in the open air." In the rest of the article Lewis miniaturized Fremstad's life story, much as Cather had done in "Three American Singers." The next week Fremstad appeared in one of *Every Week*'s key features, a themed photospread in which a long caption accompanied each photo. "They Come to Us from Every Nation," the headline proclaimed of prominent Americans who came to the U.S. as immigrants. A second photo of Fremstad chopping wood is accompanied by a biographical caption that begins with Fremstad's first public appearance in Stockholm and follows her with her family to Minnesota and then to New York. "Every year one thousand girls come to New York to study music," Lewis explained, "but 999 go back home and teach school. Young Olive Fremstad didn't go back—she went right on and on, clear up to the footlights of the Metropolitan." Lewis's caption for a photo of S .S. McClure essentially miniaturized Cather's ghostwritten autobiography of him. The caption recounted how McClure had come to the U.S. at age nine and acquired an education despite his family's poverty, and started "the first newspaper syndicate in America" at age twenty-seven, "the enterprise which founded his fame as an editor."[71]

Cather published fiction in *McClure's* before, during, and after her editorial stint there, but she contributed no fiction to *Every Week*—the tone of its fiction was more populist and popular. However, Lewis did entice her to contribute a nonfiction article, "Wireless Boys Who Went Down with Their Ships," which celebrated Harold Bride of the *Titanic* and other radio operators who sacrificed their lives to save passengers on sinking ships. The article appeared in August 1915, putting cash into Cather and Lewis's coffers in time for their first southwestern trip together. On their way west the two women stopped over in Lincoln and spoke to a *Nebraska State Journal* reporter. Cather described the "magazine situation in New York" as "interesting and precarious," in a state of "crisis" because of the "over-production of cheap magazines, the business depression and a feeling among business men that the magazine advertising bubble has burst." She improbably described McClure's withdrawal from *McClure's Magazine* as a prescient move allowing him to live a life of ease. Lewis was less voluble about being the managing editor of a cheap magazine, but she made sure readers in Lincoln knew that *Every Week* had "already gained an enormous circulation" after "running only a few months."[72]

The junior staff of *Every Week* that Lewis hired and managed was an interconnected and ever-changing group of Greenwich Village Bohemians in their twenties. Anne Herendeen, one of the earliest hires, graduated from Wells College in her native Upstate New York and had cut her teeth as a journalist in the Twin Cities. When she moved to New York City in 1914, she became active in feminist social and political circles, among other things joining the feminist luncheon club Heterodoxy. Minnesotan Brenda Ueland, Herendeen's classmate at Wells, started working for *Every Week* in late 1915. The year before, Ueland and Herendeen had shared a tiny apartment in Greenwich Village, frequenting its Bohemian haunts wearing fashions of their own devising and their hair cropped short. There were only two men on the editorial staff, whom Herendeen remembered after both had died as "delightful deviates . . . bless them." John Chapin Mosher, a young Williams College graduate from Albany, joined the *Every Week* staff in 1915. Outside the office he immersed himself in the Village's avant-garde theater community (the Provincetown Players staged two of his one-act plays during their first New York season). In 1916, John Colton, Ueland and Herendeen's journalist colleague from the Twin Cities, joined the staff. Raised by American parents in Japan, Colton would soon move on to writing sensational melodramas set in Asia and then to screenwriting. In 1916, Lella Faye Secor, a western journalist fresh off Henry Ford's Peace Ship, joined the staff. She and Anne Herendeen were soon engaged in antiwar activism together. Finally, in 1918, a few months before the magazine ceased publication, Herendeen helped her friend from the Women's Peace Party, journalist Freda Kirchwey, get a position.[73]

Cather and Lewis began holding their legendary Friday teas at 5 Bank Street the same year Lewis started at *Every Week*. These teas have generally been portrayed as a salon with Cather, the novelist, at their center, but they also gave Lewis a place to mentor her young staff. As Brenda Ueland recalled, even though Bruce Barton was the public face of *Every Week*, Lewis was "our real boss." Ueland wrote her mother that she and Lewis "have a secret liking of each other. She is pretty and shy and we both have the same trouble of jerky talking. . . . [S]trange to say (for me), I love her." She remembered her as "the best boss I ever had, the most intelligent, the most just, the kindest and the bluntest." Lewis would criticize Ueland's work (the humorous captions she wrote for photographs) while "almost lisping and blushing deeply." Her criticism would have caused "an unbearable wound" delivered by anyone else, but Ueland "respected [Lewis] so much" that she rewrote her captions without complaint, feeling "grateful to her for all her guidance." Ueland felt like a "young nobod[y]" at Friday tea when music critics like Louis Sherwin and Pitts Sanborn were engaging in "highbrow talk" with Cather, who was "affirmative and masculinely intellectual," her "talk" "pleasant and fluent but very, very definite." Lewis, however, "*our* darling," as she, Herendeen, and Mosher saw her, "was always shy and quiet, gently blushing if you said something that made her laugh, and she just quietly saw to it that we had a nice time and that there was hot water for tea." Gossiping at tea, Herendeen reported that Lewis "had once written beautiful poetry but gave it up." They all agreed, "I bet she would be a hundred times better than Miss Cather!"[74]

In addition to giving up writing "beautiful poetry," Lewis had given up writing her own fiction, and this former fiction writer assumed primary responsibility for *Every Week*'s fiction program. ASM had generally included more than one substantial short story (4,000 to 5,000 words) in each issue. In contrast, *Every Week* was running a serial novel (*Who Is Marie DuPont?*, by Adele Luehrmann, began serialization in the second issue) and only one short story. Bruce Barton boasted to readers that every issue of *Every Week* would give them "*one better*" short story rather than "*five good* stories," and as "E. Lewis," the "Literary Editor" of *Every Week*, Lewis advertised for contributors, seeking "a story of modern life, preferably 60,000 to 70,000 words, with plenty of action" to run as a serial and 5,000-word short stories about "love, mystery and adventure."[75]

As literary editor, Lewis combined tact, idealism, and pragmatism. George Buckley, president of the Crowell Publishing Company (which would purchase *Every Week* in 1916), said that Lewis "had a very fine mind, really a brilliant mind: that she was one of the best judges of fiction that they had ever known; that she had rewritten a great deal of the stuff that had come in to them." The absence of an editorial archive makes it difficult to observe Lewis in action as she judged and rewrote fiction, and her work editing Cather's fiction in this period also remains inaccessible—the first extant edited typescript of a Cather novel or short story is *The Professor's House* (1925). However, two young authors, Phillip Curtiss and Conrad Richter, happened to preserve letters from *Every Week* and their literary agents who corresponded with the magazine on their behalf. These letters document Lewis's work and illuminate how her magazine editorial experiences made her an important resource for Cather as she was establishing her reputation as a novelist. Curtiss, a graduate of Trinity College in Connecticut, came to fiction writing from journalism and advertising. Even though he became a prolific and successful magazinist, he was still struggling in 1915 to establish himself as an author. Curtiss left no mark on literary history, but Richter would achieve a reputation equal to Cather's as a novelist of American frontier life. In 1915, when *Every Week* launched, however, Richter was, like Curtiss, still a struggling beginner.[76]

When Curtiss submitted "The Patrician" to ASM in early 1915, Lewis wrote to him about the editorial transition and explained that she and Barton were interested in publishing his story in *Every Week* but wanted him to revise it first. In Curtiss's story, two men who grew up in a Massachusetts mill town, the narrator and his prizefighter friend, Spike, encounter the title character, Prenny Weston. The narrator expresses surprise that Spike has become friendly with someone they both loathed as working-class boys. To explain the friendship, Spike recounts his service under Prenny in the army and how he assisted him with a plot to capture the woman whom he later marries. In Curtiss's original rendering of Prenny as a child, he was, in Lewis's words, "a sort of cry-baby, mother's-darling kind of boy." Lewis and Barton felt that this characterization made the later emergence of his "steely streak" unconvincing. "Can't you make him petted and spoiled," she queried, "and yet, at the same time, give one the idea that his unpopularity consisted rather in his being supercilious and autocratic rather than his being unhealthy and good for nothing." Curtiss jumped quickly into action, sending the revised story back days later. "I think you have done an amazingly good job in following up my suggestion," Lewis wrote, telling him that they would "raise [him] somewhat" on his usual pay (from $150 to $200) because they thought the story "an unusually good one." Lewis declined Curtiss's story "Forty-five," explaining that although she "agree[d] with" him that it was "an extremely powerful story" and "more unusual" than "The Patrician," it was not worth the $500 he asked because "we are looking for stories with strong plots," which "The Patrician" had but which "Forty-five" lacked. In writing Curtiss, Lewis acknowledged that there were different kinds of literary value, but she was being pragmatic and doing her job. She also revealed to Curtiss that under the cover of editorial anonymity she had been his editor before: "I was one of the editors at McClure's, at the time we published your 'Princess and Plumbers,' and have always remembered your work with much pleasure. I hope you are going to send us a lot of good stuff for our new weekly."[77]

Barton wrote Richter soliciting a short story after one of his short stories appeared on a "best of 1914" list. Barton himself wrote to reject Richter's first submission, but Lewis tactfully rejected his next. "Mr. Barton and I have both been interested in this story" (which story is not clear), she wrote, "but it seems to us a little too quiet and leisurely in tone to be just the sort of thing we are looking for." Expressing a desire "to have [his] name" in the magazine, she asked him to "send us the next good thing" he wrote and gently guided him toward the magazine's needs by sending several issues "so that you can get some idea of the kind of fiction we are using." In her role as editor, Lewis worked to build relationships with authors and steered them toward the magazine's aesthetic.[78]

Undeterred by rejection, Richter soon sent another story, about which Lewis wrote him at length because the story had "interested [her] more than the general run." She conceded it was "a very unusual and original piece of work" and "the idea" was "extremely original and interesting," but his "power of execution [was] not nearly adequate to [his] idea." Likening Richter's story to "the type of thing in which [Nathaniel] Hawthorne succeeded so wonderfully," she found that Richter's lack of technique "blurred" his "flashes of real inspiration and imagination." "As a marketable product," she explained, returning to a pragmatic register, "it does not stand as good a show as a story with a more commonplace idea that lies within the writer's power of presentation." "Interested" was a key word when Lewis corresponded with potential contributors of fiction. In some instances, it signaled a willingness to buy ("we" are "interested" in purchasing your story), but in others, Lewis was "interested" in an aesthetic debate. In the latter case, she wrote in the first person singular, indulging in a longer epistolary exchange, but she knew better than to open *Every Week*'s purse to buy fiction that didn't suit its audience.[79]

Early in 1916, *Every Week* purchased another story from Curtiss, "Cather," which Lewis praised, writing him, "I think Cather was the best thing you have ever done." The cleverly plotted story is told from the perspective of Stephen Langley, a successful country gentleman who was not a good student in college. Out of pity, he takes in as a sort of permanent houseguest John Cather, a brilliant college classmate who failed at teaching. Cather remains quietly at Langley's house while Langley socializes with his well-off country set. One day Langley stumbles on an unfinished letter from Cather to a woman, in which Cather boasts of his adventures in country high society. After reading it, Langley does not confront Cather about his deception but instead brings him modestly into his social world. He gives him a nice suit, teaches him to ride, and absents himself so Cather can entertain the woman to whom he is writing the letters. In the final sentence of the story, Langley and the readers learn that Cather was not deceiving his lady friend about his social life in the country; rather, he was writing an epistolary novel, and having placed his novel with a publisher, he is in a position to marry.[80]

Curtiss had no idea that the editor who praised his "Cather" was living with Willa Cather, author of *Alexander's Bridge, O Pioneers!*, and *The Song of the Lark*, and his competitor in the magazine short story market. In any event, having scheduled "Cather" for March publication, Lewis observed that they had "a hole in [their] April schedule" and would like to "follow ['Cather'] up with another story from you while that is still fresh in people's minds." Lewis and Barton were expecting a series of stories from Curtiss, but it fell to Barton to chastise Curtiss for submitting an inferior story when they were under pressure to fill space. In the midst of this conflict, Lewis once again became "interested" in an aesthetic argument. "Your letter interests me very much," she wrote Curtiss. She conceded that arbitrary length limitations for short stories were problematic. "Of course any story ought to take the amount of space that is required for the expression of its idea," she conceded, and brevity was only a virtue for "a certain kind of story that is told best in the fewest words." She maintained that magazines had gotten better about allowing for longer short stories, citing her experiences at *McClure's*, where "we used to run a story as long as eighteen thousand words in a single number." However, not all stories needed to be that long, although "once in a while one comes along and there ought to be space for it when it does." In the case of *Every Week*, its twenty-page format made "space . . . a terrible problem." She looked forward to a planned increase in page count that would allow them "to pub-lish longer stories and more different kinds of stories." Even as she rejected Curtiss's story, she left the door open for him as a contributor, telling him, "I feel that both stories of yours which we have published have been quite mem-orable studies of character, and that they stand high above the general run of magazine stories."[81]

The hoped-for increase from twenty to twenty-four pages came later in 1916. *Every Week* boasted to potential authors that they had a "chance for an-other short story every week" and that the magazine was "especially friendly to those who are on the way up. We are in that class ourselves." It took *Every Week* a while to accept the struggling and aspiring Conrad Richter, who, frustrated with his lack of success, had engaged a literary agent. Cora Paget of the Paget Literary Agency wrote him in 1917 about placing his "Swanson's Sweet Home." *Everybody's* had accepted it, but "one of the editors at *Every Week*" (certainly Lewis) had "half wanted to accept" the story but

decided against it, because the opinion in that office was that your writing and handling of your material was not as good as the ideas in your stories warranted. This editor seemed to think that your work was inclined to be long winded and too indirect, in treatment, always taking, so to speak, a long round about way, instead of a straight direct path to the incident.

Soon Paget was able to report that *Every Week* had bought his story "Nothing Else Matters" for $300. With Paget's advice, Richter had extensively rewritten the story, which neatly tied together technical details of railyard operations, the male protagonist's character development, and a wholesome romance. The very brief biography of Richter that ran with the story boasted of his railroad work experience, and Paget soon told him that *Every Week* wanted more railroad stories.[82]

Lewis dealt with many literary agents, including Paul Reynolds, whom Cather engaged to place her short stories in magazines beginning in 1916. In August 1917, Lewis wrote directly to authors whose work she had read for *Every Week*, even those such as Richter who were represented by agents, about a new "experiment" in editorial policy. She told them that the magazine might publish "two short stories of from one to two thousand words" in addition to its established "custom of running one lead story of from five to six thousand words—the best we can find in the market." She suggested that these short-short stories would be "in their way . . . as interesting and powerful as" the longer lead story. This change would both allow the magazine "to use more fiction . . . without cutting out any of our other features" and offer authors "a new, interesting form for writers to play with and experiment with." Speaking directly in the first person without the cover of the editorial "we," Lewis continued, "I think there must be a great many writers who have ideas they would like to use in this kind of story. Heretofore there has been no market for them. We hope that by offering a market, Every Week can develop a new and very interesting kind of fiction." She suggested that these stories might focus on "one incident or situation or character and develop it in such a way as to give the reader a single powerful impression"; rather than "leading through a series of events up to a climax, as a longer story does, they will seize upon one striking or significant moment in the human drama and throw it up in strong relief." *Every Week*'s fiction was certainly not highbrow, and as Lewis's correspondence with both Curtiss and Richter demonstrates, she understood that the magazine's readers were looking for the excitement of genre fiction. Nevertheless, her idealism came through in her suggestion that "French writers have succeeded in mastering this sort of thing, and I do not see any reason why American writers cannot produce equally good results. I think many of our foremost short story writers would find it a relief to get away from the conventional form that most magazines demand, and try their hand at an entirely fresh, new kind of fiction."[83]

Richter soon wrote Lewis asking how much *Every Week* would pay for these shorter stories. Lewis responded that they would use a "more or less sliding scale" as they did with other contributions, but "[i]f the idea is original and powerful enough, the thing well enough done," she didn't see why they couldn't pay as much for a 2,000-word story as a 5,000-word one. She also expanded on her rationale for the new fiction program. She felt "sure that most writers must have ideas that do not inevitably fit into the conventional magazine story length," and at both *Every Week* and *McClure's*, she had to "turn down so many stories of just this sort merely because there was no place for them according to the policy of the magazine. I think there would have been more of them and more good ones if there had been a definite market for them." No short-short story by Richter appeared in *Every Week*. Rather, "The Pippin of Pike County," a briskly paced longer tale set in a Western mining camp, was the last Richter story *Every Week* published. As in "Nothing Else Matters," the technical details of silver mining in "The Pippin of Pike County" provide a backdrop for the development of the male protagonist into a real man, and he gets the girl (and substantial wealth) in the end.[84]

As *Every Week's* buyer of fiction, Lewis successfully guided these young authors toward meeting the magazine's needs. During the years that Lewis was advising authors who submitted to *Every Week*, Willa Cather was writing magazine stories about New York office workers and about female singers negotiating the perils of celebrity. These atypical stories are Cather's least well known, written, as she often explained in letters, to bring in money while she engaged in the slow work of novel writing. As she wrote to Ferris Greenslet in late 1916, these short stories, placed in magazines by Paul Reynolds as her agent, had made her enough money that she could "afford to bone down on [her] long story," meaning *My Ántonia*, which she had just begun writing. However, even this "long story," so unlike most fiction published in *Every Week*, was informed by the work of Cather's fellow Nebraskan spending her days at the *Every Week* office.[85]

Visualizing Great Plains Immigrants in *Every Week* and *My Ántonia*

During its three-year run, *Every Week* regularly published Western genre fiction, stories not only set on the plains during the open range era but also set in the southwestern desert, in mining camps, and in the frigid farthest

West (northwestern Canada, the Yukon, and Alaska). During those same years, *Every Week's* managing editor was living with one of "America's foremost short story writers," whose *My Ántonia*, a new kind of Western, would soon establish her reputation as one of American's foremost novelists. Lewis's magazine editorial work and Cather's novel writing were not parallel activities running on separate tracks. Instead, the two Nebraskans were thinking together about their home region and how to represent it to a national audience through both words and pictures.

When Cather was nearly done writing *My Ántonia* in the spring of 1917, she began negotiating with Houghton Mifflin to have Polish American illustrator W. T. Benda illustrate her novel. Benda's illustrations had appeared regularly in *McClure's* while Cather and Lewis were on staff, and he was also doing work for *Every Week*. Lewis had featured him alongside Fremstad and McClure in "They Come from Every Nation" in July 1915. The caption next to a photograph of the illustrator at work in his studio explained that Benda

came over to this country some years after his aunt, Helena Modjeska, greatest of Polish actresses, started her big fruit ranch in southern California, with the dream of making it an agricultural community of Polish refugees. Some of the Poles who emigrated to the Modjeska ranch brought with them pokers and tin pans—necessities they despaired of finding in barbarous America. The community was a failure, but young Benda wasn't; he began to draw black-and-white studies of lovely, languorous Polish ladies—the kind that used to captivate their Russian conquerors, and that now captivated the New York magazine editors to such a degree that Mr. Benda has never been allowed to go back and settle in his native Cracow; instead, he lives immured in a studio somewhere in upper New York City. This is no place to talk shop; otherwise we should mention that our next serial, by James Oliver Curwood, is to be illustrated by Mr. Benda.

Curwood's serial *The Girl Beyond the Trail* (illustrated by Benda for *Every Week* and later retitled *The Courage of Marge O'Doone* for book publication) ran from July to September 1916. This adventure tale set in remote and snowy regions of western Canada features a wolf-dog, a trained bear, and a romance and family reunion plots enabled by an extraordinary number of coincidences. From 1915 through the early fall of 1917, Benda also illustrated short stories, drew headpieces, and created full-page designs and a cover for *Every Week*. A typical "Benda woman" appeared on the cover of the same

November 1917 issue in which Benda wrote about Ignace Paderewski for the ongoing *Every Week* series "The Most Interesting Man I Know." Unlike most who contributed to this series, Benda both wrote the text about the Polish violinist and drew a portrait of him.[86]

In the midst of Lewis's ongoing work with Benda for *Every Week* content, Benda came to dinner at 5 Bank Street in mid-October 1917 to discuss illustrations for *My Ántonia*. Benda's usual magazine illustrations (including most of his *Every Week* illustrations) were drawn in charcoal and printed in halftone. Cather found these "rather too mannered," but she had seen his pen-and-ink illustrations for Jacob Riis's *The Old Town* (1909), a book about Riis's childhood hometown in Denmark, and she wanted him illustrate her novel in the same style.[87]

In November 1917, a month after Lewis and Cather had Benda over for dinner, Cather became embroiled in a dispute with Houghton Mifflin about Benda's compensation for the pen-and-ink drawings he had been working on for a month. Ferris Greenslet's colleague Roger Scaife had first suggested illustrations to Cather during an in-person visit to New York City in the spring, but in November, he offered to pay Benda a mere $150 for the planned twelve drawings. Citing her experience at *McClure's*, Cather argued for a higher rate, but in rejecting her argument Scaife aimed over Cather's shoulder at Lewis, managing editor of a magazine that was certainly paying Benda well for his services: "Magazine[s] are in the habit of paying very much larger sums to artists. In fact, in a good many cases, they have completely spoiled the artists, and have made it practically impossible for book publishers to use their work."[88]

The conflict was eventually resolved. Houghton Mifflin did not disclose to Cather their terms with Benda, but they seem to have paid him more than $150 but below his normal rate. Benda might have felt, however, that the high-paying magazine work Lewis continued to offer him made up for it. Indeed, at the same dinner at which Cather proposed to Benda that he produce pen-and-ink drawings of Czech and Swedish immigrants for her novel, Lewis likely asked Benda to do the same for the first *Every Week* story published as part of her short-short story program. Two Benda pen-and-ink drawings accompany Elizabeth Gaines Wilcoxson's "Morning," a 2,000-word story depicting the first hour of the day for Swedish-speaking Alma and Nels (Figure 2.7). Married for a year, they had earlier moved away from their families to "a distant State where land was abundant and cheap, though hard to till" (plausibly Nebraska). In the course of their morning, Alma milks the

Figure 2.7   W. T. Benda's illustrations from "Morning" in *Every Week* magazine.

cows, feeds the chickens, and gathers their eggs, but when the husband and wife are about to go out together to sow seeds, she cannot lift the seed bag. When Nels looks at her with a puzzled expression, she confesses that she is pregnant with their first child.[89]

Cather was finishing up her novel at the same time Lewis was editing Wilcoxson's story, and Benda was working on illustrations for both simultaneously. Indeed, he clearly used the same woman as a model for his drawing of Norwegian immigrant Lena Lingard in *My Ántonia* (Figure 2.8) and his drawings of Swedish immigrant Alma in "Morning." Although the published results differ in style, Benda's delicately lined pen-and-ink illustrations for "Morning" served as a sort of early draft for his more heavily inked drawings for *My Ántonia*, which Cather wanted to resemble "old woodcuts." Through their work with Benda, both Lewis as an editor and Cather as a novelist were trying out strategies for representing Great Plains European immigrant women sympathetically to a national audience.[90]

Wilcoxson's simple and charming story differs markedly from a longer story she published in *Every Week* in 1917, and Lewis had great hopes that her new series would spur other authors to write high-quality fiction. On the same page as the opening paragraphs of "Morning," Lewis touted her

Figure 2.8 W. T. Benda's illustration of Lena Lingard knitting in *My Ántonia*.

new program as "Something New in Short Stories" and reproduced excerpts from letters from authors (including Phillip Curtiss) praising the innovation. "Apparently there is a real desire among writers of fiction in America to do something new and different in short-story writing," she wrote. "Uncommonly good stories can be and are told in the conventional magazine length. But occasionally writers get tired of this length. Instead of taking the reader through a long, complicated plot, they want to do something short and sharp—to create a single dramatic effect, give him one picture that will stay in his mind, awaken a mood that he will always remember and associate with that particular story." Introducing Wilcoxson's story, she opined, "We do not expect to get many better stories than 'Morning,' by Elizabeth Wilcoxson. Its freshness, charm, and simple truthfulness set an unusually high mark."[91]

Sarah Orne Jewett had written Cather nearly a decade earlier that her "Nebraska life,—a child's Virginia, and now an intimate knowledge of what we are pleased to call the 'Bohemia' of newspaper and magazine office life" were "uncommon equipment" for her as a writer and subjects about which she might write fiction. Even though Cather's departure from *McClure's* was belated, she was fulfilling Jewett's prophecy. In addition to writing about Nebraska in *My Ántonia*, Cather wrote, as mentioned earlier, magazine stories about office workers, including "Ardessa." Set in the magazine offices of the *Outcry*, "Ardessa" appeared in the *Century* shortly before Houghton Mifflin published *Ántonia*. Having left *McClure's*, Cather was equipped to see "the 'Bohemia' of . . . magazine office life" "from the outside," the position from which Jewett advised her to write about it.[92]

In *On Company Time: American Modernism in the Big Magazines*, Donal Harris points to "Cather's double life as editor and author" as the source of "productive friction." On the one hand, like other early-twentieth-century authors, Cather claimed "aesthetic autonomy"—the value of her work was outside the market. On the other hand, she and others forged their aesthetics in the "unapologetically successful economic and institutional worlds" of journalism and magazines. Harris locates that doubling and friction within Cather, but we might also see it in her partnership with Lewis. The Irishness of Marcus O'Malley, the *Outcry's* editor-in-chief in "Ardessa," and the fictional magazine's muckraking character have evoked for critics Cather's experiences at *McClure's*. However, the *Outcry* is a weekly, not a monthly like *McClure's*, and the brash O'Malley resembles the brash Bruce Barton, Lewis's boss at *Every Week*, as much as he resembles S .S. McClure. Cather, who had left *McClure's* several years before writing "Ardessa," could see the magazine office through Lewis's eyes. Lewis, who spent her days at the *Every Week* office and nights and weekends at 5 Bank Street, reading and talking over with Cather her novels and stories in progress, had her own double vision: she used her position as the managing editor of a cheap magazine to make a market for "a new kind of fiction," including Wilcoxson's fresh take on Scandinavian immigrants to the Great Plains.[93]

The War at Home and the End of *Every Week*

Although Lewis couched her short-short story program in idealistic terms for readers and authors, it was also a pragmatic response to the pressures World War I was putting on magazine production. *Every Week* ran its last serial novel in 1917, probably to avoid committing financially to another longer work if the magazine had to shut down before serialization concluded. Even though the young women working under Lewis were engaged in antiwar work, once the U.S. entered the war, war-related content dominated *Every Week*. John Mosher, the young staff member of whom Lewis was most fond, began to feel the pressure to enlist. As Brenda Ueland recalled, he "made jokes and burst into his spasmodic, agonized laugh. 'I have a friend,' he said, 'whose mother is very anxious for him to go to the Front, to see the stuff that is in him.'" Succumbing to the pressure, he enlisted in the Army Medical Corps. Soon after, Cather complained to Meta Schaper Cather, the German American wife of her brother Roscoe, that "the war d[ar]kens everything" in the city, making people "so bitter and horrid" and inducing prejudice against all Germans and German culture.[94]

A war-related "coal famine and a blizzard" in early 1918 landed a one-two punch on both apartment and office life for Cather and Lewis. Because their gas lines froze, they couldn't cook, and Cather wrote at the dining room table to be near a coal grate and "spen[t] all [her] time hunting coal" to feed it. Meanwhile *Every Week*'s office was "almost entirely without heat," and as Cather reported to friends in Red Cloud, "Edith's office [was] so cold she had to work in her coat and furs for weeks." Nevertheless, "[e]very Friday afternoon" they had "pleasant and interesting people" for tea, including many friends from Lincoln who came through New York, and they pulled off "some jolly little dinner parties."[95]

Cather needed to keep feeding that coal grate to feed portions of the final typescript of *My Ántonia* to Houghton Mifflin. In late June, she finally sent Ferris Greenslet the introduction, which she wrote last. Just as Cather was completing her novel, Lewis lost her job. In late May, Bruce Barton informed contributors that the directors had voted *Every Week* out of existence because the war had driven paper costs up and advertising revenues down. "Please remind Miss Lewis of my appreciation of her kind interest in my humble scratchings," a disappointed Conrad Richter wrote to Barton. After Cather sent her introduction and the galley proofs of the opening chapters of *My Ántonia* to Boston, she and Lewis headed for Jaffrey, New Hampshire.[96]

They had hoped to go west to visit Willa's brother Roscoe in Wyoming, but as she explained to him, "the horrible increase in railroad and Pul[l]man fares made Wyoming out of the question for both Miss Lewis and me." Instead, they were at the Shattuck Inn, where Cather had written part of *My Ántonia* the summer before, to read its proofs. In *Willa Cather Living*, Lewis explained that Cather "liked to read proofs out of doors whenever it was possible; and one could always find convenient rocks to sit against in the wood near the Shattuck Inn." Cather generally worked in the morning, and Lewis described mornings reading proofs in 1918 as "full of beauty and pleasure," with chipmunks "flash[ing] up and down along the trunks of the trees" and a mole "steal[ing] out of its hole near [them] and slid[ing] like a dark show along the ground." From Jaffrey Cather went to Scarsdale, where Isabelle McClung (now married to violinist Jan Hambourg) was staying. From there Cather went to Red Cloud to visit her family.[97]

Lewis recalled that while she and Cather were reading the proofs for *My Ántonia* "[t]he air seemed full of the future—a future of bright prospects, limitless horizons." However, her own future was uncertain. She was unemployed and her health was poor (she had been struggling with trachoma, an eye infection, for several years). From Jaffrey, Lewis went to Canada for a four-month vacation. In late November, she was back in New York and recovering but still unemployed. Her brother Harold offered to send her money if she was "run[ning] short . . . I don't see how you have managed it with all your doctor's bills and enforced vacation and all the trouble with your eye, and hate to think what would have happened to me under similar circumstances." She was, however, just about to apply again for a job as a copywriter at the J. Walter Thompson Co. This job, which would challenge and satisfy her for the rest of her working life, is the subject of Chapter 4. But before we follow Edith Lewis to Madison Avenue, I turn back the clock to 1915 to follow her and Cather on their first trip together to the American Southwest.[98]

3

"Our Wonderful Adventures in the Southwest"

Willa Cather and Edith Lewis's Southwestern Collaborations

A year after Willa Cather's death, Edith Lewis sent Cather's niece Virginia Cather Brockway a "parcel post box of Willa's things," including two pieces of Native American jewelry. "The little Indian necklace of turquoise and coral was one of her great treasures," she explained, because "she was especially fond of that soft blue Indian turquoise." She also sent a "Navaho bracelet" because she thought it would "remind" Virginia "of that time we all met together in Santa Fe." Although Lewis willingly parted with these items, she also feared that they might not be as meaningful to Cather's niece as they were to her. The items brought "back the most vivid pictures" of Cather—she could "hardly see them as they [were] in themselves or as perhaps they appear to another person." The necklace in particular, she explained, "seems the whole Southwest to me—our adventures down there—the feeling of the country."[1]

For Lewis and Cather, their southwestern travels together were an escape from the pressures of modern city life into a realm of adventure. Lewis used the word "adventure" elsewhere for her southwestern travels with Cather. To Stephen Tennant, for example, responding to his condolence letter after Cather's death, she wrote that she wished to "talk with" him about "many things," including "some of our wonderful adventures in the Southwest," which she had been recollecting.[2]

Cather first traveled to the Southwest in 1912, to visit her brother Douglass, then a brakeman for the Santa Fe Railway. This trip inspired the southwestern section of *The Song of the Lark*, in which the protagonist, Thea Kronborg, discovers her artistic identity while visiting cliff dweller ruins modeled on Arizona's Walnut Canyon. Lewis did not accompany Cather in 1912 or on a 1914 southwestern trip, but she and Cather traveled to the

Southwest together in 1915, 1916, 1925, and 1926, and southwestern travel became their shared passion.

Travel was also an integral part of Cather's creative cycle: composition, revision, editing, and proofreading often took place away from New York City. In the Southwest, Cather sought experiences and information necessary for her creative work, and she transformed experiences she shared with Lewis into fiction. She gave their 1915 experiences at the cliff dweller ruins at Mesa Verde National Park in southwestern Colorado to Tom Outland in *The Professor's House* (1925), and in 1925 in northern New Mexico, she and Lewis together "discovered" the life stories of Jean-Baptiste Lamy and Joseph Machebeuf that formed the basis of *Death Comes for the Archbishop* (1927).

Cather and Lewis were not the only enervated eastern city dwellers who sought adventure and regeneration in the West. In 1885, Dr. S. Wier Mitchell, a specialist in "nervous diseases," sent Owen Wister, a young Harvard graduate unhappily working at a bank, to a Montana cattle ranch to calm his shattered nerves. Wister's experiences inspired his novel *The Virginian* (1902), which set the pattern for many Westerns to follow. Dr. Mitchell sent Charlotte Perkins Gilman, who had recently given birth, to bed instead of to a western ranch, and her experience of this "rest cure" inspired her story "The Yellow Wallpaper" (1892), in which the narrator descends into madness. Cather and Lewis's choices of dress and activities on their southwestern trips suggest that they were playing cowboy rather than allowing themselves to be confined as women. During the brief open range era, western Nebraska had been cowboy territory, but when both women lived in central Nebraska in the late nineteenth century, the crop farmer rather than the cowman predominated. As Wister observed in his 1895 essay, "The Evolution of the Cow-puncher," the true cow-puncher was "not compatible with Progress" and was "now departed, never to return." Wister noted, however, one exception: New Mexico was the cow-puncher's "last domain." To play cowboy, Cather and Lewis needed to go farther west than Nebraska, to the southwestern desert, a landscape featured in Zane Grey's spectacularly successful *Riders of the Purple Sage* (1912), in which two cowboy heroes rescue two damsels from Mormons and cattle rustlers.[3]

The Professor's House and *Death Comes for the Archbishop* certainly depart from the formulas of the popular Western: their plots little resemble either *The Virginian* or *Riders of the Purple Sage*, and Cather's restrained style differs sharply from Grey's purple prose. Furthermore, literary historians have described Cather as resisting the masculine tradition of the Western and have begun recovering a tradition of Westerns written by women. However, even though women-authored Westerns appeared in *McClure's Magazine* while Cather and Lewis worked there, they viewed their southwestern experiences through the lens of the masculine Western. Cather wrote her friend Harriet Whicher, a Mount Holyoke College English professor, in October 1925 that she was "hard at work" in New Hampshire "after a glorious summer riding horseback in New Mexico—sage brush plains and aspen woods in high mountains. I wanted to go to Paris awfully in the spring, but somehow I wanted the sagebrush more. I have a regular Zane Gray [sic] mind; roughneck and low-brow is [the] name for me." While Cather was perhaps being facetious, her conceit nevertheless suggests that she and Lewis had self-consciously played cowboy, going so far as dressing the part by donning trousers to ride through the sagebrush. In this letter and elsewhere, Cather emphasized the ruggedness of her southwestern experiences and set herself apart from mere tourists. Despite the pose, however, Cather and Lewis were always tourists, participating in commodified experiences.[4]

Notably, *The Professor's House* is the earliest Cather novel for which a typed draft survives, and Lewis's handwriting appears on nearly every page—before Lewis edited the novel, Cather's prose was closer to Zane Grey's than readers accustomed to the streamlined published version might expect. Because this crucial piece of evidence is closely associated with their southwestern travels, I pause midchapter to document and theorize Lewis's role as Cather's editor. I also contest a long tradition of biographical readings of *The Professor's House* that hinge on Isabelle McClung's marriage to Jan Hambourg while ignoring Lewis's role in Cather's life and creative process. No typed draft of *Death Comes for the Archbishop* has surfaced, but a rich, multilayered archive of letters, photographs, notebooks, manuscript fragments, and inscribed copies of Cather's books demonstrates that both novels are collaborative texts. Indeed, both novels represent Cather and Lewis's collaboration in producing them by portraying affectionate bonds between men. This is not, however, a story of lesbian collaborators in the closet. Instead, Cather and Lewis's creative collaboration had the same status as the intimate relationship in which it was embedded—not a secret but also not explicitly labeled, not hidden but also not part of Cather's public performance of authorship. In this in-between space, Cather and Lewis as creative partners found space for pleasure and play.

Southwestern Adventures in Khaki

Reading proofs of *The Song of the Lark* with Cather in May and June 1915 would have whetted Lewis's appetite for her first trip to the Southwest. In late May, Cather bragged to a Houghton Mifflin staff member arranging publicity for *The Song of the Lark* that she would be "going to the big cliff ruins down at Durango, Colorado, late this summer." By late June, Cather was crowing to Elizabeth Sergeant about her "new kakis [*sic*] for the Cliff Dwellers—Just like Kurt's in Fidelio." Wagnerian soprano Melanie Kurt had recently performed in Ludwig von Beethoven's only opera at the Metropolitan Opera in New York City, and Cather's allusion suggests that she and Lewis were purchasing costumes for an adventure. Kurt had played Lenore, wife of the Spanish nobleman Florestan, who disguises herself as a young man (Fidelio) to rescue him from political imprisonment, but in the first act Fidelio is the love object of Marzeline, who wishes to marry him. As Fidelio, Melanie Kurt wore dark velvet trousers tucked into knee-high boots and a matching jacket with blouse and tie underneath (Figure 3.1), a costume both signifying her masculine role and allowing her to move freely on stage, especially in the rescue scene. Cather and Lewis's khaki suits differed from Kurt's stage costume only in texture and color (Figure 3.2). While an adolescent, Cather had sported a short masculine haircut and called herself "William," but she grew her hair out in college and wore conventional feminine attire. Indeed, while exploring Walnut Canyon with her brother in 1912 she wore a skirt. In 1915, before the 1920s revolution in women's fashion, wearing pants was itself an adventure for the middle-aged Cather and Lewis, precisely the kind of adventure experienced by the female protagonists of *Riders of the Purple Sage*, who wear male attire while riding horseback through the sage and climbing the face of a cliff to enter a cliff-dweller ruin.[5]

In late July, a plea from S. S. McClure that Cather travel to Germany to write about the developing war in Europe for a newspaper with which he was then associated diverted her briefly from her planned Mesa Verde trip with Lewis. As managing editor of *Every Week*, Lewis was not free to travel with Cather on assignment for a newspaper. Instead, Isabelle McClung, who could speak German, was to accompany Cather. However, when McClung's father refused to let her go, Cather abandoned the European trip, and she and Lewis set out for Mesa Verde as originally planned.[6]

Figure 3.1 Melanie Kurt in costume as Fidelio, from Henry Edward Krehbiel, *More Chapters of Opera, Being Historical and Critical Observations and Records Concerning the Lyric Drama in New York From 1908 to 1918* (1919).

Cather and Lewis boarded a train in New York in early August and changed in Chicago to the Burlington bound for Denver. They stopped briefly in Lincoln, where they spoke to a *Nebraska State Journal* reporter about their plan to "spend a few weeks in camping in southwestern Colorado and Arizona." From Lincoln, the train headed southwest, bypassing Red Cloud but joining up with the Burlington main line in Oxford Junction. "From the train windows," Lewis remembered, "we followed the Republican River—the river of Willa Cather's Red Cloud childhood—to its source, as it wound like a snake back and forth from one side of the tracks to the other," with "orange milkweed . . . in bloom all along the way."[7]

When they arrived in Denver on August 8, Cather signed them into adjacent rooms on the ninth floor of the Brown Palace Hotel. Ninth-floor rooms were modest, but the travelers were not staying long and could still

Figure 3.2 Willa Cather at Cliff Palace, Mesa Verde, in 1915, wearing a khaki trouser suit, cowboy hat, and boots. Courtesy Archives and Special Collections, University of Nebraska–Lincoln Libraries.

enjoy the grand Italian Renaissance–style central courtyard and the abundant water supplied to rooms by the hotel's own artesian well. Decades later, Lewis described this trip as purely for pleasure: Cather "loved the Southwest for its own sake. She did not go there with any express purpose of writing about it—of 'gathering material, as they say, for a story.'" In August 1915, seated in the hotel's elegant drawing room, its walls ornamented with white onyx columns and wainscoting and its ceiling ornamented with a painted mural, Cather told a young female reporter for the *Denver Times* a different story. She frankly admitted (in Margaret Harvey's paraphrase), that she was "go[ing] near Durango . . . to see the old homes of the cliff dwellers, which [she] plans to use in her next novel."[8]

In line with this single-minded pursuit of literary material, she and Lewis ignored the five-day circle route from Denver to southwestern Colorado recommended to tourists, opting instead for a more direct route. The evening of August 9 in Denver, they boarded a Denver & Rio Grande train. Two hundred miles later, at 4 a.m. on August 10, Cather was awake when the train "crawl[ed] out of the La Veta Pass." Later that day, they changed to the D&RG narrow-gauge line at Antonito. Because there were no sleeper cars on the narrow-gauge trains, Cather and Lewis disembarked the same day in Durango to spend the night before taking the last short leg of a D&RG spur to Mancos on August 11. Even this two-day journey from Denver to Mancos was dramatic, "not a dull moment," as Cather later wrote. "All day you are among high mountains, swinging back and forth between Colorado and New Mexico, with the Sangre de Cristo and Culebra ranges always in sight until you cross the continental divide at Cumbres and begin the wild scurry down the westward slope."

Mesa Verde, a portion of which had been made a national park in 1906, loomed over them once they reached Mancos. Mesa Verde is not a singular outcropping in a flat landscape; rather, it is part of the larger Mancos Formation, "2000 feet of gray shale, limestone, and thin sandstone deposited in the great sea which completely divided North America . . . about nineteen million years ago." The Mesa Verde Formation consists of hills and a series of flat-topped mountains with canyons eroded between them. The office of the park superintendent, Thomas Rickner, was then located in Mancos, where Cather and Lewis spent at least two days making travel arrangements, quizzing locals about Mesa Verde, and enjoying the town itself. A rugged wagon road into the park had been completed in 1913, and when automobiles followed horse-drawn wagons in 1914, they provided a faster, but still rugged, even terrifying, journey. Cather and Lewis, however, were following in the footsteps of Richard Wetherill, the son of a local ranching family who had "discovered" the Cliff Palace ruin in 1888. Rather than go into the park the most modern way, then, they opted to hire a team of horses and a driver.[9]

From the tent camp provided for park visitors, Cather and Lewis could see Balcony House, one of the smaller excavated ruins, across Spruce Canyon. Oddie Jeep, the married daughter of the park superintendent, ran the camp, and her husband, Fred Jeep, served as Cather and Lewis's guide. Modern visitors enter cliff ruins from the top of the mesa, using ladders and paved paths. In 1915, however, visitors had to either climb up from the canyon bottom or descend from the mesa top, sometimes using the hand- and footholds carved into the rock by the cliff dwellers. Female visitors to Mesa Verde could rent "divided skirts," but Cather and Lewis had no need of this service. Lewis photographed a smiling Cather climbing the cliff face in her

Figure 3.3 Willa Cather climbing using the ancient hand- and footholds at Mesa Verde in 1915. Courtesy Archives and Special Collections, University of Nebraska–Lincoln Libraries.

khaki adventure suit, looking like Melanie Kurt as Fidelio or Bess in *Riders of the Purple Sage*, who wears similar masculine attire while using the hand- and footholds left by cliff dwellers to explore their ruins (Figure 3.3).[10]

Lewis recalled spending a whole day at the large Cliff Palace ruin, "the cliff dwelling . . . described in the Tom Outland part of *The Professor's House*, cooking our lunch there and drinking from the spring behind the cliff houses." Surviving photographs of the two women together are rare, but like many tourists, they handed the camera back and forth between them. One photo shows them in their matching khaki suits, each posed sitting on the same wall at Cliff Palace (Figure 3.4). Only Lewis's more slender build and their hats differentiate them from one another. Indeed, while Lewis wore a more formfitting, smaller-brimmed woman's hat, Cather wore a cowboy hat. Richard Wetherill and his brothers, who later helped him excavate some of the Mesa Verde ruins, were cowboys,

Figure 3.4 Edith Lewis (*left*) and Willa Cather (*right*) at Cliff Palace, Mesa Verde, in 1915. Courtesy Archives and Special Collections, University of Nebraska–Lincoln Libraries.

and Cather dressed the part to explore the same ruins. Lewis sketched pots made by the Ancient Puebloans of Mesa Verde in a crude bound volume she picked up on their way to the park, likely in Mancos (Figure 3.5). These sketches suggest that she and Cather had met archaeologist Jesse Walter Fewkes and viewed the artifacts he had excavated from the ruins.[11]

Although Cather and Lewis had Fred Jeep to themselves as a guide for about a week, when a large group of tourists arrived, he handed them off to his nephew, who had just returned from three years of medical school in New England. Around August 23, James Rickner proposed to guide them to a recently discovered, unexcavated ruin. He first led them down from the rim of what is now called Chapin Mesa on a "very rough trail"—"we had in many places," Lewis recalled, "to hang from a tree or rock and then drop several feet to the next rock." They then hiked along the "wide, grassy bottom" of Soda Canyon and climbed up the opposite canyon wall to the ruin. Rickner had

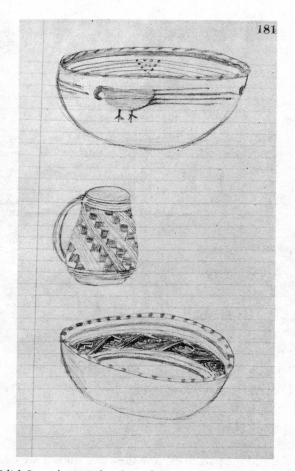

Figure 3.5 Edith Lewis's 1915 sketches of pots made by the Ancient Puebloans of Mesa Verde Courtesy Archives and Special Collections, University of Nebraska–Lincoln Libraries.

not brought the ropes needed to climb back up to the top of Chapin Mesa on the same trail on which they had descended, however, so he led them farther south down Soda Canyon and proposed that they hike north up Cliff Canyon (up the other side of Chapin Mesa) to Fewkes's archaeological camp. Unfortunately, the floor of Cliff Canyon was "just a mass of broken rocks all the way, some of them as big as a house," so Cather told Rickner to go to the camp alone while she and Lewis awaited assistance. Lewis recalled their time waiting as peaceful. They climbed up onto a "large flat rock at the mouth of Cliff Canyon," settling themselves comfortably and feeling assured that rattlesnakes would not surprise them. "We were tired and rather thirsty," she remembered, "but not worried, for we knew we should eventually be found. We did not talk, but watched the long summer twilight come on, and the full moon rise up over the rim of the canyon. The place was very beautiful." When the men from Fewkes's camp arrived, the women still had a strenuous climb up the rocky Cliff Canyon to the camp. When they arrived there at 2 a.m., the men hitched up a wagon and drove them back to the tent camp, and at 8 a.m., their team and driver arrived to take them back to Mancos.[12]

They were not yet done with acquiring information about Mesa Verde, however. Clayton Wetherill, who had helped his brother Richard excavate the ruins, had recently arrived in Mancos for a visit. Cather and Lewis sought him out to hear "the whole story of how Dick Wetherill swam the Mancos river on his horse and rode into the Mesa after lost cattle, and how he came upon the cliff dwellings that had been hidden there for centuries." Through both experiences and conversation, Cather had gained the "material" she needed to write her planned new novel.[13]

"To Be on the Alert for Every Landmark": Taos, the Pueblos, and the Black Mesa

Cather and Lewis wanted to imagine themselves experiencing Mesa Verde in the nineteenth century, but the story of their misadventures traveled at twentieth-century speed. The *Denver Times* published an item on August 25 and the *New York Times* published its story the next day. In the New York paper, Cather and Lewis became the subjects of low comedy, two urban New Women out of their element in the Wild West. "Miss Willa Sibert Cather, a former editor of McClure's Magazine, and Miss Edith Lewis, assistant [*sic*] editor at Every Week, had a nerve-racking experience in the Mesa Verde wilds," the brief article begins, describing both as "exhausted" and Cather as having suffered "severe sprains" after she "wandered all night in a rocky cañon [*sic*]."[14]

They remained oblivious to this publicity because they started immediately by train to northern New Mexico: they probably returned to Antonito to board the narrow-gauge heading south. Disembarking at Taos Junction, nineteen miles south of Taos, they needed to engage motor stage driver John Dunn, who had a monopoly on transporting passengers from the junction to Taos proper. An "immeasurably tall and lean" man "with a drooping, tobacco-stained mustache and melancholy eyes," Dunn exaggerated his nasal "Yankee drawl" to "ma[k]e people laugh." Dunn drove Cather and Lewis slowly down into the dramatic Rio Grande Gorge, a yawning gap in the middle of the flat desertland, across the river, and back up the other side of the gorge to Taos.[15]

Although reaching Taos was challenging, a summer artists' colony was thriving there. Traveling exhibits put on by the Taos Society of Artists attracted more than a hundred artists for all or part of the summer in 1915. Cather and Lewis had friends who were part of the colony, Ernest Blumenschein and Herbert Dunton, both of whom had done illustration work for *McClure's*. After "discovering" Taos in the 1890s, Blumenschein had established a studio there in 1910, encouraging Dunton, who studied with him New York City, to come out as well. Lewis had interviewed Mary Greene Shepard Blumenschein, Ernest's wife, for *Every Week* after one of her paintings won the Shaw Prize at the New York Academy Exhibition for "the most meritorious work of art produced by a woman." Mary Blumenschein proclaimed that "[w]omen have something quite definite and special to contribute to illustrative art in America today," and urged them "to avoid imitating men" and to do the "type of work [that] comes most naturally to them." To her, this meant painting "young and pretty girls" who embodied "the ideal American type of young womanhood, compounded of audacity, intelligence, and charm." In 1915, Mary's husband spent only summers in Taos because she found the rugged "frontier" atmosphere unsuitable for establishing a home and raising their child.[16]

Cather and Lewis embraced what Mary Blumenschein rejected, seeking more rugged and typically masculine southwestern experiences. In Colorado, they had climbed and hiked and had been driven, but in New Mexico they drove their own wagon and rode horseback. Cather had been to northern New Mexico before, but the landscape was new to Lewis. "It was necessary to be on the alert for every landmark," she remembered, "otherwise we were likely to lose our way" on long rides through the countryside. Nevertheless, she explained, "Each Mexican village had its own vivid identity and setting, did not look like all the other Mexican villages. Each little church had its special character." In the same crude volume in which Lewis had sketched pots at Mesa Verde, she drew idiosyncratic maps of these travels, which provide details about their movements not documented in letters.[17]

In her map of the Taos vicinity, Lewis followed cartographic convention by drawing rivers, canyons, and roads and locating settlements in relation to them. She departed from convention, however, by including tiny sketches of buildings and other landmarks. In Lewis's sketch of Taos Pueblo, the historic multistory adobe dwelling looks precisely as Mabel Dodge Luhan (who in 1915 had not yet moved to Taos) would describe it in *Edge of the Taos Desert*, like "two piles of brown cubes, like children's building blocks, that rose in pyramidal-shaped masses." Lewis also drew the front of the adobe church at Los Rancho de Taos (painters and photographers were already busy making the enormous adobe buttresses at the rear of the building into icons of twentieth-century art). In her miniature sketch of the central plaza of Taos proper, however, she stripped it of all detail.[18]

Lewis's map of the Española Valley (Figure 3.6) is more idiosyncratic but also more informative. Rather than sketch a range of topographical features and networks of roads, she selectively represented a journey. She drew a tiny train next to the name of the town of Española—evidently she and Cather had taken the train from Taos Junction to this town. Lewis drew the arched bridge over the Rio Grande that took travelers from Española east to Santa Cruz, but she omitted the river, keeping her focus on their journey. Above the words "Santa Cruz," Lewis made a disproportionately large sketch of the historic Santa Cruz de la Cañada parish church, including associated buildings and rows of trees planted

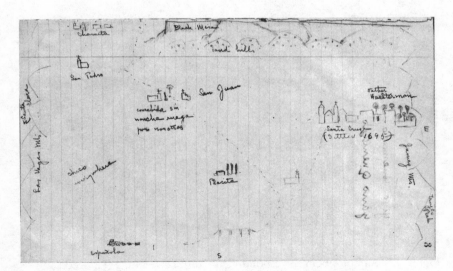

Figure 3.6 Edith Lewis's 1915 map featuring Ohkay Owingeh (then called San Juan Pueblo) and the Black Mesa. Courtesy Archives and Special Collections, University of Nebraska–Lincoln Libraries.

in European fashion. Below "Santa Cruz," Cather added to Lewis's map the information "(settled in 1695)." Above her drawing of the church, Lewis wrote "Father Haelterman," commemorating their visit with Gisleen Haelterman, the Belgian-born Catholic priest who both served the parish church and drove out to minister to the Española Valley Indian Pueblos. As Cather later remembered, Father Haelterman was "[o]ne of the most intelligent and inspiriting persons" she found in her southwestern travels. He served "eighteen Indian missions," driving to them "with a spring wagon and a pair of mules. He knew a great deal about the country and the Indians and their traditions."[19]

The rest of Lewis's map of the Española Valley suggests that, equipped with information from Haelterman, she and Cather recrossed the bridge over the Rio Grande and drove their hired wagon north to Ohkay Owingeh (then called San Juan Pueblo). In the late nineteenth century, a French priest was assigned to the pueblo's parish church (formerly a mission church). By 1912, he had knocked down the historic adobe church and had built in its place a brick neo-Gothic structure, naming it after Our Lady of Lourdes (Figure 3.7). Lewis represented the angular building and its chapel across the road,

Figure 3.7 A photograph corresponding to Edith Lewis's map (Figure 3.6), including the two church buildings and the Black Mesa. Ohkay Owingeh (San Juan Pueblo), New Mexico, ca. 1935–40. Courtesy Palace of the Governors Photo Archives (NMHM/DCA), #188484.

incongruously situated among single-story adobe dwellings, in much less detail than she did Haelterman's church, suggesting that she and Cather merely passed the buildings on their way farther into and past the pueblo's lands, where they visited, as noted on Lewis's map, the village of Chamita and the Capilla de San Pedro Church.

The train station, bridges, roads, and church buildings are in the middle of the page, while Lewis placed topographical features on the sides and top of her map. She vaguely indicated mountains to the west (misleadingly labeled Las Vegas) and to the east (Jemez), but a land formation she labeled "Black Mesa" looms over the map. Lewis drew the mesa in great detail and out of scale, giving it outsized significance. Also known as Mesa Prieta (Dark Mesa), this thirty-six-square-mile basalt mesa runs ten miles from southwest to northeast (Lewis represented it as running west to east) at the confluence of the Rio Grande and the Rio Chama. The tens of thousands of petroglyphs on the mesa's surface (one of the highest concentrations in New Mexico) testify to a long history of human habitation in the area.[20]

Cather and Lewis had spent nearly three weeks together exploring southwestern Colorado and northern New Mexico, but their paths soon diverged. They traveled down to Lamy, south of Santa Fe, so Lewis could board the Santa Fe Railway to begin her journey back to New York and her office job. On her part, Cather went on to Wyoming for a brief visit with her brother Roscoe and his family (he and his wife, Meta, had just had twin girls), and then to Red Cloud for a long visit with her parents and to Lincoln for a short one before she and Lewis were reunited in New York in late October.[21]

Mesa Verde Wonderland

Both Cather and Lewis soon wrote about their Mesa Verde experiences, putting revealingly different spins on them. When Cather was in Red Cloud and Elizabeth Sergeant had already read about their Mesa Verde adventure in the *New York Times*, Cather characterized the experience as "rough" and "difficult" but "glorious." Indeed, she considered it fortunate that the experience of getting lost in the canyon had been "thrust upon" her because she "learned so much" without "break[ing] any bones." "I was on my horse again four days afterward," she boasted, and despite bruises wanted "to go right back into that canyon and be mauled about by its brutality. . . . It's a country that drives you crazy with delight." In contrast, Lewis's "Mesa Verde letter" to Achsah Brewster made the experience sound "magical and restful as well as inspiring." "I can remember," Brewster wrote in response to Lewis's description, "as a child my fascination at seeing some replicas of a cliff-dwellers village, with all their utensils. The real things out in the great cliffs must be beyond words."[22]

In the immediate aftermath of their 1915 trip, Cather put aside the planned novel she had described to Margaret Harvey in Denver in favor of a southwestern travel book. The advertising for the Santa Fe Railway gave Cather and Lewis's friend Ernest Blumenschein free transportation to Taos "with the understanding that he employ some of his hard-earned talents in art to entice people to take the Santa Fe west, for a trip to New Mexico or Arizona to view the region's exotic scenery." The Santa Fe also bought his paintings to use in advertising. During their trip, Cather and Lewis were in contact with the passenger traffic manager of the Denver & Rio Grande (Frank Wadleigh), who was tasked with increasing ticket sales by promoting tourism in the region. Wadleigh put the Taos Pueblo on the front cover of his tourism brochure promoting the 1916 season, *Beautiful Historical Taos: A Wonderland for Tourists*, and Rancho de Taos Church on the first page—Lewis had sketched both on her Taos map. Wadleigh promoted as tourist attractions both "Indian and Mexican life as it has existed for centuries, the magnificence of the scenery" and the "large colony of artists who each year spend their summer in Taos," explaining that together they gave Taos an "atmosphere found nowhere else in the United States." He advertised Cather and Lewis themselves as attractions. After his long list of regular residents of the artists' colony, including Blumenschein and Dunton, he hopefully included "Miss Cather and Miss Lewis" in a list of "first-timers."[23]

Cather wrote to Ferris Greenslet, her editor at Houghton Mifflin, that "the general Traffic Manager" of the D&RG had lent her "the jewels" of its art collection, "glorious photographs of the Cliff Dweller ruins on the Mesa Verde." She also boasted that she had "a hundred splendid photographs of the wonderful Taos region and all the Rio Grande pueblos about Espanola." "Do you still want a book on the Southwest?" she queried Greenslet, suggesting that she "might induce the Santa Fe Railway to furnish some transportation," enabling her to "run about to some of the more distant places in Arizona" the next summer "and finish the whole thing off, giving the story of the Santa Fe Trail along with the rest." It would be, she assured him, "the only reasonably good book on that country ever done," better than the one for which travel writer Ernest Peixotto was doing shallow research in 1915.[24]

Cather was more than willing, then, to put herself at the service of railroad promotion of tourism in the Southwest. In the fall or early winter, she tried her hand at a portion of her proposed travel book, writing an essay published in the *Denver Times* in January 1916 that promoted Mesa Verde as (just like Taos) a "Wonderland" within "easy reach" of tourists traveling by rail. Because she was promoting tourism, Cather glossed over the challenges (the harrowing drive into the park) and the rusticity (the primitive conditions at the tent camp). Even as she promoted the national park as a sort of commodity tourists might purchase, she burnished the Wetherill "discovery" of the ruins with a Romantic glow. Expressing "envy of the entrada of Richard Wetherill" into the canyon from which he first glimpsed the Cliff Palace ruin, she portrayed the Mesa Verde ruins as "the highest achievement of stone-age man—preserved in bright, dry sunshine, like a fly in amber." She made no mention of the Wetherills' excavating and profiting from the ruins.[25]

In the fall, perhaps before Cather wrote this essay, Lewis wrote about Mesa Verde for *Every Week*. Placing Cliff Palace in the midst of other "Lost Cities" (Babylon, Astur, Boro Budur, pre-Conquest Mexico City, Pompei, and Mercur), Lewis wrote a long caption for a photo of Cliff Palace:

> This is what two-cow-boys, hunting for stray cattle on the Mesa Verde, in Colorado, accidently stumbled on one day—a whole city, with walls and towers, built up in the wall of the canon [*sic*]. And that was how the Mesa Verde cliff-dwellings came to be discovered, the oldest prehistoric ruins in America. The more enterprising of the two cow-boys, whose name was Richard Wetherill, wasn't satisfied with discovering one city. He and a younger brother spent five winters on the Mesa, and discovered twenty or more cliff cities, to say nothing of a few cart-loads of pottery and flint weapons, which they sold to scientific societies for upward of $30,000. After that the government got busy and decided to make a government reserve of Mesa Verde.

Rather than present Cliff Palace as a "high cultural achievement" at which Richard Wetherill wondered, Lewis focused on the cowboy's ambition and commercial acumen as he sought out more ruins and profits from the sale of excavated artifacts.[26]

It is tempting to categorize Cather and Lewis's experiences in Colorado and New Mexico in 1915 as *either* a Romantic, idealistic adventure *or* a business venture, but these were two sides of the same coin. Cather aspired to be an artist and had made the momentous decision two years before to write full time, but writing was also what she did for a living. As she explained to Margaret Harvey in Denver, good fiction was based on experience and knowledge, but writing was "like any other work," subject to market forces of supply and demand. It required "labor" and perseverance in the face of rejection: a publisher or editor might simply be "overstocked," she explained, and a writer, like a tailor, should not give up after one potential client rejected a work sample. Likewise, by writing about Mesa Verde for the magazine of which she was the managing editor, Lewis turned the trip into a work trip, but southwestern travel was also her escape from modern office life into a romanticized fantasy of southwestern history.

"The Blue Mesa, Full of Love and Hate": 1916 in Northern New Mexico

Cather toyed with her planned southwestern travel book through 1916, but the idea of putting the ancient cliff dweller ruins into a work of fiction also returned. In the back of Lewis's 1915 travel journal, near her map of Taos and sketches of the Mesa Verde pots, Cather wrote a list of titles, all heading in the direction of the theme and setting of what would become "Tom Outland's Story" in *The Professor's House*:

> Youth's Adventure
> A Young Adventure
> The Blue Mesa
> The first lapp [?]
> The first half

She and Lewis never returned to Mesa Verde, but they returned to Taos in 1916. Lewis had wanted to visit Earl and Achsah Brewster in Italy again, but as Achsah conceded when responding to Lewis's change of plans, the war would have made her trip unsafe. Willa's brother Roscoe had invited them to visit his family in Wyoming, but she explained to him that "Edith wanted very much to return [to Taos], where we had a delightful week last summer."[27]

At the end of June 1916, Cather wrote Greenslet from Denver that she was on her way to Taos, "the pueblos, and the Black Mesa"—that is, to the locations Lewis represented in the maps she had drawn the year before.

Cather pleaded with Greenslet not to let anyone else write a southwestern travel book for Houghton Mifflin before she did, but she also observed that she was "rather absorbed in another notion. You will probably hear about it later." She and Lewis enjoyed five luxurious days at the Brown Palace Hotel despite "gritting hot" weather in the Mile-High City. By July 8, they were at the only hotel in Taos, the modest Columbian on the central plaza. Cather reported to Harrison Dwight, with whom she became acquainted as a *McClure's* contributor, of being "forty miles from the railroad" in a "pink adobe" hotel "up in the mountains" in "a Mexican town of three thousand without a 'frame' home in it, and lovely little towns lying everywhere about us." She later recommended the Columbian to Elizabeth Sergeant but put the distance from Taos Junction by the "[g]ood automobile stage" at thirty-five miles. She and Lewis could "get excellent horses," she wrote her brother Douglass from the Columbian. "Edith is a showy rider, and I can at least manage to get about on a horse and don't much mind a rough trail." Clearly, Cather could pitch the experience of Taos differently to different audiences.[28]

Cather was disgruntled by Isabelle McClung's April 1916 marriage to violinist Jan Hambourg. Writing Roscoe the same day she wrote Douglass about the horses, she described Jan Hambourg as "a very brilliant and perfectly poisonous Jew." Despite—or perhaps because of—her disappointment, she also, as she wrote to Roscoe, had "a new idea for a novel" she wanted "to talk over with" him. "The trouble about this story," she explained, "is that the central figure must be a man." She "wish[ed]" Roscoe had "kept a diary" on a "Yellowstone trip of long ago—It's a little that kind of story."[29]

In 1916, Cather and Lewis stayed in the Taos region for about three weeks, including at least five days at the Columbian Hotel early in their stay. Thereafter they left no traces of their movements. Perhaps they had hired a wagon and a camping kit to travel along the Rio Chama, where there were no train stations or hotels. As usual, Lewis had to leave before Cather did. The first half of the installments of James Oliver Curwood's Canadian Arctic adventure tale, *The Girl Beyond the Trail* (discussed in Chapter 2), would have been fully prepared for serialization in *Every Week* before she left, but she had to leave her own desert adventures for the humid heat of New York City to prepare the second half for publication.[30]

Cather went from northern New Mexico to Red Cloud, and from there she wrote Greenslet that she was putting aside the travel book for "a story of the Southwest, and the title will probably be 'The Blue Mesa' or something of that sort, and it will be full of love and hate." Houghton Mifflin was increasingly publishing popular Westerns, and Greenslet responded enthusiastically. "'The Blue Mesa, Full of Love and Hate' sounds, as Mrs. Fields used to say, 'ripping,'" he replied. He was "keen" to see it, had "put it down" on their spring publication schedule "encircled in red," and felt sure it would sell twice as many advance copies as *The Song of the Lark*. Indeed, "The Blue Mesa Full of Love and Hate" sounds like the title of a sensational Zane Grey novel. However, by October, Cather was, as she wrote Greenslet, doing little more than "making notes" for it, and by March 1917, she conceded to Greenslet's colleague Roger Scaife that she had "put aside the notes for 'The Blue Mesa' to take up another novel."[31]

Cather's novel set in late-nineteenth-century Nebraska, *My Ántonia*, narrated by a man but with a woman at its center, displaced the southwestern cowboy tale of love and hate. After *My Ántonia* appeared in late 1918, Cather began "wrestling . . . a little" with "The Blue Mesa" again. She reported to Roscoe that "the commonplace way to do it is so utterly manufactured, and the only way worth while is so alarmingly difficult." As she would later explain to Grant Overton, literary editor at *Collier's Weekly*, which serialized *The Professor's House*, "Tom's story seemed the natural beginning of what she had to tell," but working on it she discovered that "Tom's story was monotonous, and except as a piece of high adventure, meaningless." Stumped about how to make her protagonist's story meaningful, she let the Southwest as fictional subject matter and a travel destination sink from view. She took up Tom's story again only when "it came to her that Tom was significant only as he affected other lives." Cather was saved from publishing "The Blue Mesa" as she originally conceived it, which might have been something like a Zane Grey novel, but as we shall see, Cather and Lewis's original impulse to dress up and play southwestern cowboys runs just below the surface of *The Professor's House*.[32]

Interlude: "It Takes Two People to Write a Book" and "Writing . . . and This Queer Business of Living"

Willa Cather did not finally return to her "Blue Mesa" story until 1924, and she and Lewis did not return to the Southwest until 1925. In the interim, travel to places other than the Southwest and other writing projects occupied the two women. In 1917, the war made even domestic travel difficult. Cather went west in June to receive an honorary degree from the University of

Nebraska. After a flurry of correspondence, Lewis joined her in Red Cloud in July for her first visit there. Three weeks later, they boarded a train to Denver to escape the Nebraska heat, but they did not continue farther south or west. In the years 1918 through 1923, they spent time together in Jaffrey, in France, and on Grand Manan Island (this Canadian island as a vacation home is the subject of Chapter 5). On Grand Manan in the summer of 1924, Cather wrote the first draft of Book 1 of *The Professor's House*, "The Family." Because she had worked on "The Blue Mesa" story years before, she worked very quickly, completing several drafts of the entire novel by December.[33]

Critics and biographers have read *The Professor's House* as symptomatic of Cather's midlife crisis spurred, in part, by the loss of Isabelle McClung to Jan Hambourg. Books I ("The Family") and III ("The Professor") of the novel take place in the present of the title character, Godfrey St. Peter, who feels alienated from his wife and from his two adult daughters. He is also reluctant to move out of the shabby rented house his family long occupied and into the new, modern house built with the prize money he received for his multivolume history of the Spanish Conquistadors. Louie Marsellus, the Jewish husband of Godfrey's daughter Rosamund, is key to biographical readings of the novel: Jan Hambourg took Isabelle away from Cather, and so, it would seem, she caricatured him. Conversely, through Godfrey's longing for his dead former student, Tom Outland, Cather expressed her longing for the absent Isabelle, "dead" to her because she had married.[34]

Following Elizabeth Sergeant's lead in her memoir of Cather, scholars have most often characterized Lewis as a domestic figure. When Sergeant described Cather's "personal life" in the 1920s, she noted that whenever she visited 5 Bank Street, "Edith Lewis, who now worked at the J. Walter Thompson Company, was always at dinner. One realized how much her companionship meant to Willa. A captain, as Will White of Emporia said . . . must have a first officer, who does a lot the captain never knows about to steer the boat through rocks and reefs." This portrait of Lewis as the unobtrusive first officer steering the domestic ship of which Cather was the captain has been influential (while Sergeant's mention of Lewis's employment at a major advertising agency has been ignored). When Lewis appears at all in biographical readings of *The Professor's House*, it is as Augusta, the dour and sexless sewing woman who rescues Godfrey from suffocation in his gas-filled study in the final pages of the novel.[35]

Lewis was not, however, in the least domestic. She was a well-compensated professional woman, who spent long hours at the office. As Cather complained to her mother in December 1919, after Lewis had been working at the J. Walter Thompson Co. for a year, "You know I have no maid this year, and as Edith is away from eight-thirty in the morning until six-thirty at night, most of the housekeeping falls on me." And Cather had not really "lost" Isabelle. She spent long stretches of time with the Hambourgs without Lewis, and Lewis, Cather, and the Hambourgs had an ongoing, if complicated and uncomfortable relationship.[36]

We may never fully understand how the four people in this tangled web understood their relationships to one another, although a February 1923 letter from Cather to the Brewsters seemingly reveals a painful truth. Like all letters, it was embedded in the context of particular relationships. Cather had known Achsah casually for nearly two decades but had only recently come to know her and Earl better. During Cather and Lewis's 1920 European trip (Figure 3.8), they were together in Paris (and saw the Hambourgs together). Lewis then traveled to Sorrento to visit the Brewsters while Cather went to Cantigny with the Hambourgs to visit the grave of her cousin, G. P. Cather, who had died in battle in France. In Cantigny, Cather wrote part of *One of Ours* (1922), a novel inspired by G.P.'s life and death. Cather was supposed to

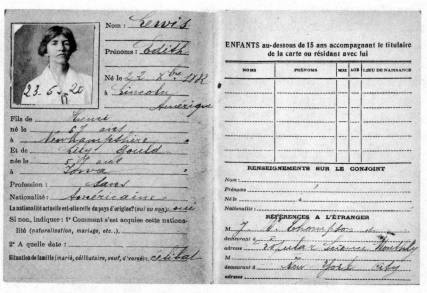

Figure 3.8 Edith Lewis's French identity card from her trip to Europe with Willa Cather in 1920. Courtesy Archives and Special Collections, University of Nebraska–Lincoln Libraries.

join Lewis in Sorrento, but because of postwar food shortages, she abandoned this plan. Instead, Cather and Lewis were able to spend only a short time with the Brewsters in Naples at the end of their European sojourn. Though brief, this visit fostered a new level of intimacy between the two couples.[37]

When Cather wrote the Brewsters in February 1923, she was getting ready for a long visit with the Hambourgs in their suburban Paris home. The Brewsters had been in France since their return from Ceylon in the fall of 1922, and they had met and befriended the Hambourgs. Cather was acutely aware of the implications of this new friendship for Lewis. "I beg you both," she wrote the Brewsters, "to write often to Edith while I am gone." She continued conspiratorially:

> I must tell you a secret that is a little difficult to tell: Edith does not like the Hambourgs at all—never has. They irritate her, rub her the wrong way; Isabelle even more than Jan. I think it's been hard for her to face that they were seeing you this winter when she was not. We are like that about the people we love best sometimes, we have a kind of loving jealousy about them. It has always been difficult about the Hambourgs, because they are old and dear friends of mine, and yet they do darken the scene for Edith whenever they appear—put rancours in the vessel of her peace, as Macbeth said. I think the way that likes and dislikes interweave is the most disheartening thing about life anyway. It's nothing Edith can help; their personalities simply hurt her. She feels that their attitude toward her is rather patronizing, but there I feel sure she is mistaken.

By disclosing a confidence to the Brewsters, Cather was negotiating her *own* growing relationship with them. However, Achsah, Lewis's oldest and closest friend, certainly already knew that Lewis found spending time around Isabelle Hambourg painful and awkward.

The Brewsters were about to visit the U.S. for the first time since their 1910 marriage, and Cather urged them to spend as much time as possible with Lewis "to make up to her for my absence." "As you know," Cather continued, "she does not care for a great many people, and for them she cares very much." Near the end of her letter, Cather hinted at what she left unsaid: "Dear friends, there are so many things I wish to say to you—about painting, about writing, about ourselves and this queer business of living." Cather was able to say these things to them in person after she arrived in France, leaving no written trace. Nevertheless, she closed this letter in the first-person plural, aligning herself and Lewis as a couple sending good wishes to another couple: "We both send you our dearest love and wish you happy working-days with all the deep satisfaction they bring."[38]

But where, then, do we find Lewis in *The Professor's House*, the novel Cather wrote in 1924 after her long visit with the Hambourgs in 1923? In describing Cather and Lewis's relationship, Elizabeth Sergeant cited an another pearl of wisdom from William Allen White, the Pulitzer Prize–winning editor of the *Emporia Gazette*: " 'It takes two to write a book,' was another line of his creed." We find Lewis in *The Professor's House*, then, at the intersection of "writing" and this "queer business of living" rather than in domestic labor: her hand-writing appears all over a working typed draft of the novel. Rather than read the novel through the Hambourgs, I read it through Cather's relationship with Lewis, her expert editor and her traveling companion on the south-western trips that provided crucial raw material for her fiction.[39]

"The Thing Not Named": Edith Lewis Edits *The Professor's House*

In *The Work of Revision*, Hannah Sullivan argues that the typewriter transformed the approach of early-twentieth-century authors to writing and revision. Most modernist authors did not compose directly at the typewriter. Instead, they drafted by hand and revised after their texts had been typed be-cause the "visual defamiliarization" produced by seeing their words in type prompted "the kind of self-critical, self-disowning rereading that promotes revision." Sullivan describes the typed page "with extensive manuscript scrawls, cross-outs, and speech bubbles inserting large portions of new text" as the "classic document of modernist revision." She concerns herself prima-rily with modernist authors as self-editors, however, "willful and controlling about the state of their texts" rather than open to editorial intervention by others. Cather's composing and revising practices testify to the importance of the typewriter, but not only because Cather revised her own words once she saw them in type. Rather, the typed versions of Cather's texts served as an invitation to Lewis, an experienced magazine editor accustomed to working over typescripts of other people's works, to take up her pen and dig in.[40]

Cather typically wrote her early drafts in pencil; then, with her pencil draft beside her, she herself typed a new draft, liberally revising as she typed. Cather likely learned to type when she was a journalist in the 1890s—her presence in the newsroom was exceptional, but male journalists typed, too. In contrast, the younger Lewis never learned to type. This was perhaps a strategic choice on her part because in the early twentieth century, typing was increasingly seen as women's work, and even a graduate of an elite women's college could be relegated to the secretarial track if she had acquired clerical skills. What Lewis *had* acquired at *McClure's* and *Every Week*, and which she continued to develop while writing advertising copy, were sharp editing and writing skills; thus she, or Cather, or both marked revisions on the early draft (or multiple drafts) of Cather's fiction that Cather herself had typed.[41]

Cather could produce serviceable typescripts, but producing clean carbons with a finicky manual typewriter was difficult. Because Cather often wanted two or even three carbons at later compositional stages, she had a professional typist retype marked-up early drafts. Beginning in the mid-1920s, Cather employed Sarah Bloom, who also held a full-time salaried position as a secretary, to do this work for her. *The Professor's House* happens to be the earliest surviving typed draft of a Cather novel or short story, but as Lewis's editing work described below makes clear, this was not her first time editing Cather's prose. Cather clearly trusted her judgment, granting her full authority to proceed independently. This was also not the last time Lewis edited Cather. Typed drafts of most of Cather's novels and several of her short stories and essays published after 1925 survive, and Lewis's handwriting appears on the typed drafts of most of these works.[42]

The surviving draft of *The Professor's House* is relatively early, and Cather herself typed all parts of it. Like many of Cather's other surviving drafts, it is a patchwork: it incorporates a few short segments cut and pasted from an earlier version into a later, relatively continuous typing. Lewis extensively edited the main document in ink, while Cather's few penciled edits appear mostly on the inserted earlier segments. In the summer of 1924, Cather wrote "The Family" on Grand Manan, where she had no typewriter, so she typed and Lewis edited Cather's typing after their return to Manhattan in the fall. As demonstrated by Lewis's rewriting, revising, or clarifying of her own initial edits, she was acting on her own authority and exercising her own editorial judgment rather than copying Cather's edits from some other, now-lost document, and Cather let Lewis's revisions stand without reversing any of them. At the end of Chapter 16 of "The Family" (the second-to-last chapter of that section), Cather jotted a note to "Miss Bloom," instructing her to "[m]ake two carbons from here on through the story." Sarah Bloom retyped the document at least once before typesetting of the novel began in February 1925.[43]

Lewis made significant changes to the *Professor*-in-progress, pruning wordiness, condensing or eliminating descriptions of characters' internal thoughts, and sharpening and realigning key images. In Cather's typed draft of the early chapters, when Godfrey St. Peter surveys the attic study in his old house, which he shares with the seamstress, Augusta, and the sewing forms she uses to produce dresses for his daughters and wife, he thinks, "It was just there, under Augusta's archaic 'forms,' the two speaking, structural paradoxes, that he had always meant to put the filing cabinets he had never spared the time or money to buy." Lewis revised this to "Just in that corner, under Augusta's archaic 'forms,' he had always meant to put the filing-cabinets he had never spared the time or money to buy." Her changes are both stylistic (eliminating the wordy "It was," specifying "that corner" for the vague "there," eliminating the later "that") and substantive (removing Godfrey's internal commentary on the dress forms).[44]

The novel is exceedingly vague about the town where "The Family" and "The Professor" take place—its most salient features in the novel as published are its location on the shores of Lake Michigan and the state-supported university where Godfrey teaches. In Cather's original typed draft of another key scene that takes place in Godfrey's study, Lewis made a small revision that both changed the college town and reverberated through the novel's network of symbols. Godfrey has been working through the night after an unpleasant conversation with his daughter Kathleen about claims by Professor Crane, a colleague in physics, to profits from Tom Outland's invention of an important gas later commercialized in the wartime aviation industry. In the early morning, "factory whistles blowing" interrupt Godfrey's concentration and turn his thoughts back to the ill feeling between his daughters. Lewis crossed out "factory whistles" and substituted "the Angelus . . . ringing." These bells, associated with the annunciation of the Virgin Mary, ring at Augusta's Catholic parish church, and Augusta later saves the professor from suffocation. This was the only mention of the factory whistles blowing in the college town as Cather originally imagined it. Because of Lewis's revision, the town lost its factory, but the novel gained a symbolically resonant image.[45]

The novel withholds for several chapters the story of how Godfrey and his wife, Lillian, met in France and how his marriage led him to take a teaching position at a university he does not respect. Lewis meticulously revised the paragraph in which Cather finally revealed this backstory. Cather had typed that "French people" thought Lillian was an "English girl," not "an American," because of "her gold hair and fair complexion" and "her reserved and almost forbidding beauty," and "because she was reserved and imperious in manner." Lewis crossed out Lillian's "reserved and imperious manner" and turned her "forbidding beauty" into "her really radiant charm." Lewis also made Lillian speak more subtly in a later scene in which Godfrey stages a historical *tableaux vivant* featuring his sons-in-law, Louie Marsellus and Scott McGregor. Cather had typed that Lillian "said something about heavy-handed caricature being rather tiresome now-a-days, when even cartoonists were becoming subtle." In Lewis's revision, Lillian herself speaks subtly and even ironically: she "said dryly that she was afraid nobody saw his little joke."[46]

Most of Lewis's edits survived through subsequent rounds of revision, appearing in the novel as published, and even her changes that did not may have been jettisoned later by Lewis herself. Lewis made one of her most telling revisions to the opening of "The Professor," just after "Tom Outland's Story" concludes. Cather had typed the following summary of Godfrey St. Peter's ruminations about his life: "The most disappointing thing about life, St. Peter thought, was the amazing part that blind chance played in it. After one had attributed as much as possible to indirect causation, there still remained so much, even in a quiet and sheltered existence like his own, that was irreducible to any logic." Lewis boldly substituted one new pithy sentence for Cather's verbose two: "All the most important things in his life had been determined by chance, St. Peter thought" (see Figure I.2). By the time the text had been typeset and galley proofs printed, either Cather or Lewis had reordered the clauses and changed one key word: "All the most important things in his life, St. Peter *knew*, had been determined by chance" (emphasis added). By the time the novel was between covers, the sentence had become "All the most important things in his life, St. Peter *sometimes reflected*, had been determined by chance" (emphasis added). It is difficult to imagine the final section of the novel opening with Cather's discursive and tortuous sentences about determinism rather than Lewis's elegant and direct substitution. In the case of these revised sentences, it is actually Lewis's language that readers have known for nearly a century as characteristic of Cather's style.[47]

Later in the final section of *The Professor's House*, Lewis was equally ruthless in paring away long passages describing the professor's ruminations about the past he nostalgically longs for and the present and future he dreads. In "The Professor," after St. Peter has spent much of the summer alone in the old house, he receives a letter from Lillian telling him that she, Rosamund, and Louie are returning early from Europe because Rosamund is pregnant with her first child. Soon after, the gas heater in his study nearly asphyxiates him. His near-death experience might be construed as a suicide attempt, and Cather had ascribed thoughts to the recovering Godfrey that lent credence to that supposition:

> This morning, no it was now yesterday morning, after Lillian's letter had unloosed terror upon him, he had sat a long while at the table where Augusta was now reading, and thought and thought; trying to see where he had made his mistake, what he had done amiss, that he now wanted to run away from everything he had so intensely cared for. He must have been very stupid yesterday. It was clear enough.

At first, Lewis toyed with condensing this train of thought, carving out words and phrases, but then, in black ink, she finally deleted the entire passage.[48]

Lewis also made many careful adjustments to the voice of Cather's New Mexican cowboy, who, like the title character of *The Virginian*, speaks an oddly formal vernacular in "Tom Outland's Story." When Tom meets Roddy Blake, Tom is a call boy for the railroad in the fictional town of Pardee, New Mexico. Because he needs to keep track of the men whom he might call to work at a moment's notice, he observes a late-night poker game in which Roddy plays. Cather had "as many more standing about the walls" observing the poker game in which Roddy is winning substantial sums—Lewis made them "a crowd of fellows." Describing the end of the game, Cather typed, "The boys were fussing about one fellow, Rodney Blake, who'd come in from his engine without cleaning up." Lewis turned the boys into "The crowd" that "was fussing" and expanded the contraction to "who had."[49]

When Tom becomes ill with pneumonia, he and Roddy leave Pardee and their railroad jobs to become cowboys so that Tom can recover. Lewis made some of her most extensive revisions and deletions in a passage in which Tom first describes the mesa adjacent to the land on which the cattle graze, where they later find the cliff dweller ruins (Figure 3.9):

> That Mesa was one of the landmarks we always saw from Pardee. Landmarks mean more in a flat, semi-desert country than they do any-where else. For one thing, you can see them better in that clear air and brilliant light, and their stability is a comfort in a sandy land that is half blown away every spring. To the northwest of Pardee, over toward Utah, we had the Mormon Buttes, three sharp blue peaks, like the mountains in geography books.

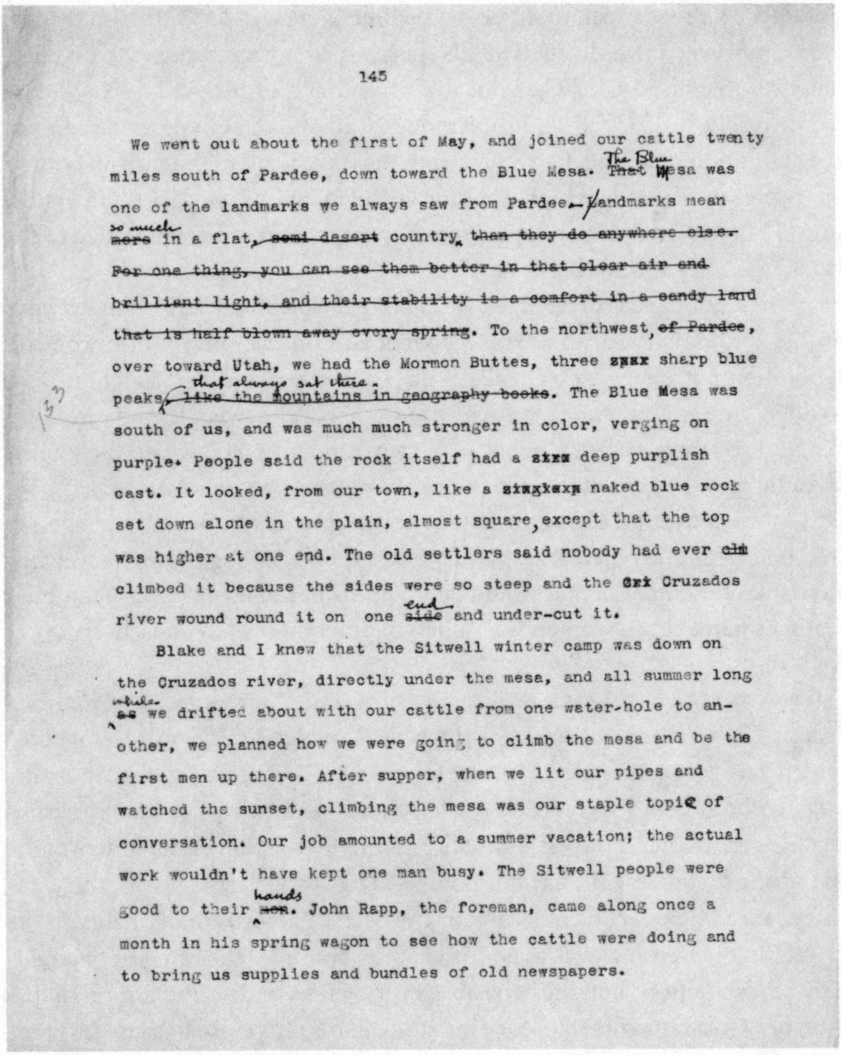

145

We went out about the first of May, and joined our cattle twenty miles south of Pardee, down toward the Blue Mesa. *The Blue* That Mesa was one of the landmarks we always saw from Pardee. Landmarks mean *so much* more in a flat, ~~semi-desert~~ country, ~~than they do anywhere else. For one thing, you can see them better in that clear air and brilliant light, and their stability is a comfort in a sandy land that is half blown away every spring.~~ To the northwest, ~~of Pardee,~~ over toward Utah, we had the Mormon Buttes, three ~~zxxx~~ sharp blue peaks *that always sat there.* ~~like the mountains in geography books.~~ The Blue Mesa was south of us, and was much much stronger in color, verging on purple. People said the rock itself had a ~~zixx~~ deep purplish cast. It looked, from our town, like a ~~zixgkxxx~~ naked blue rock set down alone in the plain, almost square, except that the top was higher at one end. The old settlers said nobody had ever ~~clm~~ climbed it because the sides were so steep and the ~~Grx~~ Cruzados river wound round it on one *end* ~~side~~ and under-cut it.

Blake and I knew that the Sitwell winter camp was down on the Cruzados river, directly under the mesa, and all summer long *while* ~~as~~ we drifted about with our cattle from one water-hole to another, we planned how we were going to climb the mesa and be the first men up there. After supper, when we lit our pipes and watched the sunset, climbing the mesa was our staple topic of conversation. Our job amounted to a summer vacation; the actual work wouldn't have kept one man busy. The Sitwell people were good to their *hands* ~~men.~~ John Rapp, the foreman, came along once a month in his spring wagon to see how the cattle were doing and to bring us supplies and bundles of old newspapers.

Figure 3.9 A page from the typed draft of *The Professor's House*, with Edith Lewis's revisions in pen. Tom Outland is describing the Blue Mesa. Courtesy Archives and Special Collections, University of Nebraska–Lincoln Libraries.

Lewis reined in Tom's bout of philosophizing description, having him state flatly, "Landmarks mean so much in a flat country." Tom's early schooling was scant, so what would he know about geography textbooks? Instead, Lewis had him describe the "sharp blue peaks that always sat there." When Tom first enters the secret canyon that bisects the Blue Mesa and finds the cliff dweller ruins, however, Lewis livened up his speech in a way appropriate to his character. Cather used Cliff Canyon, the rugged site of her and Lewis's Mesa Verde rescue in 1915, as her visual model: Cather had Tom describe some of the "huge boulders" that had fallen from the mesa walls to the canyon bottom as "twelve or fifteen feet high, yet they lay piled on one another like a load of gravel." Lewis gave Tom an appropriate metaphor to indicate the size of the boulders: "they were as big as hay-stacks."[50]

In these sequences of changes, we can see the productive friction between author and editor. Caroline Fraser's reflection on the end result of the collaboration between Laura Ingalls Wilder as author and her daughter Rose Wilder Lane as editor applies equally to Cather and Lewis: "the unique combination of their skills . . . created a transcendent whole." The dichotomy of author and editor does not fully capture the dynamic between Cather and Lewis, however. Cather began by writing words in pencil, but she edited herself as she typed and then revised typed versions of her texts, while Lewis wrote sentences that would later appear in the novel published under Cather's name. Each woman was, albeit in different proportions, both writer and editor.[51]

Two years before Lewis made these cuts and changes to *The Professor's House*, Cather wrote an essay for the *New Republic*, "The Novel Démeublé," which has come to define Cather's aesthetics. "Whatever is felt upon the page without being specifically named there," Cather wrote, "that, it seems to me, is created. It is the inexplicable presence of the thing not named, of the over-tone divined by the ear but not heard by it, the verbal mood, the emotional aura of the fact or the thing or the deed, that gives high quality to the novel." In one sense, Lewis as editorial collaborator is "the thing not named" in Cather's fiction, but she is visible everywhere in *The Professor's House*. Notably, Godfrey refuses to leave his study in his old house because he is editing Tom Outland's diary for publication, and in this diary Tom recorded his excavation of the cliff dweller ruins in the canyon running through the Blue Mesa. In Chapter 2 of "The Professor," which Lewis edited, the narrator tells us that St. Peter finds Tom's "plain account" of his experiences "almost beautiful" because of "the things it did not say," including anything about "the young explorer's emotions." In some respects, Godfrey in his attic study is a representation of Cather herself. As she wrote "The Family" in 1924, she, like Godfrey, was in her early fifties—she was fifty, soon to turn fifty-one, while he is fifty-two. As a result, when Lewis edited this chapter, she edited

Cather in two senses: she edited Cather's literary representation of herself in Godfrey and she edited Cather's typed words on the page. In another sense, we might understand Godfrey sitting at his desk, his editor's pen in hand, as Cather's portrait of Lewis. In an affectionate inside joke, she invited Lewis to edit an image of herself as Cather's editor.[52]

In either scenario, both women were enjoying the gender play that characterized their 1915 and 1916 southwestern trips, which Cather made explicit to Lewis by incorporating her 1915 travel journal into the novel. In "Tom Outland's Story," Tom explains to the professor how he and his friend Roddy Blake, cowboys turned amateur archaeologists, kept records of their "excavating": "We numbered each specimen, and in my day-book I wrote down just where and in what condition we had found it, and what we thought it had been used for. I'd got a merchant's ledger in Tarpin, and every night after supper, while Roddy read the newspapers, I sat down at the kitchen table and wrote up an account of the day's work." When Tom is in Washington trying to interest the Smithsonian in the ruins, Roddy sells the cataloged objects without telling him. Despite Tom's protest that he never thought of the objects in terms of monetary value, he wrote his "account" in a "merchant's ledger," suggesting that he was always thinking of them as commodities for sale.[53]

In August 1915 in Mancos, Colorado, fictionalized as Tarpin, Lewis also bought a bound blank volume in which she had sketched Mesa Verde pots and drawn maps (see Figures 3.5 and 3.6). The volume, bound in cloth-covered boards, measures 7½ by 11¾ inches, a proportion typical of legal and accounting documents, in contrast to the size of the paper, 8½ by 11 inches, on which Cather typed *The Professor's House*. "Record" is stamped at the center of the front cover, the lined pages inside are prenumbered, and tables of information on "carrying capacity of a freight car" for agricultural commodities, a "short method for calculating interest," "years which a given amount will double at several rates of interest," quantities of seed required to plant acres of specified crops, and so on, are printed on the endpapers. The volume was designed, then, for farmers or small-town merchants to use as a ledger book for recording business transactions. Playfully aligning Lewis with Tom Outland, Cather put a volume resembling Lewis's travel journal into Tom's hands. Godfrey has this "merchant's ledger" in his attic study because he is editing Tom's "diary" written in its pages. "There was a minute description of each tool they found," the narrator explains, "of every piece of cloth and pottery, frequently accompanied by a very suggestive pencil sketch of the object and a surmise as to its use and the kind of life in which it had played a part." Lewis thus edited Godfrey editing Tom's diary in a "merchant's ledger" modeled on an object in which she had drawn suggestive pencil sketches of Mesa Verde pots. Furthermore, in 1915, Cather and Lewis, like Tom and Roddy, mined their time in the cliff dwellings for both aesthetic and material value. *The Professor's House* thus intricately reflected back to Cather and Lewis their repeated interchanges of roles as they produced the novel.[54]

Cather and Lewis Ride Again: 1925 at the San Gabriel Ranch

In 1925, Cather and Lewis felt drawn again to the Southwest, but they waited until the corrected galley proofs for *The Professor's House* had gone back to the printers before departing. On their way they briefly detrained in Lincoln on June 9 to chat with friends. Rather than come down from Colorado into New Mexico as they had before, this time they detrained in Lamy in mid-June and reappeared in Santa Fe a week later. Cather and Lewis had reservations to spend a week at the San Gabriel Ranch in Alcalde, New Mexico, beginning June 24, and page proofs and business correspondence were scheduled to meet them there. First, however, they "loaf[ed] about" for a few days at the Hotel LaFonda, a 1920 Pueblo Revival–style building on Santa Fe's central square (the Atchison, Topeka and the Santa Fe Railway had recently acquired it from the original owners, who had failed to make it profitable).[55]

Although the two women persistently characterized themselves as nontourists, the San Gabriel was a high-class dude ranch, expensive enough that visitors' credit ratings were checked before their reservations were accepted. The ranch was owned and managed by Roy and Carol Pfäffle, a married couple that might have walked out of the pages of *The Virginian*, in which the cowboy marries the genteel New England school marm. Roy Pfäffle, the son of German immigrants, left Iowa after his father's death to support his mother and sister by cowboying in New Mexico, while Massachusetts-born Caroline Bishop Stanley studied piano at the New England Conservatory of Music and had taught piano at a girls' boarding school. In 1916, at the end of a desert trek for which Roy was the guide and Caroline a dude on vacation, they married. They managed dude ranch properties for others until 1920, when they acquired an existing ranch in Alcalde, near the confluence of the Rio Chama and the Rio Grande, midway between Taos and Santa Fe, and christened it the San Gabriel Ranch.[56]

The ranch combined gentility (Caroline played the Steinway grand piano in the main ranch house for guests) and western roughness with a Spanish colonial-era flair. The ranch office opened onto the town's small plaza, where *penitentes* performed their rites at the small parish church, and the Pfäffles had renovated as guestrooms the colonial-era single-story adobe buildings and the small courtyards they surrounded, called patios. Cather and Lewis may have met Roy Pfäffle in 1916, when he owned a livery stable in Española, and Elizabeth Sergeant was acquainted with Carol Pfäffle, but the San Gabriel was no word-of-mouth secret. Rather, the Santa Fe Railway distributed the ranch's advertising brochures through its "America's Most Famous Fifty Square Miles" campaign. The ranch's 1925 brochure featured photographs of high-hatted cowboys performing rope tricks, riding barrels, and gambling against a backdrop of adobe buildings, with a lone Native man, his hair braided and wearing his blanket, looking on impassively (Figure 3.10). In its text the brochure also prominently featured the Pajarito Plateau, a volcanic plateau in the Jemez range eroded to form canyons and mesas.

Figure 3.10 A photo reproduced in the San Gabriel Ranch's advertising brochure. Edward H. Kemp, photographer, "Cowboy's shooting craps, San Gabriel Ranch, Alcalde, New Mexico," ca. 1923–25. Courtesy Palace of the Governors Photo Archives (NMHM/DCA), #151373.

Both the Bandelier National Monument (near Los Alamos) and the Puye cliff dwellings (closer to Española) are on the plateau. "[W]ithin fifteen miles" of the ranch, prospective guests were informed, they could "wander among the prehistoric ruins of the ancient Pueblo peoples" on "the famous Pajarito Plateau with CLIFF DWELLINGS and PREHISTORIC RUINS by the thousands."[57]

Even though Cather evoke the Wetherill discovery of the Mesa Verde ruins in "Tom Outland's Story," her fictional cowboys discover their ruins in New Mexico, not Colorado. Cather and Lewis did not return to Mesa Verde to read the page proofs of *The Professor's House*, but their surroundings at the San Gabriel evoked all of the key elements of "Tom Outland's Story"— the northern New Mexico landscape, the cowboys and cattle (dude ranches needed cattle as well as paying guests to be economically viable), and ancient cliff dweller ruins. Cather generally worked only two or three hours in the morning, leaving the rest of the day for recreation. At the San Gabriel, she and Lewis could read page proofs in the morning and ride out on good horses after lunch. Put another way, they could be author and editor in the morning and New Mexican cowboys in the afternoon.[58]

The page proofs arrived at the ranch on schedule. The printers commissioned by Alfred A. Knopf, Inc., had produced the galley proofs from an edited typescript known as the "setting copy." The printers sent these galley proofs—a trial printing from typeset text not yet configured into pages—to the author with the setting copy so she could check the accuracy of the typesetting and mark corrections (Cather and Lewis had completed this step in New York before leaving). Cather often, however, actually revised her fiction in galley proofs. After the printers incorporated corrections and changes from the galleys and configured the text into pages, the process was repeated, except this time the author compared the page proofs with the corrected galleys. The extant galleys of *The Professor's House* are an uncorrected extra set, but Cather's handwriting—not Lewis's—appears on the surviving corrected galleys of other works. Lewis's role in the process, then, was the "copyholder," who read aloud from the setting copy or the corrected galleys, while Cather's was the "proofreader," who marked corrections onto the galley or page proofs.[59]

Lewis would have read all of *The Professor's House* aloud at the San Gabriel, but her reading aloud of "Tom Outland's Story" at the ranch carried particular meaning: they had carefully scheduled their travel so that they could enjoy the special pleasure of reading the page proofs there. Although in "The Family" the professor edits Tom Outland's diary of his discovery and excavation of the cliff dweller ruins, "Tom Outland's Story" is not Tom's diary. Instead, the professor is remembering an occasion years earlier when Tom told him his cowboy tale "full of love and hate" on a New Mexico mesa.

We might imagine Lewis and Cather in late June 1925 sitting outdoors in the cool of the morning in the shade adjacent to one of the patios at the San Gabriel Ranch (Figure 3.11). Lewis is reading aloud from the galleys of *The Professor's House* they corrected before leaving New York and Cather is marking corrections and additional final changes on the page proofs. The Black Mesa (Mesa Prieta), which Lewis had sketched a decade earlier in one of her maps, is close by, just across the Rio Grande to their northwest; its long, low profile forms part of their horizon line. No canyon filled with cliff dweller ruins bisects this mesa. Nevertheless, as Cather and Lewis viewed it in 1915 and as Lewis sketched it, it more closely resembles Tom's fictional

Figure 3.11 A photo reproduced in the San Gabriel Ranch's brochure with the title "A last chat before the Pack Trip starts." Edward H. Kemp, photographer, "Group in the corner of patio, San Gabriel Ranch, Alcalde, New Mexico," 1923. Courtesy Palace of the Governors Photo Archives (NMHM/DCA), #112304.

Blue Mesa than the Mesa Verde formation does. In addition to its prominence in a flat landscape, Tom describes the top of Blue Mesa as "higher at
one end," and with "the profile of a big beast lying down; the head . . . higher
than the flanks," and "the Cruzados river wound round it at one end." The
Black Mesa is much longer than the fictional square Blue Mesa, but it, too,
is higher at one end, and the Rio Grande winds along beside it. They had
returned, then, to a real place that had given them pleasure in 1915 and 1916
and which had inspired Cather to create the fictional Blue Mesa.[60]

When Godfrey contemplates Tom's diary, he senses "the ardour and excitement of the boy" in his austere written account of his excavations, "like
the vibration in a voice when the speaker strives to conceal his emotion." As
Cather sat at a dude ranch in northern New Mexico in the shadow of the
Black Mesa marking the page proofs of her novel, she and Lewis doubled
Godfrey and Tom: Cather took the part of Godfrey as listener while Lewis
read aloud Tom's soliloquy of his experiences on the Blue Mesa, the vibration of her voice bringing alive Tom and his emotions. "[T]he overtone
divined by the ear but not heard by it" might, as Cather argued in "The Novel
Démeublé," give "high quality" to a novel, but Lewis was more than an over-
tone: throughout Cather's career, when she and Lewis read proofs together,
it was Lewis's voice that Cather heard—she was the voice of Cather's fiction.
And while at the end of *The Professor's House* Godfrey St. Peter finds himself
facing the prospect of a future "without delight," Godfrey's creator was about
to embark on a delightful new adventure with her creative partner.[61]

Mabel Dodge Luhan's Persistence and Cather and Lewis's Return to Taos

The San Gabriel Ranch specialized in leading long pack trips into the desert,
and perhaps Cather and Lewis thought they might take a desert trek after
they finished proofreading. Repeated invitations from Mabel Dodge Luhan
to come visit her in Taos, however, changed their plans and gave rise to discoveries and experiences that fueled *Death Comes for the Archbishop*, a novel
that fictionalizes experiences of Archbishop Jean-Baptiste Lamy and Joseph
Machebeuf, his friend and fellow French priest, in nineteenth-century New
Mexico. After the novel was published, Cather explained that Lamy "had become a sort of invisible personal friend" during her travels in New Mexico
because she heard so many stories about him and admired the cathedral he

built in Santa Fe. Her curiosity about "the daily life" of such a "well-bred" man "in a crude frontier" society was finally satisfied in 1925, she explained, when she stumbled "upon a book printed years ago on a country press at Pueblo, Colorado: *The Life of the Right Reverend Joseph P. Machebeuf*, by William Joseph Howlett, a priest who had worked with Father Machebeuf in Denver." The book, which included translations of letters Machebeuf sent home to his sister, a nun in France, "reveal[ed] as much about Father Lamy as about Father Machebeuf, since the two men were associated from early youth."

In *Willa Cather Living*, Lewis cast this moment of discovery more dramatically. Writing that Cather went to New Mexico in 1925 with "no definite design for a novel," she described how in Santa Fe

> in a single evening, as she often said, the idea of *Death Comes for the Archbishop* came to her, essentially as she afterwards wrote it. From that time on it completely took possession of her, filled all her waking thoughts. She knew exactly what material she needed in order to write the story as she wanted to write it, and she seemed to draw it out of everything she encountered.

Lewis gave Cather something like Godfrey St. Peter's moment early in his career when he conceives of the design of his history of the Spanish Conquistadors. On a boat "skirting the south coast of Spain," with "the ranges of the Sierra Nevadas tower[ing]" on the coast, "the design of [St. Peter's] book unfolded in the air above him, just as definitely as the mountain ranges themselves. And the design was sound. He had accepted it as inevitable, had never meddled with it, and had seen it through." In 1925, however, the encounters with places and people, living and dead, that inspired *Archbishop* were not as tidy or Romantic. Although the novel is often characterized as a Santa Fe novel, and although Cather may have read Howlett's book there before she and Lewis made their 1925 trip to Taos, much of the novel is set in and around Taos rather than in the Bishop's seat of power, and it is in Taos that Latour encounters the resistance and conflicts that propel the novel's plot. If Cather and Lewis had not accepted Luhan's invitation, Cather still might have written *Archbishop*, but it would have been a different novel.[62]

Lewis set off the chain of events that led to Luhan's invitation. In the 1910s, Cather may have been slightly acquainted with Luhan (Dodge at the time), who then held a salon in her grand house off Washington

Square. In the 1920s, however, Luhan was living in Taos, where she was trying to build an arts community around herself. In 1923, British novelist D. H. Lawrence and his wife, Frieda, first visited New Mexico at Luhan's invitation. The Lawrences had met the Brewsters in Italy in 1921, and the four traveled together to Ceylon in late 1922. On the Brewsters' 1923 trip to the U.S., Earl Brewster wrote Lewis in July from his Ohio hometown asking, "Have you seen the Lawrences? They arrived in NY July 15th. Achsah gave them your address and I presume they will have called. Just a line came from him this morning saying that they would be in New Jersey for a while." Lawrence's publisher had rented a cottage for D.H. and Frieda in New Jersey, and they spent most of their time there reading proofs. Cather was in France with the Hambourgs, and the Lawrences do not seem to have visited Lewis in her absence. However, in March 1924, the Lawrences, accompanied by the painter Dorothy Brett, returned to the U.S., and as D.H. wrote Earl Brewster in February, "I should very much like to see [Cather]."[63]

The Lawrences and Brett arrived in New York City on March 11, and early in their stay, D.H. left a concert midperformance to go to 5 Bank Street alone, staying so late that Frieda and Brett were concerned that he had gotten lost. Instead, as he told them, he "liked Willa Cather," "had a nice time," and "she has invited [them] all to tea the following day." "We are sitting in Willa Cather's room," Brett recalled in her 1933 memoir, addressed to the dead Lawrence in the present tense. "Miss Lewis has been showing me some pictures" (perhaps the Brewsters' paintings hanging in the apartment). Brett continued:

> They are very kind and hospitable. The tea is very good. And you are teasing Willa Cather about art. She is serious, probing you about your ideas; you are evading, mischievously. "I hate literature and literary people," you say. "People shouldn't fuss so much about art. I hate books and art and the whole business." The more amazed, the more indignant Willa Cather becomes, the more you storm against art.

In *Willa Cater Living*, Lewis reported that Cather found the Lawrences "very attractive," especially D.H., who was "in his sunniest mood" and mostly talked about his adventures in Ceylon with the Brewsters rather than about literature. "When they said goodbye," Lewis concluded, "they spoke of our all meeting again in New Mexico." For her part, Cather wrote her Pittsburgh friend Elizabeth Vermorcken that although both D.H. and Frieda were "unusual and charming and thrilling," they had tired her out.[64]

The Lawrences preferred Mexico, where they spent much of 1924, to New Mexico, and initially they were not sure they would return to the ranch Luhan had given to them in exchange for the manuscript of D.H.'s novel *Sons and Lovers*. In the spring of 1925, Frieda improbably thought that Cather might rent the ranch and occupy it herself. However, in April, a doctor ordered D.H. to Taos, where the dry air and high altitude were thought to be good for his lungs.[65]

After the Lawrences had settled into their ranch, Luhan issued her first invitation to Cather. Cather resisted, explaining in late May 1925 that she planned to visit the Grand Canyon before spending time at the San Gabriel—maybe she and Lewis did go to the Grand Canyon, but maybe it was just an excuse. "I hardly think my friend and I will get to Taos at all," Cather continued, bringing Lewis into the question, "but if there is any chance of our doing so, I'll signal you and ask whether you have a house for us. I doubt whether we will stay in any one place long enough to begin housekeeping. I would like to see you in Taos, though, and your own house there." When Cather and Lewis arrived in New Mexico in June, Cather continued to put Luhan off. "My friend and I have just drifted about down here," she wrote from Lamy. "We'll be at the San Gabriel Ranch near Española while I read the proofs of my new book, then we'll go to the country about Albuquerque." She again suggested that they might come through Taos but not long enough to settle in as Luhan's guests. Luhan persisted—she presented herself at the San Gabriel Ranch on Wednesday, June 24, but Cather and Lewis were still making their way to Española by train and did not arrive at the ranch until the evening, after Luhan had gone back to Taos.[66]

Luhan was, after a fashion, a collector of distinguished artists, but she was not merely attempting to acquire Cather for her private artists' colony; she was also seeking Cather's help with her memoirs. Cather wrote Luhan from Alcalde on Thursday that she expected to finish reading proofs by early the next week and inquired whether she and Lewis might rent Luhan's guesthouse "on a cash basis" because "[y]ou see Miss Lewis and I are travelling together, and while my advice about your manuscript might (possibly) be worth my board and keep, I doubt whether I could stretch my wisdom far enough to cover two people." Expressing puzzlement at why Luhan "thought [she] wanted to keep us" because they were not "very exciting visitors," Cather told Luhan to call Alcalde at an appointed hour on Sunday if she really *did* want to "keep them." Undeterred, Luhan telephoned, and on Tuesday, June 30, she and Tony Lujan, her Taos Pueblo husband, drove to Alcalde to pick up the two women.[67]

When Cather and Lewis arrived in Taos, Luhan gave them space and privacy by putting them in the Pink House, a modest adobe a few steps from Luhan's own larger house. Instead of isolating themselves, however, Cather and Lewis spent much of their time with Mabel and Tony, and with two other guests, Mabel's friends Mary Hubbard Foote and Ida Rauh. Foote had first met Luhan in Florence when she was studying painting there, and she later established herself as a successful portrait painter with a Washington Square studio. In the 1920s, however, she was living in Switzerland so that Carl Jung could analyze her. Rauh was an actress, activist, sculptor, and poet, who had also formerly been part of the Greenwich Village scene, but in the summer of 1925 she was living in Santa Fe with painter Andrew Dasburg. Cather and Lewis knew the Taos region well from their 1915 and 1916 trips, but pursuing the historical Bishop Lamy and encountering it with new friends, they saw it with fresh eyes.[68]

"The Fine Reality of the Summer": Two Weeks in Taos at Los Gallos

Wednesday, July 1, their first full day staying at the compound Mabel Luhan had christened Los Gallos (the roosters), Cather and Lewis walked into Taos in the morning, and in the evening Tony Lujan took them to the nearby Taos Pueblo. Tony used Mabel's large touring car to drive her guests around the region. As Lewis later described him:

He was a splendid figure, over six feet tall, with a noble head and digni-
fied carriage; there was great simplicity and kindness in his voice and
manner. . . . Tony would sit in the driver's seat, in his silver bracelets and
purple blanket, often singing softly to himself; while we sat behind. . . . He
talked very little, but what he said was always illuminating and curiously
poetic.

On Thursday, he drove Cather and Lewis east and north, through Fernandez Canyon to the Cimarron Canyon and Ute Park, and on Friday, they headed south with Mabel, looking for historic houses and finding two on the road to Las Trampas.[69]

Mabel had a corral and an alfalfa field to supply hay for her horses, which Cather and Lewis enjoyed riding during their visit. As they had at Mesa Verde in 1915, the two women handed the camera back and forth to take pictures of each other, but this time they were on horseback. In two photos mirroring one another (the horizon line behind Cather descends from left to right, while behind Lewis it descends from right to left), the desert landscape is nearly featureless—only dry grass and low sagebrush are visible (Figure 3.12). They wore matching khaki suits and riding boots and sturdy leather gloves covering their hands and wrists. Lewis, as at Mesa Verde, wore a low-crowned, small-brimmed hat, while Cather again wore a cowboy hat. Cather sat her quiescent horse awkwardly, while Lewis sat her more lively horse erectly and stylishly. The movement of Lewis's horse blurred her photograph of Cather. In a second photograph of Lewis, she and her horse had turned to the left, making visible her right hand and the riding crop with which she controlled the horse—she was precisely the "showy rider" Cather described

Figure 3.12 Edith Lewis (*left*) and Willa Cather (*right*) on horseback in the desert. Courtesy Archives and Special Collections, University of Nebraska–Lincoln Libraries.

Figure 3.13 Edith Lewis on horseback in the desert (*left*) and Willa Cather on horseback, her horse standing in a stream (*right*). Courtesy Archives and Special Collections, University of Nebraska–Lincoln Libraries.

to her brother Douglass in 1916 (Figure 3.13, *left*). In a second picture of Cather, her horse stood in a shallow stream, and the corral, barn, and a stand of trees behind her testify to the presence of more water nearby (Figure 3.13, *right*). Hills rise gradually behind the barn.[70]

On Saturday, they saddled up to ride to Taos Pueblo, while on Sunday morning they rode into the hills beyond the pueblo to Glorieta Grove (*glorieta* being Spanish for "bower" or "arbor"). In *Edge of the Taos Desert*, Mabel depicted Tony taking her to this "old sacred grove of cottonwoods up the canyon beyond the Pueblo," but the grove was no sacred secret. Rather it was an established tourist attraction, included in the same Taos tourist brochure that had listed "Miss Cather and Miss Lewis" as first-timers in the Taos artists' colony in 1915. After their Sunday morning horseback ride, in the afternoon Tony drove them north and west to Arroyo Hondo via Arroyo Seco, and they picnicked in Twining Canyon, the site of an abandoned mining camp.[71]

On Monday, Tony finally drove them past Arroyo Hondo and toward Questa, up to the mountain ranch where the Lawrences lived in a primitive homesteader's cabin, cultivating crops and keeping chickens (Brett had her own one-room cabin nearby). The Lawrences were pleased that Cather and Lewis had made the "hard" trip up the mountain to visit them. They and Cather talked about "the mechanics of writing," and Cather later sent D.H. *The Song of the Lark*, probably because of its Arizona section. D.H. complained to the Brewsters that Cather was "a bit heavy-footed," but he also conceded "she has strength." On her part, Frieda told a friend that although "everybody said" Cather "was blunt and abrupt . . . we got along famously." Lewis appears in none of these accounts, but perhaps she was sitting quietly with Brett, whose deafness made her timid, speaking into her ear trumpet while the more forceful Cather and the forceful Lawrences conversed loudly.[72]

In 1925, Cather and Lewis's friend Herbert Dunton was still living and painting in Taos, and on Tuesday they called on him at his studio. His marriage had ended amicably, and although his wife and daughters lived in Santa Fe, his girls spent summers enjoying the rugged life in Taos, including horseback riding. Unlike his friend Ernest Blumenschein and other founders of the Taos Society of Artists, who painted Native Americans and southwestern landscapes, Dunton painted animals and cowboys and, on occasion, cowgirls. Even though Cather and Lewis could have walked the two miles to his studio, they fittingly chose to arrive on horseback. That afternoon, Tony drove them to Los Ranchos de Taos, site of the iconic San Francisco de Assisi Church Lewis had drawn on her map a decade earlier.[73]

After Cather and Lewis's morning horseback ride into Taos with Foote on Friday, July 10, in the afternoon Tony and Mabel drove the two women and Ida Rauh to a cave above Arroyo Seco on the side of Lucero Peak. The Lawrences had visited the cave with Mabel and Tony in 1924, and D.H. used it as a model for the ceremonial cave in "The Woman Who Rode Away" (1925). Perhaps he had urged Cather and Lewis to make sure to see it. This was one of Cather and Lewis's more rugged experiences in 1925, echoing their dramatic Mesa Verde experience of 1915 and proving crucial to the historical novel coalescing in Cather's mind.[74]

Luhan would later describe a wintertime trip with Tony to this cave in *Winter in Taos*, and when Lewis later read the book in manuscript she recognized it as the cave she and Cather had visited. In *Winter in Taos*, Luhan described Arroyo Seco as "a little community under the rocky north wall of a round mountain, exposed to all the sunshine and over-looking the sloping valley—it really breathed of coziness and contentment, like a cat purring in the sun." The "dark cave" on the peak's face, however, she described as an ominous "aperture" that the pine trees on the slope could not hide. Mabel begged Tony to take her to this "ceremonial cave of long-forgotten days, where sacrifices were made behind the waterfall that veils its recessed altar."

"[R]anks of perfect little Christmas trees" grew near a brook outside the cave, but as they approached the cave they "turned into tall pines that darkened the way" until "the woods seemed to grow sinister and haunted and to lose the lightsome feeling they had down below."[75]

In *Winter in Taos*, when Tony and Mabel approached the cave's entrance, the ice pillar formed by the waterfall obscured their view, but once they were inside, the "light came in green and subdued, and we found a large, dry chamber of rock with a high, domed ceiling, and with the sides sloping upwards to meet it." Tony showed her "steps, apparently rough hewn out at the back wall, leading up to a ledge; and above the ledge and far above us, impossible to reach without a long ladder, there was the faint painting of a sun." Together they "climb[ed] up the side of the cave" and from a "flat ledge" looked out through the trees into the sunny valley. In the cave, however, "it was entirely different from the life down below, which sparkled and shone and laughed—for here a brooding spirit dwelt in eternal gloom . . . save for the irrevocable fall of the water past the entrance." In July 1925, no ice pillar would have formed at the cave's entrance, and Lewis remembered the place very differently: "the wooded country just before you get to the cave" had "an almost fairy-like beauty, fresh and full of trickling streams with white stones." As Tony was driving Mabel, Cather, Lewis, and Rauh away from cave, his car fell into a ditch above Arroyo Seco, dispelling any residual gloom with low comedy.[76]

Cather and Lewis's Saturday was less dramatic than their Friday. In the morning they rode horseback into the foothills behind Los Gallos (it may be these hills that are visible in one of the photographs of Cather on horseback), and in the afternoon Tony drove them on narrow bumpy roads to Ojo Caliente (hot springs) (if they brought bathing costumes, they might have taken a soak). Rather than return the way they had come, they went east, driving down into the Rio Grande Gorge and back up to return via Llano Quemado, Los Ranchos, and Talpa. In Lewis's brief day-by-day account of the two weeks she and Cather spent at Los Gallos, she wrote "Padre Martinez" in the margin next to this second Saturday. As Tony Lujan drove them around the Taos region, they were pursuing a nineteenth-century figure whom Cather would make Bishop Latour's primary antagonist in *Death Comes for the Archbishop*. Cather would give Lamy and Machebeuf new names, but in fictionalizing history, she would use the real names of key figures associated with Taos, including Padre Antonio Jose Martinez, Padre Mariono Lucero, and Kit Carson.[77]

Their heads filled with new experiences, ideas, and information, and questions about history, Cather and Lewis paused their frantic activity for two days to "read Prescott" in the Pink House. In *The Conquest of Mexico* (1843), William Hickling Prescott narrated the history of the region (New Mexico having been part of Mexico) through the sixteenth century, the closing era of Spanish conquest and exploration that Godfrey St. Peter takes as his subject in *The Professor's House*. Prescott's account does not continue into the nineteenth century, the historical epoch Cather fictionized in *Archbishop*, but the novel frequently flashes back to this earlier era, which Prescott covered in his second volume: "Modern Mexico—Settlement of the Country—Condition of the Natives—Christian Missionaries—Cultivation of the Soil—Voyages and Expeditions."

Cather and Lewis resumed their rides and drives on Wednesday, when Tony Lujan drove them back toward the Rio Grande Gorge, and on Thursday, Mary Foote joined them for a drive to the Old Taos Pueblo, circling back via Ojo Caliente. During their last two days at Los Gallos, Cather and Lewis again rode horseback into the foothills, and Tony drove them through the Taos Canyon and yet again to the Rio Grande Gorge, which they clearly found irresistible. On Saturday, July 18, John Dunn picked them up at Los Gallos and drove them back down into the gorge on their way to Taos Junction. Their trunks fell into a mud hole created by a New Mexico summer monsoon, and Dunn spent half an hour dragging them out. They would have missed their southbound train to Santa Fe had it not been running late.

Pursuing Nineteenth-Century Priests in Early-Twentieth-Century New Mexico

While Cather and Lewis had been lukewarm about visiting Luhan, they came away committed enthusiasts, and both wrote Luhan praising letters the day after they reached Santa Fe. The "Tom Outland's Story" section of *The Professor's House* had begun appearing serially in *Collier's Weekly* while they were in Taos, and in Santa Fe, as Cather reported to Luhan, she found waiting for her "an astonishing collection of letters" from "hard-boiled publishers and solemn professors" who said that it had "g[iven] them a pulse." In "The Family," Louie Marsellus remarks on a gift that Tom Outland gave to the professor's daughter Rosamund, a bracelet she was wearing the first time he met her: "A turquoise set in silver, wasn't it? Yes, a turquoise set in dull silver." Louie's words appear as an epigraph on the novel's title page, and as many critics have observed, the epigraph describes the novel's structure—the dull silver of "The Family" and "The Professor" surrounds the turquoise of "Tom Outland's Story." Luhan had given Cather a bracelet just like the one in the novel. Louie's quotation appeared less prominently as a chapter epigraph in the serial, which had not yet finished its run, so Cather and Lewis must have told Luhan about the entire arc of the plot or let her read the whole novel in their extra set of page proofs. "I love it," Cather wrote to Luhan of the bracelet (perhaps the same bracelet Lewis later gave to Cather's niece). Linking the object in real life to the fictional one, Cather continued, "I think your giving it to me was a good omen for the book." With Luhan's guidance, Cather and Lewis were also moving forward with more reading and experiential research for *Death Comes for the Archbishop*. "I'm still hard on the trail of my old priests," Cather wrote. She had "found a lot of interesting things that morning" that she promised to tell Luhan about later. She and Lewis were also about to travel farther west, "though of course," Cather affirmed, "we'd like to start right back to Taos!" She closed her letter "one of your 'hangers-on' hereafter! Admiringly yours."[78]

Lewis wrote Luhan that "Taos was the most beautiful part of our travels. I liked everything there; our little house, and the flowers, and the horses, and our drives up canyons. But the best thing was to meet someone that I could admire so much. That is more exciting even than beautiful country. Thank you for all your wonderful kindness to us both. I shall never forget it." Lewis also made clear that she and Cather were following Luhan's advice as they continued their historical research. "Miss Cather is still pursuing Father Martinez," Lewis wrote, "through all the books in the Museum. Each new book tells a new story. We sit up late at night reading about priests. Tomorrow, we are driving to Chimayo, as you suggested, and the next day we go to Lamy."[79]

In Santa Fe, Lewis purchased a small school composition notebook and wrote her name on the cover. In the opening pages, while her memory was still fresh, she made a day-by-day list of her and Cather's activities in Taos. She also wrote lists of names: names of towns around Taos, Spanish names of people they met in Alcalde and Taos, names of Native American children, and names of animals at Taos. Other pages of the notebook testify to the shared research and reading both she and Cather were undertaking in Santa Fe and about which each had written to Luhan. Toward the back of the notebook, Lewis recorded conversational Spanish phrases, including religious sayings, and took notes on the lives of Lamy, Machebeuf, Carson, and

Martinez. Cather also used Lewis's notebook, taking notes on the history of Santa Fe and the Navajo War and recording important dates in the history of the Catholic church in the region.

After they left Santa Fe, in addition to visiting the Hispano settlement of Chimayo, Cather and Lewis traveled west to two Pueblo communities, Laguna and Acoma—all of these communities would appear in *Archbishop*. Despite the promotion of tourism to the area, getting to locations far from a railroad station—or even getting to a railroad station—could prove difficult, especially in monsoon season. Cather had visited Laguna with her brother Douglass in 1912 (the Santa Fe line ran right through the middle of the community), but she got no closer to Acoma than buying Fred Harvey Co. color postcards of it, which she sent to Elizabeth Sergeant and Lewis.[80]

In 1925, Cather and Lewis were stuck at Lamy for three days because of a washout at Trinidad to the west. Lewis fondly remembered the "wonderful Harvey Houses, set like jewels along the Santa Fe railroad," and El Ortiz in Lamy, with fewer than ten guest rooms, was the smallest jewel. Together, the Santa Fe's architect, Louis Curtiss, and the Harvey Company's interior designer, Mary Jane Colter, had created a fantasy version of a Spanish hacienda. Colter covered the floors of the main lounge with Navajo rugs and the walls with Spanish religious paintings and furnished it with heavy carved pieces. The guest rooms opened onto an enclosed patio with hanging vines, planter boxes, and a fountain. In 1910, when the hotel was still new, Owen Wister spent a week there with his family, and he wrote the manager praising it as "like a private house of someone who had lavished thought and care upon every nook." Sitting in the patio watching the pigeons pecking in the grass, Wister considered El Ortiz a "little desert oasis among the desert hills," tempting him to give up his planned travels.[81]

When Cather and Lewis were finally able to leave the genteel fantasy of El Ortiz, rain delayed them three more days at the small railroad village of New Laguna, two and a half miles west of the Laguna Pueblo. Lewis remembered the adobe structures as "beautiful," the Laguna people as "handsome," and the "costumes" of the women as "beautiful," but the hotel was "the roughest and dirtiest we had ever stopped in." There was dirt on unswept carpets, and there were holes in their bedroom windows and "burnt matches and cigarette papers . . . scattered all over the floor." They had to go down a flight of stairs and through a long dark hallway to go to the bathroom, and the proprietor fed them only canned food, which they supplemented with cheese and crackers from the Indian trader's shop across the street.[82]

As Cather reported to Luhan, a Laguna man who had attended the Carlisle Indian School in Pennsylvania finally agreed to drive them to Acoma "through eighteen miles of lake and mud" produced by a "cloud-burst every afternoon." Lewis later wrote in *Willa Cather Living*, "There is no need to tell of that journey" to Acoma because "Willa Cather has told it in the *Archbishop*." In Cather's 1909 *Harper's* magazine story, "The Enchanted Bluff," children in a Nebraska small town imagine being the first to climb to the top of a mesa in New Mexico on which there are Indian ruins. Lewis observed that Cather "had been looking forward to" her journey to Acoma "all her life." "As we passed the Mesa Encantada (the Enchanted Bluff)," Lewis recalled, "we stopped for a long time to look up at it. It looked lonely and mysterious and remote, as if it were far and distant in time—thousands of years away."[83]

The inhabited Acoma Mesa, rather than the uninhabited Mesa Encantada, was their destination, however. There was no road to the mesa top, so Cather and Lewis had to walk up one of the traditional trails. In 1924, architect John Gaw Meem made his first ascent of Acoma, and he recalled that he "started apprehensively up the precipitous trail," intimidated by the "giant rocks on either side . . . over the little trail winding upward." When he reached the top, he was "keyed up" and "awfully glad to see civilization again" in the form of the Acoma pueblo village and "the huge mass of the church towering above" him at the edge of the village. Ambitious Spanish missionaries had forced the Acoma people to build the San Estevan Del Rey Church, carrying timber from far away for its impressive roof. By 1924, however, it was "a spectacular deteriorated building situated in a sublime landscape." In the fall of 1924, Meem, supported by the Committee for the Preservation and Restoration of New Mexico Churches, worked with the Acoma people to stabilize the roof of the massive adobe building with concrete—Cather and Lewis would have seen this restored roof. At the San Gabriel, Cather and Lewis had played cowboy, but in response to their visit to Acoma, Cather played Indian, writing "Pueblo Indian Song," a dramatic poem (not published in her lifetime) in the voice of an Acoma speaker. She and Lewis had come through muck and the mire to Acoma, but the speaker of her poem "lay in cloud-kissed Acoma / and dreamed of" of her beloved in a time of drought, when the sky is "blazing blue," the "red rock mesa cracked for thirst," and the cisterns collecting the community's water are dry.[84]

After their dramatic adventure at Acoma, Cather and Lewis traveled to Denver, where they met up with Cather's mother and her sister Elsie and took "a very comfortable apartment" in the "new and very good" Hotel Olin. Catering to an older woman in poor health and their own taste for modern comforts after their strenuous New Mexico experiences, Cather and Lewis went "to the theatre and [took] walks and motor rides," as Cather wrote to Luhan. Cather also encouraged Luhan to persevere with her work on her memoir and praised her as a host: "My weeks with you in Taos stand out as the fine reality of the summer."[85]

On August 3, Lewis had to start her journey back to New York and the salaried office job that financed her long vacations with Cather. Cather, however, remained in Denver, where she soon presented herself at the Denver Public Library to ask for research assistance. The head of reference was on vacation, so an assistant, Louise Guerber, was assigned to help her. Cather befriended the young librarian, taking her out to tea and accepting her invitation to drive her around the surrounding countryside. Willa's brother Roscoe came in from Wyoming with his wife, Meta, and his three daughters, and Cather invited Guerber to join them all for dinner at the Olin. After dinner, as Guerber recorded in her diary, Cather "was just full of her new book and fathers Macbrebouf [sic] and Lamy and she told us a great deal about the Southwest, the mission churches and about the old days." Cather also showed off another "turquoise set in silver" (in this case a ring in "a square setting") and a turquoise necklace.[86]

Willa Cather accompanied her mother home to Red Cloud, an easy journey on the main line of the Burlington between Denver and Kansas City, but there she got sick and gave up her plan to travel to Grand Manan to work. Instead, after she got back to New York she went to Boston to try to persuade her former publisher, Houghton Mifflin, to sell her backlisted novels with the firm to her new publisher, Alfred A. Knopf, Inc. (the effort failed). From Boston she went to the Shattuck Inn in Jaffrey, which she still found a congenial place to write. In early October, she wrote Alfred Knopf from Jaffrey about how pleased she was with the sales of *The Professor's House* and about how "The Bishop" was "behaving well up in this part of the woods."[87]

Perhaps Cather had taken the school composition notebook Lewis had acquired in Santa Fe up to Jaffrey. There is no surviving typed draft of *Death Comes for the Archbishop*, but in the notebook—in a section that came after Lewis's travel diary of their experiences in Taos and before her and Cather's research notes—Cather wrote an early pencil draft of a long passage about Don Manuel Chavez, a historical figure who appears in Book 4 of the novel. The position of this document in the notebook makes clear how this shared record of travel and research informed Cather's writing. The names of Latour and Vaillant's mules, Tranquillino and Contento, appear in Lewis's lists of names she encountered in Alcalde and Taos, for example, while the details of the life of Padre Martinez that Lewis recorded all appear in the novel. Cather was not just drawing on recorded information, however; she also drew inspiration from memories of the travels she shared with Lewis. The notebook, then, reveals how inextricably Cather and Lewis's shared travels intertwined with Cather's creative process—the *Archbishop* is nestled deeply in the middle of their record of their experiences and collaborative research.

"Running About" New Mexico and Arizona in 1926

By December 1925, Cather and Lewis were thinking about returning to New Mexico. Cather wrote her brother Roscoe asking whether "you could bring your ladies down to New Mexico in the car in June and run about for a couple weeks with me?" She and Lewis were not planning a pure pleasure trip, however, but a research trip. They had spent most of their time in 1925 in and around Taos, so they needed to spend more time in and around Santa Fe, where important parts of *Death Comes for the Archbishop* are set.[88]

Louise Guerber had taken a job in New York at the Metropolitan Museum of Art library, and Cather invited her to Friday tea at 5 Bank Street in April. There she met people from the East and from the West or, like Lewis and Cather, both. Lewis's friends Rudolph and Filomena Ruzicka came down from Dobbs Ferry. Bookstore owner and newspaper critic Fanny Butcher was visiting from Chicago. Eunice Chapin, a University of Nebraska graduate who worked as a magazine editor in New York, was there. William Allen White and his wife were visiting from Kansas, while C. A. Dawson Scott was in from England. Albert Donovan, Cather's student in Pittsburgh who had become a New York accountant, was there, as was Elizabeth Sergeant. "Met Miss Lewis," Guerber wrote in her diary, "who is charming in a very feminine and graceful way." Cather felt such confidence in Guerber's judgment that soon after she came to tea, Cather let her have the typed draft of the first part of *Archbishop* for two days. The two then sat in Central Park to talk it over. Cather was hoping to serialize the novel in a magazine before the Knopfs published it, so in late April, she sent the earlier chapters to literary agent Paul Reynolds. Notably, these early chapters are *not* set in Santa Fe—she urgently needed to travel there so she could finish writing the novel.[89]

Cather and Lewis started their westward trek on May 15. They again announced their intention to visit the Grand Canyon, but shortly before they departed, Cather's father telegraphed insisting that they stop in Red Cloud. After two days there, they started for Denver, staying at the Brown Palace two days before heading to New Mexico. They paused for a day at Lamy, enjoying El Ortiz, before taking the train to Gallup, near the New Mexico–Arizona border. Lewis, the overtaxed office worker, had caught a "nasty cold" as they traveled through a heat wave in Nebraska, so she may have missed the dramatic red rocks near the tracks as the train approached Gallup. Cather had faith in the power of the West to cure her. As she wrote Luhan, they had "very comfortable rooms" at El Navajo, yet another Harvey hotel adjacent to a Santa Fe line railroad station, where Lewis was "very happy and relaxed in bed for two days." Whereas the tiny El Ortiz was a fantasy Spanish hacienda, the more modern and severe architecture of the much larger El Navajo (sixty-five guest rooms) vaguely evoked the angular architecture of Pueblo dwellings. Mary Jane Colter filled the hotel with Native American artifacts, including wall art reproducing designs from sacred Navajo sand paintings. While Lewis lounged in her room (which also featured Navajo rugs, pottery, and baskets), Cather "made several strange and terrible acquaintants" in the town, which she described as "the Hell of a place," full of "low types."[90]

The Santa Fe and the Harvey Co. had made El Navajo so large precisely because Gallup was an ideal jumping-off point for ancient and modern Native American sites to the west. While Lewis was still convalescing, she and Cather made a day trip to Zuni Pueblo, but they waited before making the arduous trip to Canyon de Chelly in Arizona. Chinle, the Navajo reservation town near the canyon's mouth, was a considerable drive through the desert on rough and dusty (or muddy if it rained) dirt roads. "We can't do it unless Edith gets over her cough," Cather wrote Luhan, "for the drivers tell me it's a harder trip than it's advertised to be." Two days later, Lewis was well enough for the drive to Chinle, where they were outfitted with horses and packs to ride into the canyon. Meanwhile, as Cather wrote to Blanche Knopf, they were waiting "for good weather to start on a long hard horseback" ride into the canyon, "where motor can't go, thank God!"[91]

They first viewed the canyon from its rim, but they rode in at its wide sandy mouth—one of them took a snapshot of the other as she rode ahead into the narrowing canyon. Cliff dweller ruins of a similar vintage as the Mesa Verde ruins were (and are) located in the walls of Canyon de Chelly. As at Mesa Verde, those who built these dwellings migrated elsewhere, but at Canyon de Chelly, Navajos took up residence on the canyon floor. The river that had formed the canyon no longer flowed along its bottom, but a high water table and seasonal snowmelt flowing down the canyon walls made it suitable for raising crops and livestock. It was spring, lamb season for the Navajos' flocks, and cotton was blowing from the cottonwood trees. Cather and Lewis's horseback ride may have been rugged, but the canyon also presented a sort of pastoral ideal, especially for Cather, who fondly remembered her father raising sheep during her Virginia childhood.[92]

As they had in 1925, Cather and Lewis alternated rugged travel with modern comforts. From Chinle, they returned to Gallup, where they boarded the train to Lamy and arrived at the Hotel La Fonda in Santa Fe on June 4. Simultaneous with her research and writing of *Archbishop*, Cather had been rushing to finish *My Mortal Enemy*, a grim short novel set in early-twentieth-century New York. She had instructed Knopf to send the galley proofs for *My Mortal Enemy* to Gallup, but a comedy of errors delayed their arrival until just before she and Lewis departed for Santa Fe. Their first order of business at La Fonda was thus to read the proofs and send them back to New York City. They then moved quickly on to absorbing the atmosphere of Santa Fe and to visiting locations that would appear in *Archbishop*.[93]

The hotel was a block from the cathedral built by Archbishop Lamy. After Cather and Lewis's time at the hotel in 1925, the new owners had followed their usual practice and leased it to the Fred Harvey Company, and Mary Jane Colter was just beginning the process of making it over into an elegant, romanticized fantasy of nineteenth-century Santa Fe. The Harvey Company was making the hotel viable by using it as a center for its "Indian Detours," touring car excursions that enabled cross-country rail passengers to see the sights in the region quickly over the course of a few days. These tours, which had just started in the spring of 1926, were so successful that the railroad and the Harvey Company were planning a significant expansion of the hotel. Cather complained to Luhan that "the Indian Detourists abound and the motor horn is the worm that dieth not." She and Lewis, however, were as much tourists as the passengers in the honking touring cars. Even though they made individual arrangements to see sites rather than being driven by Harvey guides, they saw many of the same sites as the Detourists did and had been enjoying the aesthetics and amenities of the Harvey hotels.[94]

Despite Cather's complaints, she and Lewis settled into work on *Archbishop*. It was likely at this time that a young Paul Horgan, who many years later wrote a Pulitzer Prize–winning biography of Lamy, accidentally stumbled on Cather and Lewis on a balcony at La Fonda. As he recalled:

> In the deepest corner of the porch were two steamer chairs, and upon them reclined two ladies whose concentration I disturbed. They were busy with papers and pencils. I have an impression of many accessories—note-books, opened volumes, steamer rugs against the vagrant breezes which feel cool to someone out of the sun in Santa Fe. . . . [T]he nearer of the two ladies turned upon me a light blue regard of such annoyance and distaste at my intrusion that I was gone too quickly to take more than a sweeping impression of where I had been.

Nevertheless, Horgan recognized one of the "ladies" as Cather and presumed the other to be her "secretary." Embarrassed by the haughty stare, he did not introduce himself, but a year later, when *Archbishop* came out, he reflected on the fact that "she was working only a hundred yards from [Lamy's] cathedral, whose humble beauties she was the first to recognize."[95]

Cather's fellow author Mary Austin, who had recently relocated to Santa Fe, proved an important resource for Cather and Lewis as they sought to see sites outside of Santa Fe. Austin's niece, a recent Wellesley College graduate, could drive, and Austin offered her as their driver. Austin, her niece, Cather, and Lewis together drove to the Pecos ruins northeast of Santa Fe, a drive that elicited from Lewis, as she later wrote Austin, "many pleasant memories." The Cicuye (Pecos) people had occupied and built on the site from the 1400s until 1838, when their much-diminished community moved to the Jemez Pueblo.[96]

Once Roscoe Cather and his family arrived, on June 14, Willa Cather and Edith Lewis put work aside to enjoy New Mexico with visitors who were seeing it for the first time. Because Roscoe had driven in his personal car from Wyoming, they were able to range far. The week that the two couples—Roscoe and Meta, and Willa and Edith—spent touring in and around Santa Fe integrated Lewis further into at least one branch of Willa Cather's family, making her a member of it as much as Meta was. Having spent more than a month away, however, Lewis had to go back to work in New York City on June 23. Roscoe and his family took her to the train station and snapped a picture of her with their twin daughters before she boarded the train (Figure 3.14). When Roscoe's family started their drive to Wyoming the next day, Willa found herself alone.

Figure 3.14 Edith Lewis with Margaret and Elizabeth Cather in Santa Fe in 1926. Courtesy George Brockway.

As soon as Roscoe and Meta finished their drive home to Casper, they sent Lewis a note, and she was grateful for their thoughtfulness at the end of her three-day train journey. On their way back to Wyoming, the Cathers had stopped in Taos. "Didn't you all think it was beautiful?" Lewis queried. "I wish I could have heard the twins' comments. I wonder if you saw Mrs. Luhan's place, where Willa and I stayed." New York City contrasted sharply with New Mexico. Indeed, it seemed to Lewis "awful after all that beautiful open country. It is cool, but the sky hangs right down over your head, a dirty gray color, thousands of people rush past you with tense, stony looks as you walk along the street, and instead of hearing meadow larks, you hear the radio." She harkened back to "our ride to Española," calling it "one of the loveliest trips I ever took. Tell the twins to be sure to send me their pictures, and not to forget that we are all going to learn Spanish." The twins were still little girls in 1926, but by the time Lewis saw them again in 1936, when they summered on Grand Manan with her and Willa, they were young women.[97]

Mary Austin had left town before Roscoe's family arrived, leaving her house keys with Willa Cather so that she could get away from La Fonda in the mornings to write. As she wrote to both Austin and Roscoe on June 26, she found "my Bishop there waiting for me" every morning at Austin's house. Willa Cather was also, as she reported to her mother two days later, feeling "plenty lonely" after the departures of Lewis and of Roscoe's family. She had planned to go back up to Taos to work while staying in the Pink House, and

Mary Foote, whom Cather found "good company" in 1925, was also supposed to be there. Mabel and Tony Luhan were not there, however—Tony
was ill in the hospital, and Mabel was with him—and after a short time at Los
Gallos, Cather changed her mind and departed for the East.[98]

"To Edith Lewis, Who Discovered the Archbishop with Me"

While Lewis had found New York cool and gray in June, the weather changed
after Cather got there. By "the first dreadful week of August," she was looking
for a cooler place to work. She couldn't get a room in Jaffrey, so she asked
Marian MacDowell if she could come stay at her colony in Peterborough,
New Hampshire. As Cather wrote Louise Guerber, she at first found the artists' colony atmosphere awkward but found some of her co-residents tolerable, and she was "enjoying the Bishop again, after weeks of separation."
Cather left the MacDowell Colony for Jaffrey in early September. Before
Lewis joined her there for another month's vacation, she first traveled
to Grand Manan Island to buy land on which to build their own vacation
cottage.[99]

The two women were together again, then, as Cather worked happily in
Jaffrey on her novel based on their recent adventures in New Mexico and
Arizona. And after Knopf published the novel in book form in the fall of
1927, Cather presented a copy to Lewis inscribed, "To Edith Lewis, Who discovered the Archbishop with me." Many of the places they had visited and the
experiences they had had appear in the novel. They had visited a ceremonial
cave with Tony Lujan; Bishop Latour visits a ceremonial cave with Jacinto.
Jacinto is from the declining Pecos Pueblo (an anachronism, as Cather
concedes in a footnote, as the Pecos Pueblo had already been abandoned before the U.S. took possession of New Mexico); Cather and Lewis had visited
the Pecos ruins with Mary Austin and her niece. Cather and Lewis visited
Acoma Pueblo, where the mission church's roof had recently been restored;
in Cather's novel Latour says mass in the mission church, feeling oppressed
by the Acoma parishioners and the church's ponderous roof. As noted earlier, Cather gave Lamy and Machebeuf new names when she fictionalized
their lives, but the characters associated with Taos and vicinity appear under
their own names. Taos Padre Martinez, whom Cather demonized, wields his
power in opposition to the new bishop. Cather and Lewis drove out to Arroyo

Hondo several times with Tony Lujan; Padre Lucero of Arroyo Hondo, who joins Martinez in opposing the Bishop's authority, is an equally unsavory character in Cather's novel. Cather portrayed Kit Carson, who had a house in Taos, as largely admirable. The only fault Cather attributed to Carson was his leading the U.S. government expedition that drove the Navajo off their land, including Canyon de Chelly. Latour feels gratified at the end of the novel that the Navajo have been allowed to return and are living and farming peacefully in the canyon; Cather and Lewis's 1926 pack trip into Canyon de Chelly, where they witnessed the Navajo living and farming in the canyon, was their last southwestern horseback adventure, although at the time they did not know that it would be.[100]

Later, Cather turned a copy of the illustrated edition of *Archbishop* into a sort of scrapbook, pasting related materials into the volume. For example, a reader whose father had met Kit Carson in Santa Fe in the 1860s sent Cather a carte de visite of him, and Cather pasted both the reader's letter and the photograph into the front of the book. Cather also pasted on the blank pages before "The Vicar Apostolic" section of the novel the two mirror image photographs of herself and Lewis on horseback in the desert that they had taken of each other in 1925 when they were staying at Los Gallos (Figure 3.12) (in a copy of the first edition of the novel, Cather pasted the other photograph of Lewis on horseback [Figure 3.13]). By pasting the photographs of herself and Lewis in her personal copy of the novel, Cather put them both in the novel, just as Kit Carson is in the novel, but rather than appearing as themselves, two twentieth-century career women on vacation, they appeared as Latour and Valliant, who, like them, rode through the desert together.[101]

As Marilee Lindemann observes in *Willa Cather Queering America*, *Death Comes for the Archbishop* is "in the smallest and largest senses and to a greater extent than anything else [Cather] ever wrote—a love story," a narrative "fully and frankly . . . given over to telling the story of Latour's love for Vaillant . . . [and] completely . . . driven by the rhythms of 'their life together.'" Mabel Luhan never saw Cather's personal copy of *Archbishop*, but in Taos in 1925 she had befriended both Cather and Lewis and clearly understood that they were a couple. Just as Latour discovers that a powerful river flows under the rock in the ceremonial cave where he and Jacinto take refuge in a storm, Luhan discerned the subterranean current powering Cather's novel. As Luhan wrote in the 1950s in a reminiscence about Taos in the 1920s, "The book that came out of Willa when she left Taos was better loved than all her other books. Perhaps there is more love in it."[102]

* * *

When Cather and Lewis were at the Shattuck Inn in September 1926, the *Forum* magazine was preparing to promote the imminent serialization of *Archbishop*. Eunice Chapin, then assistant editor of the *Forum*, sent proposed promotional copy to Cather for review. Cather wrote to Chapin that it was "a mistake" to focus on "landscape," because the novel focused on "movement" rather than "ornamental descriptive writing." She enclosed the following promotional copy to replace what she had been sent:

> Miss Cather's new narrative, Death Comes etc. recounts the adventures of two missionary priests in the old Southwest. Two hardy French priests find themselves set down in the strange world at the end of the Santa Fé trail, among scouts and trappers and cut-throats, old Mexican settlements and ancient Indian pueblos. The period is that immediately following the Mexican War, and the story is a rich, moving panorama of life on that wild frontier.

When Lewis wasn't riding through the desert with Cather, imagining herself to be a cowboy or a missionary priest, she was a modern career woman working long hours at the J. Walter Thompson Co. Nearly seven years into her advertising copywriting career in 1926, she certainly had a hand in writing this promotional copy for Cather's novel, just as she had a hand in the experiences that inspired it. As demonstrated in the next chapter, which focuses on Lewis and Cather together in New York City in the 1920s, this is not the only instance of crossover between Lewis's advertising career and Cather's fiction writing. The two were as intertwined as their southwestern travels were with *The Professor's House* and *Death Comes for the Archbishop*.[103]

4

"The Thing Not Named"

Edith Lewis's Advertising Career and Willa Cather's Fiction and Celebrity in the 1920s

In March 1926, Willa Cather's *My Mortal Enemy* was published as a "novelette complete in one issue" in *McCall's*, a national-circulation women's magazine affiliated with a dress pattern company whose patterns were featured in the magazine. The magazine provided an introductory caption for the novella on its first page:

> The age of innocence—when our modern social world was young—is a time to which our authors seem to be turning for relief from the uncompromising materialism of today. Surfeited with frenzied finance, jazz, flapperism, and the other concomitants of a motor-car civilization, they seem to be seeking some earlier day where, in a lovelier, more spacious world, there was still room for high romance. No one has caught and reproduced the tone of that far-off time with more tenderness and fidelity than Miss Cather in this charming and subtle study of a haunting woman of that era. In her pages there breathes again the very sprit of those old days in New York when Madison Square was the heart of Manhattan.

Listing the real theatrical figures who appear as characters or who are mentioned in *My Mortal Enemy*, the caption goes on to praise Cather's portrayal of "old-world manners and the quiet leisure of lovely living" in a work of fiction that "recaptures the far-away and long ago, and is, in every stroke, the work of a consummate artist with words."[1]

The caption both evaded the darker side of the "high romance" depicted in Cather's novella and ignored its settings outside of Manhattan. Narrator Nellie Birdseye recounts the late-nineteenth-century romance, relayed to her by her Aunt Lydia, between Myra Driscoll and Oswald Henshaw in Parthia, Illinois, which had culminated in their elopement and Myra's disinheritance by her wealthy uncle. In New York, where a teenage Nellie visits them around

1905, the Harvard-educated Oswald has an office job with a railroad, and he and his wife live in genteel poverty. Myra is jealous of Oswald's attentions to other women, and she murmurs under her breath to Nellie after she tips a cabdriver extravagantly, "[I]t's very nasty, being poor." The second half of the novella takes place a decade later in California, where Nellie moves to teach college and where she finds herself in the same down-market residential hotel as Myra and Oswald. Myra, ill and disabled, resents Oswald and their shared poverty. "Money is a protection, a cloak," she tells Nellie; "it can buy one quiet and some sort of dignity." After Myra's death, Oswald protests that they were happy in New York, but her aunt's bitterness haunts Nellie, and her reflection on it concludes the novella:

> Sometimes when I have watched the bright beginning of a love story, when I have seen a common feeling exalted into beauty by imagination, generosity, and the flaming courage of youth, I have heard again that strange complaint breathed by a dying woman into the stillness of night, like a confession of the soul: "Why must I die like this, alone with my mortal enemy?"[2]

In the same issue of *McCall's* in which *My Mortal Enemy* appeared, Woodbury's Facial Soap ran an advertisement, part of a two-year campaign that the J. Walter Thompson advertising agency called a "group testimonial plan." Thompson surveyed categories of elite-class women, mostly young, and an advertising copywriter at Thompson then mined the responses of satisfied Woodbury's users for quotable quotes. The copywriter also wrote striking captions and introductory copy to draw magazine readers in. "At the Universities of Michigan, Wisconsin [and] Chicago alone," the headline of the March 1926 ad boasts, "nearly 2,000 girls use this soap for their skin." The central illustration (published in black and white in *McCall's* and in color in other magazines) shows distinctly modern young women, with short hair and wearing short dresses, engaged in conversation with dapper young men in evening dress. The image is captioned, "Fraternity dances—and the thrill of popularity, of success," and the ad copy proper describes:

> Thousands of girls—girls dark and fair, long-haired and bobbed, graceful and *gauche*—shy girls, audacious girls, dreamy girls, provocative girls—in endless and fascinating variety they pour through our great mid-Western universities. They are at an age when life seems a wonderful adventure—and

success, admiration, the approval of others more desirable than it will ever seem again. Latin verbs, yes; but what girl of twenty does not at heart believe supremely in the importance of a lovely fresh rose leaf complexion?

In April, the Woodbury's group testimonial campaign moved on to the Colony Club, "the smartest club in New York." The ad copy opens with a scene of guests arriving for a debutante dance: "Gold slippers above the asphalt pavement . . . the flash of jewels under the softness of furs . . . the purring of motor cars, crowding the curb . . . drift of music through the heavy, half-opened doors." Even though these women "can afford the most costly personal luxuries," the copy explains, Woodbury's Facial Soap, priced twenty-five cents a cake, is "pure enough and fine enough" for these "distinguished," "elegant," and "fastidious" consumers.[3]

The fiction in *McCall's* and other women's magazines in the 1920s was surprisingly heterogeneous—works by Zane Grey, Gene Stratton Porter, Joseph Hergesheimer, and Rudyard Kipling appeared in *McCall's* in 1926. Nevertheless, the publication of *My Mortal Enemy*, a darkly nostalgic novella by a "consummate artist of words" about the bitter end of a grand romance, seems jarring in a magazine full of advertisements for breakfast cereal, soup, cold cream, laundry soap, ice boxes, toothpaste, house plans for suburban bungalows, sanitary napkins, linoleum, and ham. Unlike Cather's novella, the Woodbury's advertisements, which sought to convince young women that using the soap would spark romance and happy endings, seem perfectly at home in this feminized, commercial context. Nevertheless, *My Mortal Enemy* and the Woodbury's Facial Soap ads shared an invisible connection. Advertising copywriters did not sign their work, but from 1923 until 1929, Edith Lewis was the sole copywriter at Thompson for Woodbury's Facial Soap, as well as for Jergens Lotion, both products of the Andrew Jergens Co. of Cincinnati. In the 1920s, then, Edith Lewis was writing advertisements that built up fantasies of heterosexual romance while Willa Cather was writing fiction that deconstructed these fantasies.

Cather and Lewis's writing pulled in opposite directions in other ways as well. Cultural historian Roland Marchand argues that advertising in the 1920s, which persuaded people to embrace the new and speed up the pace of consumption, was a key force in "making way for modernity." In order to carry out this mission, he explains, advertising copywriters used "parables" to teach consumers about the value of consumer goods and to persuade them to purchase an advertised product. The "parable of the democracy of goods" is at the center of the Woodbury's group testimonial campaign. Rather than feel envious of the elite women in the ads, middle-class white women (almost always the target market for ads in women's magazines) were taught that "the wonders of modern mass production and distribution enabled every person to enjoy the society's most significant pleasure, convenience, or benefit." In this case, women could achieve the same benefit (beautiful skin) as their social betters by purchasing the same soap they did.[4]

Lewis began working at the J. Walter Thompson Co. in January 1919. Soon thereafter Cather issued two sharp critiques of commodity culture. In her 1920 essay "On the Art of Fiction," Cather opined, "Writing ought either to be the manufacture of stories for which there is a market demand—a business as safe and commendable as making soap or breakfast foods—or it should be an art, which is always a search for something for which there is no market demand, something new and untried, where the values are intrinsic and have nothing to do with standardized values." Two years later, in "The Novel Démeublé" (1922), Cather distinguished her own art from popular forms, analogizing "[t]he novel manufactured to entertain great multitudes of people" to "cheap soap or a cheap perfume, or cheap furniture." The masses who preferred quantity over quality, she complained, "want change, a succession of new things that are quickly threadbare and can be lightly thrown away." Implicitly invoking a mass of childish female consumers, she asked rhetorically, "Does anyone pretend that if the Woolworth-store windows were piled high with Tanagra figurines at ten cents, they could for a moment compete with Kewpie brides in the popular esteem?"[5]

At roughly the same moment, then, Lewis embraced advertising as a career and Cather rejected modern consumerism. This convergence seems to register a tension or conflict within their relationship—while Cather mocked the production and selling of cheap soap, Lewis sold cheap soap. However, this tension could also be productive, even playful, as the two women engaged in an implicit dialogue with one another about the pleasures and perils of modern materialism and the desires it could engender.

Furthermore, rather than take as gospel truth modernist artists' claims that they stood outside the market, literary historians have increasingly turned their attention to the interface between the literary market and commodity culture. As Aaron Jaffe observes, scholars have come to the formerly "unthinkable" conclusion that as "producers of culture, modernists were keenly involved with the exigencies of making a place for themselves in the world and for their products in the cultural marketplace," in part through the mechanisms of celebrity culture. In Cather's case, her published critiques of the market cannot be taken at face value—she cared a great deal about the advertising, marketing, and sales of her books. Loren Glass argues in his analysis of literary celebrity that this kind of "posture of disdain for the mainstream audience" was "a virtual requirement for any author aspiring for high cultural consecration," and such a posture could, paradoxically, function as "a marketable image," as it did for Cather.[6]

Lewis's advertising career is not mentioned in any Cather biography, however. Even David Porter's *On the Divide: The Many Lives of Willa Cather*, which takes as its subject Cather's ambivalent relationship to advertising and self-promotion, relegates Lewis's copywriting career to a subordinate clause. Instead, Porter portrays Cather as seeking ever tighter control over the marketing of her books and the presentation of herself to the public.[7]

In light of her deep involvement in Cather's creative process as her editorial collaborator, however, Lewis's career as an advertising copywriter demands attention. Cather never wrote fiction with a particular magazine venue in mind: she wrote what she wanted to write, and then she let her agent, Paul Reynolds, or later her book publishers, Alfred and Blanche Knopf and their staff, place her fiction in whatever magazine would pay the highest price. Because women's magazines had the highest circulations, they often paid the highest prices. If she had targeted them, as her old friend Dorothy Canfield Fisher did, she might have made considerably more money. As editorial collaborator, then, Lewis helped Cather achieve her aesthetic vision for a particular piece rather than shape it for a particular venue.

Nevertheless, both Lewis and Cather were, in a real sense, writing for women's magazines in the 1920s and 1930s. Lewis had given up bylined publication of fiction and poetry, but as the Woodbury's ads quoted above demonstrate, copywriting was *writing*. Cather was the named author of short stories and serial novels that appeared in the same venues as Lewis's advertising copy, and Lewis's invisible editorial hand also shaped Cather's fiction published in women's and other magazines. In this period, each woman significantly increased her earning power. Combining forces, marrying advertising with literature and commerce with art, Cather and Lewis both achieved professional success beyond what each might have achieved alone.

In Lewis's ads, as in most 1920s advertisements directed at women, female consumers were invited to look at and appraise themselves through men's eyes. Lewis's advertising campaigns for women's beauty products and her articles in trade publications about the philosophy of advertising thus present a fresh context for interpreting Cather's fiction of the 1920s, a significant portion of which Cather wrote from the male point of view (*My Mortal Enemy* being an exception that proves the rule). And, finally, Lewis's advertising work also gave her expertise useful in shaping not just Cather's fiction but her public persona: Lewis contributed promotional copy for Cather's books and used her expertise in working with photographer Edward Steichen, whose photographs were featured in Jergens and Woodbury's ads, to help shape Cather's image as a particular kind of celebrity in the 1920s.

"One Has to Advertise": Willa Cather and Edith Lewis Embrace Advertising

In 1915, while she and Lewis were in Taos, Cather wrote her brother Douglass complaining that her writing career was stalled and she might give it up. "[I]n my business," she explained, "one has to advertise a little or drop out—I surely do not advertise or talk about myself as much as most people who write for a living." She was protesting too much—her trip was a research venture, and at its beginning she had made sure to have a journalist interview her in Denver to promote the imminent publication of *The Song of the Lark*. From 1915 to 1918, while Lewis was managing editor of *Every Week*, Cather wrote frequently to Ferris Greenslet and others at Houghton Mifflin suggesting advertising and promotional strategies for her novels, and she became increasingly disaffected by what she saw as her publisher's failure to promote her novels aggressively enough. As she wrote Greenslet in May 1919, she was considering an offer from "one firm" (certainly Alfred A. Knopf, Inc.) that had "outlined an advertising scheme which seems to me excellent. They believe that the aim of a[d]vertising is not so much to sell one particular book, or to be careful to come out even on one book, as to give the author a certain standing which would insure his future and interest in his future books." Cather wanted Houghton Mifflin to focus more on promoting her, not the publishing house, as the source of a certain kind of fiction. Put another way, she wanted them to promote her name as a brand.[8]

Cather did not jump ship from Houghton Mifflin until 1920, however. In 1919, she was working on a new novel, ultimately published in 1922 by Knopf as *One of Ours*, and she was willing to give Greenslet another chance at adequately promoting her fiction. Notably she called in a newly trained copywriter for reinforcement. As she wrote Greenslet in late August 1919, "Miss

Lewis" had "put down some valuable advertising copy in a note book" while they were both at the Shattuck Inn in Jaffrey, New Hampshire. Even before Lewis officially commenced her advertising writing career, she had written promotional copy for *My Ántonia*. In December 1917, when Houghton Mifflin was preparing a mockup of the book to be used by the firm's salesmen, Cather wrote Greenslet that "Miss Lewis pulled this off yesterday." Greenslet thanked Cather for sending Lewis's "excellent blast," presumably language to be used on the dust jacket. By 1919, then, when Cather was seriously considering leaving Houghton Mifflin for Knopf and when Lewis was in the first year of her career at Thompson, both women had embraced the value of advertising.[9]

Lewis had been offered a job at Thompson in 1915 but had declined it in favor of a position as managing editor of *Every Week*. Just after Thanksgiving in 1918, back from a four-month vacation in Canada to recover her health, she filled out a new Thompson job application. Perhaps feeling that her career had not advanced as quickly as she had hoped, she, like Cather, lied about her age: she claimed to be thirty-four (she was thirty-six and would soon turn thirty-seven) and left blank the space provided for the date of her college degree. Responding to a series of questions about her "personal characteristics," she touted her "power to visualize new ideas & understandings" and "make decisions quietly, but act on them deliberately." She also boasted, "I cannot remember ever having abandoned anything I set out to do," "I have often supplied the driving power for a whole office-ful of people," and "difficulties attract me." Her ultimate career goal, she explained, was to become "the head of a large, successful working organization." Specifying that she was seeking a position as a copywriter, she claimed that she would succeed at this work "because my publishing experience gives me unusual advantages in the way of training" and that she was applying to Thompson in particular "[b]ecause it has an extremely high reputation among publishers [and] because I like the tone of the organization, and because I like the personnel so far as I know it." She responded no to the question "Can you operate any sort of office machine?" Answering yes could land a female applicant, even a college-educated, experienced magazine editor, in the secretarial pool. Lewis's childhood friend from Lincoln, Frances Maule, clearly understood the risk of admitting that she had secretarial skills when she applied for a position at Thompson in 1920. "While I realize the injudiciousness of doing so," Maule wrote in response to this question, "I must confess to being able to operate a typewriter and a multigraph."[10]

Lewis's application immediately interested the agency. Within a week of applying, she had interviewed with one of the senior women copywriters, Aminta Casseres, and her references had been called. George Buckley of the Crowell Corporation (which had owned *Every Week* magazine) praised Lewis as "a very fine executive and good on detail and follow up" with "a very fine mind, really a brilliant mind." Buckley promised to ask Bruce Barton, editor in chief of *Every Week*, about Lewis's writing abilities. Coincidentally, Barton and two men he had met through the United War Work Committee were about to start a new advertising agency. In December, Lewis talked to Barton about his plans, which made her, as she reported to Casseres, "more than eager to go into advertising work." On January 3, 1919, Casseres wrote to offer Lewis an open position, telling her she could begin as soon as she wanted. Lewis accepted Thompson's offer and declined one from Barton's new agency, Barton, Durstine, and Osborne. She had asked Thompson to match her $80-a-week salary as managing editor of *Every Week* ($4,160 a year, or about $64,000 in 2018 dollars), and the agency evidently met her demand.[11]

Thompson was a large, complex, and compartmentalized organization, with people in multiple departments carrying out the work necessary to create and place advertisements. As a copywriter, Lewis was responsible for the text, including long paragraphs, headlines, and captions. At Thompson, writers were organized into "copy groups" under "copy heads," and writers worked together on accounts assigned to the group. The mechanical department created or commissioned the artwork, designed the type, and created the layout in which the copy was embedded (Thompson did not create a separate art department until the late 1920s). Consumer research carried out by the research department might suggest new advertising appeals, while its studies of newspaper and magazine readership influenced decisions concerning ad placement. Buyers in the scheduling department purchased space from newspapers and magazines to run ads, while the traffic department coordinated the logistics of this whole process, from conception through execution and placement. The account representatives served as the executive-level contacts with the clients—copywriters were invisible to clients—and although in the 1920s women at Thompson wrote copy, they were not account executives. Lewis had disclosed on her application that she had no sales experience, and because Thompson considered direct contact with consumers a crucial training ground for copywriting, she was likely sent out for a few months to work behind the cosmetics counter at a department store or to knock on doors for consumer research.[12]

At Thompson, copywriting was gender-segregated. Female copywriters made up the Women's Editorial Department, founded and managed by Helen Lansdowne Resor, in which they wrote exclusively for products classified as "women's products" (a category that included beauty products but also products associated with housework and caring for children). Women were assigned exclusively to women's products because they ostensibly possessed "the woman's viewpoint," which enabled them to persuade other women to purchase the products. As Kathy Peiss observes in *Hope in a Jar: The Making of America's Beauty Culture*, this logic "implied that women secured their jobs and succeeded in advertising not through professional training and achievement, but by virtue of their womanly empathy." Nevertheless, with Helen Resor at its helm, the Women's Editorial Department made Thompson the largest agency in the U.S. in the 1920s. In the New York office in 1925, twenty-two women wrote for sixty-two accounts, while nineteen male copywriters worked on only eighteen. Furthermore, women's magazines, where most women's products were advertised, had among the highest circulation numbers. Thompson and its female copywriters thus had a symbiotic relationship with these magazines and with their millions of readers.[13]

Within the gender-segregated confines of the Women's Editorial Department, many women—including Lewis—found challenging and well-paid professional work. In the 1960s, Ruth Waldo, one of the longest-serving women at Thompson, defended the earlier gender segregation at the agency as advancing women's careers:

> When a woman works for a man or in a man's group, she becomes less important, her opinion is worth less, her own progress and advancement less rapid. Then she does not have the excitement and incentive to work as hard as she can, nor, in a men's group, does she get the full credit for what she does. But with the knowledge and confidence of Mrs. Resor's support, a woman at Thompson could advance in her own group without having to complete with <u>Men</u>, for recognition of her ability. She has greater independence and freedom; a woman's ideas could be judged on their value alone.

Waldo elaborated that the combination of Helen Resor and Stanley Resor (Helen's husband and the agency's president) was crucial: Stanley Resor

"appreciated ideas on their own merits without concern about who originated the idea."[14]

Producing an advertising campaign, like editing a magazine, was collaborative work. After she retired, Lewis recalled that when she still worked in
an advertising office, she felt "like a player in a football game." The work was
also anonymous. As psychologist John Watson, hired to direct research at
Thompson, observed in 1929, once a piece of advertising copy was "finished,"
the question of "who wrote it?" could be impossible to answer. "The group
wrote it—the whole agency wrote it," he explained. "The most anyone can say
is that he wrote on the account." Nevertheless, for a time Lewis was an unusual case as a sole copywriter on two major accounts.[15]

Lewis quickly embraced advertising as a career and Thompson as an
employer, bringing and offering to bring friends and associates into her
new profession. When Frances Maule, Lewis's childhood friend and fellow
Greenwich Village resident, applied for a job at Thompson in 1920, she
explained that she was applying because she "[h]ad an introduction to Mrs.
Riser [sic]"—certainly, it was Lewis who introduced the experienced journalist and women's suffrage organizer and publicist to Helen Resor. Lewis
also encouraged former *Every Week* staff members to join her at Thompson.
In 1924, as Brenda Ueland explained to her mother, Lewis, whom she
described as "a person of importance" at the "large advertising firm,"

> tells me that if I wish, she will hire me and train me in this. As it is quite
> an undertaking to train a person there, if I go to work for her I must make
> up my mind to stay there for a long time. There are several advantages to
> working there. They have large handsome offices in a building near the
> Grand Central Station. They pay very good salaries and have a large staff of
> agreeable and intelligent people.

Ueland ultimately didn't accept this offer, but Lewis had made copywriting
at Thompson sound alluring. In 1928, Lewis got another *Every Week* staffer,
Anne Herendeen, hired on a temporary basis to help with the Woodbury's
Beauty Survey (discussed later).[16]

As her correspondence with magazine contributors suggests, Lewis was
pragmatic about audience, and that pragmatism translated well to advertising. In 1924, she was asked to interview Helen Goodspeed, a University of
Chicago graduate who had published book reviews in the *New Republic*, for
a copywriting position. As reported in an internal memo, Lewis was "very

much impressed" with Goodspeed's "considerable intelligence" and "very pleasing personality." She was cautious, however, about her prospects as a copywriter because "Miss G. has written the sort of thing that appeals to a more or less restricted class of people—literary or cultured, more or less." Lewis wondered "if Miss G. could be trained or would train herself to write for the kind of people who would be interested in food, cooking, Rinso [a laundry soap for which Thompson produced ads] and such like." Whatever her doubts about Goodspeed, clearly Lewis had already been trained to write—or had trained herself to write—with an audience of ordinary consumers in mind.[17]

In the spring of 1942, Willa Cather seemingly dismissed the audience for Lewis's advertising copy in a letter to her sister-in-law, Meta Schaper Cather. Forwarding Meta two examples of ads Lewis wrote for the *American Weekly* magazine, she explained, "This the [*sic*] kind of advertising work Edith does. The text and sketch are both hers. It's very interesting work and requires a great knowledge of types and printing—and of the dullness of the average human mind." During the war years, Lewis moved into art direction while continuing to write copy (thus Cather's praise of her "great knowledge of types and printing" and attribution of "the sketch" to her), but Cather also seemingly damned the readers of Lewis's advertisements as intellectually inferior to *her* readers.[18]

Notably, such dismissals of the intelligence of consumers—the intended audience for advertisements—were widespread inside the advertising community. Some described advertising as missionary work aiming to educate consumers and make their lives better, but others were more cynical, understanding themselves as using their superior intelligence and advertising tradecraft to manipulate gullible consumers. Thus Lewis's colleague William Esty argued at a 1930 Thompson account representatives meeting that their place was not to bring consumers up to a higher level; rather, they should admit among themselves that "what we are really saying is that the great bulk of people are stupid." As Marchand observes, the perception that "consumer citizens" were overwhelmingly women often inflected this scorn. Admen thought of the audience to whom they addressed ads "as an emotional, feminized mass, characterized by mental lethargy, bad taste, and ignorance." This is precisely the kind of scorn Cather directed at the feminized masses who would choose Kewpie brides over priceless ancient artifacts in "The Novel Démeublé". Thus in writing to Meta Cather about the "lowness of the average human mind," Willa may have been echoing Lewis's representations of her own work and her thinking about the audience for the advertising copy she wrote: Lewis could be a professional dedicated to her craft without respecting the consumers she sought to persuade.[19]

Aspiring writers often took advertising copywriting jobs, but most did not last long. Both poet Hart Crane and novelist John P. Marquand passed through the Thompson agency in the early 1920s while Lewis was there; Marquand satirized the agency in his novel *H. M. Pullman, Esquire* (1941). F. Scott Fitzgerald famously spent a few unhappy months writing streetcar jingles for the Colliers Street Railway Advertising Company, part of the Barron Collier Agency, before quitting and retreating to St. Paul to drastically revise the novel that became *This Side of Paradise*. Those who stuck it out nevertheless recognized their kinship with writers of fiction and poetry, making that kinship the subject of frequent comment in the advertising trade press. For example, in 1916 in the advertising trade journal *Printers Ink*, Henry Beers, Jr., wrote about what he called the "narrative style" in advertising copy. Because of severe space constraints, he explained, every word in advertising copy had to "[pay] a pretty heavy freight," and the advertising writer would thus do well to "borrow his brother artist's fire" in order to "make each syllable sing." In 1917, in *Printers Ink*, Charles Stirrup claimed that the advertising writer had to outdo the literary writer. Writing ad copy "calls for more careful thought than any other form of literary effort" because every word "represents . . . money." Thus a "conscientious copy-writer" would not allow copy out of his hands until he had "exhausted his best efforts upon it. It calls . . . for much more drastic revision than any other writing. It demands more condensation." In "On the Art of Fiction," Cather argued:

> Art . . . should simplify. That, indeed, is very nearly the whole of the higher artistic process; finding what conventions of form and what detail one can do without and yet preserve the spirit of the whole—so that all that one has suppressed and cut away is there to the reader's consciousness as much as if it were in type on the page.

In the advertising trade press, influence was generally imagined to run from the literary to the advertising sphere—the copywriter should learn lessons from his "first cousin" the story writer. In Cather's case, however, her compressed style was the product of her collaboration with an advertising copywriter, who practiced her tradecraft of "drastic revision" and "condensation" on Cather's fiction.[20]

"You Can Write as Emotionally about Ham as about Christianity": Lewis's Woodbury's Facial Soap Copy and Cather's Aesthetic Theories

When Lewis first began working on the Woodbury's account she may have been part of a copy group, but by the mid-1920s she came to occupy the peculiar position as a copy group of one. As a result it is possible to do what is normally impossible: identify the authorship of copy for a product's ads with certainty. Stanley Resor, the president of Thompson, had brought the Woodbury's account to the agency in 1910, when he was still head of the agency's Cincinnati office. An approach he had pioneered—promoting Woodbury's as an effective treatment for various skin conditions—was still being used a decade later. The first trace of Lewis's work on the account is a March 1921 internal company newsletter article about newspaper ads for the soap. Lewis (under the byline "E.L.") wrote about a subtle shift in the newspaper campaign for Woodbury's:

> an attempt . . . to give freshness to the standard treatment advertisements without fundamentally altering their character. Special pains have been taken, in the setting of the advertisements, to give importance and interest to the treatment itself. In place of the old-fashioned borders, simple ruled borders have been used. The headlines have been given more of a news character for example, "<u>There is constant danger</u> in an oily skin" has replaced the former standard heading "<u>Oily skin and shiny nose—how to correct them!</u>". For the first time, in the art work, we have tried using girls' heads without indicating the treatment in the illustration—that is, the girl is not holding a cake of soap or a hot washcloth to her face, or bending over a bowl of steam.

Lewis's brief article illuminates the collaborative process of creating the described advertisement—the copy, including headlines and captions, is carefully integrated with visual and design elements, and both the copy and Lewis's account of the writing of it emanate from a collective "we."[21]

In a 1923 essay published in Thompson's client newsletter, "The Emotional Quality in Advertisements," Lewis theorized the kind of writing she was producing for Woodbury's ads. She also slyly took up and repurposed Cather's aesthetic proclamations, demonstrating her awareness of the difference between her writing (addressed to "the kind of people . . . interested in Rinso") and Cather's writing (for an audience of "a more or less restricted class of people—literary or cultured, more or less"). In "The Novel Démeublé" (first published in the *New Republic*, the high-toned, intellectual magazine in which Helen Goodspeed published her book reviews), Cather argued against the overfurnished materialism of the realist novel and for the superior aesthetic value of "[w]hatever is felt upon the page without being specifically named . . . the inexplicable presence of the thing not named, of the over-tone divined by the ear but not heard by it, the verbal mood, the emotional aura of the fact or thing or deed." She challenged the idea that catalogs of "material objects" or explanations of "mechanical processes" or "the methods of operating manufactures and trades" constituted literary realism. Instead, she asked rhetorically, "is not realism, more than it is anything else, an attitude of mind on the part of the writer toward his material, a vague definition of the sympathy and candor with which he accepts, rather than chooses, his theme?"[22]

In "The Emotional Quality in Advertisements," Lewis, like Cather, argued that carefully crafted prose carries an emotional aura. For Lewis, however, this aura served the purpose of provoking consumers' desires to buy material goods. In her essay, Lewis also entered into a debate within the advertising trade about "reason why" versus "emotional" appeals. Which were more effective, advertisements that logically described the benefits of a product ("reason why") or ads that appealed to consumers' desires ("emotional")? Lewis refused to accept the distinction, explaining that "[a]ll good advertisements are emotional," and the emotional quality of an ad depended "on the writer's ability to feel strongly about the material" rather than "the material the writer is handling." Citing the example of Gibbon's *Decline and Fall of the Roman Empire*, she claimed that it was more emotional than "most magazine fiction." Without emotion, Gibbon's history would be "something like the World's Almanac—a mere catalog of names and figures." Emotion was essential to all writing, but even more so to advertising writing, she argued, "because . . . you must not only interest your reader—you must induce him to act on the strength of the interest and sympathy you can arouse." Some objects carried natural emotional appeals that were easily dramatized in ads (she listed as examples "food, furniture, clothes, vacation trips"). Products such as "a cake of soap," however, "would be difficult or even impossible to present in such a way as to make, in themselves, any appeal to the imagination." Faced with cakes of soaps that, to the consumer's senses, appeared largely fungible, the copywriter had "to get an emotional response by appealing to the uses, by making the reader feel what wonderful things it will do for her."[23]

Referring specifically to the advertising for Woodbury's Facial Soap (ad copy she herself was writing), Lewis conceded that the uses of the soap as a treatment for skin conditions were an important, longtime element of the ads, but she qualified this statement: "it has been necessary to reinforce the emotional appeal by going outside these uses; by creating situations that bring strongly before the reader's imagination the social disadvantages of a bad complexion, the social incentives for a good one." Lewis called it "a mistake . . . to imagine that 'emotion' means a man and a woman, or a mother and a child." She continued, adding a touch of dry wit, "Soup can produce emotion; you can write as emotionally about ham as about Christianity." She helpfully provided a list of emotions that might add "freshness and spontaneity of treatment," including "fear, appetites, humor, interest, love of luxury, and so forth."[24]

When she wrote "treatment" advertisements (like those in the newspaper campaign she described in the company newsletter in 1921), Lewis had to muster enthusiasm for devising new ways to describe established methods for using the soap to treat undesirable skin conditions. However, Thompson alternated those treatment advertisements with what they called "sentimental" ones, which featured images of heterosexual couples, the man's arm around the woman, both facing toward the viewer, under the slogan "The Skin You Love to Touch." This appeal, generally credited to Helen Lansdowne Resor (from her earlier years as a copywriter), was newer than the treatment appeal but was nevertheless well established by the 1920s. Denise Sutton observes that this copy appeal seems "oddly . . . aimed at a male audience" rather than at women. A woman reading a magazine was, Sutton hypothesizes, "being encouraged to imagine a 'secondary reader,' the man who will, thanks to Woodbury's Soap, be enticed to touch her skin. The slogan is a message of male desire for a woman with skin he loves to touch."[25]

Lewis had no part in coining Woodbury's slogan, but she worked within its established logic, inviting female consumers to gaze at and appraise themselves through men's eyes. "You, too, *can have the charm of 'A skin you love to touch',*" proclaimed the headline of an October 1922 Woodbury's ad, at the center of which is a Walter Biggs illustration of a man with one hand around a woman's waist and the other stroking her arm. The ad copy exclaimed, "That mysterious charm which is only found in the skin of a beautiful woman— you too, can possess it! You, too, can have a soft, clear, radiant complexion.

Each day your skin is changing—old skin dies and new skin takes its place. This is your opportunity!" The opportunity was to buy a cake of Woodbury's Facial Soap, which had a booklet wrapped around it describing a "treatment" that would work wonders on a woman's skin in a week to ten days. In this and similar advertisements, the Woodbury's name appeared only in ordinary small type, and the soap itself was not represented visually. Thompson characterized this as "editorial style," in which ads were crafted to resemble adjacent editorial content.[26]

Because the Woodbury's slogan was well established, most readers would have recognized the slogan in this ad as an implied reference to the brand name, but many Woodbury's ads from the early 1920s took the editorial style to an extreme. Take, for example, a May 1922 ad with the headline "Nothing quite effaces that momentary disappointment" (Figure 4.1). In the illustration a man stands close to a woman in a box at the theater, and he gazes at her face as he helps her remove her wrap. Together the copy and the illustration created what Roland Marchand calls a social tableau. The ad also deployed another one of the great advertising parables, the "parable of first impressions." "Instinctively," the copy explained, "perhaps without even stating it to himself—a man expects to find daintiness, charm, refinement in the women he knows. And when some unpleasant little detail mars this conception of what a woman should be—nothing quite effaces his involuntary disappointment." In this ad (and others in this series described later), nothing alerted the reader that she was confronting a soap advertisement until she was several paragraphs into the small type of the "editorial" matter. The emotions, however, were front and center. The cake of Woodbury's soap, depicted visually in use in the treatment ads and as an icon at the bottom of the page in some sentimental ads, was invisible. Instead, we have (to apply Cather's aesthetic theory across domains) Woodbury's Soap as "the thing not named" which was nevertheless "inexplicabl[y] presen[t]" through its conjured "emotional aura."[27]

Other Woodbury's Facial Soap headlines from 1921 and 1922, all derived from the copy proper, asked women to imagine men watching and judging them: "A man's first impression of a woman"; "His unspoken thoughts when he looks into your face,—*what are they*?"; "All around you people are judging you silently"; "Strangers' eyes, keen and critical, *can you meet them proudly—confidently—without fear*?" In "The Emotional Quality in Advertisements," Lewis argued for "emotions" beyond "a man and a woman," listing a broader palette of emotions—"fear, appetites, humor,

Figure 4.1 A May 1922 Woodbury's Facial Soap advertisement in the *Woman's Home Companion* designed to mimic adjacent magazine content and disguise its status as an ad.

interest, love of luxury, and so forth"—that could make advertisements more "fresh." However, in the early 1920s Woodbury's ads, the darker emotions of fear, appetites, and love of luxury were inextricably tied up with heterosexual romance.[28]

Around the time that Lewis was writing copy for these advertisements, she was using her expertise to write dust jacket copy for Cather's novel *One of Ours* and facing an even greater challenge of not-naming. Cather did not want the novel advertised as a war novel; Lewis complained to Cather about her proposed approach to promoting the book, and Cather relayed Lewis's complaint to Alfred Knopf: "Miss Lewis says that it's very difficult to write an ad for a story when the author insists that the theme of the story must not be whispered in the ad!" Under the signature of Alfred Knopf on the front of the first edition dust jacket, Cather was praised as "our greatest living woman novelist," and *One of Ours* was identified as "an authentic masterpiece—a novel to rank with the finest of this or any age." However, it was Lewis, not Knopf, who wrote this praise and who described how the protagonist, Claude Wheeler, "a sort of young Hamlet of the prairies," found release from the "baffled energy" of his "nature" through an unspecified "final adventure."[29]

"The Skin You Love to Touch": Men Looking at Women in Lewis's Woodbury's Facial Soap Group Testimonial Ads

From 1921 to 1923, Lewis, probably as part of a copy group, was writing within already-established appeals for Woodbury's Soap. In 1923 and 1924, however, her role changed in two ways: she became sole copywriter for both Woodbury's and Jergens Lotion, and she began devising new copy appeals and executing new campaigns. The Woodbury's group testimonial ads of the mid-1920s described at the beginning of this chapter had their origins in consumer research begun in 1922 when the Thompson research department surveyed women "to determine if there have been any changes in the Woodbury's market. What classes and age groups are using WOODBURY'S. Is our appeal today directed to all who should be using the product?" While the door-to-door investigation covered women of all classes (divided, as was the firm's usual practice, in descending order of income, into A, B, C, and D), Thompson supplemented this investigation with a mail survey of Wellesley College students and women faculty members. As they noted in their report, "The [students] are in the main from the homes of upper middle class families." Not only did the survey of Wellesley students yield an extraordinarily high rate of return (more than half responded), their responses indicated a high rate of Woodbury's use (54 versus 30 percent in the broader survey). The Wellesley students also expressed great enthusiasm for the product.[30]

In 1924, Thompson launched a successful campaign for Pond's Cold Cream using testimonials from American society women and minor European royalty. Although the campaign continued for years, the formula quickly became stale and stretched credibility—did Marie of Roumania really use Pond's Cold Cream to make herself fascinating, or was she laughing all the way to the bank with the $10,000 she was paid for the right to use her name and likeness in its ads (even as she was endorsing other products)? When Stanley Resor pitched a new campaign to the client in November 1924 using sample ads drawing on the Wellesley College survey results, he worked to distinguish the proposal from the celebrity endorsement model, calling it "a testimonial campaign in a new form. It is by groups of people rather than by individuals—groups of so personal and yet so wide an interest, that the interest should really be national in scope." The groups proposed were female students at "the national women's colleges" supplemented by large state universities; "the season's debutantes in the principal cities"; actresses; women guests at fashionable resorts; women passengers on transatlantic steamers; and wives and daughters of U.S. senators. When William Groom of Thompson's Cincinnati office conveyed the response of Jergens' corporate secretary (Frank Adams) back to Resor, the difference from the celebrity endorsement was key to their enthusiasm: "Of special advantage, it seems to me, is the strong note of conviction you get out of reading this copy on what the soap does for you. . . . Frank's comment on the example piece of copy was: 'Stanley has hit upon a copy plan which is as interesting and just as fresh and new as the original Woodbury plan in 1911.' "[31]

Lewis's colleagues in the New York office knew that she was sole copywriter for the Jergens accounts, but both she and Helen Resor, head of the Women's Editorial Department, were invisible to the Andrew Jergens Co. As far as the company was concerned, everything, including the copy and the ideas behind it, came from the mind of their man, Stanley, who, because of his long relationship with the company, worked directly with them rather than delegating to an account representative in Cincinnati. From 1925 to 1927, the Thompson research department sent to Lewis (and only Lewis) the survey reports for each of the classes of female consumers Resor had enumerated (except steamer passengers and senator's wives and daughter). Lewis then mined these reports both for impressive aggregate numbers and for individual women's words enthusiastically describing what Woodbury's did for their skin.[32]

Andrew Jergens Co. was also a substantial client warranting direct super-vision of the account by the agency president. During the years that Lewis was sole copywriter for Woodbury's and Jergens, the annual combined ad-vertising appropriation for the two brands was more than a million dollars. Woodbury's Facial Soap ads often ran in color on full pages, including back covers, and sometimes as two-page spreads—thus that appropriation was over $800,000. In contrast, Jergens Lotion ads were mostly in black and white and sometimes only on half pages, so that appropriation was generally about $200,000. During all of this time, the Resors, the two most powerful people at Thompson, were Lewis's day-to-day contacts on both the Jergens and Woodbury's campaigns. The fact that the Resors entrusted her with first the ongoing Woodbury's campaigns and then the Jergens Lotion campaign (when Thompson launched national advertising for it) suggests that they saw her as especially skilled at writing copy for beauty products.[33]

During the first year of the Woodbury's group testimonial campaign, Lewis wrote quasi-sociological copy. Take, for example, a two-page color ad, which ran in June 1925 women's magazines about Woodbury's users at two women's colleges, Smith and Bryn Mawr (Figure 4.2). Under the headline

Figure 4.2 Woodbury's Facial Soap "group testimonial" ad for which Edith Lewis wrote the copy, from the June 1925 *Ladies Home Journal*.

"Five Hundred & Twenty Girls at Smith and Bryn Mawr tell why they are using this soap for their skin," Lewis began her copy:

> We wanted to know how the American college girl takes care of that clear fresh skin of hers. What soap does she use? Why does she choose it? And what are the qualities about it that especially appeal to her? It was to learn the answers to these questions that we selected two of the most representative groups of American college girls for a special investigation.

In this and the other ads during the first year of the campaign, heterosexual romance appeared only in the illustrations. In the Smith and Bryn Mawr ad, a large image of a man paddling a canoe in which a young woman lounges, trailing her hand through the water, runs diagonally across the centerfold, but the other illustrations depict only women: one shows three women together in front of a college building, and the three others depict women using Woodbury's Soap. The primary message of the ad was not "use this soap and a man will desire you" but "use this soap, and you can share an experience with the privileged class of women endorsing the product."[34]

As Lewis later explained at a special agency-wide meeting on testimonials in advertising, the promise of a sample set of Woodbury's products was enough to spur college students to fill out the questionnaires. The agency found, however, "that we could not send a simple questionnaire to a debutante and expect her to fill it out and return it to us." Instead, they had to use paid investigators to corral the debutantes and elite resort and hotel guests and record their answers for them. Thompson held the meeting at which Lewis spoke because testimonial ads were coming under attack as misleading, and she explained how they avoided having the investigators skew the results: "We tried to insure the honesty of the results by simply paying the investigator $2 a questionnaire whether the answer was 'no' or 'yes,' whether a person used or did not use the soap."[35]

In 1926, as described at the beginning of this chapter, the appeal in the group testimonial campaign shifted—the illustrations became more modern and the copy more literary and focused on romantic situations. Lewis's skills as a copywriter, her setting of romantic and glamorous scenes, became more important as the groups of women offering testimonials became harder to pursue. In the image for a July 1926 ad featuring women at Bar Harbor and Newport (Figure 4.3), a woman languishes on a deck chair, a book falling out of her hand, while a man in a blazer and white flannel trousers stretched

July, 1926 — *The Ladies'* HOME JOURNAL

IN THE FASHIONABLE SUMMER COLONIES
I AT NEWPORT AND BAR HARBOR

*169 women tell why they find
this soap best for their skin ~*

Figure 4.3 Second-stage Woodbury's "group testimonial" ad for which Edith
Lewis wrote the copy, from the June 1926 *Ladies Home Journal.*

out behind her gazes sidelong at her exposed neck. "The Italian ambassador
arrives," Lewis began her caption. "Dinners, dances, bathing-parties . . . The
Brazilian envoy arrives." Lewis continued the list, focusing primarily on
men's activities in "the Newport season!," which, she advised readers, was

more "picturesque" and "*insouciant*" than in the winter, like a "wonderful cubist pattern, all dazzling movement and color." Having introduced the distinguished men, those who do the looking, Lewis moved on to the objects of the men's gazes, women who were "like tropical flowers in their brilliant sports frocks; their cheeks touched to carnation by sun and wind, arms and throats delicately sun-browned." Once she had set the scene, Lewis introduced these flapper flowers, who might have stepped out of *The Great Gatsby*, as Woodbury's users.[36]

"Hit Hard by Beauty": Men Looking at Women in Cather's Fiction

In the spring of 1925, F. Scott Fitzgerald, who professed himself to be "one of [Cather's] greatest admirers," wrote her to exonerate himself from "an instance of apparent plagiarism" in his new novel, *The Great Gatsby*. When Cather's *A Lost Lady* was published in 1923, he explained, he read it with "the greatest delight" and particularly admired a passage near the end in which Niel Herbert, the point-of-view character, reflects back on his feelings about Marian Forrester, the "lost lady" of the title:

> Her eyes, when they laughed for a moment into one's own, seemed to promise a wild delight that he has not found in life. "I know where it is," they seemed to say, "I could show you!" He would like to call the shade of the young Mrs. Forrester, as the witch of Endor called up Samuel's, and challenge it, demand the secret of that ardour; ask her whether she had really found some ever-blooming, ever-burning, every-piercing joy, or whether it was all fine play-acting. Probably she had no more than another; but she had always the power of suggesting things much lovelier than herself, as the perfume of a single flower may call up the whole sweetness of spring.

Fitzgerald explained that "a month or two before" he read *A Lost Lady*, he "had written into my own book a parallel and almost similar idea in the description of a woman's charm" (a passage about Daisy Buchannan, after whom Jay Gatsby pines and about whom the narrator, Nick Caraway, becomes disillusioned). Fitzgerald conceded that his "expression" was "neither so clear, nor so beautiful, nor so moving" as Cather's, but he was concerned enough about the similarity that he asked several friends to compare the two passages.

They advised him to retain the passage in his novel, but he nevertheless sent Cather pages from the original draft of what became Chapter 1 of *The Great Gatsby* to demonstrate to her that he had written his words before reading hers. Cather replied swiftly and graciously, telling Fitzgerald that she had "read and hugely enjoyed" *Gatsby* before receiving his letter and that his language had not made her think at all of her own novel:

> So many people have tried to say that same thing before either you or I tried it, and nobody has said it yet. I suppose everybody who has ever been swept away by personal charm tries in some way to express his wonder that the effect is so much greater than the cause,—and in the end we all fall back upon an old device and write about the effect and not the lovely creature who produced it. After all, the only thing one can tell about beauty, is just how hard one was hit by it. Isn't that so?[37]

This interchange points to a notable aspect of Cather' fiction during the years that Lewis was writing ads for women's beauty products: Cather presents her fictionalized worlds primarily from the point of view of male characters. For *My Ántonia*, Cather created a first-person male narrator, Jim Burden, but in her fictions of the 1920s, she reported the perceptions of central male characters in the third person. In *One of Ours*, when the protagonist, Claude Wheeler, is sick with an infection and his friend Enid comes to visit him, "wearing a flowered organdie dress" and a "floppy straw hat" with "a big lilac bow," he "wished that Enid would not talk at all, but would sit there and let him look at her." During Enid's many return visits, Claude "lay looking at her and breathing in a sweet contentment," a feeling that leads him to court and marry her, much to his later regret. In *A Lost Lady*, readers view Marian Forrester almost exclusively through the eyes of Niel Herbert, nephew of a lawyer and judge in the town of Sweetwater, and the novel traces the evolution of his feelings for her from his childhood through his young manhood. As a young boy, coming to consciousness after having fallen out of a tree, he dreamily contemplates this "lovely lady," noting that "[i]nside the lace ruffle of her dress he saw her white throat rising and falling so quickly." As a young man reading law in his uncle's office, he thinks to himself that Marian Forrester's "skin had always the fragrant, crystalline whiteness of white lilacs." Several years later, on a trip home from the East, where he has gone to study at Harvard, he realizes that "[i]n the brilliant sun of the afternoon one saw that her skin was no longer like white lilacs,—it had the ivory tint of gardenias that had just begun to fade," and he observes lines of strain around her mouth. In her final years in Sweetwater, Marian resorts to rouge.[38]

In *The Professor's House*, Godfrey St. Peter spends an astonishing amount of time looking at and critically appraising his wife and daughters, whom readers first encounter through his critical eyes. His wife he sees as "very fair pink and gold. . . . The tints of her face and hair and lashes were so soft that one did not realize, on first meeting her, how very definitely and decidedly her features were cut, under the smiling infusion of colour. When she was annoyed or tired, the lines became severe." Although most people find his older daughter, Rosamund, "brilliantly beautiful," the professor disagrees, finding her physically ungraceful. He knows, however, that all eyes focus on her "smooth black head and white throat, and the red of her curved lips that was like the duskiness of dark, heavy-scented roses." Much more to Godfrey's taste is his "pale" younger daughter, Kathleen, whose "wide cheekbones" cast "curious shadows . . . over her cheeks."[39]

As demonstrated in the preceding chapter, Lewis carefully reshaped and condensed Cather's prose in *The Professor's House*, including Godfrey's appraisals of his wife and daughters. As Cather's editorial collaborator, Lewis helped enforce stylistic compression and simplicity of language in Cather's fiction, but Lewis's copywriting and Cather's story-writing also shared a set of aesthetic practices and cultural concerns. Lewis's ad copy designed to persuade female consumers to buy beauty products was, like Cather's fiction of the 1920s, saturated with the masculine point of view. In *Living up to the Ads: Gender Fictions of the 1920s*, Simone Weil Davis locates "*metaphors for personhood*" of the adman, the female vehicle, and the female consumer in both advertisements and literary works from the 1920s U.S., including fiction by F. Scott Fitzgerald and his wife, Zelda Sayre Fitzgerald. Davis devotes a chapter to how the ad*women* of the Women's Editorial Department at Thompson disrupted the gendered logic of advertising, but she criticizes Lewis for "helping to create and foster heterosexist subjectivity when she was herself a lesbian."[40]

In judging Lewis's advertising work this way, Davis does not account for the queer potential of the scenarios of gazing in the campaigns for which Lewis wrote copy. The male gaze does not frame all of Lewis's ads or Cather's fiction of the 1920s: some of Lewis's ad copy communicates woman to woman, without the intervening male gaze, and Cather's *My Mortal Enemy* and "Uncle Valentine" (1925) both have first-person female narrators. Furthermore, in the heteronormative culture of 1920s America, centering their writing in the male point of view was one avenue for both Cather and Lewis to express an appreciation for female beauty and a desire for women. Using this point of view also allowed them to engage in a playful dialogue with one another as they constructed pleasing scenarios of gazing at women that were both public (published as novels and advertisements) and private (they read and responded to each other's work in ways invisible to the general public). As Patricia Johnston hypothesizes in her analysis of Edward Steichen's explicitly erotic advertising photography in the 1930s, women may have found viewing these images of female nudes "liberating," "may have taken an active, erotic pleasure in viewing other women's bodies." Similarly Lewis and Cather made available to their women readers the pleasure of gazing at other women's bodies. And as a result of Lewis's work on the Jergens Lotion account, she had the opportunity to put Cather in front of Steichen's camera, simultaneously constructing an iconic public image of Cather and enjoying the private pleasure of looking at Cather through Steichen's lens.[41]

The Story of Hands in Cather's Fiction and Edith Lewis's and Edward Steichen's Jergens Lotion Ads

In Cather's fiction of the 1920s, men gaze at women's faces but also at their hands, the condition of which indexes their class status and age. In *A Lost Lady*, Marian Forrester's hands fascinate the young Niel Herbert because of their beauty and her diamond rings. When she cares for him after his fall from the tree, he enjoys the touch of her "soft fingers" and watches as she takes off her "glittering rings," "shed[ding] them off her fingers with a quick motion as if she were washing her hands, and dropped them into Mary's broad palm." The meaty hand of the servant who receives the rings signifies her status as the one who does the heavy work in the house, while Marian's delicate hands tend to the injured nephew of the judge and do only the delicate work in the kitchen. Later, the ultimate sign of Marian's debasement and fall from financial security is that she must do her own housework. In *The Professor's House*, when St. Peter and his wife are arguing about Tom Outland's legacy and the way Louie Marsellus has appropriated it, he pauses: " 'Nice hands,' he murmured, looking critically at them as he took [the coffee cup], 'always such nice hands.' " As Godfrey muses several months later, his wife's income from an inheritance from her father had enabled her to avoid "pinch[ing] and be[ing] shabby and do[ing] housework, as the wives of some his colleagues did." Godfrey ultimately faces the future with resignation, but Lillian's "nature was intense and positive. . . . If her character were reduced to an heraldic device, it would be a hand (a beautiful hand) holding flaming arrows—the shafts of her violent loves and hates, her clear-cut ambitions."[42]

Woodbury's was a facial soap, so the Woodbury's ads for which Lewis wrote copy focused on women's faces, but Jergens Lotion, also, as mentioned earlier, manufactured by Andrew Jergens Co. of Cincinnati and the other account for which Lewis also became sole copywriter, was marketed as a hand lotion. Lewis's longtime colleague Ruth Waldo explained at a 1932 creative staff meeting:

> The advertising on Jergens has had more continuity than most accounts. On most accounts, when you look back over ten years of advertising, you would find at least one or two main changes in the copy theme. Jergens had one, in the first year, because an investigation was made after it had been running a few months which indicated that we ought to change it. On the basis of that investigation, the main copy theme of Jergens was worked out and has been continued ever since, because the people working on it (Mr. and Mrs. Resor and Miss E. Lewis) were fortunate enough to get a copy theme so absolutely right for the product and what women wanted of it that our sales have shown a very excellent increase each year over the year before.

Waldo commented in a similar presentation in 1931 after she displayed and commented on Jergens Lotion ads from 1923 through 1930 (all of which featured photos by Edward Steichen and copy by Lewis), "In all these ads Miss Lewis's copy gives the story an unusually human, moving quality."[43]

Before 1923, Benzoin and Almond Lotion had long been an unadvertised product of the Andrew Jergens Co., but after many years of pressure from Stanley Resor, the company agreed in 1922 to rebrand and advertise the product. As Lewis explained about this initial campaign in a 1926 account history, "[A] special attempt was made . . . to surround the product with an atmosphere of class." Initially aiming the ads "directly at women of fashion and social distinction," they hoped to "reach, indirectly, all classes of women." The ads thus featured "[p]ortraits of aristocratic young women in evening dress" by the "distinguished young portrait painter" John Carroll, while the accompanying copy focused on the medicinal "correctness" of Jergens for the skin generally. Sales increased as a result of this first round of national advertising for a previously unadvertised product, but other brands making similar claims dominated the market.[44]

After the initial campaign, as Waldo later explained, Thompson's research department undertook an "extensive investigation of the lotion market," using women's magazines to distribute questionnaires to their readers. Thompson discovered that although 70 percent of women were using lotion on their hands, none of the advertised brands, including Jergens, focused on this use. Thompson launched this investigation in early 1923, precisely when Cather was worrying that her long trip to France to visit Isabelle and Jan Hambourg would wound Lewis's feelings (see Chapter 3). Lewis was not, however, sitting idly in New York City pining for Cather. Rather soon after Cather departed, Lewis embraced the challenge of devising a new advertising strategy based on this new market research.[45]

Unlike the 1922 Jergens Lotion campaign (or, indeed, unlike the campaigns Lewis worked on for Woodbury's Facial Soap from 1925 to 1930), the new Jergens Lotion campaign spoke directly to middle-class women, not indirectly to them through appeals to upper-class women. As Lewis explained in the 1926 account history, in order to build an identity for Jergens as a lotion for the hands,

> it was clear that we must aim our copy directly at the women who use their hands most; that is, women of the great middle class who do their own housework. The copy was to do two things—to make these women conscious by every possible means, of the enormous wear and tear on their hands, caused by housework, and to convince them of the unique effectiveness of Jergens Lotion in overcoming this wear and tear and keeping their hands smooth, white and soft in spite of housework.

The Resors and Lewis decided to adopt a "new and forceful" strategy for conveying this point about wear and tear on women's hands, namely "using photographic close-ups of hands in action." The ads for which Lewis wrote the copy thus presented the problem in the photographs (hands doing housework) and the solution in the copy (how the special healing ingredients in Jergens Lotion would protect and heal the hands of women who did their own housework).[46]

Before the client and the agency committed themselves to this approach, however, they experimented. In the early 1920s, photographs rarely appeared in advertisements, but Helen and Stanley Resor wanted to change that, so they engaged Edward Steichen for the Jergens campaign as a test case. Steichen had been both a painter and a fine art photographer, but in the 1920s he wholeheartedly embraced commercial photography as an art form. As Patricia Johnston explains, "Steichen insisted on collapsing the distinctions between the fine and popular arts, challenging modernist ideas by denying the polarity of fine and applied arts." Furthermore, he fully understood and embraced the fact that his paycheck from Thompson "depended on the ability of his photographs to sell goods." At the time he took on the Jergens commission, he was under exclusive contract with the Conde Nast corporation for celebrity portraits for *Vanity Fair* magazine and fashion photography for *Vogue*, for which Conde Nast paid him $35,000 a year. This commitment did not preclude, however, his taking on advertising work.[47]

The challenge the Resors and Lewis presented to Steichen interested him. As he later recalled, he was "distressed" when he looked through magazines and saw "how little and how badly photography was used" in advertising. Later in his time working for Thompson, he complained about copywriters and designers trying to micromanage his photographic process. However, he was always deeply interested in the idea an advertising photograph was supposed to convey. As he said at a representatives meeting at Thompson in 1928 (with Lewis in the audience), "I think the photographer should have all the freedom he can have, except as regard the idea of it, that has to be kept closed in."[48]

Because the Jergens campaign was experimental in both its copy appeal and its use of photographs, in the early summer of 1923, Helen Resor and Edith Lewis went to Steichen's studio to convey their idea to him. The Thompson offices were then in the Murray Hill Building at Madison Avenue and Thirty-Eighth Street, while Steichen's studio was in the Beaux Arts Studios on West Fortieth Street, so they probably walked the half mile from one to the other. Helen Resor went further than conveying the idea to Steichen in words, however—she embodied the idea by donning a gingham apron to serve as Steichen's photographic model. Steichen "took the job," he recalled, because "the agency proposed an interesting idea for Jergens Lotion. . . . The idea was to photograph the hands of a woman who did her own housework. Among the situations suggested, I liked particularly that of peeling potatoes." He remembered Helen Resor only as "Mrs. Stanley Resor, wife of the president of J. Walter Thompson," rather than as the head of the Women's Editorial Department. In any event, he liked the aesthetics of the potato-peeling photograph so much that he would reproduce it in his autobiography. Wearing her apron, Helen Resor also held a glass pitcher with a cloth, as if drying it after washing it. In both pictures and in later ones in the series, Steichen shot in black and white using his large 8- by 10-inch view camera.[49]

The first ad using the new copy appeal, which ran in November 1923, bridged the old and new approaches: Steichen's photograph of Helen Resor's hands drying a glass pitcher held close to her checked apron appeared in the bottom half of the ad, but the top half featured a painted portrait of an elegant woman (Figure 4.4). Next to the portrait, Lewis's long caption warned, "Nothing betrays a woman's age so surely as her hands," and she counseled readers that "you can also have smooth, white, youthful-looking hands, if you give them the same care you give your face." Lewis thus picked up the cultural judgment against signs of aging in women that drives an aging Marian Forrester in *A Lost Lady* to rouge her cheeks. The bottom half of the Jergens

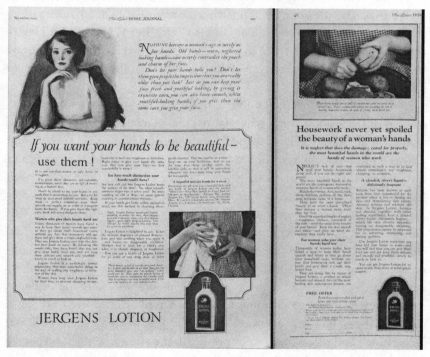

Figure 4.4 Two experimental advertisements for Jergens Lotion from the 1923 *Ladies Home Journal*, November (*left*) and December (*right*). Both feature photographs of Helen Lansdowne Resor's hands by Edward Steichen and copy by Edith Lewis.

Lotion ad made the housework appeal under the headline "If you want your hands to be beautiful—use them!" "It is not use that makes an ugly hand," Lewis's copy explained, "it is neglect." Women who used Jergens Lotion *"every time they had their hands in water"* could keep their hands "smooth and supple, as an artist or a surgeon keeps his hands." "See how much distinction your hands really have!" a sub-headline exclaimed, by ordering "a beautiful trial size bottle for 6 cents."[50]

The focus of the December 1923 Jergens ad was housework only (Figure 4.4)—the elegant woman disappeared. Under Steichen's photograph of Helen Resor's hands peeling potatoes, Lewis's headline counseled, "Housework never yet spoiled the beauty of a woman's hands." Returning to the theme of the first ad, Lewis identified neglect rather than housework as the culprit. Indeed, she explained, "The most beautiful hands in the world are the courageous, expressive, sensitive hands of women who work—Hands that sweep, dust, mend, cook, dress children, perform all the thousand intricate tasks of a home. They have the same disciplined beauty as an artist's hands. Often, they express a woman more truly than her face." One hears, perhaps, in Lewis's copy an echo of Cather's claim in a 1921 interview that "[t]he old-fashioned farmer's wife is nearer to the type of the true artist and the prima donna than is the culture enthusiast."[51]

Ironically, in the imagined universe of these Jergens ads, the only "work" women did was housework, while Lewis, the woman who wrote the copy, worked in an office and lived with Cather, who wrote for a living. Lewis and Cather routinely employed domestic servants and resorted to doing their own housework only when they were between maids. They didn't need Jergens Lotion to disguise the fact that they did their own housework—nor did Lillian St. Peter in *The Professor's House*, she of the beautiful hands. This did not make Lewis exceptional at the Thompson agency: a 1936 internal study discovered that 66 percent of the agency's copywriters employed domestic servants. Indeed, the agency was anxious about the fact that its employees were very unlike the average consumers who were the audience for their ads. Certainly, Helen Resor, who was raised by a widowed mother in Kentucky, knew how to peel a potato, but as the head of the Women's Editorial Department and wife of the agency president, she also certainly hired people to cook and clean for her and her family.[52]

Nevertheless, the advertising trade press praised the new Jergens Lotion campaign for its freshness and "sincerity," and the Resors were so pleased with Lewis's writing for the campaign that they gave her a thousand-dollar

Christmas bonus (more than $14,000 in 2018 dollars). As much as the Resors (and Lewis) valued the aesthetics of these ads, effective selling was more important, so as Lewis explained in the account history, in January and February 1924 they tested consumer response by creating a "split run" of ads. Ads in all issues of a given women's magazine featured copy with the new appeal (focusing on the damage housework did to a woman's hands and how Jergens Lotion remedied it), but headlines and illustrations diverged. Half of the ads used a painted illustration in the style of the previous campaign with "a headline purely on the beauty appeal," and the other half used a Steichen photograph of a woman's hands "with a headline in harmony with the picture." Both versions had a coupon a reader could use to send away for a product sample, and the research department tallied coupon returns to see which version "pulled" more. Would readers of the January *Ladies Home Journal* prefer an illustration of an elegant woman holding a large feather fan over her shoulder with one hand, while she toyed with her long strand of pearls with the other, under the headline "No one would ever think she used her hands for housework"? Or would they prefer a photograph of the hands of a woman threading a needle in order to darn socks, which rest in her lap with her wooden darning egg, under the headline "Can a housekeeper ever hope to have beautiful hands?" (as in all the housework photos, the woman's clothing is visible—here a housedress—but not her head and face). As it turned out, the coupon returns were dead even. Convinced that they "at least ran no risk" in using photographs rather than drawn art, the client agreed to the housework appeal in both text and photograph "as being much more original and sincere and having a fresher note."[53]

While Lewis was working on the Jergens test campaign with the Resors and Steichen, the Brewsters and their ten-year-old daughter, Harwood, came to visit her. Cather was gone for six months, so the Brewsters stayed with Lewis at 5 Bank Street twice during their long American visit, first for several weeks in the early summer and then for a few days before their return voyage to France. A financially flush Lewis was generous with her perpetually poor painter friends. She took them out for a fancy hotel lunch, on an open horse carriage ride and picnic lunch in Central Park, and to a performance of *Rain*, the sensational Broadway melodrama coauthored by John Colton, formerly one of Lewis's assistant editors at *Every Week*. A professional model had succeeded Helen Resor for the planned split-run ads for early 1924, and the hand model became a source of contention between Lewis and the Brewsters. Harwood later recalled "one rather heated discussion" when Lewis came home "one day having spent sometime [*sic*] getting photographs taken of a lady's hands for an add [*sic*]." Harwood's parents "were horrified at the amount paid to this person just to have her hands photographed. Whereupon Edith argued that it was not a very satisfying way of making a living. The artist loves his work and therefore should not expect to 'make' money on what he enjoyed doing." The tempest passed, and "[w]hen the Brewsters left—Edith was on the pier waving goodbye."[54]

Neither Lewis nor Steichen settled for pleasure as compensation. Instead, both embraced commercial art. As Steichen said to his brother-in-law, poet Carl Sandburg:

> Practically all artists who do commercial work do it with their noses turned up. . . . They want to earn enough money to get out of commercial art so as to take up pure art for art's sake. . . . That viewpoint doesn't interest me; I know what there is to know about it—and I'm through with it. I welcome the chance to work in commercial art. If I can't express the best that's in me through such advertising photographs as "Hands Kneading Dough," then I'm no good.

Lewis, for her part, presented the idea for "Hands Kneading Dough" to Steichen and wrote the copy (Figure 4.5). "Usefulness, service for your hands," her headline read, "but charm and loveliness, too." Women whose hands become rough, dry, chapped, and discolored from being frequently in water could keep their hands "smooth, white, silky-soft, with that charm and grace which every woman wants her hands to have—which no amount of usefulness quite makes up for," she counseled, if they used Jergens Lotion.[55]

In late 1924, the Resors offered Steichen his first renewable, exclusive contract for advertising photography, guaranteeing him at least $15,000 a year. In a decision that caused some dissension at an agency where collective anonymity was the norm, Steichen was allowed a credit line for some of his photos: just his last name in all capital letters appeared at the lower right-hand corner in many photos in the Jergens and other campaigns. And as Cather boasted to Achsah Brewster in February 1924 (by which time the Brewsters were back in Europe and Cather was back in New York), not only had Lewis gotten a Christmas bonus in December 1923 but "a month later [they] raised her salary again! You have to deliver goods to make a New York business firm treat you like that, I assure you." Cather linked Lewis's reward

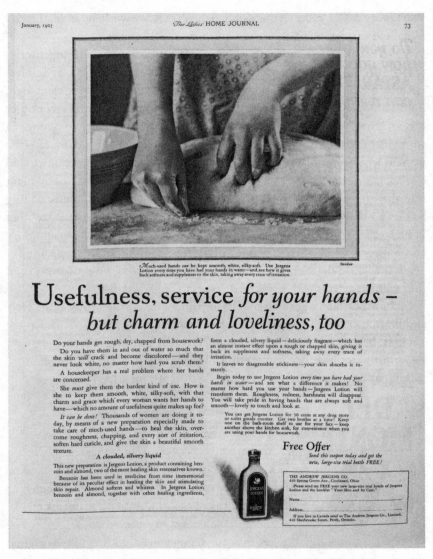

Figure 4.5 A January 1925 *Ladies Home Journal* Jergens Lotion advertisement featuring Edith Lewis's copy and Edward Steichen's photograph.

from the most powerful people at Thompson to her own success as an author, explaining that *One of Ours* and *A Lost Lady* "keep right on selling, so we're indulging ourselves in lots of little luxuries and <u>not</u> splurging. It's so good to be at home again, Achsah, and I know you are saying the same thing in your heart every day." Unlike Cather's or Steichen's creative work, however, Lewis's remained anonymous.[56]

Steichen's photographs and Lewis's words continued to work together to tell women who did their own housework that they could have lovely and fascinating hands if they used Jergens Lotion. For the first year of the campaign, both photographs and copy focused exclusively on housework. "A mother cannot 'save' her hands," Lewis cautioned in text below a Steichen photo of a woman's hands washing the hands of a toddler. "She misses too much—the woman who is afraid to use her hands," Lewis chided, her precept illustrated by Steichen's photograph of a woman preparing to transplant a potted plant into the ground. Below Steichen's photograph of a woman's hands mixing batter in a bowl, Lewis enumerated some of the "Dozens of times a day" that "a housekeeper has to wash and dry her hands": "Your hands are all floury and buttery—when the telephone rings! You're in the midst of cleaning—when the baby falls and bumps her head! You're putting up preserves—and the postman arrives with a special delivery to be signed for!"[57]

In the Woodbury's advertisements for which Lewis wrote copy in the early and middle 1920s, the social tableaux of men critically gazing at women are obvious. In the early Lewis-Steichen Jergens ads, in contrast, male judgment was mostly implied. Lewis sometimes wrote male judgment into her copy, picking up a trope from *A Lost Lady*, as in the copy for a 1924 ad:

An artist can find beauty even in the rough, red, neglected hands of a drudge. But the ordinary observer doesn't see beyond that rough, calloused surface, to beauty of line and structure beneath. Hands that are red and rough and chapped are ugly hands to him. Don't let your hands get the look of hard-worn, over-worked drudges! You *can* use your hands for homely household tasks, and still keep them exquisite—lovely to touch or look at!

Very quickly, however, the Jergens campaign evolved, adding to the original appeal what Lewis called in the 1926 account history a "sentimental situation." These ads juxtaposed the existing Steichen photographs of women's hands doing housework with new ones of women's hands glamorously adorned for an evening out and being gazed at or stroked approvingly by men. In Steichen's photographs for this phase of the campaign, men's faces are sometimes partially visible, but only women's arms and hands are visible. "What a pity to let it all go—the dazzling whiteness, softness, grace, that give a woman's hands their wonderful charm," Lewis exclaimed in a Jergens Lotion advertisement ad-stripped in the March 1925 *Woman's Home Companion* with the second installment of Cather's story "Uncle Valentine" (Figure 4.6). Steichen's photo of a woman stirring batter reappears in a smaller size next to his new photo, in which a woman pins a boutonniere on a man's tuxedo lapel.

Figure 4.6 A Lewis and Steichen advertisement for Jergens Lotion ad-stripped in the March 1925 *Woman's Home Companion* with Willa Cather's short story "Uncle Valentine."

Only the woman's hands and arms appear in the frame, but the lower half of the man's face is visible, and the angle of his chin suggests that he is gazing down at and appraising her hands. "But let your hands be something more than useful servants!" Lewis advised in the accompanying copy. "Keep that quality of charm in them that makes their lightest touch something lovable, remembered!"[58]

In 1928, Steichen's photos of housework hands were retired, and the ads featured only his new large photos of women's glamorous hands, decked out in jewels, like Marian Forrester's hands as remembered by Niel Herbert. Middle-class women were still the target audience, but their housework disappeared from both image and text in favor of an emphasis on the whitening and soothing properties of Jergens Lotion. These ads made explicit what was always implicit—only *white* female consumers were being addressed. In a September 1928 ad headlined "White Hands," for example, Lewis advised women that "[t]his fragrant, silvery preparation does away with redness or tan." While a suntan was appropriate against a "background of green grass, blue sky," it was "out of place and *gauche*" in the fall "when seen indoors, among intimate, sophisticated surroundings." Jergens Lotion solved this problem, Lewis explained, by restoring whiteness and smoothness to a woman's hands.[59]

A Face for a Face: Cather as a *Vanity Fair* Celebrity

By 1927, Edith Lewis had been writing Jergens Lotion copy telling the story of hands for more than three years, and during that time she regularly tasked Edward Steichen with getting her ideas across in images. By 1927, Willa Cather had achieved a level of celebrity that made her a candidate for a photographic portrait by Steichen to be published in *Vanity Fair* magazine. Thus Lewis was in a position to propose the *Vanity Fair* session and to devise the idea that Steichen's portrait would convey.

Fame and celebrity are arguably distinct, and modern celebrity would not exist without photography. As John Cawelti explains, celebrity is "a kind of immediate fame," "largely in the present and its mark is being known as a person. The test of artistic fame is that one's words or images remain in the minds of men; the test of celebrity is being followed everywhere by a photographer." Novelist John Dos Passos complained about his friend F. Scott Fitzgerald's "brash enthusiasm" for precisely this kind of celebrity. He recalled that Fitzgerald and his wife, Zelda, were "celebrities in the Sunday supplement sense of the word"—photographers followed them everywhere to take pictures that appeared in the photo pages of the Sunday newspaper. Dos Passos confessed that he himself was "as ambitious as the next man; but the idea of being that kind of celebrity set [his] teeth on edge."[60]

Celebrity sketches of Fitzgerald and Cather by the same person and both published in 1926 demonstrate the degree to which Cather's engagement with celebrity culture diverged from Fitzgerald's. John Chapin Mosher, who interviewed them both, had been one of Lewis's assistants at *Every Week*. After serving in World War I, he lived in Paris, where he shared an apartment with composer Virgil Thomson and painter Eugene Chown, and then the Chicago area, where he was an English instructor at Northwestern University. By 1926, he was back in New York City on the staff of a new magazine, the *New Yorker*, where his profile of Scott Fitzgerald appeared in April. Mosher described Scott and Zelda Fitzgerald as "the best looking couple in modern literary society" and Scott as "so affable and perfectly at ease with all the world" because he was "the best host of the younger set, and as a much photographed and paragraphed author." Mosher opened the sketch on a Riviera beach, where he heard "whispers" about the author's drinking in Paris, and he recounted how Scott once drove his publicity manager into a lake. Scott Fitzgerald purported to be mystified about how he managed to spend his "thousands and thousands" in monthly literary earnings, but he also claimed to have "known poverty" when he was working in advertising in New York City. "It was then that he saw," Mosher reported, "that advertising did not pay, and he threw up that job, and went home to St. Paul to write a novel." "Statistics show," the waggish Mosher observed, "that 12,536 young men annually throw up their jobs and go back home to write a novel. This has all come about since Fitzgerald set the example, for the book he wrote that winter was *This Side of Paradise*, and he was launched." Mosher's portrait of Fitzgerald turned darker in its final paragraphs, which made clear why the article was published under the title "That Sad Young Man." "The popular picture of a blond boy scribbling off bestsellers in odd moments between parties is nonsense," Mosher explained. "He's a very grave, hardworking man, and shows it. In fact, there is definitely the touch of melancholy often obvious upon him." Mosher nevertheless saw the irony in Fitzgerald's being an author "who cannot live on thirty thousand a year, and yet who earns every cent he has."[61]

By the mid-1920s, in the wake of her increased fame resulting from her 1923 Pulitzer Prize for *One of Ours*, Cather had begun declining speaking engagements and turning down other requests more often than previously. Although she did not withdraw completely, she was not an easy "get," but Lewis's friendship with Mosher and Cather's acquaintance with him during his years on *Every Week* might have inclined her to speak with him on the record. Perhaps Lewis suggested it, both as a means to promote Cather's works and to help her friend reestablish himself as a magazinist. Rather than interview Cather for the very modern and ironic *New Yorker*, however, Mosher interviewed her for the Boston-based *Writer*, which proclaimed itself "the oldest magazine for literary workers," and Mosher portrayed Cather precisely as a literary worker rather than a celebrity, an author who couldn't drive her publicity manager into a lake because she employed no such person.

"Fame has no glamour for Willa Cather," Mosher began, although her years working at *McClure's* had given her inside knowledge about the "machinery by which the great are revealed to the world, and by what strategies many of them contrive to keep before the public eye." As a result, Mosher claimed, even though Cather had become famous as an author, she simply refused to live as a public figure. Turning away "celebrity hunters," she "sees the people she wants to see" and stayed in New York "for the music . . . and of course for the demands of her business." The Nebraska of her childhood memory was her only reality. "When she speaks of this country it is with great longing and homesickness," he explained, even as her "small sitting room may be crowded with critics, artists, editors, each caught in the strait-jacket of the New York intelligentsia." In Mosher's profile of Fitzgerald, the author's wife and four-year-old daughter were omnipresent, but Lewis, the advertising copywriter and Mosher's dear friend, appeared nowhere in his portrait of Cather. Perhaps he bowed to social taboo (although Lewis's co-residence was no secret to all those people crowded into their parlor at 5 Bank Street for Friday afternoon tea). However, putting Lewis into the picture would also have spoiled the picture she herself was helping to create of Cather as an artist detached from the machinery of publicity.[62]

Although Cather was not followed everywhere by crowds of photographers, she did consent in 1927 to have Edward Steichen photograph her for *Vanity Fair*, an entanglement in the machinery of publicity that, paradoxically, contributed to her image as a writer detached from publicity. As Michael Schueth observes, *Vanity Fair* "intermixed full-page portraits of well-known Hollywood and Broadway stars with the less well recognized, putting a glamorous face to writers, intellectuals, and composers while at the same time giving an intellectual flair to the Hollywood celebrity." Also notable was *Vanity Fair*'s engagement with modernist art and artists. The magazine refused, as Faye Hammill argues, "to set modernists apart from other kinds of celebrities or to separate their work from other forms of cultural production." For example, both T. S. Eliot and *Vanity Fair*'s editors seriously considered debuting his long modernist poem *The Waste Land* in the magazine's pages.[63]

In addition to full-page celebrity portraits, the magazine published photospreads encompassing smaller, captioned photographs, including the magazine's "We Nominate for the Hall of Fame" feature. By periodically running a "We Nominate for the Hall of Oblivion" feature, *Vanity Fair* positioned itself, Hammill argues, as "a tasteful arbiter of modern celebrity," offering "discriminating judgments between worthy and unworthy stars." In the early 1920s, Cather had published a critical appreciation of Martin Andersen Nexø's *Pelle the Conqueror* in *Vanity Fair* and had herself been lauded in several photospreads, including one in the "Hall of Fame." However, Edmund Wilson, then a contributing editor, ultimately dismissed her fiction as retrograde, and mentions of her disappeared from the magazine. Steichen's portrait of Cather thus marked her return to *Vanity Fair*'s pages after a five-year absence.[64]

Steichen usually did not choose which celebrities he would photograph and met them for the first time in his studio. The Cather portrait session, however, seems to have been an unusual case. As Cather wrote to her niece Mary Virginia Auld on February 19, 1927, reporting "news" about the goings on at 5 Bank Street, "Steichen, the photographer of the Rich and Great, is coming to dinner tonight. I have a new dinner dress, and a rather gorgeous new afternoon dress." Cather gave no hint that she herself might be among the "Rich" or "Great," and perhaps Lewis had merely extended a dinner invitation to her friend and colleague. Perhaps the idea that Steichen would photograph Cather for *Vanity Fair* originated over dinner rather than being the occasion for it.[65]

Lewis became ill with appendicitis not long after Steichen came to Bank Street for dinner, however: she had an emergency appendectomy the first week of March and spent two weeks in the hospital recuperating. The photographer and his second wife, actress Dana Desboro Glover Steichen, sent the convalescent "wonderful flowers," black and bronze tulips (flower breeding was one of Steichen's many passions). "I didn't know there <u>were</u> any black tulips, outside of Dumas," Lewis wrote in thanks, "[a]nd the bronze-colored ones are almost as strange and fascinating. It was lovely of you to send them to me." Lewis expressed regret, however, that she had not been able to be present in Steichen's studio "when the photographs were taken. Please, Mr. Steichen, don't let them be the last ones." She closed the letter jointly, from one couple to another couple, "Miss Cather and I both send you our warmest greetings."[66]

Three photographs, two of which were published in *Vanity Fair* in 1927, survive from what was, alas, Steichen's only portrait session with Cather. The first appeared in an April photospread titled "Harvesters in the Field of Fiction." Cather shared the page with Louis Bromfield, Carl Van Vechten, John Erskine, Edna Ferber, and Ernest Hemingway. One of Steichen's photos of her, cropped to an oval shape, appeared prominently in the center of the page. "One of the most telling of American novelists and a stylist of precision and beauty," the caption told readers, "Willa Cather shows, in her most recent book, *My Mortal Enemy*, the same expert simplicity which distinguished her earlier novels, particularly *My Ántonia*, *One of Ours* (the Pulitzer prize winner in 1922 [*sic*]), and *The Professor's House*." Steichen's credit line appeared with this small photograph, but Cather received the full Steichen celebrity treatment in July, when a full-page version of a different pose appeared with a longer caption under the headline "An American Pioneer—Willa Cather. The Noted Novelist Has Just Completed Her New Work 'Death Comes for the Archbishop.'" This full-page photograph was placed prominently at the front of the magazine's editorial matter, after the many pages of advertisements (none of Lewis's ads appeared in *Vanity Fair*, as most ads placed in the magazine targeted male consumers).[67]

In both published Steichen photographs of Cather, she wore a white middy blouse, the sleeves rolled, with a black silk tie, and she pulled her hair back in a bun; her part is slightly off center and a few strands of gray are visible over her ears. In the April version, Steichen lit her from her left side, casting the right half of her face in shadow. She crossed her arms at her midriff as she looked directly into the camera with the faintest glimmer of a smile. This version is widely and inaccurately identified as *the* Steichen *Vanity Fair* portrait of Cather, but it is not. For the full-page version published in July (Figure 4.7), Cather sat in a scroll-back chair turned slightly to the side, but she was nevertheless looking toward the camera. Steichen lit her from her right side this time, but the effect was less dramatic and in key with her expression: her

Figure 4.7 Edward Steichen's portrait of Willa Cather in the July 1927 *Vanity Fair*. Edward Steichen, Vanity Fair © Conde Nast.

impish grin extended to her eyes. The lighting made a large pinky ring on her left hand shine—perhaps a silver ring she acquired in the Southwest—and her hand appears substantial, not refined like the glamour hands Steichen photographed for the Jergens Lotion ads.[68]

This full-page photograph of Cather is recognizable as having been taken in Steichen's studio: she sat in the same chair H. L. Mencken did for his portrait published in the February 1927 *Vanity Fair*, and the same lighting effects—wide vertical bars of dark and light—appear behind both of them. In other respects, however, Steichen's photographs of Cather diverged sharply from the hundreds of other celebrity portraits he made for *Vanity Fair* in the 1920s and 1930s. He often depicted his subjects at work. People from the world of theater or Hollywood wore costumes and engaged in stage business, and George Gershwin gazed at the camera from behind his grand piano. When Steichen's subjects were not in costume, the women wore elegant and fashionable clothes, and the men (H. L. Mencken, Sherwood Anderson, even prizefighters) wore coats and ties. In contrast, there are no visual cues to Cather's profession as a writer, such as a pen or a book in her hand, and her dress was strikingly casual. She did not don her recently acquired "dinner dress" or "rather gorgeous afternoon dress" mentioned in the letter to her niece. Instead, as Michael Schueth suggests, her casual clothing and pose evoked a much older image, Walt Whitman's famed frontispiece to *Leaves of Grass*.[69]

Cather's casual clothing also set the Steichen portraits apart from other studio portraits of her, which she had taken periodically and which she directed her publishers to send to newspapers and magazines reviewing her books. In these formal studio portraits, Cather almost always dressed up for the camera. In early author photos she wore dressy clothes and fashionable hats. Beginning in the 1920s, she abandoned the hats but continued to wear fussy or elegant clothes. For Rinehart Marsden in Omaha in 1921, she wore a jacket embroidered with striking folkloric motifs at the collar, cuffs, and pocket flaps. She sat for Nickolas Muray, Steichen's rival as a celebrity and society portrait photographer, several times in the 1920s. For one Muray session she crossed her arms and wore a pullover blouse, but the blouse was of colored silk with contrasting white collar and cuffs. For two other Muray sessions she dressed more elaborately: for one she donned a silk top embroidered with metallic thread, and for the other she draped a kimono-style robe, elaborately appliqued with flowers, over her shoulders (Figure 4.8). Her expression is stern in all three portraits, the last of which was published in Knopf's biographical pamphlet about Cather in 1926 and continued to be featured in the many revisions of the pamphlet through the 1930s.

Although some have been tempted to read the middy blouse and tie Cather wore to Steichen's studio as gender-bending or "western," apart

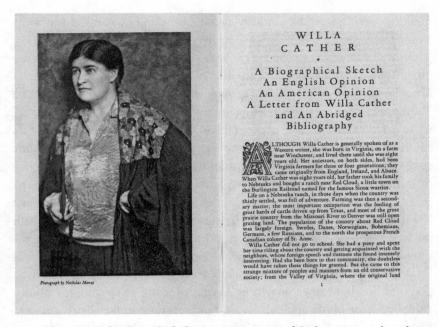

Figure 4.8 An early 1920s Nickolas Muray portrait of Cather as reproduced in a biographical pamphlet circulated by Alfred A. Knopf, Inc. Courtesy Archives and Special Collections, University of Nebraska–Lincoln Libraries.

from the fact that Cather was wearing them, in 1927 they carried no such significance. Rather viewers would have recognized her clothes as sportswear (and high-quality sportswear—Cather bought her middies at Abercrombie & Fitch). Teenage girls wore middies as the top half of their gym costumes, and an adult woman like Cather might opt for a middy if she didn't want the fuss of buttons and the tighter cut of a shirtwaist. Readers of *Vanity Fair* would not have known, however, that the combination of middy blouse and tie had been Cather's preferred casual attire for decades. In dozens of snapshots (as opposed to studio portraits), she wore a middy blouse and tie, mostly a straight tie, as in *Vanity Fair*, but sometimes a knotted soft tie. She wore the combination with skirts and sensible shoes to ramble around Jaffrey, New Hampshire, and under cardigans on cooler days. Both she and Lewis were wearing middies and ties under their matching khaki trouser suits in photographs taken both in the Southwest and on Grand Manan (see Figures 3.2, 3.3, 3.4, 3.12, 3.13, and 5.1). Snapshots do not show Cather at work writing, but she doubtless wrote wearing a middy and tie, especially when she was away from New York.[70]

Cather's expression in the Steichen photos also sets them apart from her other studio portraits, for which she did not smile. For Steichen, she smiled—not a broad-toothed grin, but a genuine smile. As Steichen explained at a Thompson Representatives meeting in early 1928, he had to "get enthusiastic" when a sitter came in to be photographed because if he didn't, "I cannot do anything with the person. Before I start getting anything out of it, the person's got to be lit up." Cather had been put in front of Steichen's camera, like one of the hand models for Lewis's Jergens Lotion campaign, and Steichen's credit line in *Vanity Fair* was the same as that for his advertising work, just STEICHEN (see Figure 4.5). Cather was wearing clothes associated with the travels she shared with Lewis, including the southwestern trips that inspired *Death Comes for the Archbishop*. Perhaps what "lit up" Cather's face was not imagining the anonymous audience of *Vanity Fair* viewing Steichen's photo of her, but rather imagining Lewis's pleasure at viewing the photograph. Because of her appendectomy, Lewis was not in Steichen's studio as he photographed Cather, but she was metaphorically there, peering over Steichen's shoulder. Steichen and his wife sent Lewis flowers because she was recuperating from surgery, but perhaps the photographer was also sending his friend a bouquet to thank her for having maneuvered her partner into a portrait sitting and to celebrate the success of the enterprise. And perhaps the portraits were themselves a sort of gift from Steichen to Lewis. Wealthy and prominent people not selected to appear in *Vanity Fair* paid Steichen $1,000 for a portrait session. Because *Vanity Fair* paid him, he charged Lewis no fee for a photographic portrait of her famous partner, although she did have to share the results with tens of thousands of strangers.[71]

The long caption accompanying the July 1927 photo alternated between *Vanity Fair*'s typically breezy style and more serious critical pronouncements. Notably, as in the photograph, Cather was framed as a noncelebrity celebrity. The caption praised her "twenty-four years of scrupulous craftsmanship" and judged her "the heir apparent to Edith Wharton's lonely eminence among America's women novelists." Celebrating "her position in American letters" as "an absolute one by right of sheer artistic stature," the caption also declared her to be "beyond the categories of literary schools and genres." Implicitly drawing on her own aesthetic manifestos, the caption praised her "transparent" style that "conceals in its overtones a vast and subtle interplay of ironical intelligence." She was, the caption avowed, an artist who wrote according to the dictates of art rather than the popular taste. However, the image, headline, and text also doubled as an advertisement for *Death Comes for the Archbishop* (the novel is not mentioned in the caption but appears prominently in the headline). Appearing in *Vanity Fair* this way, Cather exploited the market even as she critiqued it, and Lewis, behind the scenes and pulling some strings, was a crucial resource in burnishing Cather's persona as a disinterested artist and a particular sort of celebrity—one who appeared in public through interviews and photographs while proclaiming that she cared nothing for fame.

After her portraits appeared in *Vanity Fair*, Cather inscribed copies of three of her novels to Steichen. Implicitly acknowledging the advertising value of Steichen's portrait for *Death Comes for the Archbishop*, she inscribed a prepublication copy, "For Steichen, and I awfully hope he'll like it. Willa Cather August 29 1927." She inscribed *My Ántonia*, "For Steichen / from his admiring Sitter / Willa Cather." Most evocatively, she inscribed *A Lost Lady*, "For Steichen / A face for a face / Willa Cather." Through his lens Steichen had captured Cather's face, and through her novel (and from Niel Herbert's perspective) Cather had captured the face of Marian Forrester. And although the Jergens Lotion ads for which Lewis wrote the copy and Steichen took the photographs kept women's faces out of the frame, Lewis would soon task Steichen with capturing women's faces for the Woodbury's Beauty Survey.[72]

"Who Are the *Real* Woodbury Beauties?": Edith Lewis Makes F. Scott Fitzgerald Sell Soap

The Woodbury's group testimonial campaign wrapped up around the time that Steichen's portrait of Cather appeared in *Vanity Fair*. For a time Thompson returned to alternating "treatment" and "sentimental" ads for Woodbury's, but soon Lewis was helping to devise a new kind of testimonial campaign for the twenty-five-cent soap, a beauty contest in which the winners would testify to what Woodbury's did for their skin. At first, the Andrew Jergens Co. resisted the idea "on the basis that it was cheapening to Woodbury, and that it was devoting too much interest to the contest and not enough to the product." The Resors and Lewis then devised a workaround, the "Woodbury's Beauty Survey," in which, the agency assured the client, "the testimonial of each winner would be featured prominently, and that therefore the product would get as much attention as the personalities themselves."[73]

As Lewis wrote in the internal company newsletter in early 1929, just as the campaign was launching in the major women's magazines, the "survey" was designed to discover "Who are the *real* Woodbury beauties? Out of all the hundreds of thousands of women who buy Woodbury's Facial Soap—which ones are the outstanding examples of our slogan 'A Skin You Love to Touch'?" Lewis also described the structure and behind-the-scenes machinery of the survey not revealed to the public. Women were spared "the crudity of entering themselves" in a beauty contest. Instead, Thompson contacted local Junior League chapters and asked members to nominate their friends and acquaintances. This "survey" structure was also designed to "disregard the conventional boundaries and include every type of American woman" by asking for nominees in the categories of "loveliest debutante, sportswoman, wife, co-ed, mother, woman in the arts, high school girl, woman in the professions, sub-deb, bride, grandmother, and business girl." Thompson then "persuaded" (that is, paid) three "distinguished American men" (John Barrymore, Cornelius Vanderbilt, Jr., and F. Scott Fitzgerald) to act as judges. Woodbury's treated each beauty survey "winner" to an all-expense-paid trip to New York City, including a shopping expedition to Bergdorf Goodman's, followed by a portrait session in which Steichen would photograph her in her new clothes.[74]

By 1929, Thompson had created a "Personalities Department" to handle endorsements, and Lewis got Anne Herendeen, formerly one of her assistants at *Every Week*, hired on a temporary basis to assist with the high volume of work associated with the beauty survey. Nevertheless, as the copywriter Lewis was still responsible for much of the work related to handling the personalities associated with her campaign. In the copy for each ad, she described the woman's life and quoted her in the first person, suggesting that she interviewed the women when they came to New York. She also likely would have accompanied them to Steichen's studio or, in some cases, on location to ensure that his photographs conveyed the same idea as her copy.[75]

In the copy Lewis wrote for the Woodbury's Beauty Survey, she lovingly described in rich visual detail the beauty of each woman, often specifying colors not visible in Steichen's black-and-white photographs (Thompson's mechanical department colorized some photographs). Lewis described Miss Lillian Moriarty, the "sportswoman," as being

> as full of contradictions as she is of bewitchment and charm. She has close-cut, curling, bronze hair, a pure, fair skin,—no touch of rouge,—a laughing

child's mouth. Her eyes are her most unusual feature—unusual both in setting and expression. They are rather long, set wide apart, of a curious shade
of blue. Their calm, rather remote, far-seeing gaze gives the only clue to her
pre-occupation with one of the most dangerous of sports.

Moriarty's "sport" was flying, and Steichen photographed her in her leather
jacket and aviator's cap in front of a biplane. Lewis's description of "The
Loveliest of Wives" evoked Marian Forrester in *A Lost Lady*: she was "tall,
slim as a wand, with beautiful bright brown eyes, full of golden lights, and
a skin like a Maréchal Niel rose. Her face, seen in repose, is grave and rather
dreamy. When she smiles it breaks into a look of enchanting mischief—of
lovely archness." Mrs. George Franklin Hester was so fully absorbed in being
a wife that her own given name did not appear in the ad, only her husband's.
Steichen photographed Mrs. Hester both in his studio, her satin gown and
necklace and bracelets shimmering against a dark background, and on
a New York sidewalk as she was speaking to a man whose back was to the
camera. Julia Evans (Figure 4.9), an amateur dramatist from St. Louis who
was "serious" about acting and hoped to pursue it professionally someday,
was "the most beautiful woman in the arts." Lewis described her "beauty" as
"very distinguished, very individual, with something rich and golden about
it that somehow suggests the rippling play of light on Western wheatfields."
W. T. Benda, who illustrated *My Ántonia* and had done illustration work for
Every Week when Lewis was managing editor, turned in the 1920s to the art
of making theatrical masks. Certainly it must have been Lewis who suggested
that Steichen pose the aspiring midwestern actress with what the caption
called "the famous Benda masks."[76]

Nickolas Muray, not Steichen, took the uncredited photos of the celebrity judges, which were used in an advertisement introducing the beauty
survey (Figure 4.10) and in some of the later advertisements introducing
each category winner. Muray posed two of the judges as if they were
doing the work of judging. Vanderbilt sat on the edge of a desk or table
on which photographs rested, seeming to pick one up as if to examine it
more closely, while Fitzgerald was seated behind a desk or table, gazing
intently at one photograph he held in his hand while others were arrayed
on the surface in front of him. In some of the ads introducing the winners,
the photographs of the judges were placed so that their gazes seemed to
frame the images of a woman: they loomed over her or leered at her from
the side.[77]

Figure 4.9 Woodbury's Beauty Survey advertisement from the September 1929 *Woman's Home Companion*, featuring Edward Steichen's photograph of Julia Evans and Edith Lewis's copy.

Lewis's words, in turn, framed the men who gazed upon and judged the women. F. Scott Fitzgerald, Lewis explained in the ad introducing the survey, was a judge "because, as the most brilliant of America's younger novelists, he was the first to discover and portray a new type of American

Figure 4.10 A February 1929 *Woman's Home Companion* advertisement introducing the Woodbury's Beauty Survey, featuring photographs by Nickolas Muray and copy by Edith Lewis.

girl. Because at the age of 23, he woke up to find himself famous as the author of *This Side of Paradise*. Because no other man of his time writes so sympathetically, skillfully, fascinatingly about women." Lewis did not ventriloquize the voice of Fitzgerald or the other men. Instead, Lewis used the same literary technique in this advertising copy that Cather used in several of her novels in the 1920s: she wrote from the male perspective but in the third rather than the first person. Cather first tried to write *A Lost Lady* in Niel Herbert's voice, as she had written *My Ántonia* with Jim Burden as the first-person narrator, but she changed course and wrote in the third person but primarily from Niel's perspective. By making this choice, Cather put distance between herself and Niel while still giving readers access to his gaze. Readers see Marian through Niel's eyes, but they also see Niel through the eyes of a critical observer who is, metaphorically, peering over his shoulder. Similarly, in the Woodbury's Beauty Survey, Lewis both constructed Fitzgerald (an author who had apologized to Cather for his apparent plagiarism of *A Lost Lady*) as a judge of female beauty and described women's beauty from the presumed perspective of Fitzgerald and the other male judges. In helping to devise this campaign and in executing it, Lewis also put the "winners" in the same position that she had put Cather less than two years earlier: in front of Steichen's camera. The winners of the Woodbury's Beauty Survey did not bring celebrity to the soap—rather, being selected *made* them celebrities. Having been chosen because of their beauty (and high socioeconomic status and whiteness), their job was to sell the soap that had made them beautiful.[78]

The male celebrity judges were also, obviously, helping to sell soap, although Fitzgerald tried to distance himself from his return to his old role as adman. In an essay published in the *Princeton Alumni Weekly* shortly after the campaign launched, Fitzgerald seemingly disavowed his participation, even though in writing about it he inevitably drew attention to it. In the essay, he collapsed 1920, when he was a nobody writing ads to be posted in streetcars (his most notable achievement being a jingle for a laundry, "We keep you clean in Muscatine"), and 1929, when his celebrity image appeared in the Woodbury's Beauty Survey. When "Mr. Fitzgerald" asks "Mr. Cakebook," his advertising agency boss, for money, Cakebook offers, "You let us use your picture and your name as one of the judges in this contest and we'll call it a thousand dollars." Fitzgerald points out that the task will take time and he has a family to support, and Cakebook increases the offer to $1,500. "And it's understood that I'm in no sense to endorse this product." "Perfectly," Cakebook replies. "You merely pick the prettiest girl." As Kirk Curnutt argues, Fitzgerald's essay, titled "Ten Years in the Advertising Business," revealed Fitzgerald's "remorseful recognition that he never escaped the advertising business," that although he was no longer working as a copywriter he continued selling, only "the commodity he has sold has merely been himself." Fitzgerald told the story of his brief career in advertising over and over again to interviewers, including Lewis's friend John Mosher. Maybe the idea of drawing the perpetually cash-strapped celebrity author and erstwhile copywriter into her campaign amused Lewis, the dedicated adwoman.[79]

The Woodbury's Beauty Survey came to an inglorious end. Despite the large advertising budget, the overall sales trend line for Woodbury's during the 1920s had been downward: the market was highly competitive, and the company was up against ten-cent soaps for which similar claims were being made. There was hope that the beauty survey would boost sales, but sales declined, and in June, the client charged Thompson with studying market conditions to find a solution to the decline. Coincidentally, Lewis and Cather had already scheduled their first long stay in their new cottage on Grand Manan from early July through early September, so Lewis was not there as the investigation was carried out. On November 5, 1929, when Lewis was back in the office, Jergens notified Thompson that it was on probation for the Woodbury's account, and the beauty survey campaign ended abruptly in November with the "Loveliest Sub-Deb." The ads Lewis planned featuring a "woman in the professions," a grandmother, and a "business girl" did not appear. Her full plan, if it hadn't been cut short, would have done what Frances Maule advocated in the Thompson client newsletter in 1924. Citing "the old suffrage slogan" "Women Are People," she urged copywriters to get beyond "the good old conventional 'angel-idiot' conception of women." Many women might be housewives, she explained, but they were also society women, clubwomen, and businesswomen, the last being "an ever-increasing class with an entirely different set of needs from the woman at home."[80]

When a new advertising manager took over at Andrew Jergens Co. in late 1929, he wrote a long memo to his boss comparing the Jergens Lotion and Woodbury's Facial Soap campaigns to the detriment of the Woodbury's ads. His analysis demonstrated no awareness that the same copywriter had written all of the copy for both. Pointing out what he saw as the deficiencies in the Woodbury's ads, he praised the Jergens Lotion ads as combining both an informative "reason why" appeal and an emotional appeal: "The Lotion advertising seems to have the happy composite of appealing both to logic and instinct. Woman is curious. She desires to know why, and the proof. Woman instinctively covets means of acquiring charm and chic, and appeal to men. Lovely, alluring hands are one means."[81]

"Desire . . . Is the Magical Element"

In *The Professor's House*, Godfrey St. Peter is mystified by the women in his life, but he nevertheless continues to watch and appraise as the relationship between his daughters degenerates into a stew of envy and jealousy over money and the things it can buy. After returning from a shopping expedition in Chicago with Rosamund, his wealthy older daughter, he explains to his wife that he failed to buy a necessary new winter overcoat as a reaction against Rosamund's "orgy of acquisition." Even though the novel invites readers to be critical of the women in the professor's life, their desires—including their consumerist desires—propel them into the future. Early in the novel, as he is remembering his first meeting with Tom Outland as a student, he reflects, "A man can do anything if he wishes to enough. . . . Desire is a creation, is the magical element in that process. If there were an instrument by which to measure desire, one could foretell achievement." In writing advertising copy, Lewis exercised an invisible power over consumers' desires. As newspaperman William Allen White observed in an address to the Advertising Club of New York in January 1927, "The real revolutionist is the advertising man, whose stimulation of mass desire and demand results in mass production and buying." More than twenty years before, White had been one of the judges who had selected Lewis's story "Chains of Darkness" for publication in *Collier's Weekly*. In 1926, a year before he gave his speech about advertising, he had been to tea at Bank Street—perhaps Lewis, the adwoman, chatted with him about her work while pouring tea.[82]

In May 1930, Andrew Jergens Co. removed Thompson from the Woodbury's account, but it allowed the agency to continue producing advertising for Jergens Lotion. The client was not pleased with the results of the Woodbury's campaign but did not know who was writing the copy. Thompson thus could—and did—retain Lewis without jeopardizing the Jergens Lotion account. Indeed, Lewis continued working as a copywriter at Thompson until she retired. She may have been devoid of the womanly "instinct" to appeal to men that the advertising manager of Andrew Jergens Co. identified as central to the ads she wrote for Jergens Lotion, but as her job application to the J. Walter Thompson Co. a decade earlier had made clear, she had a desire to succeed professionally. By 1929, she had made herself into a highly skilled advertising professional, and she continued to be one until she retired.[83]

In a fast-paced work environment with frequent staff turnover, both her long service and her reserve made her stand out. Former colleagues interviewed for an oral history of the agency in the 1960s (who did not seem to know she was still alive and living on Park Avenue) described her as "one of our best women writers" and "an extremely brilliant writer." She was also remembered, however, as an "extremely shy person who would blush deeply when meeting anyone," "very reserved, conservative," and "unassuming and quiet." On her job application, she had expressed a desire to become "the head of a large, successful working organization," but even as women at Thompson began working as account executives in the 1930s, Lewis remained on the creative side, perhaps because of this shyness and reserve. One female colleague from the Women's Editorial Department remembered that "[a]ll of us always felt sorry that she had to work on the Woodbury account" because "she had many blemishes and a terrible complexion herself." She did not, these colleagues judged, have "a skin you love to touch." However, that she wasn't married did not set her apart from other longtime female copywriters—neither Ruth Waldo nor Aminta Casseres married. Furthermore, her relationship with Cather was not hidden. "She lived with Willa Cather for a very long time," Florence Baldwin recalled; "they were devoted to each other."[84]

On her part, Cather expressed no regret about choosing to share her life with an advertising professional who simultaneously wrote concise heterosexual romantic fantasies for Woodbury's Facial Soap and Jergens Lotion and edited Cather's fictions about the bitter ends of such romances. Instead, Cather's boasts to the Brewsters and to Meta Schaper Cather suggest that she took pride in Lewis's work and recognized that it required a professional expertise that she herself lacked. As she wrote to Alfred Knopf on a rare occasion when she agreed to provide a jacket blurb for someone else's book (in this case, Joseph Kessel's *Army of Shadows* [1944]), "Miss Lewis always jeers at me when I attempt to write advertising, but this is not professional, it is simply how I feel about the book." And perhaps in late 1928, when Lewis was working on the soon-to-appear Woodbury's Beauty Survey, they chuckled together over the fact that Lewis was making F. Scott Fitzgerald sell soap and manipulating his male gaze as he chose "the prettiest girl."[85]

The career in which Lewis excelled, however, cost her something. She periodically fled from its pressures by traveling with Cather far away from Manhattan and from cheap beauty soap. Of course, Lewis financed her travels with her spoils from Madison Avenue. The gender segregation at

Thompson allowed women copywriters to achieve professionally, but driven career women like Lewis still wrote ads grounded in the presumption that all women "instinctively" wanted to "appeal to men." Cather and Lewis traveled to the Southwest, Europe, and Canada together, but on Grand Manan Island, they made a second home for themselves. Every summer that they traveled there and joined the all-woman resort community of Whale Cove, they not only put physical distance between themselves and New York City but left behind such patriarchal presumptions about women's desires.

5

"Edith and I Hope to Get Away
to Grand Manan"

Work, Play, and Community at Whale Cove

In the summer of 1922, Willa Cather and Edith Lewis first visited Grand Manan, a Canadian island at the mouth of the Bay of Fundy. Earlier that summer Lewis had accompanied Cather when she lectured at the Bread Loaf School of English in Vermont. They both needed peace and quiet that summer: Cather wanted to write, and Lewis was anxious to get away from the pressures of the office. They rented Orchardside Cottage from Sarah Jacobus, the co-proprietor and manager of the Whale Cove Inn, and one could hardly imagine a place more different from New York City in the summer than a quiet cove with a simple inn surrounded by rustic cottages—and that was precisely the point. Even in August, nights could be brisk, and the weather coming in off the Atlantic Ocean varied constantly. "There was solitude without loneliness," Lewis recalled in *Willa Cather Living*. "One could walk for miles along the cliffs without meeting anyone or seeing any mark of human life."[1]

Despite their earlier thoughts of becoming frequent visitors to or part-time residents of New Mexico, after their 1926 trip they never returned to the Southwest. Instead for nearly two decades they firmly located themselves as regular summer residents of a women-only rustic resort community on an Atlantic island. The time Lewis and Cather spent on Grand Manan enjoying outdoor recreation and the sociability of a community of like-minded women renewed them and made their urban life in New York City possible. When they chose to build their own cottage, the other cottage owners and renters, women mostly from New York and New England, were steps away, and they, like Cather and Lewis, took at least some of their meals in the common dining room at the Whale Cove Inn. Because Cather and Lewis chose a site surrounded by trees on three sides and overlooking the ocean on the fourth, they claimed space, quiet, and privacy to focus their joint attention on the production of Cather's fiction. Cather and Lewis also shared multiple nodes of connection to these women, who mirrored back to them versions of themselves and their place in the world as middle-aged working women who came of age in the Progressive Era and whose lives revolved around their relationships with other women rather than being structured by heterosexual marriage.[2]

Cather and Lewis did not participate in any of the lesbian subcultures of Manhattan in the 1920s and 1930s, when, for example, lesbian tearooms appeared in Greenwich Village. Nor was Grand Manan a secret lesbian community where women came to express a sexuality they could not express in closeted lives lived elsewhere the rest of the year: even though there were other romantic couples at Whale Cove, pairs of sisters and widowed women were also part of the community. Nevertheless, Whale Cove functioned as a women-only subculture for Cather and Lewis, where their sister colonists quietly recognized and accepted them as a couple and where they could escape the cultural norms of femininity that permeated Lewis's advertising work. Many of the women of Whale Cove invited friends and family to visit them, and in the 1930s, when Cather and Lewis were firmly established as cottage-owning summer residents and after both had lost their parents, they cultivated relationships with the younger women in their families (but *only* the women) by inviting them to be their guests at Grand Manan.[3]

The Women of Whale Cove

Whale Cove was "discovered" in 1900 by three young women from suburban Boston. Sarah "Sally" Jacobus and Sarah "Sally" McAllister Adams were both graduates of the Boston Normal School for Gymnastics (BNSG). The BNSG was a classic single-sex Progressive Era institution, which offered a two-year course designed to develop students' physical fitness and to train them to teach sports, games, Swedish gymnastics, and calisthenics to other women and to children. Graduates of the school taught in public and private schools, supervised public playgrounds, and provided one-on-one instruction in gymnasiums (a precursor to physical therapy), but if they chose not to teach or left teaching for marriage, their training had given them healthy bodies that suited them for healthy pregnancies and for raising healthy children.[4]

This schooling inspired Jacobus and Adams, accompanied by Jacobus's friend Marie Felix, to take a tramp steamer up from Boston into the Bay of Fundy in order to search for a place where they might pursue vigorous outdoor recreation. Jacobus, an 1897 BNSG graduate, was central to the development of the Whale Cove Inn and was a presence on Grand Manan for more than forty years. Born near Pittsburgh, by the time she enrolled in BSNG her family had moved to Auburndale, a village within the town of Newton, Massachusetts. After graduating, Jacobus taught physical training at public schools in the Boston area. Adams graduated from BNSG in 1894 and returned for a year of advanced study after teaching in Massachusetts and Virginia. She then taught for two years in Pittsburgh before returning to Boston in 1900 to work in a private gymnasium. Marie Felix had earned a diploma from Fanny Farmer's Boston Cooking School in 1895 and lived in Auburndale with family, helping to manage their households and care for their children.[5]

Fifty years after their first visit, Felix recalled that the three found on Grand Manan the ' "un-touristed' vacation" they sought. They hired a local boatman to sail them around the island and returned in 1901, asking their boatman about available properties. "He knew of a house we could buy," she recalled, and they "rushed that evening" to see "the small, shabby, rather desolate embric of Whale Cove Cottage." In December 1901, they purchased the "very small house and a twenty acre strip of grass and woodcot." In the summer of 1903, after local carpenters repaired the house, they took possession. Their first guest was Sally Jacobus's BNSG classmate Alice Butler Coney (known as Peter), who was from Cincinnati and who returned there after graduation to work in a private gymnasium. Coney was the first of many visitors, and in response Jacobus, Adams, and Felix expanded the original building, bought additional adjacent land and buildings (Orchardside and Cooperage) when they became available in 1909 and 1913, and planted an orchard and garden. "In self-defense," Felix recalled, "we were keeping an inn." In 1909, however, Adams moved west with her new doctor husband, and Peter Coney bought Adams's share in the Whale Cove property, maintaining a notable aspect of the community: the women who owned property there were not married and shared homes on the island and off with other unmarried women.[6]

When Cather and Lewis first rented Orchardside Cottage in 1922, the community was in transition: women in the core group and friends they had drawn in were acquiring or building their own cottages near the inn. Cather and Lewis were connected in many ways to this expanded core group of property owners. Sisters Alice and Mary Jordan became Cather and Lewis's closest neighbors and friends at Whale Cove. Mary was born in Bombay,

India, in 1869, and Alice the next year in Maine when their seafaring family returned home. Following relatives who had abandoned the maritime industry, their family moved to Auburndale in 1881. In 1895, one of Alice and Mary's cousins married Marie Felix's sister, and Marie joined the Ranlett household in Auburndale. Mary Jordan graduated from Smith College in 1892 and co-founded the Kimerley School for Girls in New Jersey with a Smith classmate. Rather than attend college, Alice taught for several years before joining the staff of the Boston Public Library, where, through on-the-job training, she worked her way up to head of the Children's Department. Alice and Mary visited Whale Cove as early as 1904, and Alice was an enthusiastic regular visitor for two decades. As a vigorous woman in her thirties, she used to don knickers and use cables to let herself down the face of dramatic sea cliffs, then climb back up hand over hand. Around 1910, she persuaded her widowed mother to join her for a summer visit, and Mrs. Jordan raved about how the dramatic beauty and weather of the island "renew[ed] our bodies and souls after the weeks in the hot dusty city" of Boston, allowing her, an "elderly person," to walk four miles a day, while Alice walked two or three times as far. Mary Jordan finally returned to Grand Manan in the early 1920s because "Al" wanted her sister to join her in building a summer cottage. After contemplating the scenery for several days, Mary conceded, "I don't see why Al shouldn't have a house here if she wants it." Alice purchased high land looking over a pasture for $250 in September 1922. Charles Green, the same local carpenter Cather and Lewis would later hire, built their cottage, and in 1924 Alice acquired adjacent land for $300, giving them privacy and room for a large vegetable garden. The sisters would share the bounty from this garden with Cather and Lewis for the occasional meal they prepared in their cottage. In 1939, Alice and Mary together acquired additional adjacent land, including a stretch of shoreline.[7]

Catherine Merideth Schwartz and Ethelwyn Manning first acquired property at Whale Cove in 1924. Rather than build a new cottage, they acquired land with an existing house and barn. The Whale Cove group was compact, but their plot lay at the opposite end from Lewis and Cather's cottage, on the Whistle Road toward the village of North Head. Manning later recalled seeing Cather on the road in front of their house, returning from shopping in the village and struggling to carry her packages. New Jersey–born Manning graduated from Smith College in 1908 and from the Training School for Children's Librarians at the Carnegie Library in Pittsburgh in 1910. As a children's librarian she held positions in Brooklyn, Massachusetts, and in

Iowa. After her family moved to Newton, she lived with them while studying at Simmons College in an early college-level library science program, from which she received a B.S. in 1917. Alice Jordan lectured at Simmons on children's librarianship, and Manning surely studied under her. Shortly after Manning earned her B.S., however, she took a position as head cataloger at the Amherst College Library, where she worked until Helen Clay Frick (whom she likely knew in Pittsburgh) plucked her out of obscurity in 1924 to make her the head of the Frick Art Reference Library in New York City.[8]

Manning's move to New York reunited her with Schwartz, her Carnegie classmate. A Pittsburgh native several years Manning's senior, Schwartz enrolled in the Training School for Children's Librarians in 1908 without a college degree, likely after working at the library. Schwartz held various children's librarian positions in the Pittsburgh Carnegie system from her 1911 graduation until 1917, when she became a children's librarian at the New York Public Library Hamilton Grange Branch in Upper Manhattan. From 1924 on, Schwartz and Manning shared both a cottage on Grand Manan and an apartment in Midtown Manhattan. That they maintained their friendship from Manning's departure from Pittsburgh in 1910 until their New York reunion in 1924 and then lived together for the rest of their lives testifies to their mutual devotion. They were, however, an odd couple. Manning celebrated her escape from the "dirty," "trashy" work of children's librarianship and gloried in her "thrilling" work at the Frick and her connection to the library's wealthy patron. Those who knew her on Grand Manan in the 1950s and 1960s remembered her as lively, feminine, and flirtatious. In contrast, Schwartz devoted her life to working with the poor, minority, and immigrant children who patronized public libraries, and she documented New York immigrant life in watercolors. She was remembered as painfully shy but "masculine" and handy with tools.[9]

In the 1920s or early 1930s, Marie Felix and her then-widowed sister, Adele Felix Ranlett, acquired a building they called the "Barnlet" and relocated it to land on the Whistle Road. During this period Peter Coney shared summer quarters with Sarah Jacobus in the main inn building, of which Jacobus became the primary manager. Peter's sister Grace also visited the island. By 1920, Jacobus had moved from the Boston area to New York City, where she first worked at the YWCA and shared an apartment with her mother and (at least at the time the census taker appeared) with Peter Coney. Soon Jacobus took a position at the New York Public Library Circulation Department, and until 1931 she worked at the library for three seasons and spent her summers on Grand Manan. Peter Coney died in an automobile accident in 1929, and Grace died a few years later. As a result Jacobus and Felix inherited Peter's life interest in her third of the inn property. In the early 1930s, Felix transferred part of her share of the inn property to Jacobus, who built a cottage on the water for herself and her mother and became a year-round island resident.[10]

Renters came from similar occupational groups as the owners. Librarians—educated professionals who were modestly compensated—found Whale Cove particularly attractive. Theodosia McCurdy, Alice Jordan's colleague at the Boston Public Library, came with Jordan the year before her cottage was built. Sarah Jacobus got her job at the New York Public Library (NYPL) on the recommendation of Whale Cove renter Florence Overton, head of the Circulation Department and the highest-ranking female librarian in the library system. It was likely Overton who recommended Grand Manan to Cather as a quiet place to work. Overton and Alice Jordan were Cather's age, but younger librarians also enjoyed the colony. Margaret Bonnell, a 1917 graduate of Smith College, graduated from the NYPL training course and worked in the reference cataloging division there before moving on to other library positions in New York City. Henrietta Quigley, a 1937 Pratt Institute library course graduate and librarian in the Circulation Department, was a longtime summer renter who came to Grand Manan with Nan Peters, with whom she also shared a Greenwich Village apartment and an interest in bird-watching. Phyllis Osteen, an NYPL branch librarian, and Lucy M. Crissey, who left a position at the NYPL to become assistant to the dean of the Columbia University School of Library Service, similarly lived together in Manhattan and birdwatched as summer renters at Whale Cove.[11]

Educators, social workers, writers, and visual artists also rented at Whale Cove. Poet Grace Hazard Conkling, an 1899 graduate of and English professor at Smith College, came at least one summer in the late 1920s, as did her fellow Smith English faculty members Mary Ellen Chase (a New England regional novelist) and Margaret McGregor. Chase and McGregor shared a home on the Smith campus as they had earlier when both taught at the University of Minnesota. Marion Edwards Park, president of Bryn Mawr College from 1922 to 1942, found her way to Grand Manan in the 1920s; she had earlier been dean of Simmons College and likely knew the Jordan sisters. Margaret Byington, a social worker and author of an influential exposé of the living and working conditions of steelworkers in Homestead, Pennsylvania, summered at Whale Cove. Helen Clark Fernald, a widowed children's book author and friend of the Jordan sisters, summered at Grand Manan from the

1930s, as did British-born children's book author and illustrator Winifred Bromhall. Marjorie Harrison, a British journalist who wrote books about Canadian immigration and the Oxford Group Movement, spent time there. Among Whale Cove renters, Eloise Derby and her friend Miss Frith (likely Louise Frith) were outliers, wealthy socialites with no paid occupation or family responsibilities. Derby hailed from Boston and lived most of the year in France; Frith was from New York City, and they probably first met at the fashionable Maine resort town of Bar Harbor.[12]

Sabra Jane Briggs, a graduate of the Boston Museum Art School, was on the fringes of the Whale Cove community. She was a New York–based illustrator and interior decorator until the early 1920s, when she moved to Grand Manan, opened a guesthouse in North Head, and took up painting and pottery. She sometimes took dinner in the Whale Cove dining room, where she met Cather and Lewis and was invited to visit their cottage. In 1936, Briggs moved to Grand Harbour, several miles south of North Head, and established the Anchorage. Like the inn at Whale Cove, the Anchorage was an inn surrounded by cottages, and it attracted a similar (although younger) clientele.[13]

Lewis and Cather consistently referred to their fellow Whale Cove summer residents, whether proprietors of the inn, cottage owners, or renters, as "friends." Their occupations as an advertising copywriter and critically esteemed novelist set them apart, but geography, social class, and education connected them. Cather could have chosen to become a regular at the MacDowell Colony (where she was a resident briefly in 1926), but Lewis would not have been welcome there or at a similar formal artists' colony. Instead, the two together chose a community of women who were alternate versions of themselves, what they themselves might have been if they had chosen more typical career paths as women in both of their families had. And the Whale Cove women welcomed them into the community and respected their privacy by not appearing at their cabin uninvited or grilling Cather about her writing. "Her cottage was a workshop," Sabra Briggs recalled of Cather. "I felt very definitely that she was here to work. I never went down to call unless I was asked." Briggs and others *were* asked, however.[14]

Derby and Frith violated these unuttered rules. When they were seated at a table with Cather and Lewis in the inn's small dining room, the four got along well for a couple of nights, talking about "Paris and restaurants and that sort of thing." However, Frith then asked Cather whether she had based an incident in *A Lost Lady* (1923) (Ivy Peters blinding a female woodpecker) on fact. In the 1960s, Derby gleefully shared stories about Cather's standoff-ishness, but others' accounts (and Cather's and Lewis's own letters from the time) paint a very different picture of their integration into the social life of the community rather than their separation from it.[15]

Cather and Lewis also referred to as "friends" Ralph and Alice Beal and Willie Thomas, year-round, native-born residents whom they paid to maintain and clean their cottage and do other work for them. The relationship between the Whale Cove women and the Grand Manan locals who served them was, as in most resort communities, sometimes uneasy and based on mutual misunderstanding. The island's residents had an ambiguous national and cultural status. The first white settlers on the island were Loyalists who fled to Canada during the American Revolution and to whom the British crown awarded land grants. However, the island is closer to the state of Maine than to the mainland portion of the Canadian province of New Brunswick, of which the island is a part. These circumstances made the year-round residents more culturally American than Canadian, and the Whale Cove women were over-whelmingly American (the sole Canadian at Whale Cove seems to have been someone Cather referred to only as Miss Gissing, "who manage[d] a fash-ionable girls' boarding school in Canada"). And yet conservative Protestant congregations and temperance lodges dominated the social life of the geo-graphically isolated island. All in all, then, the locals were detached from the twentieth-century American culture the Whale Cove women represented. By 1920s U.S. standards, Cather, Lewis, and their American friends at Whale Cove were middle-of-the-road rather than radical, but locals nevertheless found baffling these unmarried American women who sometimes smoked, drank, and wore pants.[16]

Making a Home at Whale Cove

In 1921, Cather had hoped to travel to Grand Manan from Toronto, where she was visiting the Hambourgs, but the trip failed to come off. Instead, Cather and Lewis did not make their first trip until August 1922. Because they were already in Vermont, they traveled via Montreal to St. John's, New Brunswick, where the ferry service to the island departed. From the start, Cather's time on Grand Manan was intimately tied to her writing. When her novels appeared in the fall catalog of her publisher, early copies were shipped to Grand Manan. Thus on August 16, 1922, she inscribed an early copy of

One of Ours to Lewis. During their monthlong first visit that year, Cather wrote rapturously to friends and family about the island's natural beauty and the work she was accomplishing. She wrote Dorothy Canfield Fisher that she was a " 'paying guest' with friends who have a place on the sea," and she praised the combination of "quiet and solitude all day" with "pleasant people, a few, to meet at dinner." Cather also wrote that she had "pull[ed] out a long-short story which seemed to have died on [her] hands." On her next visit, in 1924, Cather inscribed a copy of that "long-short story," *A Lost Lady* (1923), to Sarah Jacobus "from a grateful author. . . . Part II of this story . . . was written in the Month of August 1922." Cather did not want to perform being an author while on the island, but the fact that she wrote there was no secret. During her first visit she also wrote a preface for a reissue of her first novel, *Alexander's Bridge* (1912), signing the preface in print, "Willa Cather, Whale Cove Cottage, Grand Manan, N.B., September 1922."[17]

Cather and Lewis gloried in the island's cliffs, trees, and weather. Cather described to Fisher long walks "on the fine wooded cliffs hanging over the sea" and portrayed herself as writing her letter "off in the woods, sitting on high cliffs that hang over a summer sea." August 1922 was pleasantly chilly. "I am sure you would be delighted if you knew what a comfort your woolen scarf has been to me this summer," Cather wrote to her mother. "It is about my shoulders this minute, as I sit under a pine tree on the cliffs up over the sea, writing to you. I never go to walk without it." In snapshots Lewis took of Cather during their early visits to Grand Manan, what is probably that scarf often appeared (see Figure 5.1).[18]

Cather learned early on that Whale Cove was both an ideal and a challenging place to work. "This is a fine place to work," she wrote Alfred Knopf a few days into her first visit, describing her rapid progress on *A Lost Lady*. Nevertheless, although she almost always wrote on the island, she did not force herself to keep to a schedule as she often did in New York. "Working periods come and go, like the tides in this treacherous Bay of Fundy," she wrote to British author and critic Frank Swinnerton in 1924. "[T]here's no controlling them or prognosticating them." Being on a rustic Canadian island also made it difficult to send and receive packages. In 1922, the proofs of Knopf's revised edition of her early book of poetry, *April Twilights*, took several weeks to reach her because the Knopf office had misread her handwriting, addressing the package to "Grand Manor." Furthermore, the mail boat served the island only three times a week, and the package was mailed in a way that required Cather to take delivery and pay duties at the customs

Figure 5.1 Cather (*right*) and Lewis (*left*) on Grand Manan in the early 1920s. Courtesy Archives and Special Collections, University of Nebraska–Lincoln Libraries.

office—she had to travel in a hired car to the southern end of the island to do this. By returning to New York in September, she and Lewis avoided similar troubles with the limited edition of *One of Ours*, which Cather had to autograph.[19]

In the summer of 1923, Cather was in France with the Hambourgs, so she and Lewis did not go to Grand Manan. However, in 1924, the charms of the island drew them again. Furthermore, since 1919, they had been living under the threat that subway construction might lead to demolition of 5 Bank Street, and in 1924, there was again confusion about whether they would have to move. They were thus happy to get away, and Lewis was, as usual, feeling exhausted by her office job. "How well I understand the weariness you are feeling in the midst of the confusion you are in in the apartment," Edith's mother, Lillie, wrote her in late July, "and the rush of work at the office to get ready to leave, & I shall be so glad when it is finished & you are really off for the Grand Manan . . . and I do hope nothing will happen to interrupt your vacation and a real rest." For $25 a week, she and Lewis again rented Orchardside Cottage, which Cather described to Frank Swinnerton as a "little house" "in an apple orchard that drop[ped] off into the sea" thirty yards from the window of the room where she wrote. During this second visit, Cather and Lewis likely saw the newly built cottage of the Jordan sisters and perhaps Manning and Schwartz's newly acquired residence, giving them a vision of what they themselves might do.[20]

Cather again found Whale Cove a productive place to work. As she wrote to her friend playwright Zoë Akins, "I've been working awfully hard on a quite new novel, and have nearly got half way through the first writing of it." But she also told Akins that she was doing more than writing. "Miss Lewis and I have a lovely little cottage all to ourselves," she wrote. "We've had every kind of weather <u>but</u> heat; sun and and [sic] wind and splendid stunning fogs." Even the outer edges of a hurricane that battered the island excited Cather as they went "walking lots, and cruising round among lighthouses and bell-buoys." She thanked Akins for "the tan-colored hunters [sic] suit you gave me two years ago, as it sheds the water from grass and branch better than anything else I have. For really bad weather I wear knickerbockers." Photographs Cather and Lewis took of each other on Grand Manan in the early 1920s (Figure 5.1) evoke their pleasure in dressing up for outdoor adventure on an Atlantic island. They wore what they did in the Southwest—brimmed hats, khaki trouser suits, and middy blouses with ties under their jackets—and they similarly passed the camera back and forth. In two matching photos, Lewis's neutral expression and arms resting at her side contrast with Cather's grin and the rustic walking stick she used as a prop.[21]

In 1925, Cather and Lewis went to the Southwest rather than Grand Manan, but Cather made sure to mail an early copy of *The Professor's House* to Sarah Jacobus on September 16, writing in it, "The first part of the first Book, 'The Family' was written at Orchardside last summer." In 1926, Cather and Lewis again went to the Southwest. After Lewis returned to New York, Cather had planned to stay at Mabel Luhan's ranch to work on *Death Comes for the Archbishop*, but she left sooner than she had planned. In August, she was accommodated at the last minute at the MacDowell Colony in Peterboro, New Hampshire. It had become clear that construction of a new subway station would definitely begin the next winter, so while Cather was in New Hampshire, Lewis went to Grand Manan on her own to purchase land and make arrangements to build a cottage: they would have a home together there that no subway construction could disturb. From Cather and Lewis's first summer in their own cottage in 1928 (after they finally lost their Bank Street apartment, in 1927) until late 1932, when they moved into an apartment at 570 Park Avenue, their Whale Cove cottage was the most homelike place they shared. Cather consistently described it as a home. As she wrote to her Pittsburgh friend Elizabeth Morehead Vermorcken in September 1928, just after returning from Grand Manan, "I've been at Grand Manan for the last two months, an island off the coast of New Brunswick, where Miss Lewis and I have built a little home." At the top of a black-and-white snapshot of their cottage, tinted in water colors by Lewis, that Willa sent to her brother Roscoe's family, she wrote, "This is our little home."[22]

But first they needed to build that little home. On September 7, 1926, Lewis paid $325 for a plot that was close by the Jordan cottage and which had a view of the cove that gave the inn and cottages their name. Peter Coney referred Lewis to a local carpenter, Charles Green, and with him she staked out the cottage. Rather than provide him with plans, she instructed him to build a copy of Orchardside Cottage, which she and Cather had enjoyed in 1922 and 1924. Orchardside began as a foursquare cottage with a dormer roof, but at a later date a narrower building with a lower hipped roof had been joined at a right angle and set back from the front door of the original cottage. Mimicking this vernacular nineteenth-century building and others in the Whale Cove group, Cather and Lewis also had their twentieth-century vacation cottage sided with unpainted dark wood shingles. The cottage's siting gave them a view of the cove from their two front-facing doors and three windows, and the wooded slope rising behind the cottage provided privacy. The location would also cause them countless troubles because winter snowmelt pooled in their crawlspace, rotting out floorboards and leaving the house and its contents damp.[23]

The cottage's central room was the living room, which was flanked by Lewis's bedroom on the north side in the foursquare cottage and Cather's on the south in the ell. All three of the rooms had east-facing windows with unobstructed views of the cove. Their small kitchen (equipped with an icebox and small woodstove) and a dining area were in the rear, facing west toward the slope and retaining wall. Both of their bedrooms had bathing alcoves, but they had no interior bathroom, only an outhouse. Ralph Beal, who maintained the cottage for them year round, hand-pumped water from their well to a cistern behind the house, and gravity carried cold water from there to the kitchen sink and to a shed behind it rigged for shower bathing. In 1928,

Lewis paid $125 for more land behind their cottage, ensuring their privacy and protecting their water supply.[24]

A joint telephone and telegraph cable was laid to the island in the late nineteenth century, but Grand Manan had no electric service until 1929. Cather and Lewis, however, did not connect their cottage to these services even after they became available. During the long summer days in the Bay of Fundy, sunlight streamed in through their windows, making additional lighting unnecessary; after sunset they relied on kerosene lamps, candles, and firelight. Two fireplaces, one facing the living room and the other facing Lewis's bedroom, shared the cottage's single chimney. The attic space in the dormer above the main cottage was unfinished but had a solid board floor. Cather put her writing desk at the attic window in the north-facing gable end, where she could glimpse the Bay of Fundy through the trees and had a sliver of an unobstructed view of the cove to the east. The attic's sloping dormer roof line gave Cather the physical space she had long preferred for writing, and during her preferred morning writing hours it was cool and comfortable. By putting her desk in the attic, Cather also spared Lewis the noise of a typewriter. Lewis hated the distracting noise of typing at her office in New York when she was trying to write advertising copy, and the quiet downstairs or on their front lawn allowed her to concentrate while she polished Cather's prose or pursued her other interests.[25]

Both women loved botanizing, and the island was rich in wildflowers. Aided by Ralph Beal they cultivated flowers around their property, literally rooting themselves on Grand Manan. Wild roses grew on the edge of the property, a large trellised pink rosebush they named "Dorothy" flourished near the front door, and Lewis planted a yellow rosebush, a grafted plant that later went wild. Hardy hollyhocks, flowers beloved by the Czech immigrants Cather knew in her Nebraska childhood and mentioned in *My Ántonia*, grew up toward the eaves on the south wall near Cather's bedroom window. Cather and Lewis planted marigolds and monks' hood in a small flowerbed on the northwest corner outside the kitchen and purple portulaca in the crevices of their retaining wall. On the front lawn of their cottage, they placed a sundial—if they weren't working, they could sit in their steamer chairs facing the cove and watch the time pass, much as an aging Captain Forrester in *A Lost Lady* contemplates his sundial.[26]

Cather and Lewis found furnishing their cottage home challenging because duties charged by the Canadian government made shipping furnishings from the U.S. expensive. Nevertheless, they enjoyed taking gifts from friends and family there, homey and simple objects that might have seemed out of place in a New York apartment. Willa Cather's sister Elsie gave her a length of heavy printed cretonne fabric, which, as Willa reported to her mother, Lewis thought would "be lovely for Grand Manan," probably to cover their east-facing bedroom windows—because they were so far east and north, the sun rose early. Cather, who had no firelight in her bedroom, used the "silver candlestick" Blanche Knopf gave her to "light[] [her] to bed every night." Cather wrote to Mollie Ferris, her old friend from Red Cloud, about the "two holders" she had made for her "years ago." "I keep them hanging by the fire place in my cottage at Grand Manan," she explained. "They are useful and pretty as when you first sent them to me." To another friend from Red Cloud, Lydia Lambrecht, Cather wrote of bringing a quilt Lambrecht's daughters had made to Grand Manan, where it looked "lovely . . . on my hand-carved walnut bed that came over from England."[27]

A decade after they moved in, Lewis described the house's interior to Harwood Brewster Picard (Achsah and Earl Brewster's daughter):

> It is far from "artistic" for we have had to furnish it mostly with Canadian goods—and they are much uglier and more badly made than American manufactured things. Because of the duty, one has to pay almost double on anything sent in from the States. This year we sent a little chair from New York—it was $7.95 when we bought it, and had cost over $16 by the time we got it up here. So for the most part we have contented ourselves with the simplest possible furniture from Saint John's—kitchen chairs and table, which we have painted, braided rugs which we have bought here on the Island, curtains made from odds and ends of material we happened to have by us. But after years of coming here, we have succeeded in making it very comfortable, and I do not think there is a lovelier spot anywhere in the world.

One account places Indian rugs from the Southwest in Cather's bedroom. Perhaps by transporting the rugs there, she communicated both that Grand Manan was equal to the Southwest as a site of adventure and that she and Lewis had chosen Grand Manan over New Mexico as their summer home.[28]

Once they had their own cottage, Cather and Lewis could come and go any time without worrying about reservations. Nevertheless, each time they traveled to Grand Manan, they were generally rushing to finish up work in New York before the summer heat set in. Once they got to the island,

however, changes in the weather were as dramatic as the Bay of Fundy's
world-renowned tides. As Lewis wrote to her old friend Rudolph Ruzicka,
a Czech American wood engraver and type designer, "[T]he weather is the
supreme fact in everyone's life, and that is more variable and various than
I have ever known it anywhere." Frequent rain and fog made the rocky island "as green as Ireland and as cool as England," Cather wrote to Zoë
Akins, "right for leather coats, sweaters, leggings etc," even in July. Cather
praised the "comfort" of nightgowns her mother had made for her. "They
are a little heavy for town wear," she wrote her mother in 1928, "but were just
what I needed in the country." Cather warned her twin nieces, Margaret and
Elizabeth Cather, before their first visit, "[D]on't forget rain coats. On our
island one must be able to enjoy rain because there is often so much of it,
and the woods are lovely in rain." Both Lewis and Cather recommended elk
skin moccasins for walking and climbing wet rocks along the cliff tops. The
rain and fog sometimes made their cottage so damp that they leaned their
packages of Lucky Strike cigarettes on the andirons of the living room fireplace to keep them dry enough to light. The weather also dampened other
kinds of paper: it stained their wallpaper and made it difficult to mark proofs
for correction. After Cather marked proof corrections and endorsed each
page in ink, she and Lewis had to spread the pages around the attic until the
ink dried before they could pack them up for shipping.[29]

The island's geographic isolation was both one of its strongest attractions
for Cather and Lewis and an obstacle when they had to conduct business.
Writing to Charlotte Stanfield during an early visit, Cather praised the "quiet
cottage with a splendid work room all to myself, and pleasant friends to meet
at dinner," but she proclaimed "[b]est of all" the fact that "mail comes only
three times a week, on a little steamer from the Canadian shore." The island
had no newspaper of its own, and residents did not pay much attention to
the mainland papers, which arrived three days late. "The nice carpenter
who built my house and has taken care of it for four years, said gently the
other day that he wished he knew what paper I wrote for, as he would like to
subscribe for it," Cather wrote to Dorothy Canfield Fisher in 1931. "You see
I have found a place where I'm let alone." She wrote to Zoë Akins with similar
satisfaction, "Newspapers always three days late, mail three times a week, no
radio on this island. World-affairs never touch us."[30]

Each time they left New York City for the island, Lewis committed herself
only vaguely to a return date, and in late August or early September, letters
and telegrams from the J. Walter Thompson Co. would begin arriving asking

her about her plans or urging her return for a new project. In August 1932, Howard Kohl, traffic manager at Thompson, wrote that he was "sorry, indeed, to break in on your vacation" but the agency needed her back in early September to work on the Lux Toilet Soap account. Lewis explained in her response that she had tried to send a telegram, but "the cable from this Island to the mainland has been broken for several weeks (they go out every day in boats to grapple for it) and there is no way to send telegrams except to ask the captain of the steamship which calls here to carry it over to the mainland." The steamship's thrice-weekly schedule compounded the delay. Lewis promised to come back in mid-September, "sacrific[ing] the beautiful month of October here (although if you knew how much I am enjoying life you would never have the heart to ask me) and come back prepared to devote myself heart and soul to the Lever Brothers" (the company that made Lux Toilet Soap).[31]

"Family Portraits": *Shadows on the Rock, Obscure Destinies*, and Literary Collaboration

Charles Cather, Willa Cather's father, died in March 1928. In *Willa Cather Living*, Lewis recalled that in the ensuing summer (the first in their own cottage), "Grand Manan seemed the only foothold left on earth. With all her things in storage—with not even a comfortable writing-table to write at—Willa Cather looked forward fervently to her attic at Grand Manan. No palace could have seemed so attractive to her just then as that rough little cottage, with the soft fogs blowing across the flowery fields, and the crystalline quiet of the place." Absent from Lewis's reminiscence are her own losses during their first decade of Grand Manan visits, when she, like Cather, grappled with the final illnesses and deaths of her parents and with other family disruptions. Two books, the novel *Shadows on the Rock* (1931) and the collection of three stories, *Obscure Destinies* (1932), emerged in the wake of these losses. Although both bore only Cather's name on their title pages, they emerged out of Cather and Lewis's shared experiences of grief and through a literary collaboration that took place on or was associated with their residence on Grand Manan.[32]

The difficulties in Lewis's family began well before Cather's father died. After Edith's sisters Ruth and Helen graduated from high school in Winchester, Massachusetts, they attended the Sargent School for Physical

Training in Cambridge, which operated on precisely the same model as the Boston Normal School for Gymnastics. Henry and Lillie's oldest child, Harold, traveled frequently as an electrical engineer for Westinghouse, so after Helen and Ruth graduated and accepted teaching positions elsewhere, Henry and Lillie shared an apartment in Cambridge with their son. Lillie took in boarders during the war to bring in much-needed money, and Henry was distressed at being financially dependent on his son.[33]

In 1919, Helen became director of physical training at Brooklyn Heights Female Seminary, across the Hudson River from Manhattan, and Ruth also took a position there. In New York, Helen became reacquainted with a neighbor and elementary school classmate from Lincoln, Harold Philip "Phil" Morgan. The couple married in Cambridge in June 1920, and in 1921, they moved to Lincoln, where they lived on South Twenty-Seventh Street with Phil's parents. Then, in October 1921, Harold Lewis married his much younger secretary, Alice Griffin, and the couple soon established their own home. Edith was now sufficiently comfortable financially to send money to her parents, including a check that she mailed from Grand Manan to Cambridge in 1922, but it soon became clear that Harold and Lillie could not live on their own. In late 1922, Henry moved to central California, where Helen and Phil Morgan had relocated, and Lillie moved in with Ruth, who continued to teach at Brooklyn Heights Seminary. As Cather wrote to Earl and Achsah Brewster in early 1923, "This has been a hard winter for [Edith]—her family has made such heavy demands upon her"—and their demands would continue to be heavy.[34]

Just after Edith Lewis and Willa Cather had returned from Grand Manan in 1922, Lillie Lewis visited 5 Bank Street, where Cather inscribed a copy of the recently published One of Ours, "For Lillie G. Lewis, Willa Sibert Cather, Five Bank Street, September 16th, 1922." Lillie dreaded the stairs at the Brooklyn Heights subway station (it was the deepest station in New York), so she did not make regular return visits to her daughter's Manhattan apartment during her years in Brooklyn. Instead she addressed plaintive letters to Edith, commiserating with her about the continuing challenges her daughter and "Miss Cather" faced in retaining a maid to clean and cook for them and about Edith's need to get away from the stresses of her job. Both Helen and Harold soon had children, bringing joy into the Lewis family at a difficult time. From California, Henry sent Edith pictures of Helen's daughters, and Edith visited her little nieces Ruth and Elizabeth, Harold's daughters, in Massachusetts. A snapshot shows her laughing with her nieces in their sandbox (Figure 5.2),

Figure 5.2   Edith Lewis with her nieces Ruth and Elizabeth Lewis in the mid-1920s. Courtesy Family of Ruth Lewis Trainor.

and she also delighted in sending them books, sometimes inscribing them with original verse.[35]

The intertwined chain of deaths of Willa Cather's and Edith Lewis's parents began with Henry Lewis. He died of a stroke in California on June 14, 1926, the same day Willa's brother Roscoe and his family came down from Wyoming to join Willa and Edith in Santa Fe. His coffin traveled all the way across the country to be interred in the Lewis family plot in New Hampshire—perhaps the train carrying it passed through New Mexico on its way. In the summer of 1927, Cather and Lewis planned to go to Italy rather than to Grand Manan (their cottage was still under construction). Shortly before they were scheduled to sail, Cather sent an inscribed copy of *Death Comes for the Archbishop* to Sarah Jacobus, acknowledging in her inscription their cottage-under-construction by identifying herself as "your friend and neighbor." As Cather wrote to Mabel Dodge Luhan in mid-September, however, "We had planned to be in Rome at this date, [but] Miss Lewis, and I and are in—New Hampshire!" They had had to change their plans multiple times, first because her father's heart trouble had unexpectedly prolonged her earlier visit to Red Cloud, and then because they had spent time packing up their Bank Street apartment before the building was demolished, and, finally, because "Edith's mother had a stroke in Springfield," where she had been visiting her son's family. Vacationing at the Shattuck Inn allowed Lewis "to be somewhere near her mother" and a "dead tired" Cather to avoid the trauma of "embark[ing] for Italy alone."[36]

Once Cather and Lewis got back to New York, they moved into a suite of rooms at the Grosvenor, a residential hotel in Greenwich Village, and Lewis took the train up to Springfield most weekends to visit her mother in the hospital. In December 1927, while Lewis was still making these regular train trips, Cather went for a long holiday visit to Red Cloud. Just seven days after she started her journey back to New York in late February 1928, her father died. She reversed course and was in Red Cloud for his funeral in early March. Willa then packed her mother off to California to visit her son Douglass, while Willa stayed in Red Cloud to make repairs and improvements to her parents' house in anticipation of her mother's returning to live there. She wrote to Roscoe from Red Cloud in April, "Edith's poor mother is still dying—it is surely a long hard way." Lillie Gould Lewis, age seventy, died on May 8, 1928, in Springfield. Although she had been living apart from her husband for several years, they were reunited in death: she was buried next to him in the Lewis family plot in New Hampshire. When Willa wrote Roscoe in April about Lillie Lewis's long, slow death, she did not know that her own mother, still visiting Douglass in California, would suffer a stroke in December, becoming stranded there, and that Virginia Cather's way from her stroke to her death would be even longer and harder than Lillie Lewis's.[37]

Events in the wake of Charles Cather's and Lillie Lewis's deaths launched Cather unexpectedly into her second historical novel about Catholic North America. Although Cather and Lewis first traveled to Grand Manan via Montreal, on their next two trips she and Lewis likely took a train to Lubec, Maine, for the ferry to Campobello Island, where they could catch a steamer plying the Bay of Fundy. In 1928, seeking a different travel experience, they decided to travel via Quebec. Cather was grieving her father's death and had suffered a bout of influenza, so she was not well in the months before their trip. She wrote to Sarah Orne Jewett's sister Mary that she was "a used up thing . . . not sick any longer, simply no force, two or three hours a day are all I'm good for," but "an able bodied friend" (Lewis) would be traveling with her. As she wrote to Carrie Miner Sherwood, "[t]wo doctors and two nurses" had cared for her because she "had a high temperature for five days that simply burned [her] up." Lewis was not there to nurse her, she explained to

Sherwood, because she "was away, up in New England burying her mother. This has surely been an awful year for me." However, when Cather and Lewis arrived in Quebec City and checked into the Hotel Frontenac, it was Lewis, grieving the death of her mother and probably exhausted from work, who fell ill. Diagnosed with influenza, she was ordered to bed for a week. Lewis's illness delayed their trip to Grand Manan and left Cather roaming the city alone and reading a copy of Francis Parkman's history of French Canada she found in the hotel library. She had been at loose ends with no plans for a new novel, but because of her wanderings during Lewis's illness, she conceived the idea of a novel set in seventeenth-century Quebec.

Once they finally arrived on Grand Manan, Cather wrote Carrie Sherwood that it was

> a bowery, flowery isle this year! Every bit of it that is not pine woods is one soft, fluffy hayfield, full of daisies and bluebells. Our little house seems so pretty this year, and there is such peace and silence about it. The front yard is just a daisy field that drops 200 feet into the sea. The sea is really a part of our front yard. I so hope and pray for a few weeks to rest and write here.

Cather opened her letter asking Sherwood to send a can of furniture wax to the island, but, she explained,

> I've grown superstitious. Probably before your furniture wax can reach me something dreadful will have happened and I will be throwing my clothes in a trunk and hurrying to some other part of the world. The dear friend [Peter Coney] who helped Miss Lewis and me build this little house and who did so much for our comfort here, was killed in an automobile accident in Florida last winter. Father's death was like the falling of a prop; every k[in]d of disaster has come since.

As Lewis recalled Cather's mental processes that summer, "I think her mind often went back to [her father's] gentle protectiveness and kindness, the trusting relationship between them, in the old days in Virginia. Something of that perhaps entered into her conception of the apothecary *Euclide Auclair* and his little daughter."[38]

Lewis's family history and the recent loss of both her parents also inflected the novel Cather was just beginning. Henry Lewis's Huguenot ancestors lived in northern New England in the eighteenth century, when it was a contested border region between French and British colonies. In 1754, Peter Labaree, Edith Lewis's great, great grandfather, was taken captive by Native American allies of the French and transported to Montreal, where he was indentured as a carpenter. After he gained freedom from his indenture, the French held him as a prisoner of war, but he escaped and walked back to Charlestown, New Hampshire. Lewis certainly knew of this family history—her middle name was Labaree, and her sister Ruth Putnam Lewis was named after Peter Labaree's wife, Ruth Putnam Labaree. Furthermore, some of Henry Lewis's ancestors were among the Loyalists given land grants on Grand Manan in the late eighteenth century. In fact, Edith Lewis may have unknowingly bought the Whale Cove property from a distant relative.[39]

Cather and Lewis's travels in 1928, 1929, and 1930 took them repeatedly through these northern New England and French Canadian regions associated with Lewis's family history. Edith's father, Henry, traversed these same regions by train many times in the late nineteenth century, both when he was seeking New England capital for his midwestern business enterprises and when he took his new wife on their honeymoon journey from Iowa to New England. The full name of Edith's New Hampshire–born father, to whom she was devoted and against whom she rebelled during her Nebraska adolescence, was Henry Euclid Lewis. Surely Henry's illness and death in California after two disappointing decades in Massachusetts was heartbreaking for his daughter, and her mother's more recent death in 1928 would have brought back her grief at her father's passing. Even as Willa Cather modeled the exemplary father in *Shadows on the Rock* on her own father, by naming her fictional father Euclide Auclair she also made a loving gift to Edith Lewis, a token to prompt memories of her own beloved father when she read the novel.

Cather made another research trip to Canada on her own in the fall of 1928 after she and Lewis left Grand Manan (Lewis returned to her job in New York). Cather was thus ready to dig into her new novel when they traveled to Grand Manan in July 1929. Before they built their own cottage, Cather apparently worked primarily on the early stages of composing on the island, which entailed writing longhand in pencil. After they settled in their own cottage, Cather could leave possessions there from year to year, so in 1929 she brought a used typewriter she had acquired years before and left it behind for future use. In late July 1929, shortly after she and Lewis arrived, Cather typed a letter to Alfred Knopf's secretary asking for three hundred sheets of typing paper and a few sheets of carbon paper. With a typewriter and associated supplies in place, she dove into the work of *Shadows on the Rock*. Because the Atlantic damp was aggravating her neuritis, Cather was forced, contrary to her usual procedure, to "compos[e]" her new novel "on a machine." She did not type the two surviving drafts on Grand Manan, but she spliced a fragment of a page typed on her Grand Manan typewriter into one of them, and Lewis almost certainly edited this lost earlier typed draft while they were there. Much later, when Lewis was very old, she told her nurse that she did more than edit this novel, that she, rather than Cather, wrote one of its chapters. Whether or not this memory was accurate, it testifies to Lewis's particularly strong engagement with *Shadows on the Rock*.[40]

In September 1929, Cather and Lewis met Mary Ellen Chase and Margaret McGregor, Smith College English professors who were visiting Whale Cove with an eye to building their own cottage. Edith Lewis's cousin Mary Delia Lewis was Chase and McGregor's colleague; Mary Virginia Auld, daughter of Cather's sister Jessica, had just graduated from Smith; and another niece, Virginia Cather, daughter or Roscoe and Meta, was about to begin her first year there. The two couples thus had many points of connection. Chase later recalled that Cather had "great physical energy and vitality" and "spent hours each day in clearing away undergrowth" near the cottage "with an axe. Her hands were broad and strong, and she made excellent use of them . . . in talking, too, spreading out her thumbs and fingers as far as they could go, raising her wide-open palms backward toward her shoulders in moments of interest or excitement." What she talked of was her novel in progress. "That's just what the book is going to be . . . Shadows," Chase recalled Cather telling her. "It won't have a trace of what is called *movement* or *suspense*. It will just have people and a lot of *things*." Chase and McGregor did not join the community—McGregor died a few years later, and Chase and fellow Smith faculty member Eleanor Duckett made their summer home on Petit Manan Point in Maine rather than on Grand Manan.[41]

Cather and Lewis stayed well into the month of September in 1929. Mabel Luhan, not knowing where to write the homeless Cather and Lewis, wrote Lewis care of the J. Walter Thompson Co., where her letter sat unanswered until October. "We were up in Grand Manan," Lewis explained in apology, "where we lived a regular Swiss Family Robinson life—our friends who board us were not there, so we had to do nearly all our own cooking, but New Brunswick is no longer dry, so we were able to have champagne and things, and we managed to fare very well." In New York they were back at the Grosvenor Hotel. "I hate it as much as ever," Lewis groused, but it made no sense to take an apartment because Cather was making long visits to her mother in California and because they planned to take a long trip to Europe in 1930. Luhan sent a picture of her new house, which Lewis judged "perfectly lovely, only why did you not build a little one, then we could have come and lived in it. I wish we <u>were</u> going out there this summer." Instead, she and Cather were "going abroad, not to see Europe but to see our friends, we are afraid they will grow old and die. Willa wants to see her friends in Paris, and I want to see the Brewsters."[42]

Cather and Lewis also wanted to spend time in the medieval quarter of Paris, where parts of *Shadows on the Rock* are set. They sailed together on the *Berengaria* on May 14, 1930, and spent two months in Paris, where the Hambourgs lived, before they traveled south, first to Saint-Cyr-sur-Mer, where the Brewsters lived, and then to the spa town Aix-les-Bains. Nearly five months later, on September 29, 1930, they left France, sailing on the *Empress of France* to Quebec via the St. Lawrence Seaway. After an impromptu stay of a few days in Quebec City, they traveled, as planned, to Jaffrey to enjoy a New England autumn and so Cather could finish her novel. By the time they returned to New York City in November, Cather had in hand a typed draft of the novel in something like complete form. When it was published in 1931, Cather inscribed a copy, "For Edith Lewis, The first friend of this book. Willa Cather, June 19th 1931."[43]

Cather and Lewis's work on *Shadows* intertwined with the writing and editing of the three short stories collected in *Obscure Destinies* (1932), and their joint work on "Old Mrs. Harris" and "Two Friends" on Grand Manan in 1931 is richly documented. After Virginia Cather's stroke in late 1928, she could speak very little and was cared for in a sanitarium in Pasadena, where Willa Cather made a long visit in the spring of 1931. She and Lewis had wanted to leave for Grand Manan in June, but negotiations over the British edition of *Shadows* had kept them in New York City longer than they had wanted. When they finally arrived on the island in July, "rust and mould [had] got a good start" on their cottage because it had been closed up since their last visit in 1929, and it thus needed "settling" before they could get to work.[44]

One of the *Obscure Destinies* stories, "Neighbour Rosicky," had already been published in a magazine, so Cather and Lewis did not devote time to it in 1931. Cather had begun writing that story after her father's death in the spring of 1928, perhaps partly on Grand Manan, and she may have produced the first typed draft during their second summer in their own cottage, when she brought a typewriter to the island. She probably handwrote early pencil drafts of "Old Mrs. Harris" and "Two Friends" in Pasadena, but she produced her typed drafts very quickly on Grand Manan in 1931. Over the space of three weeks, Cather produced a complete typed revision of "Old Mrs. Harris," then typed a substantially revised version of parts of it, and finally, with scissors and glue, cobbled the two documents into one seventy-one-page typed text. Handing this typed text back and forth, Cather and Lewis revised it multiple times, each correcting errors, making single-word substitutions, and substantially recasting or deleting certain passages, especially those reflecting the internal thoughts of characters.[45]

In *Willa Cather Living*, Lewis wrote that "*Old Mrs. Harris . . .* might well have been called *Family Portraits*" because "Willa Cather . . . recreated certain aspects of [her father's] character, as well as of her mother and herself." Her father, prototype for Hillary Templeton, and her grandmother Rachel Boak, prototype for the title character, were dead. However, her mother and siblings were still alive as she wrote and revised the story, which is set in a house closely modeled on her childhood home in Red Cloud. The family conflicts at the story's center thus needed careful and delicate handling. Lewis had met the originals of the characters and knew the Cather family dynamics, but she had more distance from them than did Willa. In muting or deleting some of the characters' harsh judgments of each other, Lewis ensured that Cather's family would not take offense. She also furthered Cather's aesthetic aims by making the characters more sympathetic and by leaving room for readers to imagine what was not said. What Lewis carved out became, as Cather wrote in "The Novel Démeublé," what "is felt upon the page without being specifically named there . . . the inexplicable presence of the thing not named . . . the over-tone divined by the ear but not heard by it."[46]

Victoria Templeton, a transplanted southern gentlewoman modeled on Virginia Cather, sometimes seems imperious and self-centered. "The best of everything that went on the table [in the Templeton house] was her natural tribute," Cather typed. "There wasn't much, to be sure, but what there was was Victoria's." Editing Cather's typed draft, Lewis softened this characterization by lining through the second sentence with a pencil. Later, Cather describes a rare moment of privacy in the passageway between the kitchen and another room that serves as Grandmother Harris's bedroom: "But now that the children were upstairs and Victoria eating sweets somewhere, she could be sure of enough privacy to undress." The narrator had already explained that Victoria had persuaded her husband to take her to the ice cream parlor, making "eating sweets somewhere" vague and gratuitous. Lewis lined the phrase out and substituted "away." Lewis made a particularly important change to the moment late in the story when Mrs. Harris realizes she is dying. Cather first described Mrs. Harris's relief that her son-in-law is away from home as follows:

> Appearance had to be kept up when there was a man in the house; and he might have taken it into his head to send for the doctor. No words could tell the dread she had of lying on this lounge and being beholden to a family where she always paid her way. And that was not to be. The Lord would take her, and she need ask nothing of anybody. <u>The Lord is my shepherd</u>, she whispered gratefully.

Lewis drew a pencil line through the three sentences that begin "No words" and end before the quotation from the Twenty-Third Psalm. She then added a clause to the first sentence about what would have happened if Hillary Templeton had called the doctor ("and stirred everybody up") and finally crafted a brief, less judgmental reflection for Grandmother Harris before she murmurs the Bible verse aloud: "Now everything would be peaceful."[47]

In a decade of sporadic Grand Manan visits, Cather had become adept at managing the intricacies of mailing. Even though she herself first typed this long story more than once, she followed her usual course and sent the second marked-up typed draft to New York City to her secretary, Sarah Bloom, to be retyped. Cather reported exultantly to Alfred Knopf on July 31 that she had "finished the longest of the three stories I mean for the next volume, and have sent it down to my secretary to be typed. It will run about 23,000 words."[48]

Cather then moved on quickly to "Two Friends," producing two copies (a ribbon and carbon copy) from a single typing. Both Cather and Lewis worked over the ribbon copy multiple times, handing it back and forth and making and sometimes erasing changes. Yet again, Cather based the story on childhood memories, this time of a friendship between two businessmen in Red Cloud that was disrupted by political differences during the presidential election of 1896 (one supports the candidacy of William Jennings Bryan, while the other favors William McKinley). The story also reflects more broadly on the nature of memory and, in particular, the function of memories of childhood.

Cather's first typed draft of "Two Friends" was cleaner and more coherent than her second typed version of the longer "Old Mrs. Harris," and yet she struggled with the opening paragraph (Figure 5.3), typing alternative

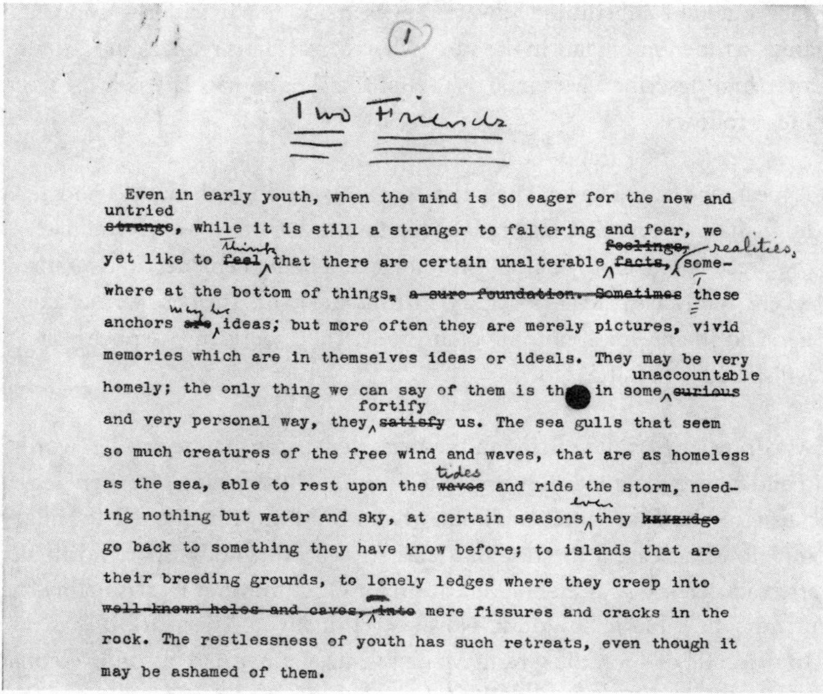

Figure 5.3   The opening paragraph of "Two Friends," typed and edited in pen by Willa Cather and edited in pencil by Edith Lewis. Because it was the setting copy for *Obscure Destinies,* Knopf copy editor and typesetter markings are also visible. Courtesy Archives and Special Collections, University of Nebraska–Lincoln Libraries.

word choices above the main line of the text as she tried to juggle a series of metaphors. And although the story is set in Singleton, Kansas (a thinly disguised Red Cloud), the images in her opening paragraph came from the rocky North Atlantic coastline she saw out her attic window:

> Even in youth, when the mind is so eager for the new and strange [or untried], while it is still a stranger to faltering and fear, we yet like to feel that there are certain unalterable facts [or feelings] somewhere at the bottom of things, a sure foundation. Sometimes, these anchors are ideas, but more often they are merely pictures, vivid memories which are in themselves ideas or ideals. They may be very homely; the only thing we can say of them is that in some curious [or unaccountable] and very personal way, they

satisfy [or fortify]. The sea gulls that seem so much creatures of the free wind and waves, that are as homeless as the sea, able to rest upon the wave and ride the storm, needing nothing but water and sky, at certain seasons they go back to something they have known before; to islands that are their breeding grounds, to lonely ledges where they creep into well-known holes and caves, into mere fissures and cracks in the rock.

First, Cather marked a few changes in the opening paragraph in pen, choosing between most of the alternatives ("feelings" over "facts," "unaccountable" over "curious," "fortify" over "satisfy") and tweaking a few other words. Next, Lewis took up her pencil—perhaps she sat out on their lawn overlooking Whale Cove—and made more changes, adjusting and compacting the final metaphor so that the seagulls rode the famous tides of Grand Manan instead of riding on waves and crept directly "into mere fissures and cracks in the rock." Together, Cather and Lewis also meticulously edited every detail of characterization of the title characters, R. E. Dillon (based on Charles Miner) and J. H. Trueman (based on William N. Richardson).[49]

The typed draft, elaborately marked in pen and pencil by both Cather and Lewis, had to be retyped before they could tackle it again. Cather thus transferred all of the edits (both her own and Lewis's) onto the carbon copy to preserve their hard work and then mailed the marked-up ribbon copy to Sarah Bloom on August 18, asking her to return her "rugged copy" with the freshly typed ribbon copy and two carbon copies. While Cather and Lewis waited for "Two Friends" to return, they set to work on Bloom's fresh typing of "Old Mrs. Harris," which had already arrived on Grand Manan. On August 24, Cather wrote the managing editor of the *Yale Review*, Helen McAfee (Lewis's Smith classmate and fellow Phi Kappa Psi member), "Edith and I have had a glorious summer up here, doing new things to our little house and taking long tramps. I've managed, among other things, to do a story I've wanted to try my hand at for a long time." Meanwhile, Bloom turned "Two Friends" around quickly, mailing it from New York to Grand Manan on August 23.[50]

In the final week of August, Cather and Lewis had their work cut out for them as they continued to polish the two stories before Cather would allow them to be circulated to magazine editors. Lewis continued her careful work muting the title character's thoughts in "Old Mrs. Harris." Late in the story, when the narrator discloses the family's backstory in Tennessee before they move to Skyline, Colorado (another thinly disguised Red Cloud), Lewis muted Mrs. Harris's emotional response to her change of status when her daughter married. "She accepted this estate unprotestingly, gratefully, as the tired apple orchards accept winter," Cather had typed. Lewis inserted "almost" before "gratefully" and lined out the metaphor.[51]

Primed by Manley Aaron (Alfred Knopf's secretary, who was handling magazine placement of the stories), Graeme Lorimer at the *Ladies Home Journal* was eager to read "Old Mrs. Harris," and on August 30, Cather promised Alfred Knopf that she would send him both stories within the week. On September 3, she mailed "Two Friends" and "Old Mrs. Harris" to New York, asking Alfred and Blanche Knopf to read them before Aaron finalized negotiations with magazine editors. "You must be having a heavenly time at Grand Manan," Blanche Knopf replied on September 10, praising the results of her work on the island and calling "Old Mrs. Harris" "one of the great short stories of all time."[52]

By the time Blanche Knopf wrote this letter, Cather and Lewis's "heavenly time" had been over for more than a week. On August 27, Cather sank into a deep depression that she could not "shake off" in the ensuing days. In the early morning hours of Monday, August 31, she had "a very vivid dream" about her mother in which she and her mother were "gathering violets . . . on a certain hillside [in Virginia] where we did use to gather them when [she] was very little." After a "sharp wakening" from her dream, at 4 a.m. Cather crossed the cottage from her own bedroom to Lewis's to waken her, saying, "Edith, I am terrified about mother." Six hours later, the first telegram about Virginia Cather's death arrived, a coincidence that Lewis "thought . . . so strange." When writing to her sister Elsie about the experience, Willa conceded that the time difference between California, where her mother died, and Grand Manan meant that "Mother had been gone some hours before I had that dream." Nevertheless, she wrote, "the dream was one of the most intense and disturbing things that ever happened to me." Just as traumatic, of course, was the loss of her mother, even if Virginia Cather had told her several times when Willa last visited her that she wanted to die.[53]

Cather's letter to Alfred Knopf reporting her mother's death crossed in the mail with his letter congratulating her on "Old Mrs. Harris." "The telegram reached me the next morning . . . several hours after the boat had left for St. Andrews," she explained. "As there was no boat out until Wednesday, I could not possibly have got to Red Cloud in time for the services." She had thus decided to stay on and keep working. However, she "muddled everything [she] touched," including sending "the unrevised copy of 'Mrs. Harris' instead of the corrected copy." She and Manley Aaron soon exchanged copies so that Aaron had the most recent version of "Old Mrs. Harris" she and Lewis had edited to share with magazine editors.[54]

In late August and early September, perhaps even in the days between the day that she received word of her mother's death and the day she sent the stories to New York, Cather and Lewis began editing Sarah Bloom's fresh typing of "Two Friends." The news of her mother's death certainly would have turned Cather's mind to her childhood in Red Cloud, but she could not travel to meet her mother's body there. Instead, she was perching on a rocky ledge overlooking the Atlantic trying to finish work on her story. Even though "Two Friends" does not depict her mother, it was still set in Red Cloud during Cather's childhood. Although both Cather and Lewis had edited the earlier typed draft of the story, Lewis did almost all of the editing of this second version (Figure 5.4), sparing Cather the pain of rereading her own depiction of a time and place when her mother was still alive.

Lewis left the first sentence of the introductory paragraph stand as she and Cather had revised it, but she worked over and pared down the rest. Cather had vacillated confusingly between describing the anchoring memories of childhood as "ideas" and "ideals" or "pictures," writing, "These anchors may be ideas; but more often they are merely pictures, vivid memories, which are themselves ideas or ideals. They may be very homely; the only thing we can say of them is that in some unaccountable and very personal way they fortify us." Carefully lining out phrases and inserting new connecting words, Lewis eliminated the confusion, making the sentences read, "These anchors may be ideas; but more often they are merely pictures, vivid memories, which in some unaccountable and very personal way give us courage." Lewis had previously worked over Cather's seagull metaphor for how our minds return to scenes from childhood so that it read, "at certain seasons even they go back to something they have known before; to islands that are their breeding grounds, to lonely ledges where they creep into mere fissures and cracks in the rock. The restlessness of youth has such retreats, even though it may be ashamed of them." Lewis further compacted and adjusted this language so that "at certain seasons even they go back to something they have known before; to remote islands and lonely ledges that are their breeding-grounds."[55]

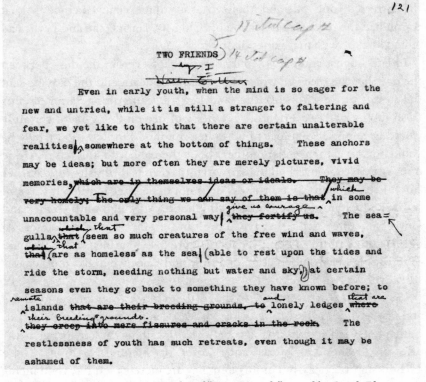

Figure 5.4 The opening paragraphs of "Two Friends" typed by Sarah Bloom and edited by Edith Lewis. Courtesy Archives and Special Collections, University of Nebraska–Lincoln Libraries.

When "Two Friends" appeared in *Obscure Destinies* in 1932 with "Neighbour Rosicky" and "Old Mrs. Harris," Cather inscribed a copy to "Edith Lewis, To whom especially belongs the story of 'Three Friends.'" Why Cather wrote "Three Friends" rather than "Two Friends" is a mystery, but her inscription expressed her gratitude to Lewis, who, in late August and early September 1931, took charge of "Two Friends" and gave Cather space to grieve her mother's death. The intensely autobiographical nature of Cather's *Obscure Destinies* stories should not obscure their resonance for Lewis as well, however. R. E. Dillon of "Two Friends" shares much with Henry Lewis during his Nebraska years: he was a banker, owned a ranch, and was an intensely partisan Democrat and personal friend of William Jennings Bryan.

Something of the strain of Lewis's relationship with her mother in the 1920s perhaps also found its way into Cather's imagination as she wrote "Old Mrs. Harris." Lillie Lewis had fallen far from her days as a Lincoln clubwoman, and although Lillie was sympathetic to Edith's demanding work life and consistently deferential to the woman she always called "Miss Cather," Lillie's letters to Edith were full of grievances against her daughter Helen's husband and her son Harold's wife. She was not a long-suffering grandmother, like the title character of "Old Mrs. Harris," but the intergenerational tensions of the story resonate with those in the Lewis family.[56]

An Island Haven for Aging Orphans and Their Families: The 1930s on Grand Manan

By September 1931, Cather and Lewis were both middle-aged orphans and still homeless in New York City: they could access their parents only through memory. They finally settled into an apartment at 570 Park Avenue in late 1932, but whenever they could they visited Grand Manan for two months or more. Lewis, who had long enjoyed sketching as an avocation, was painting in water color when they were on the island (Figure 5.5). Albert Bierstadt and his nineteenth-century contemporaries had painted dramatic Grand Manan scenes in oil, but Lewis produced watercolor sketches. She had company among the Whale Cove women: Catherine Schwartz and Sally Frankenstein (Elsie Cather's 1912 Smith College classmate, who managed the inn for Jacobus in the summer of 1931) also painted Grand Manan scenes in watercolor. Lewis also enjoyed having time to write long letters to family and friends. To Earl and Achsah Brewster she wrote stories about island life and painted the place in word pictures. In 1932, Achsah wished that she would come visit them in Europe again, but she was comforted by the thought that Lewis "would be in New Brunswick, dabbling in the dew and wrapped in morning mist" with "whales spout[ing] in [her] front yard" like "domestic pet[s]" or "garden ornament[s]" (whales sometimes swam into the cove and spouted—and thus the name Whale Cove). In 1933, Earl similarly wrote, "If you are not with us I like to think of you at Whale Cove. I wonder if you will paint again this summer, and if so, what will you paint and how you will do it? I would like to know about your painting in greater detail, and best of all to see it."[57]

Figure 5.5 A watercolor sketch by Edith Lewis of her and Willa Cather's Grand Manan cottage. OBJ-50-1000-15, Betty Kort Collection, Willa Cather Foundation Collections and Archives at the National Willa Cather Center, Red Cloud, Nebraska.

As older children in dispersed families, Cather and Lewis embraced their new roles as heads of family and invited family members to join them at Grand Manan. Improvements in transportation to the island made these visits more feasible. The Grand Manan II car ferry service, inaugurated in 1930, served Eastport in Maine and St. John, St. Stephen, and St. Andrews in New Brunswick; a new bridge also made Eastport (the easternmost point of the United States) accessible by rail. In July and August 1933, two thousand people took the ferry to the Grand Manan. Cather and Lewis did not invite anyone to stay with them in their cottage, however. As Cather confessed to Alfred Knopf, "When we built we made a special point of having no guest room, no room which could be made into one!" The cottage remained their private space for most of the day, and they paid for their guests to lodge at the inn or cottages nearby.[58]

In 1932, Cather's niece Mary Virginia Auld was their first guest. A Red Cloud native and daughter of Willa's sister Jessica, Mary Virginia found work at the New York Public Library shortly after graduating from Smith College in 1929. After completing the internal library training course, she was assigned to the Tremont Branch in the Bronx. Mary Virginia probably knew some of the other women at Whale Cove who, like herself, worked at the NYPL, making her a natural fit for the little community. "I've never enjoyed the weather and woods and my little house so much as this year," Cather wrote Blanche Knopf in July 1932. "Happiness always makes me lazy, and I've done very little but enjoy things. My little niece is with me for a month, and she always makes me gay. I've been practising cookery as a fine art now and then, as I like very special dishes with special wines." National prohibition had been instituted in the U.S., making Canada even more attractive for Cather and Lewis as wine lovers. Perhaps inspired by the presence of her young niece, Cather had, as she reported to Knopf, "begun a new book, just as an experiment; if my interest grows, I'll go on with it. If it bores me, I'll drop it. It's about a young thing, this time. If I finish it, I'll call it simply by her name, 'Lucy Gayheart.' " Lewis, who was writing advertising copy for the Eastman Kodak account in the 1930s, took up the company's technology, using it like an ordinary consumer to take snapshots of the cliffs, their cottage, Mary Virginia, and Cather. A hatless Mary Virginia wears pants, but her middle-aged aunt wears a skirt, a cardigan, and a hat (Figure 5.6). Because library work did not pay well and because Mary Virginia's parents had recently divorced, her aunt felt keenly her need for a proper vacation, and she invited her niece to return the next year. "Mary Virginia arrived yesterday to spend her vacation here," she wrote Roscoe and Meta Cather in July 1933. "She really had nowhere else to go, poor child." She also wished that Roscoe and Meta's daughter Virginia, just graduated from Smith, "was here too, for we have awfully good times. The weather is glorious and the whole island so sweet and flowery."[59]

Even though Cather complained to Zoë Akins that she was "losing patience" with the heroine of *Lucy Gayheart* because she was "a very silly young girl," Cather and Lewis were not too old to share their pleasure in the island with girls and women from their families. In 1933, Edith Lewis's sister Ruth took advantage of the new car ferry service to travel to the island, bringing nieces Elizabeth and Ruth, daughters of their brother Harold. Like Mary Virginia, Ruth was a natural fit for the Whale Cove community: she was still teaching gym and coaching basketball at a girls high school in Brooklyn (she had left Brooklyn Heights Seminary to become director of athletics at Shore Road Academy in Bay Ridge).[60]

Figure 5.6 Willa Cather and her niece Mary Virginia Auld at Grand Manan in 1932 or 1933; photograph by Edith Lewis. Courtesy Archives and Special Collections, University of Nebraska–Lincoln Libraries.

In 1934, Willa Cather encouraged her sister Elsie, a 1912 Smith College graduate and high school English and Latin teacher in Lincoln, Nebraska, to visit Grand Manan. Elsie was planning to drive from Nebraska to New England with a friend. "If you are going into Maine," Willa wrote her, "you must certainly come on and visit me at Grand Manan. It is ever so much more different from the West than New England is, simply because it <u>is</u> an island. Real islands that set far off from shore have a character all their own." Noting the lack of a guest room "in our little house," she offered "to put you and your friend up at Miss Jacobus' little colony where we go for our meals." Warning her that she herself would be "busy finishing up my book" (*Lucy Gayheart*), she nevertheless promised "nice walks together" and assured her, "Edith and I would love to have you." Elsie was not able to make the trip—as was often the case, the burden of caring for aging family members in Nebraska fell on her. "I thought you were going to have a nice trip," Cather wrote her after she learned that Elsie would be spending her summer in Red Cloud caring for their Aunt Bess, who was dying of cancer, "and I believed you would really enjoy Grand Manan."[61]

In 1938, Lewis extended an invitation to visit Grand Manan to Rudolph Ruzicka, who might have been an awkward fit for the Whale Cove community. Ruzicka was planning to travel to Canada while his wife, Filomena, and their children were visiting family in Europe, and Lewis urged him to add Grand Manan to his itinerary. "I would get you a room at the Marathon Hotel" in North Head, she wrote him, "as Whale Cove Cottage, where we go for our meals, is entirely filled with elderly ladies, mostly single, and nearly all either librarians or social workers, and I feel they would depress you, even if you could get in. But I hope you could have your dinners there with us, and afternoon tea at our place." Although Lewis wanted to take him on cliff walks and felt he "would find it an interesting experience different from anything you have known," his visit did not come off, sparing all concerned any possible awkwardness in the Whale Cove Inn dining room, where Ruzicka would have been the odd man out. Lewis nevertheless regretted that he missed the "glorious" weather that August. "I have often wished," she continued, "as I walk along the cliffs, that you could see how beautiful it is here. We become more and more reluctant to leave every day, and keep trying to plan ways in which we can manage to stay on" after the dining room closed for the season.[62]

Two long visits by Cather's twin nieces Margaret and Elizabeth (daughters of Roscoe and Meta Cather) are the most richly documented and testify to Cather and Lewis's thorough integration into Whale Cove's woman-centered community. Willa had been fascinated by her Wyoming-born and -bred twin nieces since they were babies. In 1931, she had hoped to get the twins, who were then in high school, to Grand Manan but the visit did not come off. After graduating from high school, Margaret and Elizabeth enrolled at the University of Colorado, and in 1936, they planned to attend a Delta Gamma sorority convention in Lake Placid, their farthest trip away from Wyoming since their family had joined Cather and Lewis in Santa Fe in 1926. In March

1936, Willa started consulting with Roscoe about extending their Lake Placid trip to Grand Manan, concluding her letter, "Edith Lewis is a Delta Gamma, and greets her 'sisters in the Bonds.' "[63]

Planning cross-country and international travel for green nineteen-year-old girls from Wyoming was challenging. As Willa wrote Elsie, "[I]t is very expensive to move twins through Canada and back to Detroit!" She assured Roscoe that "while they are on the Island, they would be my guests and would be at no expense," and she would "put them up not far from my cottage at a small camp where I put up Mary Virginia during the two summers when she spent her vacations as my guest." She was worried, however, about the twins not dressing appropriately. "The important thing, my dear brother, is clothes! The sort of frippery they need for Lake Placid won't do. They must bring warm sport clothes" and proper shoes because women who had attempted walking the cliffs in high heel shoes suffered "terrible accidents." Even though she had not seen the twins since 1926, when they were still little girls, she felt confident about their spirit of adventure and desire to embrace outdoor recreation: "If the twins are anything like they used to be when I knew them, I think they would get a great thrill out of that island. I always long for it myself when I am in the most 'scenic' places of Europe."[64]

In July, Margaret and Elizabeth took the train from Lake Placid into Canada and the ferry from St. John's to the island. Cather and Lewis greeted them at North Head with the local taxi and rode with them and their luggage the short distance to Whale Cove. Sarah Jacobus accommodated these able young women in the primitive loft of an old barn. Every morning, the twins met Cather and Lewis in the dining room, and after breakfast the four walked together to Cather and Lewis's cottage, where the marked trails along the cliff tops began. The middle-aged women took many supplies on hikes—small blankets, umbrellas, scarves, chocolate, and soda crackers—but the teenaged twins took nothing. "Aunt Willa knew every turn and tree," Margaret recalled; "many of the places she and Miss Lewis had named, often using names or phrases from 'Alice in Wonderland.' " They often stopped to rest at "Wendy's House," a beech tree, and they walked through "The Tangly Wood." A worn, mounded sea bluff they called "The Giants' Graves." The four returned to the inn for lunch, but afterward Cather and Lewis retreated to their cottage and left the twins to their own devices for three or four hours. Margaret and Elizabeth thought the middle-aged women napped all afternoon, but early work on Cather's last published novel, *Sapphira and the Slave Girl* (1940), was under way.[65]

At four o'clock, the twins joined Cather and Lewis in their cottage for tea, at which they served sherry and told stories about their travels and their friends. Cather also read aloud from Shakespeare, British and American poets, and Sir Walter Scott. In 1936, Lewis was reading intensively about nineteenth-century Arctic exploration, following recommendations from twentieth-century Arctic explorer Vilhjalmur Stefansson, whom Cather and Lewis had invited to dinner that February. Perhaps Lewis relayed stories from her reading, which would have suited the isolated, misty North Atlantic island.[66]

The twins enjoyed meeting the other summer residents and guests in the dining room and were especially impressed to meet Winifred Bromhall, whose books they had read as children. A few times during both summers the twins visited, Cather and Lewis had them to their cottage for dinner. By candlelight, they ate chicken fried in butter (prepared by Alice Beal) and salad with French dressing (prepared by their aunt) and drank good French wine shipped from the mainland. Cather and Lewis also hired a car to drive the four of them to Southern Head, where they picnicked on the dramatic rocky cliffs overlooking the ocean. The long drive down the island's east coast, Margaret recalled, took them past "several very small fishing villages," while at their destination, "[i]t was nothing but beautiful scenery, cliffs, wild flowers, and ocean (or the Bay of Fundy) stretching out ahead of us."[67]

The twins brought a camera to document their visit and share it with their family back in Wyoming. Taking photographs of their Aunt Willie tending her prized hollyhocks, they inadvertently captured her and Lewis together (Figure 5.7). In the first, distant photo, Cather, wearing a skirt, cardigan, and hat, looked toward the camera as she gestured at the flowers, but tall wild grass and the photographer's finger partially obstructed the lower-right-hand corner of the image. For the second snapshot, the photographer had moved closer, and Cather, who was no longer obstructed, looked down as she pruned the plant. A behatted Lewis had entered the frame on the right. Standing with her arms akimbo to Cather's left and with her torso oriented toward her, she turned her gaze in the direction of the photographer and smiled broadly. In this accidental photo, one of only two extant of Cather and Lewis together, the photographer's thumb obstructed Lewis from the waist down, so it is not clear whether she was wearing a skirt or pants.

Cather thought the twins' visit a great success, reporting to Zoë Akins that her nieces "have never seen the ocean before—never been east of Omaha! This place makes them fairly dizzy with delight." To the twins themselves she

Figure 5.7 Two photographs of Willa Cather tending to her hollyhocks taken by either Margaret or Elizabeth Cather in 1936 or 1937 on Grand Manan. Edith Lewis also appears in the photograph on the right (only one of two known photos of her and Cather together). Courtesy Archives and Special Collections, University of Nebraska–Lincoln Libraries.

wrote of the flowers around the cottage and the wonderful "blue and gold" weather every day. She also wrote of the people who missed the girls from Wyoming. "We both miss you very much and often wish you were here," she wrote of herself and Lewis. "On Friday Miss Bromhall came for tea. She and Miss Jordan and Miss Gissing and many others wish to be remembered to you." Obliquely acknowledging the absence of married women at Whale Cove, she continued, "You must both come here again, my dears, before you do any desperate thing like getting married."[68]

Released from their obligations as hosts, Cather and Lewis had moved on to pressing work, reading the proofs for *Not Under Forty*. Even though Cather and the Knopf offices had become adept at the intricacies of mailing back and forth to Grand Manan, the manufacturing department made a serious error, sending the proofs of Cather's collection of essay "express" and assigning a value of $500. Because there was no express office on Grand Manan, they were held up at Eastport before being sent to Campobello Island too late for the weekly steamer. Once they reached Grand Manan, the valuation further held them up. "Alfred had asked me to read them promptly," Cather wrote to Blanche Knopf, "and they were two weeks on the way!"[69]

The twins' visit was so successful that Cather wanted to bring them back after their college graduation the next summer. "There is just a chance," she wrote them in May 1937, "that Edith and I may go to Grand Manan this summer" because the coronation in England was making their plan to travel there impossible. She urged Margaret and Elizabeth to read Canadian history, including Parkman, to prepare for their return. From mid-July to mid-August 1937, the twins repeated the pleasures of their first visit. However, the stresses of island living, which later caused Cather and Lewis to abandon their cottage, emerged as well. When a spider bit Cather on her right hand, she needed medical treatment, and even after the bandages were removed her hand felt "stiff and awkward," making it difficult to write.[70]

After the twins left, Cather reported the Grand Manan news to them: Willie Thomas was injured in an ax accident, Ralph Beal made an epic journey to Eastport with the autographed limit pages for the collected edition of her works that Houghton Mifflin was publishing, and Margaret Bonnell's plan to spend a day at the Gannet Rock Lighthouse, which Margaret and Elizabeth had visited, was foiled by laughable notions of sexual propriety. "Yesterday Miss Bonnell telephoned . . . the keeper," Cather explained, "to ask if she might come to spend night first fair day. Keeper replied his wife away on visit for two weeks, and he was afraid Government Inspectors would not approve Bonnell's visit! These are the actual facts. She had engaged a motor boat."[71]

The "Perplexing and Inconvenient" Life on an Island

Soon, there were no more girlish nieces to attend to spider bites, and Grand Manan became more challenging for Cather and Lewis, and especially for the older Cather. The twins sent them snapshots from their second—and last—Grand Manan visit. "We love the snapshots," Cather wrote them, "especially Gannet and your barn." Lewis had taken a Kodak movie camera and color film to the island in 1937, and Willa wrote to Margaret and Elizabeth, "I must tell you how splendidly the moving pictures that Edith took at Grand Manan came out." They had no projector but viewed the film in a Manhattan Kodak shop with Yaltah and Hephzibah Menuhin. "They were perfectly splendid of you, and even of me!" she enthused, "[a]nd the woods and water were grand." While the twins were on the island, their parents moved to Colusa, California, where their father would become president of a bank (brothers Douglass and Jim were already in California). Cather suggested she might send the film to Colusa so the twins could "show your father and mother just what Grand Manan is like." Their 1937 visit was the last time Cather and Lewis hosted guests on the island. Margaret and Elizabeth soon stopped being their aunt's "darling twinnies"—they both married in 1938 (Cather and Lewis jointly sent them wedding gifts), and soon they had children of their own.[72]

The same year the twins married, Douglass Cather died of a heart attack. Willa wrote to her sister Elsie from New York in early July, "We are hoping to get off to Grand Manan next week. If I can get to working for two hours every morning, [it] will pull me together more than anything else could, even if the work is not very good. But here, I sleep badly and I can do little toward preparing to go away." After they were settled in at Whale Cove in August, Lewis responded to a letter from Harwood Brewster Picard about the death of Harwood's uncle Joe Derby (husband of Achsah Brewster's sister Lola—Lewis had also heard about the death through the third Barlow sister, Alpha). "Just a few weeks before we came up here," Lewis explained to Harwood,

> Willa's favorite brother died of the same kind of heart attack. . . . His death has been a great grief to Willa, she cannot become reconciled to it. The shock, when she first heard of it, was so great that I was much worried before we left New York. But the peace and beauty of Grand Manan have done her worlds of good, and she is a different person, after a few weeks in the cool tranquil place, where for hours at a time the only sound is the wind in the spruce trees, and the calling of the sea gulls.

Willa herself wrote to Roscoe that she had experienced nausea and vomiting from June 14 "until I got away to Grand Manan where Douglass had never been." By early September, Grand Manan had begun to restore Willa's broken spirit. "It is already autumn here, and the weather is glorious," she wrote Alfred Knopf. "I feel more interest in things every day now, and long walks in the salt air make me feel a pleasant relaxation in all one's nerves." Lewis reported on Cather's recovery to the Brewsters, then living in the Himalayan mountain region of India. "It is good to learn that you have had a restful tranquil summer—you and Willa—at Grand Manan," Earl Brewster wrote (some medical condition—perhaps a stroke—had left Achsah unable to write). Earl marveled yet again at "what a delightful place" Lewis made the island sound. "We are indeed very sorry that Willa had to suffer the loss of her brother. We miss the sea here. . . . But how wonderful the ocean must be at Grand Manan."[73]

In 1939, Cather and Lewis almost didn't go to Grand Manan. As Willa reported to Roscoe in mid-July, their well needed redrilling "and both Miss Lewis and I feel too tired to have workmen and machinery brought forty-five miles by boat from the mainland, at an expense of $500, including gasoline engine, etc. etc." Before she had sent the letter, however, she added a postscript: "We have decided to go to Grand Manan after all. I can't work when wandering about." They arrived the first week of August. At the end of the month, Lewis described in her journal "a glorious day, with a touch of Fall in the air. The flowers are beautiful in spite of more than 6 weeks of drouth. . . . Weather for past two weeks warm and foggy most of the time. An airplane flew over the cottage this morning." Elizabeth Cather Ickis had had her first child, and her Aunt Willa took "the baby's picture to Grand Manan to show it to Elizabeth's many friends there." Cather later reported to the twins that "[e]veryone here was keen to hear about the baby, Elizabeth, and to see the little picture you sent." Margaret was living in Boston while her husband, Richard Shannon, was earning an M.B.A. at Harvard. Cather gently scolded, "[Y]ou must, please, go to see Alice Jordan at the Public Library. She feels a little sad that you didn't drop in to see her last winter. I told her you were 'shy,' but that's a lame excuse."[74]

Cather and Lewis's stay on the island in 1939 was a mixture of pleasure and pain. Cather got another spider bite, this time on her left hand "with the same results as before," as she wrote Margaret and Elizabeth, and then a few days later a black fly bit her eyelid. "And I came up here to work!!" she lamented. She nevertheless enjoyed the "lovely" weather and "rather enjoyed lying in a steamer chair and putting on wet dressings." Lewis reported to the Brewsters that the crisis with their water supply had been averted. "How splendid that the bottom did not drop out of your well but that it is now a more plenteous giver of water than before," wrote Earl. Despite this happy circumstance, their cottage was "threatened by rats." Achsah wrote of their 1939 stay, "You and Job both have my sympathy."[75]

The presence of Dr. John Macaulay, a McGill-educated physician who married a fellow student and moved with her to her native island, reassured Cather. He had made a house call when the spider bit her, and a New York

City specialist later checked the bite and proclaimed that nothing was concerning. Shortly after she reported this result to Macaulay, he died suddenly of a heart attack. "It always seemed strange to me to find such a man on that little island," she wrote his widow. "Yet when he and you together told me one day how you happened to go there, and when I saw what a happy life you had lived there, I thought he had made a wise choice. I do not know any New York physician whose career I would have preferred to his. Only a fine life in the open air could have made so fine a man and so resourceful and skillful a physician."[76]

Two other tragedies affecting island locals associated with Whale Cove soon followed: Ralph Beal's son committed suicide and Willie Thomas's house burned down. Lewis wrote Sarah Jacobus when she sent $50 to help rebuild Thomas's house ($25 from herself and $25 from Cather):

> I can't tell you how grieved Miss Cather and I are at Dr. Macaulay's death—
> it seems simply unbelievable, and I cannot make myself realize that it is
> true. I feel it as a great personal loss, and I know hundreds and hundreds of
> other people must have the same feeling that I do. That splendid man. No
> one can take his place. He was one of the finest people and led one of the
> finest lives I have ever known. I feel so terribly sad to think of all the trage-
> dies coming, one after another, to Grand Manan.

"We enjoyed the time we had up there so much, in spite of accidents," Lewis wrote hastily on her first day back at work, and closed by thanking Jacobus "for all of your kindness to us this summer."[77]

Cather wrote Alfred Knopf in late August 1940, after she and Lewis had been on Grand Manan several weeks, "Living on an island was never so perplexing and inconvenient as it has been this summer." They delayed their departure for Grand Manan until Cather could give Knopf a nearly complete edited typescript of Sapphira and the Slave Girl to begin production. Cather finished the last chapter on Grand Manan, but Sarah Bloom was not available to retype it until her return from her own vacation. As Willa explained to Roscoe after her return to New York, she had also had a "severe toothache nearly all the while I was up" at Grand Manan but hadn't wanted to lose a week's writing time to a round trip on the "queer boat service" to consult a dentist in St. John's.[78]

During their 1940 visit and on their return to New York City, Cather and Lewis did not know that they would never return to the island. In an unwitting valedictory to their Grand Manan summers, Cather arranged a November 1940 luncheon at Sherry's in New York for three of her nieces, Margaret Cather Shannon, Virginia Cather Brockway (Margaret's older sister), and Mary Virginia Auld Mellen. All of them were married and living in the New York area, and two of them (Mary Virginia and Margaret) had visited Grand Manan. "After a long and very conversational luncheon," Willa reported to Roscoe, "we went to see the colored moving pictures, which Edith took of the twins at Grand Manan, thrown on a Kodak screen. Not one of the three nieces had seen these before. The pictures really are beautiful and do justice to the splendid cliffs and blue sea."[79]

In the summer of 1941, Cather and Lewis traveled to San Francisco to spend time with Roscoe and Meta Cather while her brother was consulting a heart specialist there, and in 1942, Willa's gallbladder surgery left her too weak to travel (these events are described in the next chapter). As Cather was convalescing in 1942, she received a letter from Mary Jordan that produced a "happy dream about the Grand Manan pasture and the strip of shore spruce wood you bought several years ago." Advising Mary "never to part with your gall bladder if you can," she complained of the hot and steamy weather in the city: "Miss Lewis and I would give a lot for one hour of that West Wind that always blows over the Island at this season!" Sending greetings from "us both" to Mary and her sister Alice, she closed, "The best luck we can pray for is to be your neighbors on the island next summer."[80]

In 1943, Cather first reported that the wartime food situation was "so bad" they could not possibly go to Grand Manan, but in July a doctor ordered Cather away from the New York heat. She wrote her niece Margaret in early July from Portland, Maine, "Edith is with me, and she may go on from here to Grand Manan." In late July, she wrote to Alfred Knopf that the Asticou Inn in Northeast Harbor was "not nearly so interesting as Grand Manan" but more conventionally comfortable than their home on the island and better supplied with food. Lewis would be going to Grand Manan "to look after some repairs that are to be made on her cottage there" while Cather remained at the Asticou. Their plan soon changed, however. A few days later she wrote Margaret, "I am bored to death and we start for Grand Manan on Tuesday— by the roughest and hardest way, too!" (taking a train up to St. Stephen and waiting two days for the boat). She regretted that she would not be greeted at the end of her "hard trip" by "happy little nieces I found there long ago." But the lack of a dentist on Grand Manan would yet again prove a problem. Two days later, she wrote Margaret explaining the trip was off because "[t]wo teeth which Edith had crowned in May have cropped up with a nasty ache in this damp climate." The dentist in Maine told Lewis an abscess could occur at any time, making it "pretty risky to go off to an island." "So it's all off," she concluded, "and we are bitterly, bitterly disappointed. Everything ready up there, the cottage open, and aired for two weeks and kind friends expecting us. Too bad!"[81]

For the increasingly infirm Cather, traveling to the Asticou Inn with Lewis became her only possible escape from the city heat (their final years together in New York and their vacation trips from there to Maine feature in the next chapter). During their second stay at the Asticou Inn, Cather wrote "Before Breakfast," a story set as precisely in and around their Grand Manan cottage as "Old Mrs. Harris" is set in Cather's childhood home in Red Cloud. Henry Grenfell, the central character, wakes up to "the shameless blaze of the sunrise" through his east-facing bedroom window in his cabin, which "modestly squat[s] on a tiny clearing between a tall spruce wood and the sea." Cather and Lewis, however, would never wake up there again, and "Before Breakfast" would not be published until after Cather's death.[82]

6

"We Are the Only Wonderful Things"

The Late Lives and Deaths of Willa Cather and Edith Lewis

In 1936, Willa Cather and Edith Lewis spent two months at their Whale Cove cottage, a period that included a monthlong visit by Cather's twin nieces. They had planned to stay even longer, but when the weather changed "for the worse," the two women started their long journey from Grand Manan on September 14 and were in New York by September 19. Lewis went back to work at her advertising job, but after taking care of some publishing business, Cather repacked her suitcases and headed north again to Jaffrey. On October 4, after she had settled in at the Shattuck Inn, Cather wrote her one currently known letter to Lewis. Addressed to "My darling Edith" and dated "Sunday 4:30 p.m.," it is unlike any other surviving letter:

I am sitting in your room, looking out on the woods you know so well. So far everything delights me. I am ashamed of my appetite for food, and as for sleep—I had forgotten that sleeping can be an active and very strong phys-ical pleasure. It can! It has been for all of three nights. I wake up now and then, saturated with the pleasure of breathing clear mountain air (not cold, just chill air) of being up high with all the woods below me sleeping, too; in still white moonlight. It's a grand feeling.

One hour from now, out of your window, I shall see a sight unparalleled—Jupiter and Venus both shining in the golden-rosy sky and both in the West; she not very far above the horizon, and he about mid-way between the zenith and the silvery lady planet. From 5:30 to 6:30 they are of a superb splendor—deepening in color every second, in a still-daylight-sky guiltless of other stars, the moon not up and the sun gone down behind Gap moun-tain; those two above in the whole vault of heaven. It lasts so about an hour (did last night). Then the Lady, so silvery still, slips down into the clear rose colored glow to be near the departed sun, and imperial Jupiter hangs there alone. He goes down about 8:30. Surely it reminds one of Dante's "eternal wheels." I can't but believe that all that majesty and all that beauty, those fated and unfailing appearances and exits, are something more than mathematics and horrible temperatures. If they are <u>not</u>, then we are the only wonderful things because we can wonder.

I have worn my white silk suit almost constantly with <u>no</u> white hat, which is very awkward. By next week it will probably be colder. Everything you packed carried wonderfully—not a wrinkle.

And now I must dress to receive the Planets, dear, as I won't wish to take the time after they appear—and they will not wait for anybody.

Lovingly W.

I don't know when I have enjoyed Jupiter so much as this summer

Pleasure is at the center of this letter—Cather's pleasure in escaping New York to enjoy a New England autumn, her anticipated pleasure in viewing Jupiter and Venus, and the pleasure she wanted to give Lewis by describing these things. Jupiter and Venus are the brightest planets in the sky. Because Cather was describing an astronomical phenomenon (the annual conjunction of the two planets), she specified the time of her writing, not just the day, but the reference also underscored the pleasure. In Roman myth, Venus was associated with beauty, love, and desire. The year before at the Louvre in Paris, Cather and Lewis had visited the classical galleries, where the famed Venus de Milo was on display—the statue depicts the goddess with a cloth draped low over her hips but with her breasts exposed. Similarly in *The Birth of Venus*, Sandro Botticelli depicted the goddess rising out of the sea on a clamshell, her hands modestly covering her breasts and genitals. The "silvery" sheen of the "lady" planet in Cather's letter evoked Venus's nakedness, and in order to "dress to receive" Venus and Jupiter, Cather had to first undress. Even the practical matters of the clothes and suitcases mentioned later in the letter tied into the erotics of Cather's dressing and undressing. Perhaps she would be taking off that white silk suit? Cather and Lewis occupied separate, adjoining rooms at the Shattuck Inn when they stayed their together (Figure 6.1 is a photograph of the two together in Jaffrey in 1926), but Cather specified that she was writing to her "darling Edith" from her beloved's room. She thus began the letter through Lewis's eyes and then drew her into that room for shared pleasure.[1]

Certainly, my account of Cather and Lewis's life together would be richer with access to more letters like this one. There is an oversized mythology of

Figure 6.1 Edith Lewis (standing) and Willa Cather (seated) on the lawn near the Old Meeting House in Jaffrey, New Hampshire, in the autumn of 1926. Photograph by Mrs. Josiah Wheelwright, from Theodore Jones, "Willa Cather in the Northeast (A Pictorial Biograph), 1917–1947," masters' thesis, University of New Brunswick, 1968. Archives and Special Collections, Harriet Irving Library, University of New Brunswick.

Cather and Lewis burning letters, but there is no evidence they destroyed letters as a regular practice, and more of their correspondence may yet surface. Furthermore, people seldom write letters to someone sitting a few feet away: people write letters to communicate over distance. In 1932, Cather and Lewis finally reestablished a permanent home together in New York by renting a Park Avenue apartment. In the first twenty years of their relationship, they did often spend months apart, but because Cather was facing the physical challenges of aging a decade earlier than Lewis and as Lewis was holding on tight to her advertising job, they were seldom apart in the 1930s and 1940s. The separation that was the precondition for this letter occurred during a rare October when Cather went to Jaffrey alone. More than two decades into their relationship, Cather and Lewis had become "those two," "the only wonderful things" experiencing life together (almost) every day.[2]

In 1934, they had delayed their departure for Grand Manan until Cather could send a final edited typescript of *Lucy Gayheart* to the Knopfs for typesetting. Lewis later remembered that she had been "too severe" with Cather about this short novel and had "never done it justice" while Cather was alive. She apologetically explained to Stephen Tennant, however, that Cather "never minded my being severe. She knew how I really felt." Even though Lewis scoffed at *Lucy*, in 1934 she put in her usual careful effort at polishing and refining Cather's prose. Near the end of the novel, the young eponymous heroine, a pianist who has retreated from Chicago to her Nebraska home-town, hears a performance of Michael William Balfe's popular light opera *The Bohemian Girl* in the local opera house. A declining diva incongruously sings the role of the young heroine, and the diva's performance causes Lucy to have an epiphany: "And yet she sang so well! Lucy wanted to be there on the stage with her, helping her do it." Cather had typed next, "A flood of feeling came up in her that made her chest tight and her throat ache. She wanted to flee away tonight, on wings, back to a world that strove after excellence." Certainly, the image of flight was poetic, but Lucy transits back and forth be-tween Nebraska and Chicago not through the air but on the railroad. Lewis revised Cather's prose so that "A wild kind of excitement flared up" in Lucy, who "felt she must run away tonight, by any train."[3]

In the 1930s, Cather and Lewis continued to take trains, and they crossed the Atlantic together one last time in 1935, but they could not, as Lucy ima-gines she might, travel spontaneously. Transporting Cather's aging and often malfunctioning body required careful planning and Lewis's assistance. Even as they spent more time together, both in New York and elsewhere, they con-tinued to have their own lives, and both experienced painful losses before Cather's death separated the two women permanently and left Lewis alone for twenty-five years before her own death.

Moving up to Park Avenue During the Great Depression

The Great Depression hit the advertising trade hard in the 1930s. Salaries were cut, and even though women were paid substantially less than men, agencies laid off many female copywriters in order to preserve the jobs of men, who were presumed to be in greater need of their jobs because they had to support their wives and children. The J. Walter Thompson agency kept Lewis on, however. Perhaps her habit of taking months of unpaid leave most years was partially responsible: her European travels with Cather kept her on leave for six months in 1930. When she returned to her job at the end of that year, she was overworked in the understaffed office, writing to the Brewsters that she was "a 'captive slave—toiling day and night, and Saturdays, and everything.'"[4]

When Lewis went to Grand Manan with Cather in 1931, she was not sure that she would be called back to work. As she wrote in late September to Howard Kohl, the traffic manager at Thompson, she planned to go from Grand Manan to Jaffrey in mid-October. She also offered to go to New York "at any time," elaborating that she hoped "you will need me before utter starvation sets in." In early October, Helen Resor ordered her return, and Kohl suggested she might "think of two knockout Ladies Home Journal advertisements on [the] way." Alfred Knopf's secretary had just sold Cather's story "Old Mrs. Harris" to the *Journal*, so happenstance put Lewis in the position of promoting the magazine to readers just as Cather's story had been acquired by it.[5]

In early 1932, Stanley Resor proclaimed that the agency needed to get back to basics, so all copywriters went out to knock on doors and talk to consumers. Lewis and two other female copywriters working on the Chase & Sanborn account were sent to New Haven to talk to housewives about the coffee. As Resor reported at a staff meeting, Lewis and her colleagues felt the experience gave them a better understanding of what was at stake in a new advertising campaign for the product. The Resors were also inventing work to keep staff members busy during the downturn. Helen Resor was president of the New York chapter of the Travelers Aid Society, which assisted homeless transients. In early 1932, she tasked Lewis and Edward Steichen with creating a fundraising brochure depicting these efforts: Lewis wrote up the stories of real women who had received aid and Steichen took their photographs. Cather sent a copy of the brochure to her Red Cloud friend Carrie Miner Sherwood, who assumed she was being solicited for a donation. Cather hastened to explain that she was not. Rather "we" (she and Lewis) "thought you would be interested in the splendid photographs. They were all made from real cases—people the Traveler's Aid has helped. I think the old women are lovely."[6]

Cather's response suggests how little the national financial catastrophe affected her and Lewis's lives. Ironically, Cather's literary earnings during the Great Depression reached their highest level. In 1931, *Shadows on the Rock* was a bestseller, and she was handsomely compensated for magazine appearances of the stories collected in *Obscure Destinies* in 1932 for the serialization of *Lucy Gayheart* in 1935. And even though Lewis was on the

Thompson payroll for only part of the year and salaries were down, she was an experienced writer at a top agency, and her rate of pay certainly reflected that. In 1932, the two women could well afford to leave the Grosvenor Hotel in Greenwich Village for a Park Avenue apartment. Five years earlier, when they were leaving Bank Street, Cather suggested that her "next step [would] be to get away from New York altogether," and she continued to grumble about the city during their years at the Grosvenor. However, Lewis made no move to give up her New York–based job, and if Cather wanted to continue to live with Lewis, she had to live in the city. In 1932, both women's parents were dead, so neither Cather nor Lewis was making regular visits to aging or dying parents, and Lewis's job at Thompson was secure. There was, then, no longer any reason to delay renting an apartment.[7]

When Cather and Lewis each moved to Greenwich Village in the first decade of the century, it suited their life stages and their pocketbooks. Before 1913, northbound trains heading out of the city ran above ground in a perilous smoky tunnel occupying the land that later became a broad avenue (Park Avenue). The opening of a new terminal that could serve electric trains made the desirable land east of Central Park available for development. 570 Park Avenue, a sixteen-story Georgian-style building designed by architect Emery Roth, was completed in 1916. Taking a large apartment in this elevator building suited Cather and Lewis as financially secure middle-aged women (although their Greenwich Village landlord had multiplied their rent so many times that their new rent was lower than the Bank Street rent had been when they left). They were next to Central Park, where they enjoyed walking, and the building was just a mile from the Graybar Building, adjacent to Grand Central, where the Thompson agency had relocated in the late 1920s. Lewis's commute to work was a milelong stroll straight down Park Avenue.[8]

Cather explained to Mabel Luhan in late 1932, when they were just settling into the apartment, that Lewis was "desperately busy at the office," leaving most of the tasks associated with moving into the apartment to Cather, who, if she "shop[ped] for more than a few hours at a time" bought "the most absurd things." Apologizing for the fact that Lewis had not written Luhan in so long, Cather complained that "holding an important business job in N.Y. these days means working like fury. I hope she'll resign soon." Lewis showed no willingness to do so, however. Perhaps memories of her family's financial collapse decades earlier and particularly its effects on her mother

served as an object lesson: Lillie Lewis had spent her entire life being financially dependent on others and was embittered by her fall into genteel poverty. Or perhaps Edith Lewis simply enjoyed her work and the sociability of
the office. In any event, she kept working.[9]

Lewis and Cather's new apartment was large. Its eighteen hundred
square feet encompassed three bedrooms (two very large, one small), two
bathrooms, a kitchen, a butler's pantry, a large living room, and a separate
dining room. Familiar objects from Bank Street were unpacked and displayed after five years in storage—an engraving of George Sand, a bust of
John Keats that Annie Fields had bequeathed to Cather, and paintings by
Achsah and Earl Brewster. Elizabeth Sergeant found the size of the living
room intimidating—large enough to be called a drawing room—and the
apartment as a whole dark and cheerless because the living room windows
faced the Colony Club next door. Cather, however, liked the absence of Park
Avenue traffic noise.[10]

Some of Cather and Lewis's friends had also migrated to Park Avenue.
570 is between Sixty-Second and Sixty-Third Streets, and Albert Donovan,
Cather's student in Pittsburgh and by the 1930s a New York accountant,
shared an apartment at 52 East Sixty-Fourth Street with Hugh Clark. Lewis's
friend John Mosher (Figure 6.2), film critic at the *New Yorker*, and his partner,
Philip Claflin, a Harvard-educated broker, lived at 136 East Sixty-Fourth (in
the late 1930s, Mosher and Claflin also acquired a cottage at Cherry Grove
on Fire Island). Moving to 570 also put Cather and Lewis closer to one of
their favorite dining establishments, the elegant French restaurant Voisin,
which was located on Park Avenue halfway between 570 and Grand Central.
Having her own financial resources, Lewis treated Mosher and Brenda
Ueland (both former *Every Week* staffers) to lunch there in 1935. Ueland was
divorced, raising her daughter alone in Connecticut and struggling to make
her way as an author. Ueland wrote to Bruce Barton (who had been editor in
chief of *Every Week*) about the lunch, "I saw darling Edith Lewis. She took
me and John Mosher to lunch at Voisin and we drank too much and I can remember that through the fog John Mosher rebuked me saying that NO one
any more talked the way I did about 'truth' and 'love.' But Edith Lewis stuck
up for me. She looked so elegant, charming, like Countess Mendl" (Elsie de
Wolfe, Lady Mendl, was a fashionable New York interior decorator, who, like
Lewis, did not color her striking silver-gray bobbed hair). "I love that Edith
Lewis," Ueland concluded.[11]

Figure 6.2 John Chapin Mosher photographed by Carl Van Vechten in January 1934. Carl Van Vechten Photograph © Van Vechten Trust.

Aunt Willa and Aunt Edith on Park Avenue

As adult orphans, part of the oldest living generation of each of their families, Cather and Lewis welcomed people from younger generations of their families into their new Park Avenue world, just as they did on Grand Manan. Cather's niece Mary Virginia Auld, who worked at a branch of the New York Public Library, was both their first guest at Grand Manan and a regular part of their life in New York in the 1930s. Because Mary Virginia's parents were divorced and lived far away, they were not present in 1935 when Mary Virginia married Richard Mellen, her brother Tom's Amherst College roommate. Her Aunt Willa took charge of the wedding at the Little Church Around the Corner, an Episcopal church on East Twenty-Ninth Street. Isabelle McClung was in New York in June 1935 to consult with doctors about her kidney disease, and she insisted on joining the festivities, which included a tea reception at Albert Donovan's apartment. And of course, Lewis was also there. What a queer quartet of adults supervising the union of Mary Virginia and Richard.[12]

Roscoe Cather's daughter Virginia, like her cousin Mary Virginia Auld, attended Smith College. Because her parents and younger sisters lived in Wyoming, her Aunt Willa and Edith Lewis hosted her in New York during school holidays. Their first Christmas at 570 Park Avenue in 1932, Virginia spent the days with them but spent nights in the hotel room they had booked for her. Willa Cather had declined an honorary degree from Smith in 1931 because she had already accepted an invitation from Princeton that year, but when Smith renewed their invitation in 1933, she accepted. As a result, she received her honorary doctorate and Virginia received her bachelor's degree at the same ceremony.[13]

The expense of traveling from Wyoming to Massachusetts seems to have deterred Roscoe and his wife, Meta, from attending Virginia's commencement, but she had both her Aunt Willa and "Miss Lewis" cheering her on (Cather's nieces and nephews generally called her "Miss Lewis" until they became adults and then called her "Edith"). This June 1933 trip seems to have been Lewis's only trip back to the campus since her own 1902 commencement. George and Harriet Whicher, English professors at Amherst and Mt. Holyoke, respectively, whom Cather and Lewis had met at the Bread Loaf School of English in 1922, got them rooms at the Mt. Holyoke College Faculty House in South Hadley. Staying there gave the two women some privacy before Cather stepped onto the commencement stage in Northampton. Virginia Cather had majored in English at Smith and had taken a course her junior year with Edith Lewis's cousin Mary Delia Lewis, a Smith College alumna who had been an English professor at her alma mater for some time. Their first night in South Hadley, Willa Cather and Edith Lewis invited Cather's niece and Lewis's cousin to have dinner with them and the Whichers in Amherst. Virginia Cather rode over from Northampton with Mary Lewis in her car. In Northampton, Cather and Lewis made the rounds together, attending a reception at President Neilson's house and having lunch with Virginia and another English faculty member, poet Charlotte Wilder (playwright Thornton Wilder's sister). Charlotte Wilder was a faculty resident at Baldwin House, where Virginia lived, and she and Virginia had become very close. On their walk back from town to Baldwin House, Cather entertained them all with a discourse on bullfighting in the works of Prosper Mérimée and Ernest Hemingway.[14]

Cather and Lewis had met the Menuhin family (talented children Yehudi, Hephzibah, and Yaltah, and parents Marutha and Moshe) in Paris in 1930 in the home of Jan and Isabelle Hambourg. From the start this was a friendship that fully encompassed both Cather and Lewis. Lewis's achievements as a child prodigy on the violin in Nebraska never approached Yehudi's level, but she certainly had a deeper understanding of music theory and instrumental performance than Cather did. The Menuhin children called Cather "Aunt Willa," as they called the Hambourgs "Uncle Jan" and "Aunt Isabelle," while they addressed Lewis as "dearest Miss Lewis" and "dear friend Miss Lewis." Marutha gave Cather the Russian nickname "Vassinka" and addressed Lewis as "darling Edith."[15]

Yehudi's touring schedule put the Menuhin family in New York one or two months a year, and Lewis and Cather made the most of these windows of time. In early 1931, the two women were still camping out at the Grosvenor Hotel, while the Menuhin family took a suite at the Ansonia, an apartment hotel on the Upper West Side. Yehudi and Moshe soon departed for California, where Yehudi was scheduled to perform. Cather soon also went west to visit her mother in Pasadena and to receive an honorary degree from the University of California in Berkeley, and while she was there she spent time with Yehudi. "You must be missing Aunt Willa very much," a young Yaltah wrote Lewis. She also suggested that Lewis should "be glad" that Cather was enjoying the mild climate and the scenery of Yaltah's native California. In the meantime, Marutha, Yaltah, and Hephzibah had moved into a smaller apartment at the Ansonia and invited Lewis to dinner. When the Menuhin ménage descended on Manhattan in March 1932, Cather and Lewis were both there, but Cather had the flu, and Moshe was in the hospital having his gallbladder removed. Marutha sympathized with Lewis's caring for an ill Cather and sent Lewis her own ticket "in the box with the girls" for Yehudi's recital, while she would be backstage serving as "valet to the young rascal."[16]

When the Menuhins arrived just before Christmas in 1933, Cather and Lewis were in their own apartment on the Upper East Side, allowing for richer interactions with the entire Menuhin family and especially the children. On weekdays, Cather took the children for walks in Central Park. She also decided that these multilingual children should have a better command of the English language, so she started a twice-weekly Shakespeare reading group with them. In these meetings, which persisted through the 1930s, they all sat around a table, taking turns reading the plays aloud. Lewis was unable to participate in weekday meetings but was part of the club on weekends.

As Yaltah wrote enthusiastically to Lewis in 1937, "It is so wonderful to remember the afternoon of Richard II with you & Aunt Willa and look forward
to seeing you again on Saturday. I have been so long hungry for this, that
every moment of remembrance and anticipation is precious, more than ever
before."[17]

Cather and Lewis were closer to Marutha than to Moshe. They sympathized with Marutha's efforts to protect the privacy of her children, while
Moshe worked to publicize them. Marutha was born and raised on the
Crimean peninsula and embraced her connection to Tartar culture. The
method for making kumis, a fermented mare's milk beverage she enjoyed in
childhood, came to her in a dream in 1937. As Yaltah wrote to Lewis, kumis
was "the most poetical beverage that could be made. The lightness of it and
still that immense power that makes it burst forth so lively, seems to be the
ideal, the essence of perfection," and the balance of the beverage "seems to
have expressed all mother's perfection." Marutha gave Cather and Lewis
some of her kumis, which she made with lightly sweetened cow's milk rather
than mare's milk, and they embraced this effervescent beverage as they did its
maker, attempting to make their own according to Marutha's instructions.[18]

During the Menuhin family's visits to New York, Lewis and Cather enjoyed
eating out with them at restaurants, and once they moved to Park Avenue,
they could host them for tea and dinner at home. Every January, both women
were guests at a party the Menuhin family designated Yehudi's birthday party
(even though he was actually born in April). In late 1937 and early 1938, the
family visited for three months, much longer than usual. In January 1938,
Cather and Lewis were able to take the three teenagers to two performances
of operas by Richard Wagner, *Lohengrin* and *Tristan Isolde*. Free of responsibility for her children on these nights, Marutha indulged Moshe's penchant
for Yiddish theater. Lewis wrote to Harwood Brewster Picard in February
1938 that she and Cather had seen the Menuhins more than usual and "went
to all the concerts that Yehudi and Hephzibah gave." Because of all this activity while she was "working very hard at my offices," Lewis reported that
she felt like she was "leading a sort of double life outside." "We love the whole
family so dearly," she explained, "and would forsake almost any occupation
to be with them—there is an absolutely irresistible charm in their companionship, they are so gifted and beautiful, and at the same time so simple, generous, and unspoiled."[19]

The Menuhins returned the compliment in their letters, which demonstrated that they understood and respected Cather and Lewis as a couple.

In 1936, when the Menuhins were enjoying reading Cather's essay collection *Not Under Forty*, Marutha asked "Dearest Edith" to "embrace Vassinka for us particularly tenderly." In 1937, Yaltah similarly wrote asking Lewis to "[p]lease embrace my beloved Aunt Willa for me and ask her to embrace you, also for me." She closed the letter by conveying "[l]ove from every one of us, to both of you." In 1939, writing Lewis that both she and Cather would soon get letters from Yaltah, who was recovering from a cold, Marutha observed of her daughter, "[S]he loves you, reveres you and admires you beyond words."[20]

Ethel Litchfield, a gifted concert pianist and one of Cather's old friends from Pittsburgh, moved to New York after her husband's death in 1930. Once Cather and Lewis settled into their new apartment, Litchfield became a regular guest, dining with them nearly every week. Alfred and Blanche Knopf had given Cather "an extremely fine phonograph" as a housewarming gift, and after dinner the three women listened to recordings of Yehudi accompanied by Hephzibah on piano, as well as "the last Beethoven quartets, and dozens of other favorite compositions."[21]

Lewis's biological family was also present during the years she and Cather lived together at 570 Park Avenue. Edith brought her brother Harold's daughters, Ruth and Elizabeth, to New York for a special treat one year in the 1930s, a performance by Yehudi Menuhin at Carnegie Hall. The three Lewises were seated together, while Cather was seated elsewhere, perhaps the Menuhin box. Edith's niece Ruth had been chosen early on as the girl from the next generation who would attend Smith, an education her Aunt Edith later helped finance. In the 1930s, Edith's sister Ruth was still living in Brooklyn and teaching gym and coaching basketball there, so they saw each other frequently. Their sister Helen was back in Lincoln with her husband, Phil Morgan, and their daughters. They were again living in the house where Phil grew up, four blocks south of the house where the Lewis family had lived beginning in 1883 and that Henry Lewis had signed over to his creditors in 1909. Because of complex legal disputes, the house had stood empty since then.[22]

Cather and Lewis together anchored this complex web of biological and chosen families, and everyone respected their relationship without labeling it. Even without a label, however, the two women functioned like a married couple. The last time Willa saw her brother Douglass alive, in December 1937, is telling. He had come to New York City to consult with a heart specialist, and his visit coincided with his sister's birthday. Willa wrote to their sister Elsie that, because Mary Virginia Mellen was working an evening shift at the library, she could not come to Park Avenue for her aunt's birthday dinner, but Willa "wouldn't ask anyone not 'family,' so he and Edith and I had a wonderful evening to ourselves." Cather's quotation marks around "family" suggest she did not restrict the term to her biological family: she included Lewis in that category as much as she included her brother Douglass.[23]

Lewis was not always absorbed into Cather's world. She enjoyed the imaginative escape of reading and also developed new friendships of her own. In 1936, she and Cather read the work of Arctic explorer Vilhjalmur Stefansson together and invited him over for dinner. It was Lewis, however, who maintained the connection to Stefansson and with his aid commenced a course of reading about nineteenth-century polar exploration. "No one will ever know how much pleasure I have had from all these books," she wrote him in the summer of 1936. "[I]t is not like reading but like living a second life independent of time and age, of earning one's living and running an apartment and buying clothes and keeping engagements. The dull parts do not seem dull to me, because I am not reading to get anywhere. I am there." She had written him similarly in April after she finished *The Voyage of the Jeannette* about a failed polar expedition led by George De Long: "Right now the men and events seem more real to me than the people and streets of New York, and I wake up every morning thinking of them."[24]

Not only did the *Jeannette* fail to reach the North Pole, the ship wrecked and De Long and many of his crew died in Siberia in 1881. Imagine Lewis's surprise, then, when Stefansson suggested he might introduce her to Emma De Long, the explorer's widow, who had written the introduction to *The Voyage of the Jeannette*. Stefansson had earlier sent Lewis the manuscript copy of an unpublished biography of explorer Elisha Kane by Margaret Elder Dow. Lewis's robust response demonstrated her continuing dedication to the aesthetics of writing. Although she acknowledged the worth of Dow's research, she criticized her failure to organize and synthesize it, and her criticism of Dow's style was particularly withering. "Truly, Mr. Stefansson," she wrote, "I think that is the worst kind of writing in the world." She cited as an egregious example Dow's description of "the young commander drinking his obscure and ice-chaliced draught." "I don't wonder that the polar explorer flees Woman," she quipped. "I would too, if I were a polar explorer." Reading Dow's purple prose gave her "even greater admiration for Mrs. De Long's clear, simple, straightforward introduction" to her husband's journal and "her wonderfully concise narrative."[25]

Lewis cherished the friendship that soon developed between herself and the elderly widow, and in 1937, she took time from her busy schedule to try to place De Long's memoir with a publisher. Corresponding with Stefansson early in her efforts, Lewis suggested that someone knowledgeable about the history of polar exploration (namely, Stefansson) should write an introduction to the memoir. Stefansson turned around and suggested that an introduction by Willa Cather might make the volume attractive to publishers. "No, no, Miss Cather would never dream of writing an introduction to Mrs. De Long's book," she responded testily. "She is not in this thing at all. She has never read the manuscript, nor the Voyage of the Jeannette." Lewis's efforts on Mrs. De Long's behalf failed, although she was gratified when De Long's memoir was published in 1938.[26]

Europe in 1935: Final Meetings

However awkward it had been for Lewis to spend time around Jan and Isabelle Hambourg in the 1920s, by the 1930s, she had, in a fashion, made her peace with the situation. When she and Cather spent long months in France researching *Shadows on the Rock* in 1930, they stayed in a hotel around the corner from the Hambourgs' apartment and saw them frequently. When the Hambourgs went to Germany for a music festival, Cather and Lewis went down to Saint-Cyr-sur-Mer to visit the Brewsters. After Isabelle's 1935 consultation with a New York kidney specialist resulted in a poor prognosis, she and her husband went back to Europe. Soon after the Hambourgs sailed for France in late July, Lewis and Cather followed them for what became Cather's farewell visit with Isabelle. It would also be Lewis's last visit with Achsah Brewster.[27]

First, however, Cather and Lewis went to Italy, where Cather wanted to transact some complicated business about a translation of *Death Comes for the Archbishop* in person. Lewis was a poor ocean traveler, but she had obtained a new German prescription medication for seasickness, and for the first time she was not ill crossing the Atlantic. On their arrival in Italy, she and Cather first went to Genoa but quickly left for Cortina, in the mountains, to escape the intense August heat. They finally went down to a hot and mosquito-infested Venice for the translation business, staying three weeks. The business concluded, they boarded a train together to France, but they parted company for a time. Cather went on to Paris and the Hambourgs, while Lewis went to Saint-Cyr-sur-Mer, where she checked into a hotel a bus or taxi ride away from Chateau Brun, where the Brewsters were still living.[28]

At the beginning of Lewis's visit, Achsah and Earl's daughter Harwood was still there, although she soon returned to medical school in London. Lewis arrived in time for Earl's birthday celebration, and with him and Harwood she took a day trip to Marseilles to see the Puvis de Chavannes murals at the Palais Longchamps (the painter was an important influence on both Earl and Achsah). Later, Lewis engaged a taxi to take herself, Earl and Achsah, and Geoffrey de Selincourt (a painter who was living with the Brewsters at Chateau Brun) to the monastery at Vieux Montreux, where they enjoyed the beautiful gardens. Lewis relished the weather, recording vivid visual details about it in her diary every day. It was mistral season, and the sea was "a wonderful flashing blue" with "white caps" one day, and the sunrise was a "[w]onderful apricot and gold" another.[29]

Lewis was in touch with the Paris office of the J. Walter Thompson agency, and she spent some mornings working. However, she also seems to have been working on Cather's fiction. "Got out story and read it through," she recorded one morning in her journal, "then wrote to Willa and Paris office." When Lewis wasn't well, she stayed in bed, reading Shakespeare's *Antony and Cleopatra* and D. H. Lawrence's fiction. Most days, however, her primary focus was simply enjoying the company of her friends. She looked at their paintings, they "discussed philosophical studies," and they drank tea and wine and ate meals together. Not long after she left, the Brewsters departed for India with de Selincourt. They were entirely out of money, and he had offered to pay their passage and rent a house with them when they got there.[30]

In early October, Lewis joined Cather in Paris, where the two women remained for more than two weeks. Lewis spent some time on her own, some with Cather, but also some with the Hambourgs. Monday, October 14, was fairly typical. Together, Lewis and Cather taxied to the Luxembourg Gardens to enjoy the sunny weather while eating rolls for breakfast. They then taxied back to rue Cambon for lunch at Columbin and were back at their hotel by midafternoon. The hotel was not far from where the Hambourgs were staying, so they walked over and took their friends out for a drive in a hired car. First they went to Notre Dame, then to Île Saint-Louis, and next back across Pont Royal to the Tuileries, where they got out of the car to sit and where Jan passed the time by explaining to Lewis some copyright problems he was facing. They got back in the car to drive down the rue de Rivoli, through the Place de la Concorde, to Étoile, where they stopped for tea and chocolate cake. This was not the only time that Lewis and Jan Hambourg paired together as, in a sense, the extra spouses. Isabelle was not strong, so on October 22, she and Cather simply sat in the Luxembourg Gardens together, while Lewis and Jan walked to another part of the gardens to view a statue of Frederick Chopin. More than one morning Lewis went with Cather to hunt for just the right flowers to take to the invalid Isabelle.[31]

It may have been the depths of the Great Depression back in the United States, but Cather and Lewis did not economize in Paris. Nearly every night they ate at Michaud's, drinking Hermitage vintage wine with their dinner. They went to the Louvre several times (they viewed classical sculpture on their own and modern paintings with Jan Hambourg) and attended a performance of Bizet's opera *Carmen*. Near the end of their visit, they both went for fittings at Maison Schiaparelli, where Elsa Schiaparelli's evening gowns were the height of fashion. They also prepared for their late autumn Atlantic crossing by buying warm woolen clothes. Lewis's German anti-seasickness medication entirely failed on an unusually rough crossing: she was so seasick that a nurse attended to her during the entire voyage.[32]

As Cather explained to Yaltah Menuhin, Isabelle did not want them to say goodbye as they were leaving but rather to "slip away": "It's very hard to go when I know how ill she is, and yet I feel that I cannot stay longer." The Menuhins arrived in Paris shortly after Lewis and Cather left, and Marutha reported to Lewis that Isabelle was "lucid and interested in everything" despite her illness. Indeed, Marutha explained, Isabelle, who had heard about Lewis's extreme seasickness and surgery to remove what turned out to be a benign cyst from her shoulder, seemed "to worry more about [Lewis] than about her own self."[33]

Isabelle McClung Hambourg died in Italy on October 10, 1938, and Willa Cather's world, including her writing, came to a stop. Harwood Brewster Picard had met the Hambourgs in France as a child, and Lewis wrote her about Isabelle's death. "[S]he had seemed much better and stronger than usual the first half of September," Lewis explained, "then began to grow steadily weaker, and one day a few days before her death lost consciousness—and never returned to consciousness again. I was glad that she had no acute suffering, and that it all came about so peacefully."[34]

Even if Isabelle's death was peaceful, Cather's reaction to it must have been stressful for Lewis. Cather retreated alone to the Shattuck Inn, and from there she wrote Roscoe, recounting that she had first gone there with

Isabelle and claiming that the inn was where she had "done most of [her] best work." She protested, "No other living person cared as much about my work, through thirty-eight years, as [Isabelle] did." Certainly, Willa Cather had not yet known Lewis for thirty-eight years, but Lewis's absence from this complaint is striking. Willa also wrote to Roscoe that her "classic style" had been formed by "the heat under the simple words"—where was Lewis's painstaking editorial work in crafting that "classic style"? Writing to Roscoe's daughter Margaret a few days later, Willa described Isabelle as "my best and sounded critic,—in some ways better than Edith, who knows much more about the technique of writing. I have sent Isabelle every manuscript before I published," receiving "invaluable" feedback.[35]

Soon after Isabelle's death, Jan Hambourg wrote Cather to tell her that he would be sending all of Cather's letters to Isabelle that she had carried with her during their years of moving around Europe. At first the number of letters seemed to be three hundred, but once the letters arrived in late 1939, Cather counted six hundred. Elizabeth Sergeant remembered that Cather gave the letters to Lewis to burn in the apartment building inciner-ator over the course of several weeks. Perhaps Cather read them over before consigning them to the flames. Even though Lewis and Isabelle had achieved rapprochement, witnessing Cather reading over the letters would have been painful for Lewis. Perhaps she even found some satisfaction in feeding the letters into the incinerator and watching them burn. By 1940, almost the en-tire correspondence (including Isabelle's letters to Cather, which had already been in Cather's possession) was gone, save a few stray items overlooked at Park Avenue and left behind at Grand Manan.[36]

Cather had begun work on her last novel to be published, *Sapphira and the Slave Girl*, in 1936. In the spring of 1938, she and Lewis had traveled together down to Virginia, both to cure Cather's bronchitis and to visit key sites for this novel based on Cather's family history. The two women hired a car and driver to take them around the rural landscape (neither ever learned to drive), and Cather offered a brief glimpse of their trip in the text of the novel. Describing the road up the side of a forested, mossy ravine, the narrator explains:

The road followed the ravine, climbing all the way, until at the "Double S" it swung out in four great loops round hills of solid rock; rock which the destroying armament of modern road-building has not yet succeeded in blasting away. The four loops are now denuded and ugly, but motorists, however unwillingly, must swing round them if they go on that road at all.

The deaths of Douglass Cather and Isabelle McClung Hambourg months apart later in 1938 nearly derailed *Sapphira*. Cather struggled for two more years to finish the novel. She later recalled that she had written much that "was too solidly 'manners and customs'" of the mid-nineteenth-century South because she had felt "relief of remembering them in a time of loss and personal sorrow." She then excised much of this material, putting "the discard (the excised chapters & paragraphs) on the bathroom scales," and found "they weighed six pounds." Not all of the cuts were made by Cather with scissors, however. As Lewis had many times before, she helped Cather achieve her aesthetic aims by using her pen or pencil to carve out words, phrases, and whole paragraphs. When Knopf finally published *Sapphira* in 1940, then, it seemed that their world was back to normal.[37]

"The Four of Us Together": San Francisco in 1941

In the last half dozen years of Cather's life, however, she went from medical crisis to medical crisis with little breathing room in between. While the younger Lewis was not ill as frequently as her partner, these years were difficult for her, too. Cather seriously injured the tendon in her right thumb while signing the limited edition of *Sapphira and the Slave Girl*. The injury caused her great pain and made it nearly impossible for her to write. In 1941, Dr. Frank Ober, a specialist from Boston, constructed a metal and leather brace to immobilize her thumb so that the tendon could recover. She came to rely more and more on her secretary, Sarah Bloom. Although Cather disliked dictating personal letters, she more frequently dictated even those. Bloom had a full-time office job during the week, so she came to 570 Park Avenue on Sundays. On each visit, she brought previously dictated letters for signature, took dictation of new letters, and picked up marked-up typescripts and dropped off the fresh copies for further editing by Cather and Lewis. Cather never felt able, however, to dictate her fiction, and as a result she wrote comparatively little during the 1940s.[38]

Around the time that Dr. Ober made the brace for Willa's thumb, her brother Roscoe, then living in the small central California town of Colusa, began having heart trouble and needed to consult a specialist in San Francisco. Willa proposed to him that they meet there for a good visit. In addition to her immobilized thumb, she was suffering from poor health generally, and she felt ill equipped to undertake a daunting transcontinental train journey alone. As she explained to Carrie Sherwood, she couldn't put up her hair or fasten her corsets without help.[39]

Lewis thus went with Cather, and it took the two nearly a week to cross the country—perhaps they stopped in Chicago for a few days to rest. On June 23, as they were crossing New Mexico, they watched for familiar sites from the train window, and they made a stop in Lamy, where they had stayed during some of their southwestern adventures. On June 24, they awoke to find themselves in the Mojave Desert and arrived in San Francisco later in the same day. Before they departed from New York, Sarah Bloom had written Roscoe that they would check into the Fairmount Hotel on June 28, but they actually arrived before then, perhaps to give Willa time to rest first.[40]

Willa Cather had been to San Francisco before, but it seems that Lewis had not. Their hotel was grand and showy, with a large interior courtyard, but it was also up high on one of San Francisco's hills. When Lewis awoke on the twenty-fifth, she enjoyed "[l]ooking down on San Francisco just before daylight—the houses looked transparent under thousands of floating black roofs, with a cool breeze blowing" as a large ocean liner entered the bay. After Roscoe and Meta arrived, the four established a regular rhythm to their days. As Roscoe reported to his daughter Virginia, "Willie and Edith had their breakfast in bed" every day. That did not appeal to him and Meta, but the four ate lunch and dinner together, enjoying the hotel's "remarkably good" food. After lunch, Willa took a long nap, and they did not all meet again for dinner until 7:30. In the afternoons, while Willa napped and Roscoe nursed his weak heart, Lewis explored the city on foot, visiting historic churches and climbing to the top of Telegraph Hill. The presence of the distinguished novelist in San Francisco was kept "a close family secret," Roscoe explained to Virginia: "Willie's registration does not appear on the Hotel books and all mail is sent direct to Miss Lewis. As soon as I saw Willie, I could easily recognize the advisability of this. Her hand has given her a lot of grief for months and she cannot afford the wear and tear of meeting people, even the ones she likes very much." One night, the four decided to break the pattern of hiding the famous author and went to a touring production of *Cabin in the Sky*, a Broadway musical about black life in the South with an all-black cast. Certainly, if it had become known that the author of *Sapphira and the Slave Girl* had been in the audience, it would have been news.[41]

The trip did not end on a high note for Cather and Lewis. Lewis wanted to return via the northern, Canadian route. She had been healthy and vigorous in San Francisco, but she came down with intestinal flu on the journey, forcing them to stop over in Lake Louise, Alberta, for five days. When they were ready to resume their journey, they could get only inferior train accommodations, and by the time they got back to New York, they were exhausted. In the aftermath of the trip, Cather wrote to Zoë Akins that Lewis had gone with her not by "choice" but because "she wanted to get me through" (and, indeed, the trip substituted for a summer trip to Grand Manan). Looking back on the experience, however, Lewis did not see the trip as a chore or a duty but as transformative. Cather and Lewis had spent time together with Roscoe, Meta, and their daughters in New Mexico in 1926, but this San Francisco trip was different: they were two adult couples, spending their days together. As Lewis wrote to Meta in June 1947, not long after Willa Cather's death and two years after Roscoe's, "I have always had a special feeling about the four of us together in San Francisco. It has always seemed to me that in that short time we came closer together than people usually do. I am so glad you remember all those things we did together just as I do. I am so glad I came to know and love you and Roscoe."[42]

"So Many Have Gone to War": Cather and Lewis Confront World War II

The U.S. entry into World War II in 1941 only increased the challenges Lewis faced as the younger partner of a fragile older woman even as Lewis's job became more demanding. As she explained to her niece Ruth when she regretfully declined an invitation to attend her Smith College commencement:

[A]s usual, it seems impossible for me to leave my job—or rather, my various jobs—just at this time. I have been doing a lot of rush work at the office—we are very short handed in trained people, so many have gone to the war. Also, we have no maid at home and Miss Cather is still not very strong—so that each of my days is just as full as it will hold. I don't get time even for a walk in the park!

The war also opened up work-related opportunities for Lewis. Art direction had been the exclusive province of men at J. Walter Thompson, but with so many gone to war, Lewis both wrote copy and handled the visual aspects of advertisements. She was largely responsible for a series of advertisements promoting the *American Weekly*, a Sunday supplement magazine. The advertisements, which were aimed primarily at advertisers rather than readers, celebrated the power of reading in the lives of eminent people before they achieved fame. Willa Cather sent Meta Cather an ad in this series in which Abraham Lincoln's youthful reading was said to have propelled him toward his role as the Great Emancipator. Lewis also put her reading on arctic exploration to good use, featuring Robert Peary's reaching the North Pole in one ad. The subjects of other ads included Benjamin Franklin, Thomas Jefferson, Mark Twain, Andrew Carnegie, Charles Darwin, Will Rogers, George Washington Carver, Luther Burbank, Theodore Roosevelt, Thomas Edison, David Livingstone, John Wanamaker, and James J. Hill (the U.S. railroad magnate whom Cather later praised to E. K. Brown as "a great dreamer and a great man"). Marie Curie was the sole woman in the series. A woman—Edith Lewis—was responsible for both the text and visual elements of the ads in this series, but it seems there was only one eminent woman (or the right kind of eminent woman) deemed of sufficient interest to the men who decided whether or not to advertise their products in the *American Weekly*.[43]

The U.S. entry into the war was consequential for certain consumer industries that relied on rationed ingredients. Fanny Farmer Candy, for example, commissioned Thompson to promote the purchase of war bonds under the Fanny Farmer imprimatur in order to keep the brand in the buying public's eye even if the company could not get enough sugar to produce as much candy as it had previously. Under the headline "They're going all the way," Lewis created an advertisement featuring a large photograph of smiling soldiers crowded on the deck of a ship and copy that enumerated the life stories of some men who were supposedly in that crowd: "One of them is a boy from Massachusetts. He graduated 3rd in his class at college a year ago. He was planning to be a civil engineer," and so on. Describing them as having sacrificed their lives, hopes, dreams, and plans for the war effort, Lewis finally addressed the readers of the ad, who presumably had been drawn in by the striking photograph, and asked them, "*How far are you going?*" In the logic of the ad, readers could demonstrate how far they were willing to go by purchasing war bonds. "I think this one of the best of Edith's advertisements," Willa wrote to Meta, enclosing a proof of the advertisement before it began running in 1943. "She found the photograph in Washington." As Cather had also explained to Meta the year before, Lewis's work on the Eastman Kodak account had been "shut off by the war," but she nevertheless won a 1943 award for art direction for a Kodak ad. For her part, Willa Cather was "snowed under" by letters from "nice soldier boys" who had read her books in Armed Services Editions, letters she felt compelled to answer, even if only briefly.[44]

A new friend entered Cather and Lewis's New York world because of the war. Norwegian novelist Sigrid Undset arrived in the U.S. after making a dramatic escape from Nazi forces occupying her native country. She and Cather admired each other's work and had been corresponding for a decade, but before Undset came to New York they had not met in person. The Knopfs, their mutual publishers, arranged their first meeting in 1940. When Undset wasn't traveling around the U.S. lecturing on the dangers of fascism, she lived in a modest residential hotel in Brooklyn Heights, near Edith Lewis's sister Ruth (Figure 6.3). In 1941, Ruth had finally left teaching (most recently in Bay Ridge) to become the women's activities secretary at the Brooklyn Navy Yard YMCA, a war-related position under the sponsorship of the USO. At some point during the war, Helen Lewis Morgan and her daughters also moved to Brooklyn.[45]

Figure 6.3 A 1940s studio portrait of Ruth Putnam Lewis, Edith Lewis's sister. Courtesy the Family of Ruth Lewis Trainor.

Cather and Lewis periodically invited Undset over for dinner in their spacious apartment. As Lewis later remembered, the two novelists shared a love of botany and often talked about American wildflowers. When the war was over, Undset would return to Norway with American seeds to plant in her garden. As the war continued, Cather expressed some of her darkest thoughts about the state of the world to Undset. She wrote to Undset on Christmas Day in 1943, "For the first time in my life I feel afraid—afraid of losing everything one cherished in the world and all the finest youth of the world." She also complained about the less significant hardships she and Lewis were facing. "The conditions of life grow harder every day, as you must know," she wrote Undset, explaining that "Miss Lewis" could not get a taxi to see her "two sisters living in Brooklyn . . . even in the worst weather" because drivers told her, "That trip uses too much gas."[46]

"Dying . . . Must Be a Rather Pleasant Affair": Illness and Grieving in the Early 1940s

If Lewis wondered what it would be like to lose her partner, she got a preview when Cather had her appendix and gallbladder removed in July 1942. Gallbladder attacks had been troubling Cather for some time, making it difficult for her to eat: at the time of her hospital admission she weighed only 114 pounds. As she wrote to Roscoe, in the hospital they "fed [her] entirely through [her] legs and arms" for four days before the surgery because she "couldn't keep anything on [her] stomach." These days weren't "disagreeable" to her, because she was sedated and didn't really remember them. However, "they were," she confessed, "hard for Edith because I whined so for water." The whole experience was "a kind of release from all likes and dislikes, from sunshine and shadows, which makes me feel quite sure that dying, when one comes to it, must be a rather pleasant affair. If one has lived a pretty full and pretty hard life, I think one will have had a plenty and will feel a kind of satisfaction in slipping out of it."[47]

She explained to Irene Miner Weisz that once she started eating again in the hospital after surgery, she "spoiled all their lovely blankets" by vomiting the food back up. Lewis, who had taken a leave of absence from work to care for Cather, stepped into action, having their maid cook meals in their apartment and then carrying the food in a taxi cab from Sixty-Second Street to One Hundred and Sixty-Eighth Street (where Presbyterian Hospital was located).

The two women had seen how Meta cared for Roscoe the year before, when his heart trouble made him infirm. Willa wrote to Meta that she had seen how Meta had acted "like a second physical body" to her husband. "Edith begs me to give you her love and <u>understanding</u>," she continued. "When I got sick she 'rose up.'" Friends stepped in to help as well. Yehudi Menuhin was in the city, and he took a frazzled Lewis out to lunch and telephoned Cather every day (he waited until she was discharged to visit in person). Ethel Litchfield also gave Lewis the support she needed to help Cather.[48]

Months after Cather's surgery, Lewis was still spending mornings shopping for delicacies to tempt Cather to eat, a challenge because of wartime rationing. The two women took no real vacation in 1942. All of Lewis's leave had been spent caring for an invalid, and even before Cather's surgical adventure, Lewis developed an ulcerated cornea, which required hot compresses for three hours a day. In early October, Cather and Lewis took a train up to Williamstown, Massachusetts, to spend three quiet weeks at the Williams Inn. In the country, at least, they could get "good food and <u>wonderful</u> milk."[49]

The trip was as much for Lewis's benefit as for Cather's. In early September, Lewis's dear friend John Mosher (a graduate of Williams College in Williamstown) died suddenly of a heart attack at age fifty. Mosher was remarkably open about his sexuality—so open that his employers at the *New Yorker* chastised him at least once and a straight male colleague who shared an office with him felt uncomfortable. His reputation as one of the great wits of the city may have given him license to be so open. His friend Dawn Powell satirized him in her novel *This Happy Island* as James Pinckney, who competes with another middle-aged male Manhattanite for the affections of an attractive but dimwitted young man. In his own *New Yorker* short stories, Mosher gently poked fun at himself through the recurring character of Mr. Opal, a fussy, well-to-do New York bachelor. However, Mr. Opal is not explicitly gay—the stories refer vaguely to his past romantic attachments to women who are his friends—and he occupies his Fire Island cottage alone, not with a male partner, as Mosher did.[50]

Mosher had served in World War I, but he was in his late forties by the time the U.S. entered World War II, so he did not volunteer. He reportedly told Powell when Hitler invaded Poland in 1939, "I absolutely CANNOT be dragged back and forth through that Atlantic again. Particularly not in that awful brown twill." However, Philip Claflin, his much younger partner, volunteered for service as soon as the U.S. entered the conflict, and in the wake of Claflin's enlistment, a heartbroken Mosher developed the heart disease that killed him. Certainly, Mosher had been a friend who fully understood and valued Lewis's relationship with Cather for what it was. Others—the Brewsters, Mabel Luhan, Roscoe and Meta Cather—did as well. Unlike them, however, Mosher lived in a same-sex domestic partnership. As Lewis wrote to Brenda Ueland many years later, Ueland and Mosher were her favorites on the *Every Week* staff, elaborating that she "was truly fond of" Mosher and "so regret[ted]" his "early death."[51]

Lewis suffered another painful loss in early 1945 with the death of Achsah Barlow Brewster. Achsah and Earl Brewster never left India after they moved there in early 1936, and although they had urged Lewis to come visit, her persistent seasickness made the journey untenable. Lewis thus had not seen her dear friend for ten years when she died. When Harwood Brewster Picard moved to the U.S., Lewis spent time with her and got to know Harwood's daughters, Claire and Frances. Achsah and Earl had met Claire only briefly when she was an infant, but they never met their second grandchild. As Earl and Achsah wrote to Lewis and Cather in 1942, they were "half envious of your chance to know Claire and Frances." Achsah's sister Alpha Barlow came down to New York soon after Achsah's death on February 16 to see Achsah's "special friend," Edith Lewis, who agreed to write the obituary for the *Smith Alumnae Quarterly*. Signing herself "EL," Lewis wrote of Achsah:

> She had a wonderful life. It was an artist's life throughout—not only in her beautiful paintings, many of which adorn the walls of churches and monasteries in Italy and France; she was an artist in the clothes she wore, in the food she set before her many guests, in the way she could bring together light, color, fragrance in a simple room, so that it became unforgettably lovely. She had a generosity of mind and nature that could tolerate almost any human frailty except cheapness and vulgarity. And what courage she had! I can remember her friend D. H. Lawrence telling how the poisonous snakes in Ceylon, the leopards prowling at night on the roof of their bungalow, used to terrify Achsah. But for all the large hazards of life—for living itself—she had a superb courage and gallantry. She and her husband painted happily for many years in Italy and France. In '36 they set off on the long voyage to India.[52]

Later in 1945, Cather and Lewis (both longtime smokers) were suffering from throat troubles, and they were advised to travel someplace dry and warm to recover. In 1943, when wartime conditions and medical challenges had made

Grand Manan unsuitable, they had first discovered the Asticou Inn on Mt. Desert Island in Maine. There, they were able to occupy their own small cottage on the grounds, but Maine was cool and damp. When they couldn't find suitable accommodations in Estes Park, Colorado, or a similar western resort, they headed to Maine despite the damp.[53]

Lewis had a more vigorous time in Maine than Cather did. Most days she took long walks by herself, a botany book in hand so she could identify plants. She was particularly fond of walking through the Asticou Terraces, gardens designed by Boston architect Joseph Henry Curtis, to Thuya Lodge and into the forest beyond it. Cather and Lewis both enjoyed listening to Ethel O'Neil McKenzie, a widowed Canadian pianist who summered there. Sometimes they both sat in McKenzie's studio to listen, but other times, on misty days when Lewis was walking alone, she stood quietly outside Mackenzie's studio, enjoying both the forest and the music and sketching nearby trees. Cather could walk only short distances and spent much of her time resting or working on a story based on her Red Cloud childhood, "The Best Years." As usual, Lewis also sacrificed some of her recreation time to contribute to Cather's creative work. "[W]orked with W.," she wrote in her journal for three days in late August.[54]

In early September, when they had been at the Asticou for two months, Willa received the news that her brother Roscoe had died. Ironically, she was just about to mail him the fresh typing by her local typist of "The Best Years," a story in which a fictionalized version of Roscoe as a child appears. An already weak Cather came down with influenza, but she and Lewis couldn't change their train reservations on short notice. Instead, they used their reserved tickets to Boston, where a doctor insisted Cather stay for several days before they went on to New York.[55]

Things went from bad to worse in December, when Cather discovered a lump in her left breast and was diagnosed with breast cancer. Cather and Lewis kept the true nature of her medical condition secret even from family and close friends. Considering the lingering stigma surrounding cancer and the added sensitivity concerning the location of the tumor, their decision to keep Cather's diagnosis secret is not surprising. Furthermore, Roscoe had died just months before, and Meta and their daughters were about to experience their first Christmas without him. Willa wrote Meta on December 17, "We can neither of us hope for a very happy Christmas, but I hope yours won't be too sad. You must remember that you had more of Roscoe's life than anyone else ever had, and that you made him happy." By concealing her condition from Meta and her daughters, she protected them from what might have felt like an added emotional burden at a difficult time.[56]

When Willa Cather discovered the lump, she consulted with two surgeons, who were the medical professionals with primary responsibility for breast cancer in the 1940s. Some surgeons used a microscope in the operating room to examine tissue they had just removed, and on the basis of what they saw, they might proceed with a mastectomy without obtaining the woman's consent. Other surgeons proceeded more cautiously, removing tissue for a biopsy in one minor surgery and making a recommendation for further intervention on the basis of more sophisticated histological results from a laboratory. Surgeon William Crawford White, a well-known authority on breast cancer on staff at Roosevelt Hospital, evidently followed the latter course in Cather's case, taking a tissue sample from the lump in late December or early January.[57]

On January 14, 1946, Willa wrote Meta that she had anticipated having "to go into the Roosevelt Hospital for what threatened to be a rather serious operation" but that "two eminent surgeons who have watched me pretty carefully now assured me that I will not have to go into the hospital for an operation." Either she was lying or she had not yet discussed the biopsy results with White, because two days later, on January 16, White performed a mastectomy on Cather at Roosevelt Hospital. After her discharge three weeks later, she wrote Meta that she had had surgery after all to remove "one of those useless little lumps which sometimes form on the human body," but she also assured her that it had turned out to be "quite harmless" rather than "serious." Her niece Helen Southwick, daughter of her brother Jim, lived in New Jersey at the time and brought flowers to her in the hospital and then visited her several times at home. Still, Willa managed to conceal the cancer diagnosis from her, writing that "the operation turned out very well—there was nothing ugly or alarming in the bump."[58]

Although Willa accepted visits from Helen, she did not see Roscoe and Meta's daughter Margaret when she came to New York for a week in early April with her two children. As Willa explained apologetically to Meta, a "strange nervous collapse," which had begun after Roscoe's death, had intensified, leading to frequent periods of crying, more "over pleasant things than for sad ones." In late March, her old friend Dr. Howard Taylor had come to see her and had told her that she should see no one, not even visiting nieces, so that she could have quiet and could rest. "So I am absolutely isolated," she explained to Meta, "and see no one but Miss Lewis."[59]

Yet again, Lewis had taken a leave of absence to care for her partner. As her colleague Thayer Jaccaci had written her in early February about her "forced absence," the J. Walter Thompson Co. was "most anxious to have [her] back" after her "many years" there. She was put on leave beginning March 1, "with the understanding that you will return when you feel your affairs permit you." "The arrangement you have made is very generous," she replied, "but I don't feel that I deserve to be so well treated. I hate to think of how I have inconvenienced you all." As it turned out, she would never return from her leave. Moreover, just as her leave officially began, she herself became seriously ill.[60]

By the early summer of 1946, Cather had more or less recovered, but Lewis was still gravely ill. When they traveled to the Asticou Inn in late July, they switched roles from the year before—Cather was the stronger of the two, while a weak Lewis spent the first week in bed and was not well enough for the walks she loved until September. They stayed in Boston for two weeks on their way back because their Park Avenue landlords were painting and papering their apartment. They did not get home until mid-October.[61]

Among those who visited them once they got back to New York were Lewis's old friends Rudolph and Filomena Ruzicka, who came to tea on December 17. Ruth Lewis's job at the Navy Yard had ended with the war, but in December 1946, she got a new job with the Girl Scouts. On New Year's Day, 1947, Edith reported to her niece (then married and a mother), "I have asked Ruth to meet us at a nearby Schrafft's for dinner tonight" so that she could tell them about her new job and about her Christmas visit with Harold Lewis's family in Braintree, Massachusetts (Harold was Ruth Lewis Trainor's father). Edith was pleased about her sister's new job but was worried that she might not be able to "keep well." "This last year has taught me," she elaborated, "that the most valuable material possession you can have is health—without it all of Rockefeller's millions would be of no use, in fact they would only be an added incumbrance."[62]

However, at some point, probably in early 1947, it became clear that Cather's cancer had spread to her liver, becoming what we now call Stage IV cancer. The cancer may have silently spread even before her mastectomy, and longstanding general poor health may have masked symptoms of the metastasis. In 1941, she was diagnosed with severe anemia and went through a course of thrice-weekly injections in her thigh of "liver extract" and iron solutions. This treatment was repeated in later years, including 1945, 1946, and 1947. Nevertheless, at some point, poor appetite, pain and swelling in the abdomen, and jaundice would have sent Cather to the doctor, where a physical exam and blood tests would have led to a diagnosis of liver metastasis. She had turned seventy-three in December 1946, and Lewis had turned sixty-five that same month. Once the metastasis was diagnosed, they would have understood that it was a virtual certainty that Cather was going to die many years before Lewis, although precisely how many might not have been clear.[63]

Tellingly, Cather and Lewis hired as a maid a woman who was also a trained practical nurse. They continued, however, to keep knowledge of Cather's cancer from almost everyone. Ruth Lewis and Sarah Bloom may have known, but if they did they guarded the secret as closely as Cather and Edith Lewis did. And perhaps even Edith Lewis, in a fashion, refused to accept the full implications of the spread of Cather's cancer. When Lewis was assembling a chronology of Cather's life for University of Chicago English professor E. K. Brown, whom she authorized as Cather's biographer after her death, she wrote, "During the winter and spring of 1946–47, [Cather] never lived the life of an invalid; she went out nearly every day, walked, read a great deal, dictated letters, saw a few friends, attended to all the small chores of life. Her interest in things, her talk, were full of life and spirit. It was only her bodily strength that failed." Compared with the final chapters of both their mothers' lives—strokes followed by long periods of debility before death— Cather's final months may have seemed tolerable, but she was not well and her death was imminent.[64]

Cather did manage to attend a concert by Yehudi and Hephzibah Menuhin in March 1947, even though, as Lewis conceded in *Willa Cather Living*, "it was an effort that winter for her to go out in the evening." On March 22, a few days after the concert, Hephzibah called "to ask if she might bring her husband and her two little boys to the Park Avenue apartment and introduce them." Soon after Hephzibah and her family arrived, "Yehudi turned up, with his little son and daughter," filling the apartment with "children's voices and laughter." "I would rather have almost any chapter of my life left out than the Menuhin chapter," Cather wrote to E. K. Brown in apology for not properly answering his most recent letter (they had been corresponding for a year about her work). Cather could "not write anything today except about the wonderful yesterday with those dear children (as they still are to me) and their children. Today these rooms seem actually full of their presence and their faithful loving friendship." Nevertheless, "[u]nder all the gaiety and happiness of that morning," Lewis recalled, "there was somehow a sense of heartbreak" because the Menuhins suspected they "would never see their be-loved Aunt Willa again."[65]

"That Is Happiness, to Be Dissolved into Something Complete and Great": Willa Cather's Death and Burial

In *Willa Cather Living*, Lewis wrote that on the morning of the day she died, Cather "was never more herself." Although she "was tired," her "spirit was high, her grasp of reality as firm as always." This characterization concealed more than it revealed. The whole week before Thursday, April 24, 1947, Cather had been feeling poorly. Dr. White came to examine her at 10 a.m. that morning and decided she should be admitted to Roosevelt Hospital. While Cather and Lewis were waiting for him to telephone, they had lunch and then decided to take naps. Lewis awoke from her nap and was reading when Cather appeared at the door to Lewis's bedroom complaining of a violent stomach upset. While Lewis tried to reach Dr. White on the telephone, their maid attended to Cather. Her condition continued to worsen—she felt "a terrific pain at the top of her head and base of her spine"—and at 4:30, shortly before Dr. White arrived, she died of a cerebral hemorrhage. No autopsy was performed, so when White identified cerebral hemorrhage as the cause of death on the death certificate, he must have relied on Lewis's report of Cather's symptoms in the hour leading up to her death. But what was the underlying cause of the hemorrhage? Again, without an autopsy report, we can only conjecture. Dr. White listed her breast cancer and liver metastasis on the death certificate as contributing causes, but undiagnosed metastasis to the brain is a more plausible cause of a brain bleed. Despite the brave show Cather and Lewis had been putting on, the cancer had taken her.[66]

Moments after Cather died, Ruth Lewis called her sister to make plans to meet for lunch in Manhattan when her job would bring her there. Ruth was puzzled when a man answered the phone. He identified himself as Dr. White and handed the phone to Edith, who was unable to speak. He then explained, "Miss Lewis is very much upset and can't talk as Miss Cather died just a few minutes ago. She wants to know if you can come right over." When Ruth arrived at 570 Park Avenue, Sarah Bloom had also arrived, and the undertakers were about to leave. Ruth Lewis and Sarah Bloom stayed until 11 p.m., offering support and encouragement as Edith Lewis made phone calls and sent telegrams to friends and family. One of the first they contacted was Ethel Litchfield, who hastily returned from a visit to Philadelphia and arrived at the apartment the next morning. The four women then began the difficult task of making decisions and planning a funeral for an important public figure who had stayed mostly out of the public eye in the last decade of her life and had virtually disappeared during her final years of repeated medical crises.

Lewis had reached Willa's brother Jack on the phone the evening before. The first flight that he and Willa's other remaining brother, Jim, could get from California to New York was on Monday morning, so Lewis decided to hold a small private funeral in the apartment on Monday afternoon. After nearly four decades of life shared with Cather, Lewis knew her wishes best, but she still faced challenges. Cather had been raised a Baptist, but on a visit to Red Cloud for her parents' fiftieth wedding anniversary, she and her parents joined Grace Episcopal Church. Despite being a regular reader of the Bible and culturally Christian, Cather was not a parishioner at any church in New York City, so there was no local Episcopal priest whom Lewis might ask to read scripture and the prayers for the dead at the service. Lewis was similarly without local religious connections. It was Ruth Lewis who solved the dilemma, suggesting they contact the Unitarian minister who had conducted services for their mother when she died in Massachusetts twenty years earlier. Ruth placed the call, and the Rev. Dr. Lathrop of Springfield professed himself "honored and . . . most grateful [to] be able to do something for a person who had given [him] so many delightful hours by way of her books."

But where was Cather to be buried? She had not set foot in Red Cloud since December 1931 and January 1932, when she presided over a family reunion after her mother's death. Lewis recalled that she had said she would like to be buried in Jaffrey, and one of Cather's nieces and her sister Elsie also remembered hearing her say this. The Old Burying Ground in Jaffrey was a crowded, historic one, so on the evening of Cather's death, Sarah Bloom had made a call to the Austermans, proprietors of the Shattuck Inn, seeking assistance. Fred Austerman called back the next morning to report that he had secured a plot right next to the plot where one of his twin sons, who died at age twelve, had been buried. With this crucial arrangement taken care of, Lewis and Bloom went out to select a casket, Litchfield went out to purchase garments to clothe Cather's corpse for the open-casket funeral, and Ruth Lewis stayed behind in the apartment to answer the phone and accept telegrams.[67]

About two dozen people were in the apartment for the service at 2 p.m. on Monday, April 28. In addition to Cather's brothers Jack and Jim from California, Elsie came in from Lincoln, Nebraska, where she was retired from teaching high school. Two of Willa's nieces, Virginia Cather Brockway and Mary Virginia Auld Mellen, came in from Pittsburgh and Colorado Springs, respectively, and nephew Charles came in with his father, Jim. In attendance from New York were Cather's publishers, Alfred and Blanche Knopf, and Nola Menuhin, wife of Yehudi Menuhin (who was on tour in England). Rudolf and Filomena Ruzicka came down from Westchester County. After the services, Lewis asked Virginia Cather Brockway to stay for tea so she could tell her of the circumstances leading up to her aunt's death (or what Lewis was willing to share of those circumstances). Ruth Lewis and Sarah Bloom then joined them, and the four women chatted while Cather lay in repose in the living room. "It really did not seem at all inappropriate for Aunt Willie to be present," Virginia wrote to her mother (Meta Cather), "though it does sound odd."[68]

The next day, the undertakers took Cather's body in its heavy bronze casket to the train station to begin the first leg of the journey to New Hampshire, which required a transfer to a hearse in Worcester, Massachusetts. Lewis boarded the train in New York with four members of the Cather family (Mary Virginia, Jack, Jim, and Charles). "Since one of Jaffrey's main charms for Aunt Willie was the fact that it was almost inaccessible," Virginia Brockway wrote her mother, "it seemed better not to have everyone go." Virginia stayed behind in New York City for another day with her Aunt Elsie, who had not been well. At Lewis's request the Austermans arranged for an Episcopal priest to preside at the graveside service (they enlisted Alfred Lund, Jr., son of a Presbyterian minister in Jaffrey, who came up from Brooklyn). A few additional people from Jaffrey and elsewhere in New England joined the group from New York at Cather's graveside.[69]

In June, Lewis wrote to Meta Cather from Jaffrey:

I wish you could see what a lovely place it is where Willa is lying—just at the corner of the old burying ground, with the stone wall enclosing it on two sides and on the other side a lovely hemlock tree, and a tall white birch beyond. Beyond the stone wall the ground drops to a little meadow of waving green rye and some old apple trees—and from there you look off to green fields and woods and the beautiful mountain with the light always changing on it.

She conceded that the cemetery was "wild," but she found it more "cheerful" than a carefully tended one because it was not "lonely and set apart" but instead "seem[ed] part of the village and the human life around it." In her letter of condolence, Meta, remembering the loss of her husband two years earlier, suggested that Lewis would find comfort in having "Willa's things" around her. "Everything she had, her clothes, her books, her pictures, all her little treasures, are so immeasurably precious to me," Lewis answered, and she could not "bear to live at all without them." Nevertheless, she couldn't enjoy them. Writing from Jaffrey, she asked, "How can I ever enjoy anything in this world again? Even the sunlight and these beautiful green woods seem so alien to me. She was my whole source of joy."[70]

"One thing I am thankful for all the time," she wrote to Harwood Brewster Picard the same day she wrote Meta Cather, "Willa did not have to go through a long helpless illness." In her will, Cather had left the bulk of her assets to Lewis, as well as naming her executor and literary trustee. Lewis felt a heavy sense of obligation concerning her duties as executor and trustee. "I want so much to arrange everything just as she would have wanted," she explained to Harwood. "We have had so many happy years together—she gave me such a rich wonderful life of feeling and thought—I feel that I have had more than my share. I have nothing to regret except my own inadequacies and short-comings."[71]

Lewis took great care to construct a suitable memorial for Cather at Jaffrey. In June, she attended to the formalities concerning the cemetery plot and arranged perpetual care. Two months later, in August, Rudolph and Filomena Ruzicka drove her up to Jaffrey in their car so she could select the gravestone. Lewis chose a quotation from My Ántonia (1918), part of which Cather had written in Jaffrey, about the relationship between the Nebraska pioneers and the land they settled, to engrave on the stone: "That is happiness, to be dissolved into something complete and great." Lewis prefaced the quotation with praise for Cather's public role as a writer: "The truth and charity of her great spirit will live on in the work which is her enduring gift to her country and its people." Rudolf Ruzicka, who had created the dust jacket designs for Obscure Destinies, Lucy Gayheart, and Sapphira and the Slave Girl, designed the layout and typography for the words Lewis had selected and written. Cather had long been lying about her birth year, which was 1873, and Lewis inscribed on the stone the year that Cather had given out publicly, 1876.[72]

"The Last Shock of Seeing Dear Willa Go": Edith Lewis
Grieves Willa Cather

Soon after her August visit to Jaffrey, a gallbladder attack put Lewis in the hospital. She was resisting surgery, but Marutha Menuhin, citing the example of her husband's long years of invalidism and his return to health after having his gallbladder removed in the early 1930s, urged her to have the surgery at the earliest possible moment. "You might have gone on indefinitely with an imperfect [gall]bladder," she wrote, "but the last shock of seeing dear Willa go—is not to be ignored." Lewis entered the hospital on October 18 and was there for several weeks.[73]

Lewis's grief was profound, and letter-writing to distant friends became an outlet for her grief. She began writing often to Earl Brewster, who, like Meta Cather, was two years widowed. "May the many blessed memories you have of your life with her continue to sustain and comfort you," he wrote in response to Lewis's report of Cather's final illness and death. "I know the separation will never seem easier to endure," he continued, confessing that "as age increases it is more difficult. I miss more than ever those who have been dear to me, even those of long ago." Brewster was deeply immersed in the study and practice of Hinduism, and he offered Lewis spiritual consolation: "We can still through our lives and thoughts and works have a spiritual relationship to those who have inspired us, our dearest ones, who still continue to guide and bless us. . . . I know so well how Achsah would wish me to live, and that helps me." Lewis responded by pointing, as she had in her letter to Earl and Achsah's daughter, to her "many short-comings," but Earl, slipping in and out of the present tense when he referred to his late wife, responded, "So remarkably strong, balanced and wise you have always seemed to Achsah and me. . . . Willa was indeed fortunate in having you for a companion. All this seemed so true and obvious to Achsah and me."[74]

Lewis's grief was not easily assuaged—and why would it have been? On December 31, 1947, and January 1, 1948, she wrote Earl Brewster about her inner struggle. She felt "lost in a whole new world of new thoughts and feelings," and a "continual inner preoccupation" made "all the rest seem unreal and mechanical." She also expressed envy of Brewster's life as an artist—the life she had longed for in her late adolescence and early twenties, the life she had praised in her obituary for Achsah Brewster, the life that Willa Cather had lived. "Dearest Edith," Earl Brewster protested in response, "please don't shut your eyes to the truth that you are an artist . . . and of course Achsah and I have always known it. You have done strenuous important work as an artist, I do not doubt; but an artist is not one by what he does but by what in reality he essentially is." His assurance did not, however, assuage her consciousness of "an unseen world, unseen forces which [she could] not comprehend . . . which [she felt] continually pressing upon" her.[75]

Brewster suggested he might visit his daughter in Europe and meet up with Lewis there, but he gave up that plan, and although he again suggested she might visit him in India, he also feared India might not suit her. Instead, another sympathetic correspondent, Stephen Tennant, invited her to travel with him. Cather and Tennant had struck up a correspondence in the 1920s, when the aristocratic aesthete and great admirer of Cather's fiction was in his twenties. The two had spent several days together in New York City on his 1935 trip to the U.S., and Lewis had joined them one evening—Tennant recalled Lewis's black taffeta dress and her "pretty white shingle" hairstyle.[76]

As a young man Tennant had been one of the most flamboyant of the rebellious "Bright Young People" of British high society. His one serious romance had been with the much older poet Siegfried Sassoon, who had nursed Tennant through several years of ill health caused by tuberculosis, but Tennant ended the relationship during a period when he lapsed into a serious depression. In the final months of Cather's life, Tennant was again undergoing treatment for depression, including electroconvulsive therapy. He emerged in August 1947 and wrote Lewis to offer condolences. "Willa Cather's death has been a profound & lasting sorrow for me," he wrote. In consoling Lewis he made clear, however, that he understood Lewis's place in Cather's life and her greater grief. "I loved her so deeply, and of course, always shall!" he continued, "and I cannot bear to think what sorrow is yours."[77]

Tennant's praise of Cather as an artist drew Lewis in. "You cannot know how much comfort your letter gave me," Lewis responded, "for it made me feel that you will always be her friend, and have her in your heart and in your thoughts, and never forget her." Describing the final months and days of Cather's life, Lewis wrote poignantly, "She was so herself that I could not see any danger, and I never faced the thought of losing her." Tennant was so moved by Lewis's account of Cather's final days that he "wept—burning, scalding tears, while [he] read it." Lewis continued the escalation of shared emotion, claiming that Tennant's letters

have meant more to me than anyone's. You write of Willa with such love and understanding—it is as if you were writing my own thoughts of her. I can't think of her as in the past—to me she seems more in the present than ever before—and in fact past and present seem not to have any real meaning any more—they all seem one.

Describing Cather's death as "so vast in its implications" that he could not "yet come to grips with the full desolation of it," Tennant yet again recognized Lewis's right to an even more profound grief: "And if I feel this, how much more you must feel it!" Like Earl Brewster, Tennant nevertheless proffered spiritual consolation: "People who love each other—are never quite separated, are they." He called her idea that "past and present have lost their meanings" an "illusion" because "Willa is very close to you."[78]

"I feel we must dispense with the preliminaries of acquaintanceship, and become full-fledged friends," Tennant wrote in March 1948, and he was soon urging Lewis to travel with him. She did not join him in Cyprus in the summer of 1948, as he urged, because she was too busy with her duties as Cather's literary executor. However, she continued to share her thoughts about Cather with him, and he continued to respond with sympathy. Writing of attending a piano recital by Rudolf Serkin, she confessed that she paid little attention to the music because she was thinking about Cather and about Tennant's trip to Cyprus: "The hall was packed with people, and so was the platform, but curiously there was an empty seat beside me—It reminded me very much of how we used to go to concerts. I was always so proud of her, she seemed so fine, so distinguished, so above all that crowd of people." He responded with enthusiasm, "How I love you for your thinking at the concert! No beautiful things in life are ever lost."[79]

Lewis met up with Tennant in Paris in the fall of 1948, the first of many trips with him. She was old enough to be his mother, and Tennant's biographer characterizes the "older" Lewis as a "caring, cosseting . . . nanny figure[]." Lewis was not maternal, however. Rather, she and Tennant formed a bond based on their shared sexuality and singleness, a kinship largely unspoken but nevertheless powerfully present. Mired in grief, Lewis needed, as Tennant wrote her, "to be felicitously uprooted by a friend. . . . The soul needs this wonderful latitude—to be strengthened and soothed, restored with power."[80]

In Paris, Lewis revisited many sites she and Cather had enjoyed together over the course of their several shared trips there, but traveling to Florida and Jamaica with Tennant was a new experience. In April 1949, when they were in Tampa, they "lunched at the beach" on a "wild, windy day," with "the wind lashing the awnings." This was a suitable setting for Tennant to disclose a stormy chapter in his life. Lewis wrote in her diary, "Stephen told me of the years 1927–1934" (the years encompassing his relationship with Sassoon). "I cannot write of it. His confidence in me moves me very deeply." Even though Tennant himself, not Sassoon, ended the relationship, he spent the rest of his life looking back on it longingly. Mostly, however, Lewis found Florida and Stephen sunny and pleasurable. As she wrote a few days later, she was "sad all morning until Stephen came—then no more sadness. He arrived so radiant, golden—what an incomparable nature! It is as if the air brightened when he comes into a place—as if some mysterious quality of happiness stole into it."[81]

Lewis returned to New York for a time, but in the summer of 1949, she met up again with Tennant, this time in California. She and Cather had taken the train through the Mohave Desert on their way to San Francisco in 1941. Riding through the desert with Tennant in a hired car brought back memories of Cather. "We came down into the desert," she wrote in her journal. "The Joshua trees in bloom—Willa!" Tennant had kept reptiles as pets his entire life, and he sought out encounters with them on their travels, one at a snake den in the California desert. "Stephen with the snake—one of the loveliest things I have ever seen," Lewis reflected. "It took away all horror and ugliness from the thought of snakes." From the snake den, they drove into a beautiful valley between the mountains, "an enchanted place, so full of peace and happiness." She wondered to herself, "[S]hall I ever find such peace and happiness again as I found there?"[82]

Lewis would make two other important male friends in the 1950s. Like Tennant, they were single, and although they had not, like Tennant, known Cather, they were great fans of her work. George Kates was an expert on Chinese furniture and decorative arts, and Patrick Ferry was an army nurse with a passion for book collecting. As Tennant gradually withdrew from the world and become something of a hermit at his house in the English countryside, Kates became Lewis's traveling companion. Her relationships with Kates and Ferry were not romantic any more than her relationship with Tennant was—Kates was almost certainly gay, and perhaps Ferry was as well. Rather, Cather was a sort of absent third party to these relationships. These men valued Lewis as a living connection to a great artist they admired, and Lewis valued Kates and Ferry, as she had valued Tennant, because their devotion to Cather helped keep her memory alive.[83]

"To Look After Willa's things": The Work
of Literary Executorship

Lewis never had the luxury of spending all of her time grieving. In the spring of 1948, she had finally notified the J. Walter Thompson Co. that she would not be returning from her unpaid leave of absence. She was sixty-six years old, certainly old enough to enjoy retirement, but her duties as literary executor had become a nearly a full-time job. Her grieving and her work as executor inevitably intermingled. In his letter of condolence, Stephen Tennant both offered Lewis sympathy for her loss and queried "if there is to be a life of Willa Cather written" and wondered who would write it. "I do not know of anyone comparable to her in perceptiveness & generosity of feeling capable of doing it," he elaborated, a "great enough of artist in words." Agreeing with him that it would be difficult to find the right biographer, Lewis explained that Cather had "made me literary trustee in her will" and that her will "strictly prohibited the publication of any of her letters, or any part or parts of any of her letters." It seems that Cather never discussed this provision of her will with Lewis, leaving her guessing as to her motive. "I think she dreaded the wrong kind of biography," Lewis hypothesized, "and that it was with this in mind that she made the prohibition."[84]

In any event, Lewis's first order of business as literary executor was inventorying Cather's copyrights to make sure no renewals were missed. Her next order of business, as she explained to Tennant in rejecting his invitation to travel to Cyprus, was "to look after Willa's things—there are so many of them still unfinished." Out of the latter task emerged *The Old Beauty and Others* (1948), a collection of three short stories unpublished at the time of Cather's death, and out of the former a collection of Cather's critical writings, *Willa Cather on Writing* (1949). From the start Alfred Knopf urged Lewis to put herself forward in print as an authority on Cather. He proposed that the firm draft a "definitive" note about the status of the stories collected in *The Old Beauty* for her to review but asked that she herself "draft a brief biography that should appear on the wrapper" of *The Old Beauty*. Lewis opted to draft both the explanatory text and biographical note herself, but both appeared anonymously rather than under her name.[85]

After meeting up with Tennant in Paris in the fall of 1948, Lewis decided that her new friend should write a preface for *Willa Cather on Writing*. Alfred Knopf was dubious, writing Lewis in March 1949 that he "was never sure that you were <u>sure</u> you wanted the little book of essays to have an introduction by

Mr. Tennant" and that she should not "<u>promise</u> Mr. Tennant anything . . . until you can read what he writes for the purpose." He felt that "the essays <u>don't</u> need any critical forward—but perhaps something quite personal in the way of a portrait of their author." Lewis ignored Knopf's gentle suggestions that she write a personal preface about her late partner, but her choice is unsurprising. Aside from a few advertising trade essays, she had not written for print publication under her own name for many years. Instead, she was the anonymous author of magazine paragraphs and advertising copy, and she was the editor of prose written by others (including Cather).[86]

Tennant worked for decades on his novel *Lascar* without finishing it, but he finished "The Room Beyond," the critical essay prefacing *Willa Cather on Writing*, with Lewis acting behind the scenes as his editorial collaborator. As she had written in her first letter to Tennant, he seemed to be writing her "own thoughts of" Cather, and so she would let him be her surrogate. She wove many statements from her letters to him into his essay, and on their trip to Florida in 1949, she dictated the complete text to a hotel stenographer in Tampa on the same day that he told her about his relationship with Siegfried Sassoon. She then reviewed and revised the document with him and finally sent it off to Knopf.[87]

Knopf and Raymond Preston, the firm's chief copyeditor, found the result baffling. "Mr. Preston has dealt with it in pencil and very mildly," Knopf explained to Lewis. "He has disregarded my pencilled question marks for the most part because he says that quite frankly he either does not know what Mr. Tennant is trying to say or he doesn't agree with it." Returning the marked-up document to Lewis rather than to Tennant, Knopf made one concrete suggestion for revision but otherwise left it to Lewis, asking her to "give this little manuscript your own best attention and then let me have it back in what you regard as final and satisfactory form." Knopf had seen edited typescripts of all of Cather's works his firm had published—he knew Lewis was Cather's editor, and he trusted her to untangle Tennant's preface extolling Cather's artistry. For the time being, however, Knopf gave up his attempts to get her to write about Cather under her own name.[88]

Willa Cather Living and Edith Lewis Living

I reserve for my epilogue the story of Lewis's work with E. K. Brown on an authorized biography of Cather and the period of confusion and conflict after

Brown died in 1952 before completing it. An unexpected outcome of these events was that Lewis finally agreed to publish about Cather under her own name. At Knopf's urging, she revised the narrative "notes" about Cather's life she had written for Brown and expanded them into *Willa Cather Living*, which was published nearly simultaneously with *Willa Cather: A Critical Biography*.

Lewis received many letters from friends praising her achievement in the book, with two themes of praise recurring: that the book was beautiful and that it was a book that Cather herself would have appreciated. "Oh, Edith," Meta Cather wrote, "it is a beautiful book." She was touched to see her late husband sympathetically portrayed and felt that Roscoe "would be so happy about the book" and that it was "the sort of thing that would have pleased Willie." The book confirmed the feeling she had at the moment of Willa Cather's death: that Lewis was "the one person, above all others, who knew Willie and knew how she felt about things" and was the best person to write a book about her. "How different the whole thing from the Bennett book," she observed, referring to *The World of Willa Cather* (1951), a book by Mildred Bennett focusing on Cather's childhood years in Red Cloud. "You are intelligent—cultivated—educated—The sort of person who could understand and appreciate Willa." Mabel Luhan praised Lewis's "perfect picture of Willa" and, like Meta Cather, thanked Lewis for her portrayal of her late husband: "Your words about Tony were especially touching to me."[89]

Louise Burroughs (formerly Guerber), who had met Cather at the Denver Public Library in 1925 and who was a frequent guest at Bank Street when she moved to New York, wrote that the book "deeply moved" her. She also "admire[d]" as "perfect" Lewis's "style, discrimination, exposition and restraint." "For the first time since she left us," Burroughs explained, "I was able to recall without too much pain my own, to me always incredible, experience of Miss Cather's friendship through the years from our meeting in Denver in 1925." Recognizing that Lewis perhaps had not gone to the "depth" she might have, she found it "beautifully true." She feared that for critics, the simultaneous publication with Brown's biography (completed by Leon Edel) might overshadow Lewis's. She also felt sure, however, that "Miss Cather's friends can fully realize the small miracle you have worked; can appreciate the sureness, delicacy and tact with which you have threaded your way through the intricacies and complexities of a long life. In any case one of those friends thanks you with a very full heart."[90]

Earl Brewster praised Lewis's book as "splendidly and vividly written . . . well titled Willa Cather Living." While he "admire[d] very greatly" "the absolutely complete absence of egoism with which [she] ha[d] written these memoirs, of which [she] was such a part," he liked the preface and introduction best because Lewis "seemed more there" in them. Abby Merchant, Lewis's old friend from Smith College who had lived at 60 Washington Square when both Cather and Lewis also lived there, found the evidence of Lewis herself in the book that Earl Brewster had been hard-pressed to find. She observed that the only review that had done Lewis's book justice was in the *Atlantic Monthly*, "which said in effect that you had preserved Willa's personality in amber. To me the amber was your own personality. Oh Edith I think you have made a lovely, lovely thing and I keep thinking how much Willa would have appreciated it aside from her part in it."[91]

Laura Paxton, a college friend Lewis had not seen since graduation, discerned in her reading of the book something of Lewis's regret about giving up her own ambition to be an artist. When they both lived in Hatfield House as students, Paxton and Lewis were similarly situated as the midwestern daughters of Ivy League–educated fathers. However, Paxton chose a very different life after college: she returned home to Princeton, Indiana, lived at home, stayed single, and did not pursue a career. Paxton told Lewis that reading *Willa Cather Living* "was a delight from first to last," its portrait of Cather so "vivid" that Paxton could "almost persuade" herself that she had known Cather even though she had never seen her. "How much you must miss her, even now!" she wrote with sympathy. "And what an interesting life you have had! I never heard that you knew Willa Cather—odd, isn't it?" Paxton explained that for "some years" after their 1902 Smith graduation, she "kept looking out for some story or article" by Lewis in a magazine, for she knew Lewis "wanted to write." Having read *Willa Cather Living*, Paxton reflected, "I can understand now why you did not."[92]

Lewis's memoir also attracted notice from her and Cather's friends from Whale Cove. The Jordan sisters, still sharing the Boston apartment they took in 1939 after Alice retired from the Boston Public Library and Mary from the Kimerley School for Girls, both wrote Lewis praising her book. "I have always considered that we had a great privilege in knowing Miss Cather as we did during those summers at Grand Manan," Mary wrote. "I shall always remember the walks we had across the pasture by our little vegetable patch in the sunny afternoons." Praising the "delicacy and skill" with which Lewis handled the "difficult" task of writing the memoir, Alice remarked, "I wish you might find it possible to come back to the Island." Marie Felix, still living with family in Auburndale, wrote, "I have just been reading your book and realising anew how dependent a 'genius' is on the unfailing devotion of someone else—We all at Whale Cove recognized that 'someone.'" She, like Alice Jordan, invited Lewis to return to the island: "Someday perhaps you will come back to your little Grand Manan home, though the battle with the alders is lost, I'm afraid. Such of the old ones as come back there will be delighted to see you."[93]

Lewis's pleasure in the publication of her book and its reception was tinged with sadness. Her sister Ruth, who had been so important to her in the wake of Cather's death, was terminally ill with cancer. As she wrote Alfred Knopf in February 1953, declining a dinner party invitation, "my situation is so grim just at the present that I don't see how I can. My sister cannot recover." Long subway trips to the hospital in Brooklyn four times a week left her feeling so depleted she had "no energy for anything else." She wrote Earl Brewster that she felt despair at "dark destructive forces," but he assured her she had "the power within [her] to meet" them, and he urged her not to exhaust herself with so much traveling to Brooklyn that she would "make [herself] ill from the strain," which would prevent her from helping Ruth. When Ruth was well enough to spend the summer on Cape Cod with friends, Edith was able to take up Stephen Tennant's invitation to join him in Rome.[94]

The reprieve was only temporary, however. By August, Ruth's health had "taken a turn for the worse," and she was soon hospitalized near their brother Harold's family in Braintree, where Edith visited her several times. In late December, Ruth died in her sleep, leaving Edith feeling fractured and her mind lacking "inner unity." Writing from India, Earl Brewster offered his usual Hindu-inflected spiritual consolation—"[Y]ou cannot feel sad your sister is freed from any further suffering. Death seems to me a wonderful liberation"—and because Stephen Tennant was visiting New York City, he was able to console her in person. Nevertheless, Ruth had been part of Edith's life in New York for more than thirty years, and now she gone.[95]

In the early 1950s, more than once Edith Lewis planned to travel to Grand Manan to look after the cottage she and Cather had built at Whale Cove, which she intended to leave to Cather's nieces and nephews. However, because of her health and other travel plans, and perhaps because she feared the sadness that might engulf her there, she never made it back. In 1956, L. Keith Ingersoll, the driving force behind the Grand Manan Historical Society, wrote her that trees and underbrush were overtaking the cottage, which was "quickly falling to the earth." He proposed she transfer the property to the historical society or another public association so it might be repaired and made "into a small literary museum. We would attempt to find first editions, manuscripts, or at least sufficient copies of all Miss Cather's book for quiet reading. It would be opened in the summer months for the enjoyment and enlightenment of both natives and visitors." "It just seems," he argued, "that, if the island contributed anything to your happiness and that of Willa Cather, the Island community should benefit from the cultural association which this afforded."[96]

Lewis politely, but firmly declined. "I have not of course forgotten the cottage on Grand Manan," she wrote. "I have on the contrary given much anxious thought." She had not given up on the idea of restoring the cottage but felt it required "a personal visit." She cautioned that because she and Cather "left the place intending to go back," they "left many of [their] personal things." "I should not wish any one to handle them—especially Miss Cather's things—except myself." Although she promised to "continue to think over your suggestions," she closed her letter, "I know, from my long association with Miss Cather, that she wished her books to be her true memorial—and I think I might even say the only memorial." She and others could, after a fashion, visit the cottage by reading Cather's story "Before Breakfast," which is set there, but they could not visit it as a museum. Lewis could not prevent the formation of the Willa Cather Pioneer Memorial then taking place in Red Cloud—she owned no property there—but her resistance to it was consistent with her response to the proposal to turn the Whale Cove cottage into a public memorial.[97]

Through the 1950s, despite her failure to travel to Grand Manan, Lewis remained active. She entertained many queries and visits from those seeking information about Cather, traveled with friends old and new, and read a great deal. It was a struggle, but she reconciled herself to life alone. Even before her sister Ruth died, she wrote to Earl Brewster that living alone was a great privilege because it allowed one "to think about the things you really like to think about." "[T]he world of thought and feeling has seemed to become more and more and more absorbing to me," she explained, "more inexhaustible and sustaining and how I feel the need of outside distractions less and less." Brewster agreed, responding, "[W]hat a great privilege it is, if you cannot be with those you love deeply, to be alone, to live alone."[98]

"A Long-Time Loving and Devoted Friend of the Late Authoress Willa Cather": Edith Lewis's Final Decade and Death

By the early 1960s, Lewis was old and frail. In 1961, she began suffering from a painful case of diverticulitis. Her brother Harold, who was not well himself, came down from Boston to New York to make sure that she was being cared for properly. She needed full-time nursing care so that she could receive hypodermic injections for the excruciating pain, but with that care she was able to stay in the Park Avenue apartment. She regretfully declined a request from Harwood Brewster Picard to edit her mother's memoir. As she explained, she was "so weak" that she couldn't "perform the simplest household tasks." Pointing to her shaky handwriting, she added, "[I]t is even difficult for me to write letters—though I try to write as many as I can, it is such a pleasure to get them." In 1962, she also proposed to withdraw as Cather's literary executor in favor of Alfred Knopf, but this transfer could not happen without the approval of the courts, and Knopf was not interested in assuming the responsibility anyway. The Knopf offices needed Lewis's signature for some matters, but they gradually began carrying on the work of managing Cather's literary assets without consulting her.[99]

When Lewis's diverticulitis failed to resolve itself, she had three surgeries in 1963 to address both it and a hernia. Harold had died in December 1962, but Edith's sister Helen Lewis Morgan, her last remaining and considerably younger sibling, had moved to Long Island after more than twenty years in the West. She stepped in to supervise her sister's care, including that required when she was hospitalized again in the summer of 1964 for several months. Lewis also kept in touch with and received occasional visits from members of Cather's family.[100]

In the late summer of 1965, Cather's niece Helen Southwick and her husband, Philip, who lived in Pittsburgh, visited a bedridden Lewis at 570 Park Avenue and asked about the Grand Manan cottage. Lewis encouraged them to travel to the island but warned that the cottage was in no condition to house anyone. She told them to ask Ralph Beal, the local resident who had looked after the cottage for them, for the key. When the Southwicks arrived, Beal gave them directions to the cottage and told them a key was unnecessary. They "struggled in a crouching posture through and under the alders for seemingly hundreds of yards" to a grey-shingled derelict structure from which all of the furniture and most of the doors had been stolen, with floors too rotten to walk on, the plaster ceiling falling down in Willa's former bedroom, and the roof in a sway-backed condition that seemed to foretell imminent collapse. Remarkable as it now seems, though, most of the interior walls and ceilings were intact. Almost the only indications that Willa Cather had ever been there were the typewriter stand near the attic window and the old Oliver typewriter, by then a solid block of rust, standing on one of the shelves.

Discovering that the taxes were three years in arrears, they asked Lewis to transfer the title to them. They then paid the back taxes and restored the cottage for their own use.[101]

As a result of their efforts, the cottage continued to stand, but the truth of Lewis's role as its owner and her vital presence with Cather there was fading. The Beals and women who had served in the inn dining room believed that the J. Walter Thompson Co. printed Cather's books and Lewis had been an employee of this printing house. It puzzled them that she had spent so long at Grand Manan away from her job. Others believed that Helen Southwick had inherited the cottage directly from her aunt. The cottage became "Willa Cather's cottage," "the only house she ever owned."[102]

In 1966, when a much beloved nurse, Miss Spillane, married and became Mrs. Reynolds, Helen Morgan found another nurse for her sister through an agency. This nurse, Emmeline Ruddy, seems to have worked to socially isolate Lewis in order to gain control over her finances. Even when Lewis was seriously ill and in and out of the hospital in the early and middle 1960s, she continued to write letters and receive visitors. Of the nearly six hundred Lewis letters to various correspondents I have located, one hundred are dated from 1960 through January 1966. However, I have found not a single letter dated after Ruddy became Lewis's full-time nurse. Only Lewis's sister was able to persist and continue making in-person visits—Helen Southwick was turned away. What Helen Morgan saw, including her sister being overmedicated, disturbed her enough that she began keeping a record of her observations.[103]

On August 11, 1972, Lewis finally died at home in the 570 Park Avenue apartment she had shared with Cather and where Cather had also died. Lewis was ninety, and 1972 was the year before the one-hundredth anniversary of what had been established by E. K. Brown, the biographer she authorized, as Cather's actual birth year. In 1963, Lewis had executed a will dividing most of her assets between Helen Morgan and Helen Southwick, but in 1968 she had executed a new will dividing those assets between Helen Morgan and Emmeline Ruddy. When the conflicting wills emerged, Helen Southwick contested the 1968 will, a dispute not settled until 1976.

In the immediate aftermath of Edith Lewis's death, however, Helen Morgan took control of arrangements. She placed a death notice in the *New York Times* that called her "[a] long-time loving and devoted friend of the late authoress Willa Cather"—her sister made no mention of her professional accomplishments in magazines and advertising, nor did the obituary writer for the *New York Times*. Lewis specified in her will that she wanted "my remains to be buried in my plot in the burying ground at Jaffrey, New Hampshire, near Jaffrey Common, beside my friend, Willa Sibert Cather," and her sister honored her wishes. After visitation and services at a funeral home in the town on Long Island where Helen Morgan lived, she and her daughters accompanied the body to Jaffrey for burial. Helen also followed the direction in her sister's will "that no headstone or marker be put over [her] grave."[104]

In both wills, Edith Lewis left all Cather-authored books and "all letters, manuscripts and all other handwritten and typed papers, whether written by me or by any other person," to Helen Southwick and Helen's brother, Charles Cather. Lewis made no provision in either the 1963 or the 1968 will concerning the copyrights and royalties of Willa Cather's works, because Lewis herself had only a life interest in the literary estate. It was for the courts to follow the provisions of Cather's will as to the succession of beneficiaries and to appoint a new executor (Charles Cather put himself forward and was appointed).

The stage was set for Cather's "long-time loving and devoted friend" to disappear.

Epilogue

The Edith Lewis Ghost

Edith Lewis has often been described as a nobody, a person of no importance to Willa Cather. As a result, her behavior after Cather's death has been characterized as ridiculous or hysterical and out of proportion to her lived relationship with the great novelist. In the preceding chapter, I devoted substantial space to Lewis's experience of grief after Cather's death because from the beginning of my research I have aimed to restore the integrity of her grief. My account of the life she truly shared with Cather makes it abundantly clear that she had a right to those emotions.

And yet in the years after Cather's death, many refused to see what was obvious. In this epilogue, then, I turn back to the years immediately following Cather's death to reveal how Lewis was transformed into a ridiculous specter. I focus particularly on Cather biographer E. K. Brown and Willa Cather's old friend Dorothy Canfield Fisher as they observed Lewis—or, more to the point, often failed to see her for what she was. If they had admitted what Lewis was, they would have had to confront the truth about Cather's sexuality, and because they were invested in the dead author's future reputation, they were unwilling to do so.

When Cather and Lewis began living together, the time (1908) and the place (Greenwich Village) made their choice unexceptionable. Cather's death coincided uncannily, however, with the advent of the Cold War. As historian David Johnson explains in *The Lavender Scare: The Cold War Persecution of Gays and Lesbians in the Federal Government*, "With the nation on 'moral alert' because of the Cold War, stable, monogamous, heterosexual marriages were seen as a key weapon in the arsenal against degeneracy and internal Communist subversion." Cather was dead, and Lewis was financially independent rather than a federal employee who might be fired if the nature of her relationship with Cather were revealed. However, as Johnson documents, the effects of the effort to purge "homosexuals" from government reached far beyond the civil service.[1]

Furthermore, as Terry Castle argues in *The Apparitional Lesbian: Female Homosexuality and Modern Culture*, "When it comes to lesbians . . . many people have trouble seeing what's in front of them. The lesbian remains a kind of 'ghost effect' in the . . . world of modern life: elusive, vaporous, difficult to spot—even when she is there, in plain view, mortal and magnificent, at the center." The lesbian is so "difficult to see," Castle maintains, "because she has been 'ghosted'—or made to seem invisible—by culture itself" and because she "represents a threat to patriarchal protocol." Choosing to live their lives together, Cather and Lewis had violated the patriarchal protocol. The letters between E. K. Brown and Dorothy Canfield Fisher, and then the letters between Fisher and E. K. Brown's widow after his untimely death, are haunted by this threat of Cather's sexuality, which they seek to contain.[2]

* * *

E. K. Brown, a University of Chicago English professor, really wanted to write a biography of Willa Cather. In 1937, he sent Cather an offprint of an article he had written about her, and while she characterized his article as "friendly," she also firmly corrected what she saw as his errors. In 1946, he tried again, sending her his *Yale Review* essay "Homage to Willa Cather," which she liked a great deal and which inaugurated a lively correspondence extending over the last six months of her life. Cather died on April 24, 1947, and on April 28, as death notices began appearing in newspapers, Brown wrote Alfred Knopf proposing himself as Cather's biographer. Knopf professed himself an admirer of Brown's *Yale Review* essay and was "much interested" in Brown's proposal. However, he did not "feel able to attempt to act" on it because he had to "wait until Miss Cather's literary executor [could] size up the whole situation created by her death."[3]

Brown may have heard through the grapevine of Lewis's existence, but he may have also mentally slotted her into the position of secretary, as so many did. He clearly did not know that Lewis was Cather's executor. On his part, Alfred Knopf had had very limited contact with Lewis before Cather's death and wasn't sure what course Lewis would take.

Grieving Cather's death and preoccupied with her other tasks as literary executor, Lewis did not approach Brown about writing an authorized biography until April 1948. She introduced herself concisely, making clear why any Cather biographer would have to work with her:

I have been a friend of Miss Cather for many years—we have shared an apartment together since she first came to New York. I was with her on most of her trips to the Southwest—and to Quebec, when she was writing Shadows on the Rock. We read together the proofs of all her books after The Troll Garden. In her will she left me all her papers, etc.—and made me her executor and literary trustee.

Brown eagerly accepted Lewis's invitation to write the biography. In 1949 and 1950, he visited her at 570 Park Avenue several times, and she facilitated his biographical research and writing by sending him materials, including transcriptions of hundreds of letters, and by introducing him to Cather's family and friends. When Brown asked her questions, she responded in detail, and they soon agreed that she would write detailed narrative "notes" about Cather's life for him to use as source material. Despite all of the work she did for Brown, he found her troubling. When he returned to Chicago from trips to New York, he complained repeatedly to his wife, Margaret, about Lewis's "personality" and claimed that "when he was with Miss Lewis he often had the uncomfortable feeling that Miss Lewis expected Miss Cather to pop up around the door and possibly rebuke Miss Lewis for something she had said."[4]

Lewis had included Dorothy Canfield Fisher on a list of people whom E. K. Brown should meet, but she explained to him in December 1948, "Perhaps it would be better for you to approach Mrs. Fisher directly—I have not had any communication with her for so long." Brown and Fisher began corresponding shortly thereafter, and when Brown traveled to Vermont to meet Fisher in person in the summer of 1949, they became fast friends. Apart from his research on Cather's life, the ambitious English professor found Fisher an exciting new friend (and, indeed, much of their correspondence has nothing to do with Cather). Fisher was from an academic family. Her father had been chancellor at the University of Nebraska when she and Cather first met in the 1890s, and she herself had conducted dissertation research in France for her Ph.D. in French from Columbia University (Brown's doctorate was from the Sorbonne). Fisher was also a respected and popular novelist and a member of the Book of the Month Club selection committee. On top of these professional accomplishments, she was "*Mrs.* Fisher," a wife, mother, and grandmother. Rather than complain about her to his wife, Brown praised "Mrs. Fisher" as "a wonderful woman, a wonderful woman."[5]

When Brown and Fisher met in Vermont, her husband, John Fisher (who had been Cather's university classmate), joined their conversations. After Brown left, Dorothy was anxious to report John's insight into a parallel between the lives of Cather and of Henry James:

[B]oth of them excluded from the usual "fair share" of success-in-the-flesh; both withdrawing into a touching shell of self-protective isolation from human life; both overweight and sensitive about it; both deprived all through their adult lives of the pressing immediate impact of adult emotional experiences. For neither of them, after growing up, ever had any close intimate personal relations—save those with the family circle which were part of their youth.

Brown found this comparison "extremely suggestive," describing himself as "an admirer of the art" of Henry James "but ill at ease with the personality." Brown also hoped, however, that Cather might have her "personality" rescued. He excitedly reported to Fisher his discovery of "something that looks like a romance in Willa Cather's life, in the years just before the First War." In the fall of 1949, Brown had visited with Elizabeth Shepley Sergeant, who had told him about Julio, a young Mexican man whom Cather had met on her 1912 trip to Arizona to visit her brother Douglass and about whom she had rhapsodized in letters to Sergeant. "I would be deeply interested," Brown wrote Fisher, "to know whether you think there was a change in [Cather] as a person in the years from 1912 to 1914."[6]

After the 1904–1905 conflict between Cather and Fisher over Cather's story "The Profile," the relationship between the two women was strained and their contact infrequent until Cather reached out to Fisher while she was writing *One of Ours* (she needed Fisher's expertise about wartime conditions in France). However, Fisher did not disclose to Brown her estrangement from Cather and its source. Instead, she wrote him that she was unable to answer his question because during the years in question she had been too busy promoting Maria Montessori's educational methods in the U.S. and then with her war work in France to keep up with Cather.[7]

Brown continued his near-desperate pursuit of a "romance" in Cather's life, by which he meant a *heterosexual* romance. In 1951, he was intrigued by the story of a "normal affair" between Cather and a Catholic composer, married but separated from his wife, whom Cather met during her residence at the MacDowell Colony in 1926. This story was being peddled by Nebraska-born playwright Fred Ballard, who had also been at the MacDowell Colony in 1926 and who said he was "sworn to secrecy" about the composer's identity. Edith Lewis figured in Brown's pursuit only as an obstruction to getting at the truth rather than as the answer to the riddle he repeatedly posed to himself. And Fisher continued to hold onto her authority as interpreter of Cather's life.[8]

Brown was not the only entrant in the Cather biography sweepstakes. Mildred Bennett, who had moved to Red Cloud in the mid-1940s with her doctor husband, had begun research for a biography even before Cather's death, with Carrie Miner Sherwood as her primary informant. By reading Cather's letters to Sherwood, Bennet had learned of her friendship with the Menuhin family, so in the summer of 1947 she traveled to Southern California and wrote the Menuhins proposing to interview them at their ranch. Marutha Menuhin telegraphed Lewis to ask whether she should speak to Bennett, and Lewis told her no. "The thing that gripes me," Bennett wrote to her husband back in Nebraska, "is that, if I hadn't mentioned the word biography, I would have gotten by with it." After being rebuffed, Bennett abandoned her plan for a full biography but forged ahead with a book focusing primarily on Cather's Nebraska years. In 1948, Bennett went to New York to meet Alfred Knopf and propose that his firm publish her book. Knopf sent Bennett to visit Lewis at 570 Park Avenue and asked Lewis to review Bennett's sample chapters. Lewis was unimpressed either by the quality of Bennett's research or by her prose, and on her advice Knopf declined to publish Bennett's book.[9]

Certainly, Lewis had not smoothed the way for Bennett, but as Cather's literary executor she was not obligated to help anyone pursuing biographical research, especially considering the time and effort she was investing in assisting E. K. Brown with the authorized biography. Nevertheless, Bennett developed a deep sense of grievance against Lewis. On the same trip east during which Bennett was rebuffed by Knopf and Lewis, she presented herself to Dorothy Canfield Fisher in Vermont, and the two subsequently corresponded. As Bennett wrote gleefully to Fisher in June 1949, "I have a collection of photos of Willa from baby-hood up that will make Miss Lewis most unhappy." Bennett's book, *The World of Willa Cather*, was not published until 1951, but it included several photos of Cather as an adolescent, when she called herself "William" and wore her hair in a very short masculine style.[10]

In 1948, when James Shively, a graduate student at the University of Nebraska, contacted Dorothy Canfield Fisher as part of his research for a dissertation on Cather's years at the university, Fisher had put him in touch with Knopf and Lewis. When Lewis answered Shively's questions, she asked him, as Knopf had suggested, that he promise not to publish his research as a book unless she or Knopf granted permission. He acceded to this condition, so Lewis and Knopf were thus surprised and disappointed in 1950 when the University of Nebraska Press published *Willa Cather's Campus Years*, a collection of Cather's student publications supplemented by anecdotes Shively had collected from her classmates. Even though Cather started to let her hair grow during her third year in Lincoln and adopted a more conventionally feminine style of dress, sixty years later her classmates remembered only the short masculine haircut.[11]

In the wake of Shively's book, Fisher wrote to Brown that the "effort" of Lewis and Knopf

> to respect Willa's wish to keep her girlhood days unchronicled was beginning to give rise to rather disagreeable surmises as to the cause of this wish of hers. Several people in the literary world have asked me quite horrid questions about this point—based on the idea that so great a desire to keep something hidden must mean that the "something" has a sinister color, or would be a disgrace to be known.

Fisher stridently proclaimed that Cather's "youth and girlhood and young maturity were so extremely innocent of anything even unconventional in behavior" and protested that the "vehemence in denying" had the opposite of the intended effect. She didn't particularly like *Willa Cather's Campus Years*, but she thought its publication would quell the "sinister" rumors.[12]

Lewis had provided Brown with "notes" covering Cather's entire life, but she professed that she could not offer him much about Cather's Pittsburgh years. Brown thus asked Fisher, who had visited Cather a number of times in Pittsburgh, to write her own narrative of this time and place in Cather's life. "I think it would help my portrait if you could quietly show that in the Pittsburgh years she was eager to know quite a variety of people," he wrote Fisher in early 1951, "and particularly that she was often—or least sometimes, I hope it was often—at least mildly interested in men."[13]

Fisher responded to this pointed query in an extraordinary long letter that she asked Brown to burn after reading. Expressing extreme hesitation to say something so "wounding" about Cather, Fisher nevertheless dove in because Brown would not be able to "understand the data about [Cather's] life" without the context she was providing. Cather was, Fisher explained, "one of those women who would like to know love, who <u>would</u> have loved to be married, who fully expected" to be married. Brown was young enough to be Fisher's son, so she felt the need to explain that in her generation it was considered "not nice" for a young woman to pursue a man, but "we all confidently expected that we would attract enough men to make a choice from." Cather was an exception, however: "The sad thing about Willa's life was that as she went along, year after year, she didn't" attract suitors. This was particularly frustrating for Cather, Fisher hypothesized, because she was a reasonably conventionally attractive woman, unlike their mutual friend from Lincoln, Mariel Gere (whom Brown had met). Every time Gere looked in the mirror and saw "that strange great gash of a mouth," she must have known, Fisher believed, that she was so ugly no man would ever want to marry her. Fisher realized that Brown might have been "misled by the protective don't-care-ism, which Willa put on—her masculine clothes and hair-cut, her proud aloofness and all the rest." This was just, however, a defensive posture—underneath, she longed to be a southern belle, just like her mother. "To acknowledge it openly"—that is, to explain Cather's life this way in Brown's biography—"would make Willa turn over in her grave." However, Fisher thought Cather "would much prefer any other explanation,—even one with a dark significance," than that Brown expose this painful truth.[14]

Brown did not burn Fisher's letter as requested, but she did destroy his response. From Fisher's next letter, however, it is clear that he revealed what he had learned from Cather's letters to Sergeant about Julio (Sergeant had recently given Brown typed excerpts from these), portraying him as a stereotypical hot Latin lover. "As to your news," Fisher responded,

> I had never heard the slightest whisper of it—but it is what the more experienced of us among Willa's friends used to hope for her—an encounter with somebody of another tradition, perhaps just (in the modern jargon) "more highly sexed" than most Anglo-Saxon intellectuals; who might just never notice any barriers which had kept others away.

She also wondered "with apprehension and sympathy" if the encounter with Julio was a "shock to [Cather]—for she was singularly unlearned in such things—as long as I knew her intimately that is—and she was not in her first youth, when mother-nature provides such elemental understanding through the senses." Nevertheless, she thought that Cather's experience with Julio "must have been all important."[15]

Where is Edith Lewis in all of this discussion of Willa Cather's romantic and sexual history? Where, for that matter, is Louise Pound, on whom Cather had an intense crush during her college years, or Isabelle McClung? Lewis, in the fashion described by Terry Castle, was being "ghosted," dematerialized and made a specter. Nevertheless, Cather's lesbianism was everywhere in Fisher and Brown's correspondence, the "sinister" and "dark" rumor that Fisher vigorously fought off even as she refused to name it. The sexologists of the late nineteenth and early twentieth centuries identified gender "inversion" as a sign of homosexuality. Cather's adolescence as "William" seemed to identify her as an invert, but Fisher defended her youthful "behavior" as innocent, with the implied corollary that homosexuality constituted guilt. When Fisher passed along her husband's analogy between Cather and James and otherwise focused on Cather's emotional "immaturity," she was dog-whistling Sigmund Freud's theory of homosexuality as a form of arrested sexual development.

As for Brown, he had signed up for writing a biography of a distinguished novelist, not a lesbian. Even though he omitted all mention of Cather's sexuality or any kind of romantic history from the biography he was writing, he still grasped at Julio as a straw that might save him from confronting who Willa Cather was—and who Edith Lewis was. Brown complained to his wife that the restrictions Lewis placed on him prevented him from writing the biography he wanted to write. Lewis was, he seemed to think, standing in the way of the truth about Cather's life—at least the truth as he hoped to find it, that a transformative experience of heterosexual passion had made her into the novelist whose artistry he so admired. Rather than Lewis standing in the way of the truth, however, she *was* the truth about Cather's life, a truth that he refused to see. He also made Lewis look silly for fearing the ghost of Cather, who might cow and admonish her. He couldn't acknowledge a different truth—that he and Lewis were sitting in the apartment where she and Cather had lived together for fifteen years and where Cather had died less than two years earlier, that Lewis was still deeply grieving her deceased partner and struggling to understand how she could best carry out her wishes. For Lewis, the Park Avenue apartment was filled with Cather's presence—was haunted by her—not because she feared her but because she missed her.

* * *

Even as E. K. Brown was calling for evidence that Cather was "mildly interested" in men, he was racing against the clock because he had been diagnosed with terminal cancer. Brown felt that Lewis was holding out on him.
He grumbled to Elizabeth Sergeant about Lewis's failure "to be courageous in
relating what she knows"—and Lewis did not tell him what she knew about
Cather's breast cancer. He, in turn, was holding out on Lewis: his death came
as a complete surprise to her, and left her as executor with an unanticipated
mess to clean up.[16]

After E. K. Brown's death, his widow, Margaret Brown, found that his
Cather biography was far along but not complete. How to finish the biography presented complicated technical questions. In the biographical narrative (as distinct from his critical interpretations of Cather's fiction), Brown
had relied heavily on Lewis's "notes": he not only had incorporated acknowledged quotations but also had paraphrased extensively without attribution.
In the judgment of E. K. Brown's former student Ernest Sirluck, the only
person who read both Brown's incomplete manuscript and all of Lewis's
notes before Margaret Brown returned them to Lewis, "If the book were
to be deprived of everything based <u>indirectly</u> on Miss Lewis's notes, there
wouldn't be much in the way of a biography left." However, just as her late
husband had not been willing to acknowledge how much Cather's life had
been intertwined with Lewis's, Margaret Brown was unwilling to acknowledge how much her husband's incomplete text was intertwined with Lewis's
"notes."[17]

Margaret Brown consulted both her late husband's colleagues and
Dorothy Canfield Fisher about her dilemma. Just days after her husband's
death, she wrote Fisher that she did not want "to jeopardize the book on
Miss Cather." Because "Edward has long told me of Miss Lewis's personality" and she feared Lewis might "fall apart" and cause trouble, she had
already written Lewis "a note in an attempt to calm her (no doubt) assorted
fears." Fisher responded by expressing sympathy for Brown and admiration
for how "courageously" she "set [herself] to save what can be saved of his
work." Fisher also assured Brown that she could "count on [her]" for help.
She wasn't sure she could help Brown manage Edith Lewis, however. She
claimed, "I have known her all my life—she and I were little girls together,
both playing violins in the local orchestra," and she believed herself to be
"on perfectly good terms with her." However, she also explained, "I have
seen very little of her for many many years—she and Miss Cather lived in
retirement you know."[18]

So which was it? Was Lewis someone she had "known" continuously, or was she someone she had once known but had not seen in decades? The latter is clearly the case. Indeed, Fisher's late 1947 correspondence with Knopf asking him how to handle the queries she was receiving about Cather reveals that she did not know that Lewis and Cather were still living together at the time of Cather's death. Fisher and Margaret Brown had not met in person before E. K. Brown's death (they apparently never did), nor did Lewis and Margaret Brown ever meet. Nevertheless, Fisher and Brown immediately formed a strong bond and allied themselves against Lewis.[19]

In June 1951, because Alfred Knopf had urged her to do so, Lewis put forward a proposal that she prepare E. K. Brown's manuscript for publication, including filling in the gaps at the beginning and end of it. After Margaret Brown reported this development to Fisher, Fisher responded in early July, "This proposition that Miss Lewis finish your husband's book about Willa Cather is very much more a drama than you realize, probably, young as you are." Despite her earlier admission that she hadn't seen Lewis in years, Fisher firmly claimed the authority to interpret Lewis's character and motivations:

> I have known Edith Lewis, as I think I told you, since we were both little girls. So I know very well, from a distance that is, the circumstances of Miss Lewis going to live with Miss Cather. She was a singularly attractive, sensitive, and everybody thought gifted girl who went to New York to see what she could do in the literary world. She was getting on very well, and had had some recognition, and indeed had won a prize for a short story in a contest of considerable importance. And then because she and Miss Cather had both lived in Lincoln, Nebraska, they came together. Miss Lewis fell at once completely under Miss Cather's influence and as far as her family and friends could see disappeared from view thereafter, until now when she is quite an old lady as I am. She has made every imaginable sacrifice, much more than a wife would make for her husband, because a wife has at least some legal position and definite recognition as a helper. This she has never had. So I can see that the opportunity to have a part in what will certainly be the very best book ever written about Willa Cather, means an enormous amount to her.

Lewis had not "disappeared." Rather it was Fisher who had "disappeared," moving her family to Vermont, where she, not her husband, was the primary breadwinner. Writing to E. K. Brown earlier the same year, Fisher had portrayed Cather as the sad spinster, never the object of a man's desire, but writing to Margaret Brown after E. K. Brown's death, she came close to admitting that Cather had had a wife. Even as she admitted this truth, she undermined Lewis's authority, telling a story about the supposed truth of Lewis's life that came to predominate in Cather scholarly circles for half a century: that Lewis was friendless and alienated from her family, that she was a nonentity who subordinated herself to a domineering Cather. Lewis was none of these things, nor was she, as Fisher claimed, powerless. Rather, the problem that both Fisher and Margaret Brown were confronting was that Lewis had power: as Cather's primary heir and her literary executor, she wielded a great deal of power and was in control of considerable financial resources.[20]

Brown wrote to Fisher in August, "I would be happy to let Miss Lewis finish the book, if it had might be [sic] the choice that Edward would make, no matter how I felt myself." Margaret Brown expressed some regret at how her actions affected Lewis, but she never acknowledged that she and Lewis were in the same position—both had lost their spouses and were trying to carry out their wishes. Instead, she repeatedly painted Lewis as a pathetic and hysterical old lady for whom she felt sorry. Certainly, E. K. Brown would not have wanted Cather's partner to finish the biography, and in the midst of the Cold War panic over homosexuality, Margaret Brown was not going to recognize her kinship with Lewis. Nevertheless, the impasse was finally resolved. Leon Edel, E. K. Brown's old friend and Sorbonne classmate, was put forward as a candidate to finish the biography. He gained Lewis's trust and consent, telling her, as he recalled, "that we were each mourning a friend: that we each were trying to be loyal to that friend, she to the subject and I to the biographer." At Knopf's urging, Lewis revised and expanded her "notes" for Brown into *Willa Cather Living*.[21]

Lewis certainly knew she was living in changed times, that her relationship with Cather, which so many people had quietly accepted in earlier decades, might be viewed very differently in the Cold War climate. When Philip Claflin, who had been the partner of her dear friend John Mosher, returned home from the war, he immediately married a woman, Vassar art history professor Agnes Rindge.[22] In the 1950s, Lewis was, as she had always been, circumspect and discreet. However, she was not hiding: she was still *there*. She had not tried to vanish, to make herself into the ghostly secret in Cather's life. Paradoxically, her visibility made it harder for people to see her. For some, Lewis's visibility enabled their willful blindness. Consider, for example,

Mildred Bennett's recollection of a lunchtime conversation with Louise Pound in 1957: "I . . . asked Miss Pound about the rumor of Miss Cather's being Lesbian. 'But who was her partner?,' she asked. I said I didn't know but thought perhaps she could help me. 'No,' she said, 'I can't.'" Edith Lewis lived another fifteen years, but in 1957, she had already become a ghost.[23]

* * *

Five years after Lewis's death, several members of the Board of Selectmen of Jaffrey, New Hampshire, petitioned the overseers of the Old Burying Ground to allow a marker on Lewis's grave. They apparently found it unseemly that the resting place of the "secretary to Willa Cather" was not marked, although it was not clear why this should concern them. Despite the fact that Helen Lewis Morgan, Edith Lewis's last living sibling, had established a continuing care fund with the trustees of the Old Burying Ground for the Cather-Lewis grave, the overseers allowed people with no relationship to either Lewis or Cather to place a small marker featuring Lewis's name and birth and death years.[24]

They got the birth year wrong—1882 instead of 1881. Perhaps they relied on the *New York Times* obituary (as opposed to the death announcement placed by her family), which said that she died at age ninety but did not specify her December birthdate. Lewis was buried at Cather's side, in the space between Cather's headstone and the cemetery's stone wall. However, cemetery regulations dictated that "one up-right marker, or headstone, be allowed per lot." When a second body was interred in a plot already bearing a headstone, either information concerning the second burial could be inscribed on the existing headstone, or a flat marker, "commonly referred to . . . as a foot marker" because "it is usually placed at the foot of the grave," might be added. Such a flat marker for Lewis was thus placed in the conventional location.[25]

In 1991, Cather's niece Helen Southwick (who anxiously policed the "lesbian theory" about her aunt) informed Lewis's niece Helen Morgan Schulte about this mysterious marker (Helen Lewis Morgan, Edith's last remaining sibling and the mother of Helen Schulte, had died). Helen Schulte wrote the Jaffrey town manager demanding to know why a headstone had been placed on her aunt's grave without the knowledge or consent of Lewis's surviving family. Discovering their misstep, the overseers apologized, but they were reluctant to simply remove the marker. Lewis's nieces and the overseers instead negotiated a compromise: the flat marker was moved to the head of the plot, next to Cather's upright stone, so that it accurately reflected the location of Lewis's remains.[26]

I heard stories about the relocation of Lewis's marker when I attended my first academic conference devoted to the life and works of Willa Cather, the 1993 Willa Cather International Seminar, held in Hastings and Red Cloud, Nebraska. The school bus driver who transported us around the countryside surrounding Red Cloud, often to country burying grounds, had heard about it. She suggested that someone (she had no idea who) didn't like what the placement of Lewis's stone at Cather's feet suggested about their relationship and thus had moved it. The logic of this comment was not clear to me. Did she assume that Lewis at Cather's feet accurately represented her subordination in a lesbian relationship, while if Lewis was at Cather's side, then they weren't lesbians? She also suggested that there was something vaguely Gothic about disturbing a grave by moving a marker, presumably under the cover of night.

Ten years later, in 2003, Anne Kaufman (whom I had first met at the 1993 conference) and I began researching Lewis's life, and we quickly discovered the real story of the gravesite. In 2011, at yet another Willa Cather International Seminar, this one held at Smith College, participants retraced my Mountain Day journey twenty-seven years earlier, which I describe in the introduction. In Northampton we boarded a bus for New Hampshire to visit the grave and other sites in and around Jaffrey. In 2003, the Shattuck Inn was no longer standing, and continuous torrential downpours made much of the planned itinerary impossible. While we were stranded inside the Old Meeting House adjoining the cemetery, I volunteered to tell the story of Cather's and Lewis's burials as I described them in the preceding chapter.

After I had concluded my remarks, a local resident, who had seen the arrival of the hearse bearing Lewis's body in 1972, offered an addition to my account that he thought was somehow revealing: Lewis was buried at night, when it was dark. There is a perfectly quotidian explanation for this evening burial. In 1972, it would have taken the better part of a day for the hearse to transport Lewis's body from New York to Jaffrey. Her sister and nieces who accompanied the body were not coming to Jaffrey for a vacation (and probably couldn't have gotten rooms on short notice at the height of vacation season anyway), so the interment took place immediately, and they left.

In 2013, a retired English professor worked with a local funeral home to rearrange elements of the Cather-Lewis grave. He had two small round corner markers placed at the foot of the plot, moved Lewis's marker back to the conventional location, and added a new foot marker with Cather's name engraved on it. The result was unambiguous: anyone visiting the grave can now see where each woman's remains are buried. However, the error in Lewis's birthdate persists, as does the violation of her wishes as expressed in her will.[27]

Readers who have reached the end of this book can appreciate the multiple ironies of the gravesite and its transformation over two decades. First, the selectmen of Jaffrey misperceived Cather and Lewis's creative partnership as an employer-employee relationship—although certainly they must have known that an employee would not be buried by her employer's side. Second, by placing a foot marker to commemorate "the secretary of Willa Cather," they unintentionally gave rise to the notion that Lewis was buried at Cather's feet. This myth underwrote some of the dismissals of Lewis described in my introduction, including Mildred Bennett's proclamation that Lewis "deliberately put herself at Willa Cather's feet and gloried in her position there." The collaboration between Cather's and Lewis's nieces to undo this unwarranted intrusion led some to devise Gothic tales of graveyard doings under the cover of darkness. While these shenanigans transpired above ground, Lewis's remains reposed precisely where she had wanted them to. She and Cather are side by side in death, just as they were in life. And about once a year, Venus and Jupiter conjoin in the sky, near the western horizon, before they follow the sun and slip behind Gap Mountain, leaving Cather and Lewis as "the only wonderful things" because they "can wonder."[28]

But why did Lewis request that no marker be placed? She did not explain why in her will, any more than Cather explained in *her* will why she forbade the publication of her letters. Nevertheless, both gestures seem fraught with meaning. Were they trying to hide something? In declining a grave marker, was Lewis demonstrating that she was so self-effacing, so weak and meek that she would not assert herself even in death? Lewis certainly knew about the cemetery regulations—it was she, not Cather, who bought the cemetery plot—and those regulations were designed to fit a patriarchal family model: the single surname of the patriarch on the headstone, the names and dates of those under his authority (his wife and unmarried children) inscribed under the surname on the headstone or arrayed on flat markers at the foot of the grave. Lewis, however, had used the space of the headstone to create a beautiful public memorial for Cather, writing and assembling text that covered the entire face of the granite marker (Figure E.1). There was no place to squeeze in her own name and birth and death dates without violating

Figure E.1 Willa Cather's grave marker in the Old Burying Ground in Jaffrey, New Hampshire. Photograph Andrew Jewell.

the integrity of the memorial for Cather she had created. And perhaps the only other option, a foot marker, was equally unappealing. Besides, for decades, both in her professional life in magazines and advertising and in her creative partnership with Cather, she had been the invisible hand, an anonymous author or editorial collaborator. She was already as much a part of the memorial she had created for Cather as she was a part of Cather's fiction. She didn't need a separate marker. She knew who she was, and that was enough.

Notes

Throughout the notes, Willa Cather's and Edith Lewis's names are abbreviated WC and EL, respectively. Dates are represented in the month/day/year format; for example, December 21, 1881, is 12/21/1881. Conjectured date elements are enclosed in brackets.

Letters that have been published in *The Complete Letters of Willa Cather: A Digital Edition* (cather.unl.edu/letters) are cited by their letter number in the edition, for example, WC to Alfred Knopf, 9/10/1936 (#2689). *The Selected Letters of Willa Cather*, ed. Andrew Jewell and Janis Stout (New York: Vintage, 2014), is abbreviated *SL*, and letters published in it are cited, for example, as WC to Elizabeth Shepley Sergeant, 7/28/[1915], *SL*, 206–207. For citations to materials in archival collections, Box is abbreviated B and Folder is abbreviated F. For example, Box 3, Folder 12 is abbreviated B3:F12.

Frequently cited libraries, collections, periodicals, and books are abbreviated as follows:

Beinecke	Beinecke Library, Yale University, New Haven, CT
CECC	Charles E. Cather Collection, MS 0350, University of Nebraska–Lincoln Archives & Special Collections
Dartmouth	Dartmouth College Special Collections, Hanover, NH
Drew	Willa Cather Collection, Drew University Special Collections, Madison, NJ
Duke	Duke University Special Collections, Durham, NC
EL, *WCL*	Edith Lewis, *Willa Cather Living: A Personal Record* (New York: Knopf, 1953)
EW	*Every Week* magazine
HRC	Harry Ransom Center, University of Texas at Austin
KDH	*Kearney Daily Hub*
Knopf Records	Alfred A. Knopf, Inc. Records, Harry Ransom Center, University of Texas at Austin
LC	*Lincoln Courier*
LHJ	*Ladies Home Journal*
NSJ	*Nebraska State Journal*
NYT	*New York Times*
Rosowski-Cather	Susan J. and James R. Rosowski Cather Collection, MS 0228, University of Nebraska–Lincoln Archives & Special Collections
SCA	Smith College Archives, Northampton, MA
Southwick	Philip and Helen Cather Southwick Collection, MS 0077, University of Nebraska–Lincoln Archives & Special Collections
UNLASC	Archives & Special Collections, University of Nebraska–Lincoln Libraries
WHC	*Woman's Home Companion*

Introduction

1. Marilyn Arnold, Foreword to *Willa Cather Living: A Personal Record*, by Edith Lewis (Athens: Ohio University Press, 1989); Mildred Bennett, "At the Feet of Willa Cather: A Personal Account of Edith Lewis as Protector," *Willa Cather Pioneer Memorial Newsletter* 33, no. 3 (Fall 1989): 20. O'Brien describes Lewis's grave as "smaller and humbler" than Cather's and thus a fitting emblem of her "subordination" to Cather, but she does not place Lewis at Cather's feet. *Willa Cather: The Emerging Voice* (New York: Oxford University Press, 1987), 357.

2. Joan Acocella, "Cather and the Academy," *New Yorker*, 11/27/1995, 56–72. The University of Nebraska Press published *Willa Cather and the Politics of Criticism* in 2000 and Vintage issued a mass market paperback in 2002. Acocella revived her critique when *The Selected Letters of Willa Cather* was published. "What's in Cather's Letters," *The New Yorker* book blog, 4/9/2013, https://www.newyorker.com/books/page-turner/whats-in-cathers-letters.

3. Annamarie Jagose, "Theorising Same-Sex Desire," *Queer Theory: An Introduction* (New York: New York University Press, 1997), 7–21. See also Melissa Homestead, "Willa Cather, Sarah Orne Jewett, and the Historiography of Lesbian Sexuality," *Cather Studies* 10 (2015): 3–37.

4. Eve Kosofsky Sedgwick, "Across Gender, Across Sexuality: Willa Cather and Others," *South Atlantic Quarterly* 88, no. 1 (1989): 69; Christopher Nealon, "Affect-Genealogy: Feeling and Affiliation in Willa Cather," *American Literature* 69, no. 1 (1997): 10, 11; Heather K. Love, *Feeling Backward: Loss and the Politics of Queer History* (Cambridge, MA: Harvard University Press, 2007), 40. Two important book-length queer treatments of WC present her as more modern and future-oriented but do not disrupt the notion of WC as closeted. Marilee Lindemann, *Willa Cather: Queering America* (New York: Columbia University Press, 1999); Jonathan Goldberg, *Willa Cather and Others* (Durham, NC: Duke University Press, 2001).

5. See generally Shari Benstock, *Women of the Left Bank, Paris, 1900–1940* (Austin: University of Texas Press, 1986). While analogizing Cather and Lewis to Stein and Toklas in other respects is tempting, Toklas's role in Stein's life and her creative process was quite different from Lewis's in Cather's. For biographer James Woodress (on whom Joan Acocella relies), insisting that Cather was politically conservative and denying that she was a lesbian went hand in glove. Commenting on a letter in which Cather professes herself satisfied with Franklin Roosevelt's election to a third term, Woodress opines, "[S]he almost certainly voted for [Roosevelt's Republic opponent] Wendell Wilkie." *Willa Cather: A Literary Life* (Lincoln: University of Nebraska Press, 1987), 471. Woodress's obsessive focus on unhappy marriages in Cather's fiction also seems designed to support his reading of her as a virgin isolato.

6. Alden Waitt, "Katharine Anthony: Feminist Biographer with the 'Warmth of an Advocate,'" *Frontiers* 10, no. 1 (1988): 72–77; Judith Schwarz, *Radical Feminists of Heterodoxy, Greenwich Village, 1912–1940* (Norwich, VT: New Victoria, 1986).

7. Betsy Israel quotes from her grandfather Gus's diary but does not provide his surname or the date he recorded this observation. "Village People," *NYT*, 5/6/2007, https://www.nytimes.com/2007/05/06/nyregion/thecity/06vill.html. On the letter-burning myth, Melissa J. Homestead, "Willa Cather's Letters in the Archive," *Tulsa Studies in Women's Literature* (Spring 2021).

8. Lillian Faderman, *To Believe in Women: What Lesbians Have Done for America—A History* (Boston: Houghton Mifflin, 1999), 1. On claims of WC's interest in men, Cynthia Griffin Wolff, "New Cather Biographical Data: 'Valentine' Sentiments," *Willa Cather Pioneer Memorial Newsletter and Review* 43, no. 1 (Winter/Spring 1997–1998): 60–62, and Ann Moseley, "The Arizona Letters," *Willa Cather Newsletter and Review* 56, no. 2 (Spring 2013): 17. See also Lillian Faderman, *Odd Girls and Twilight Lovers: A History of Lesbian Life in Twentieth-Century America* (New York: Columbia University Press, 1991), 53.

9. Hermione Lee, *Willa Cather: Double Lives* (New York: Vintage, 1991), 70–73. On biographers making EL a shadow, Melissa J. Homestead and Anne L. Kaufman, "Nebraska, New England, New York: Mapping the Foreground of Willa Cather and Edith Lewis's Creative Partnership," *Western American Literature* 43, no. 1 (2008): 43–44.

10. I concur with Leila Rupp that "[r]omantic friendships and Boston marriages lived on well into the twentieth century, even in circles exposed to the writings of sexologists." *A Desired Past: A Short History of Same-Sex Love in America* (Chicago: University of Chicago Press, 1999), 88.

11. George Chauncey, *Gay New York: Gender, Urban Culture, and the Making of the Gay Male World, 1890–1940* (New York: Basic, 1994), 6, [1].

12. On the queer critique of marriage, Holly Jackson, "The Marriage Trap in the Free-Love Novel and Queer Critique," *American Literature* 87, no. 4 (2015): 681–708, and Michael Warner, *The Trouble with Normal: Sex, Politics, and the Ethics of Queer Life* (New York: Free Press, 1999).

13. WC, *The Professor's House*, ts., 200, Southwick; WC, *The Professor's House* (Lincoln: University of Nebraska Press, 2002), 257.

14. EL, *WCL*, xxix; Arnold, Foreword, xxii–xxiii.

15. Jack Stillinger, *Multiple Authorship and the Myth of Solitary Genius* (New York: Oxford University Press, 1991).

16. In *On the Rocks* (2013) and *Death Comes* (2017), Sue Hallgarth has made Willa Cather and Edith Lewis into literary characters and is not bound by documented fact.

Chapter 1

1. EL, *WCL*, xxvi–xxvii. This chapter shares a title with a published article based on my early research, but it significantly expands and often corrects that account, especially concerning Lewis family finances. Melissa J. Homestead and Anne L. Kaufman, "Nebraska, New England, New York: Mapping the Foreground of Willa Cather and Edith Lewis's Creative Partnership," *Western American Literature* (Spring 2008): 41–69.

2. EL, *WCL*, xxviii–xxix.

3. WC, "148 Charles Street," in *Not Under Forty* (New York: Knopf, 1936), 57, 53, 56. First published as "The House on Charles Street" in *Literary Review*, 11/4/1922, 173–74, Key revisions EL made for book publication appear on "148 Charles Street," ts., B2:F7, Southwick.

4. University of Nebraska, Transcript and Personal Card of EL, UNLASC. Registration of births was not required, but EL's transcript is an early quasi-official document showing her birth year. See also Henry Lewis to Lillie Lewis, 8/15/1882, private collection, in which he refers to the "babies" (plural).

5. Otis Waite, *History of the Town of Claremont, New Hampshire* (Manchester, NH: John B. Clarke Co., 1895), 447; *General Catalogue and a Brief History of Kimball Union Academy* (Claremont, NH: Claremont Manufacturing Co., 1880), 76, 182, 253, 219, 243, 256; *History of the Class of 1874, Dartmouth College* (1899), n.p.; Jane Carver Field, Kimball Union Academy Archivist, email to Anne Kaufman, 8/10/2005.

6. Dartmouth Class of 1872, *Class Report, '72* (Pittsburgh: Stevenson Foster, [1903?]), 110–12; John C. Webster, *Memoralia of the Class of '64 in Dartmouth College* (Chicago: Shepard & Johnston, 1884), 73–74; *History of the Class of 1874*, n.p.; *Third Annual Report of the Board of Education of the Moline Public Schools* (Moline, IL: Kennedy, 1876), [3], and *Fourth Annual Report of the Board of Education of the Moline Public Schools* (Moline, IL: Kennedy, 1877), [3].

7. Harry E. Downer, *History of Davenport and Scott County Iowa* (Chicago: S. J. Clarke, 1910), 201. Family history more generally was derived from the biography of Daniel Gould in this volume (198–203) and confirmed by the genealogical research of Martha Trainor Day. On the development of Davenport, Timothy Mahoney, *River Towns in the Great West: The Structure of Provincial Urbanization in the American Midwest, 1820–1870* (Cambridge: Cambridge University Press, 1990), 248–49.

8. Elizabeth C. Steven, *Elizabeth Buffum Chace and Lillie Chace Wyman: A Century of Abolitionist, Suffragist and Workers' Rights Activism* (Jefferson, NC: McFarland, 2003), 66; Larry J. Reynolds and Susan Belasco Smith, Introduction to *"These Sad But Glorious Days": Dispatches from Europe, 1846–1850*, by Margaret Fuller (New Haven, CT: Yale University Press, 1991), 7–8; Elizabeth W. Brace, *Mary Elizabeth Wing: A Memoir by Her Daughter* (West Newton, MA, 1925), 6–8. A studio photograph (private collection) places Lillie in Elmira, but she likely attended Miss Thurston's Academy in Elmira rather than coeducational Elmira College. Mark Woodhouse, Elmira College Library, emails to Melissa Homestead, 2/18/2008 and 3/13/2008.

9. Thomas D. Hamm, "The Divergent Paths of Iowa Quakers in the Nineteenth Century," *Annals of Iowa* 61, no. 2 (2002): 125–50; Downer, *History of Davenport*, 201; Scott County Iowa Genealogical Society, "Marriage Records, 1870–1879, Scott County Court Hose Davenport, Iowa," mimeograph, 9/1976, 233 (the listed officiant, S. S. Hunting, was minister of the Unitarian Church; *Owen's Gazetteer and Directory of Scott County Iowa* [Davenport, IA: Globe Steam Printing, 1877], 135.

10. Henry Lewis to Lillie Lewis, 6/18/1881, 6/19/1881, 6/25/1881, and 6/27/1881, private collection; on eastern capital investment, James C. Olson and Ronald C. Naugle, *History of Nebraska*, 3rd ed. (Lincoln: University of Nebraska Press, 1997), 157, 207–208.

11. Everett E. Dick, "Problems of the Post Frontier City as Portrayed by Lincoln, Nebraska, 1880–1900," *Nebraska History* 28 (1947): 133; Henry E. Lewis, Advertisement, *NSJ*, 8/5/1881, 4; *Directory of the City of Lincoln, 1881–1882* (Lincoln, NE: Sam H. Glenn), n.p.; *Lincoln City Lancaster County Directory for 1882–3* (Lincoln, NE: Journal Company), n.p.; Henry Lewis to Lillie Lewis, 8/15/1882, 2/4/1885, and 2/13/1885, private collection.

12. Inez C. Philbrick and L. M. Pryse, [History of a liberal church in Lincoln, Nebraska], 1925, B1:F1, Unitarian Church (Lincoln, Nebraska) Records, RG1054.AM, History Nebraska, Lincoln, NE (hereinafter cited as Unitarian Church Records); Henry Lewis to Lillie Lewis, 6/19/1881, private collection; *Unity Magazine: Freedom, Fellowship, & Character in Religion*, 10/1/1882, 360; University Communications, "Biography of George E. Church (2)," *Nebraska U*, http://unlhistory.unl.edu/exhibits/show/beginnings-classics/faculty/george-e-church; Robert Manley, *Centennial History of the University of Nebraska*, vol. 1 (Lincoln, NE: Centennial Press, 1973), 23, 59, 70–71; Henry Lewis to Lillie Lewis, [late 1882], private collection.

13. "Death of Rev. E. H. Chapin," *Courier Gazette* (Rockland, ME) (clipping), [2/9/1909], B2:F7; Kate Mathews Chapin to Mrs. Hatfield, 8/25/1942, B2:F4; and Records of the First Universalist Church, 1870–1898, B3:F2, all Unitarian Church Records.

14. "Forty Years Ago Today," *NSJ*, 3/8/1923, 6; National Register of Historic Places Registration for the Guy A. Brown House, certified by the director of the Nebraska State Historical Society, 2/2/1989; deed of transfer from George E. Church and Alice A. Church to Henry Lewis, 10/29/1883, recorded 11/30/1883, Lancaster County (NE) Recorder of Deeds, 16:635; Dick, "Problems of the Post Frontier City," 139; Henry Lewis to Lillie Lewis, 2/13/1885, private collection; *LC*, 10/13/1900, 6; "Lewis Comes In," *Lincoln Evening News*, 9/24/1892, 5; "Additional Local," *Lincoln Evening News*, 10/5/1895, 8. Details concerning the house and neighborhood were derived from an examination of plat and Sanborn maps. Because it was on the edge of town, the Lewis's property was not included in these maps until well after they acquired it.

15. *History of the Class of 1874*, n.p.; *Omaha City Directory* (1885), n.p.; Barry Combs and Jim Wigton, "Central High School Historical Timeline, 1854–2012," Omaha CHS Alumni Association, omahacentralalumni.com; Brace, *Mary Elizabeth Wing*, 16; Nebraska State Census, 5 June 1885, EB502, p. 37, North half, 4th Ward, Lincoln, Lancaster County, Nebraska; *Lincoln City and Lancaster County Directory for the Year Commencing June 1, 1886* (New York: U.S. Directory Publishing Company, n.d.), n.p.; *Lincoln City Directory for 1889* (Cherrier Directory Publishing Co.), n.p.; *Class Report of '72* (Pittsburgh: Stevenson, Foster & Co. [1903]), 111.

16. Mahoney, *River Towns*, 36; on Burnham, J. Sterling Morton, Albert Watkins, and George Miller, *Illustrated History of Nebraska* (Lincoln, NE: Jacob North, 1907), 330–31, and Jim McKee, "Burnhams Left Legacy in Lincoln," *Lincoln Journal Star*, 4/7/2018; on the Harrises, Sarah Fisk Harris, *The Memoirs of Sarah Fisk Harris . . . together with certain Letters and Papers relating to her Life and that of her Husband George Samuel Harris* (privately published, 1914), n.p., and *Portrait & Biographical Album of Lancaster County Nebraska* (Chicago: Chapman Brothers, 1888), 159–61.

17. On Henry Lewis's bank positions, *Class Report '72*, 110; Arthur Bradley Hayes, *History of the City of Lincoln, Nebraska* (Lincoln, NE: State Journal Co., 1889), 318, and "May Pay Out in Full," *Lincoln Daily News*, 1/23/1896, 1; on Wing at Burnham's bank, *Lincoln City and Lancaster County Directory for the Year Commencing June 1, 1886*, n.p., [Lincoln City Directory for 1887], n.p., and *Cherriers's Lincoln City Directory for 1890*, n.p.; on Harwood, *Portrait & Biographical Album*, 159, 161.

18. Fred N. Wells, *The Nebraska Art Association: A History* (1972), 1–2, digitalcommons. unl.edu/sheldonpubs/69/; *LC*, 1/25/1891, 8, and 7/25/1891, 8.

19. Listing original members and later additions, "Men's Intellectual Clubs. Lincoln has Organization for Mental Stimulus. Round Table was the First," *NSJ*, 12/30/1906, Home Building Section, 4 (Chapin is not listed, but see "Death of Rev. E. H. Chapin"); Charles G. Dawes, Journal, 2/17/1890 entry, Charles Gates Dawes Papers, Charles Deering Library, Northwestern University; Kate Mathews Chapin to Mrs. Hatfield, 8/24/1942, B2:F4, Unitarian Church Records. Scholarship on Bryan characterizes the Round Table as having only Democratic members at its founding, with the exception of Adolphus Talbot, but my research reveals otherwise.

20. "Clubs," *LC*, 1/22/1898, 5; Lotos Club, Minute Books, vol. I., 1/16/1890, 2/27/1890, 11/19/1891, and vol. II, 12/3/1891, RG5069A.M., History Nebraska.

21. Lotos Club, Minute Books, vol. II, 1/12/1893; Harold G. Lewis, "Information for the Dartmouth College Alumni Records" for Henry Lewis, 4/18/1927, Dartmouth College Archives; *Lincoln Evening News*, 4/7/1892, 5; Lotos Club, Minute Books, vol. II, 12/1/1894.

22. Kate Mathews Chapin to Inez C. Philbrick, 1/29/1914, B2:F6, and Kate Mathews Chapin to Mrs. Hatfield, 8/24/1942, B2:F5, Unitarian Church Records; on the Weeks, "Obituary," *Railroad Age Gazette*, 10/16/1908, 1175; Constitution of the Unitarian Society of Lincoln (Lincoln, NE: Lincoln Paper House, 1891), n.p.; "The Annual Meeting, *Lincoln Daily News*, 3/28/1892, 1; "News from the Field," *Unitarian*, 11/1891, 542 and 12/1891, 592.

23. Henry Lewis to Lillie Lewis, 2/15/1885, private collection; Outline of Study of the Unity Club, Lincoln, NE, 1894–1894, B1:F2, Unitarian Church Records; on Henry's trip to New Orleans, his letters to Lillie Lewis from 4/1885 and 5/1885, private collection; EL to Ruth Lewis Trainor, 1/1/[1947], private collection.

24. University of Nebraska, *Catalogue, 1888–89*, 23–24; *Catalogue, 1889–90*, 15; *Catalogue, 1890–91*, 16; *Catalogue, 1887–88*, 21, 23; and *Catalogue, 1889–90*, 20, 21; Linus Pauling, "Gilbert Newton Lewis," *Dictionary of American Biography*, Supp. 4, ed. John Garraty and Edward James (New York: Scribner's, 1974), 487.

25. EL studying art and music, University of Nebraska, *Catalogue, 1888–89*, 25, and *Catalogue, 1894*, 38; *LC*, 9/16/1893, 3; *LC*, 5/23/1891, 8; *LC*, 8/29/1891, 8; Canfield and EL studying violin together, University of Nebraska, *Catalogue, 1892*, 39–40; "City Clerk's Report," *Lincoln Daily News*, 4/26/1893, 8; Jim McKee, "Phoebe Elliott and the Lincoln Area's First School and Teacher," *Lincoln Journal Star*, 3/3/2013; "Only Standing Room Left," *NSJ*, 6/9/1894, 6.

26. Charles G. Dawes, *A Journal of the McKinley Years*, ed. Bascom N. Timmons (Chicago: Lakeside Press, 1950), 10 (1/23/1893); "New Trust Company," *LC*, 11/11/1893, 1; Mercantile Trust Co. Articles of Incorporation, 11/2/1893, Nebraska Secretary of State Records, vol. M, 468, RG002, History Nebraska (name change to Merchants Trust Co. 3/5/1894, vol. N, 68); Tom Wing as clerk, *Hoye's City Directory of Lincoln for 1895* (Lincoln, NE: State Journal Company, n.d.), n.p.; Frank Lewis as eastern manager, *Lincoln Daily News*, 12/28/1893, 4; Olson and Naugle, *History*, 234–35, 250; "Receiver for First National," *KDH*, 10/25/1894, 1; "Lewis Gets the Other," *Lincoln Evening News*, 11/10/1894, 3.

27. Maud Burrows, "The Great Kearney Real Estate Boom, 1887–1890," *Nebraska History* 18, no. 2 (1937): 104–14; Gene E. Hamaker, "Part I. The Kearney Canal, 1875–1886," and "Part II. The Kearney Canal, 1887 and After," *Buffalo Tales* 1, nos. 6 and 7 (4 and 5/1978).

28. *KDH*, 2/5/1895, 4; University of Nebraska, *Catalogue, 1895*, 59; Buffalo County Nebraska School Census, District 7, 7/2/1895, Buffalo County Historical Society, Kearney, NE; "Our Own Arbor Day," *KDH*, 4/22/1895, 1; "An Excellent Concert," *KDH*, 1/30/1896, 3.

29. *KDH*, 10/14/1896, 3; University of Nebraska, *Calendar, 1896–1897*, 287, 302, and *Calendar, 1897–1898*, 330, 337; *LC*, 11/23/1895, 4; *Hoye's City Directory of Lincoln for 1896* (Lincoln, NE: State Journal Company, 1896), n.p.

30. Farmers Union Ditch Company Articles of Incorporation, 11/17/1896, Nebraska Secretary of State Records. E. C. Calkins had been president of the Kearney Canal and Water Supply Co. S. J. Scoutt, "The Kearney Canal," in *Buffalo County, Nebraska, and Its People*, by Samuel Clay Bassett, vol. 1 (Chicago: S. J. Clarke, 1916), 245–47. Former farmer Homer J. Allen was in the abstract and real estate business in Kearney and was also a Kearney National Bank stockholder. "Homer J. Allen," in *Biographical Souvenir of the Counties of Buffalo, Kearney, Phelps, Harlan and Franklin, Nebraska* (Chicago: F. A. Battey, 1890), 408–409. "Elm Creek Pilot Notes," *KDH*, 7/27/1897, 2, and 12/4/1897, 3 (on the head gates for an existing Elm Creek canal being replaced by new owners to "make it a dividend payer").

31. *LC*, 5/7/1898, 6, and 5/14/1898, 6; Complete record for Allison J. Cope vs. Newport Savings Bank, 37–86, District Court of Lancaster County, Nebraska, RG207, History Nebraska; *KDH*, 2/14/1898, 3. Henry Lewis's movements during this period are regularly documented in the *KDH* and the *Elm Creek Beacon*.

32. Chapin to Mrs. Hatfield, 8/24/1942; L. M. Pryse and Inez C. Philbrick, [History of a liberal church in Lincoln, NE]; All Souls Church, Constitution, in *Directory and Year Book, 1902* (Lincoln, NE: Fassett Printing, 1902), 7; *All Souls Church (Unitarian)*, [1898], B1:F3, Unitarian Church Records; "All Souls Church," *NSJ*, 12/17/1899, 15, and 6/30/1901, 16.

33. Lotos Club, Minute Books, vol. III: 2/6/1902, vol. IV: 2/11/1904, vol. III: 9/20/1900 and 11/1/1900.

34. EL to Patrick Ferry, 3/20/1956, Patrick Ferry Willa Cather Collection, Colby College, Waterville, ME; *NSJ*, 11/14/1897, 7; "Locals," *Nebraskan*, 1/21/1898, 3;

Blanche Garten, "Kappa; UN, Lincoln, Neb.," *Anchora of Delta Gamma*, 1/1/1915, 282; "Alumni and Former Students," *Hesperian*, 2/18/1898, 9; "Among the Greeks," *Hesperian*, 3/4/1898, 7; *LC*, 10/1/1898, 6; "Locals," *Nebraskan*, 9/20/1898, [3]; "Delta Gamma Anniversary," *Nebraskan*, 3/11/1898, [2]. Although both men's and women's groups called themselves "fraternities," I use the more current term "sorority" to avoid confusion.

35. Katherine H. Adams, *A Group of Their Own: College Writing Courses and American women Writers, 1880–1940* (Albany: State University of New York Press, 2001), 44–47. Adams confines her claim about multiple genres to the "advanced composition course," but my research on EL has convinced me that even a basic-level "theme-writing" course in the 1890s might allow students to write fiction.

36. All EL in *LC*: "Sunflower," 6/18/1898, 11; "Anne," 7/16/1898, 9; "The Story of Pansy," 7/23/1898, 8; "A Sacrifice," 7/30/1898, 4.

37. EL, *WCL*, xxviii; all EL in *LC*: "Mountain Echoes," 8/13/1898, 10, and 8/20/1898, 9; "Virginia," 8/13/1898, 11; "The Runaways," 9/3/1898, 8; "A Sketch," 9/10/1898, 4.

38. Joanna Levin, *Bohemia in America, 1858–1920* (Stanford, CA: Stanford University Press, 2010), 1, 125.

39. EL in *LC*: "The Portrait She Painted," 9/24/1898, 4; "Rhoda Inconsistent," 10/8/1898, 12.

40. EL, "Bohemia," *LC*, 12/31/1898, 9.

41. Barbara Miller Solomon, *In the Company of Educated Women: A History of Women and Higher Education in America* (New Haven, CT: Yale University Press, 1985), 52–53; Margaret A. Lowe, *Looking Good: College Women and Body Image, 1875–1930* (Baltimore: Johns Hopkins University Press, 2003), 105.

42. *LC*, 7/19/1890, 8; *LC*, 8/29/1896, 4; *KDH*, 9/7/1896, 3 (the referenced "Mary Lewis" is clearly her, even though she is misidentified as Henry's "sister" from "Willister, Massachusetts"); Obituary for Mary Lewis, 9/25/1937, Faculty, SCA; L. Clark Seelye, *The Early History of Smith College, 1871–1910* (Boston: Houghton Mifflin, 1923), 100; Jessie M. Anderson, "Three Freshman: Ruth, Fran, and Nathalie," *St. Nicholas Magazine*, 1/1895, 191–92.

43. University of Nebraska, *Calendar, 1896–1897*, 32, 43–44, 240; Smith College, *Twenty-Sixth Official Circular of Smith College, 1899–1900*, 93; *Nebraskan*, 10/14/1898, [2].

44. *NSJ*, 4/11/1899, 6; *KDH*, 6/8/1899, 3; *Elm Creek Beacon*, 6/9/1899 (this item mentions only "two children" and does not name Ruth and Helen, but EL was old enough to be "Miss Lewis"); *NSJ*, 6/11/1899, 10; *Elm Creek Beacon*, 6/23/1899, 7/7/1899; *LC*, 8/5/1899, 7.

45. Smith College, *Twenty-Sixth Official Circular*, 100; "Wing, Daniel Gould," in *National Cyclopedia of American Biography* (New York: White, 1953), 38: 273; Bascom N. Timmons, *Portrait of an American: Charles G. Dawes* (New York: Henry Holt, 1953), 71–72, 69; Pauling, "Gilbert Newton Lewis," 487.

46. Smith College, *Twenty-Sixth Official Circular*, 92; Helen Lefkowitz Horowitz, *Alma Mater: Design and Experience in the Women's Colleges from Their Nineteenth-Century Beginnings to the 1930s* (Boston: Beacon, 1986), 153; Alice Katharine Fallows,

"Undergraduate Life at Smith College," *Scribner's*, 7/1898, 38; *Smith College, 1893–94*, Official Circular No. 29 (Northampton, MA: 1893), 46.

47. Margaret Birney Vickery, *Smith College: The Campus Guide* (Princeton, NJ: Princeton Architectural Press, 2007), 44–46; "Elisha Ely Garrison, B.A. 1897," *Obituary Records of Graduates of Yale University Deceased during the Year 1934–1935*, 87; "Abram E. Garrison," *U.S. Civil War Soldier Records and Profiles, 1861–1865*, ancestry.com. Student head count in Hatfield derived from the list of students in *Twenty-Sixty Official Circular*.

48. Mary A. Jordan, "The College for Women," *Atlantic Monthly*, 10/1892, 544, 546; Mary A. Jordan, "Life in the Classroom: Thirty-Seven Years of It," *SAQ*, 7/1921, 281; Susan Kates, *Activist Rhetorics and American Higher Education, 1885–1937* (Carbondale: Southern Illinois University Press, 2001), 27–52; Edith Kellogg Dunton, "A Tribute," *SCM*, 6/1921, 299.

49. Lucy Marks and David Porter, *Seeking Life Whole: Willa Cather and the Brewsters* (Madison, NJ, 2009), 34–35.

50. Conclusion drawn from the student directory in the *Twenty-Sixth Official Circular*, which lists both hometowns and college residences, and a similar review of the next two circulars; "Jonathan Smith," in *One of a Thousand: A Series of Biographical Sketches of One Thousand Representative Men Resident in the Commonwealth of Massachusetts, A.D. 1888–'89*, ed. John C. Rand (Boston: First National Publishing, 1890), 559; "Cassius M. Wicker," in *Genealogical and Family History of the State of Vermont*, ed. Hiram Carleton (New York: Lewis, 1903), 73–77. Lucy Wicker appears in the 1899–1900 academic year *Circular* as boarding in town, but she wrote her father about Hatfield House life beginning in the spring 1900 semester.

51. Horowitz, *Alma Mater*, 5 (and throughout); Lowe, *Looking Good*, 45.

52. Ada Comstock Notestein, in *College: A Smith Mosaic*, ed. Jacqueline Van Voris (West Springfield, MA: Smith College, 1975), 3. I draw broadly on Horowitz, *Alma Mater*, and Lowe, *Looking Good*, for Smith student traditions. Scholars vary in their interpretations of "smashes" and romantic relationships between college women and how they shifted over time, but I do not enter this debate here as I have no direct evidence of EL's emotional life in college.

53. EL, 1902, Office of the Registrar, Transcripts, SCA. Transferred courses appear in a different color ink and are marked "S" after credit hours rather than with a grade. The columns for "First year" and "Second year" are both labeled 1899–1900. Professors' names, which do not appear on the transcripts, must be deduced by cross-referencing with the circular. All subsequent information about EL's classes was derived in this way from these documents.

54. Lowe, *Looking Good*, 1–4, 22–26, 47–47, 82–84; Achsah Brewster to EL, 3/8/1940, B6:F8, CECC; Douglas Z. Doty, "Life at a Girls' College," *Munsey's*, 9/1897, 868.

55. Marks and Porter, *Seeking Life Whole*, 35.

56. EL, "The Friend in Letters," *LC*, 12/16/1899, 9; EL, "The Light o' Life," *SCM*, 12/1899, 127, 126, 128.

57. Bertha Watters Tildsley, "Thirty Years Ago," *SCM*, 6/1921, 288; Grace Kellogg Griffith, *SCM*, 6/1921, 302; Edith Hill Bayles, *SCM*, 6/1921, 311; Tildsley, "Thirty Years Ago,"

288. Charlotte B. Deforest, in Van Voris, *College: A Smith Mosaic*, 7; Anna Hempstead Branch, "She Was a Great Teacher," *SCM*, 6/1921, 285; EL, "The Runaways," *SCM*, 3/1900, 315–19; Josephine Daskam Bacon to Gertrude Ogden Tubby, [1913], Smith College Materials—Mary A. Jordan Professorship, Mary A. Jordan Papers, SCA (the *SCM* "was made up chiefly of the results of Miss Jordan's 'Daily Themes' classes"); EL, "The Proposal," *LC*, 6/16/1900, 10.

58. "Office of the Registrar Grading Instructions," handout provided by SCA. The system changed soon after EL graduated. Louise Kingsley, "The Advantage of a System of Public Graded Marks at Smith College, *SCM*, 11/1904, 79–86.

59. Ralph Melnick, *Senda Berenson: The Unlikely Founder of Women's Basketball* (Amherst: University of Massachusetts Press, 2007), 26–28, 31–33, 57;; Josephine Dodge Daskam, *Smith College Stories* (New York: Scribner's, 1900), 20; Melnick, *Senda Berenson*, 67–68; Lucy Southworth Wicker to Casius M. Wicker, 2/25/1900, Wicker/LaVake Family Collection, MSA 750:03, Vermont Historical Society, Barre.

60. Robert Cherney, *A Righteous Cause: The Life of William Jennings Bryan* (Boston: Little Brown, 1985), 82; Lucy Southworth Wicker to Casius Milton Wicker, 2/25/25/1900. On the identity of the speaker, Jean Shaw Wilson, "Washington's Birthday," *SCM*, 3/1900, 341.

61. Constitution and membership book, 1892–1934, Phi Kappa Psi, Undergraduate Life-Student Organizations, SCA.

62. Record of the Recommendation Committee, 1900–1904, in ibid. Daskam makes this process and its social implications central to "A Case of Interference," *Smith College Stories*, 37–62.

63. Fallows, "Undergraduate Life," 50; Katherine Fiske Berry, "Letters Home," 10/28/1900 (on Edith Platt receiving her invitation), Class of 1902 Individuals, SCA; "George Barstow French," in *Supplement to the History of the Class of Eighteen Hundred and Seventy-Two* (Hanover, NH: Dartmouth College, 1921), 47–49.

64. *LC*, 10/6/1900, 8; "About College," *SCM*, 12/1900, 191; Berry, "Letters Home," 1900.

65. W. M. Paxton, *The Paxtons* (Platte City, MO: Landmark Print, 1903), 168; Melnick, *Senda Berenson*, 66–67; Lowe, *Looking Good*, 48–49; Fallows, "Undergraduate Life," 54; Laura J. Paxton to EL, 4/15/53, B6:F25, CECC.

66. Olive Howard Dunbar Torrence, "A Tribute," *SCM*, 6/1921, 298; Joan Marie Johnson, *Southern Women at Seven Sister Colleges: Feminist Values and Social Activism, 1875–1915* (Athens: University of Georgia Press, 2008), 151.

67. Johnson, *Southern Women*, 149; Lotos Club, Minute Books, 1892–1903, Phi Kappa Psi; EL, "The Interloper," *SCM*, 1/1901, 229.

68. *LC*, 3/2/1901, 7. The Chesnutt sisters entered Smith in 1897. Otelia Cromwell, the first African American student to graduate, entered after the Chesnutt sisters but with transfer credit.

69. On Henry Lewis attending to Farmer's Union business: *KDH*, 6/28/1901, 2; *Elm Creek Beacon*, 7/12/1901; *KDH*, 7/19/1901, 3; *KDH*, 7/15/1901, 2; *KDH*, 7/22/1901, 2; *Elm Creek Beacon*, 8/9/1901. On EL in Lincoln: *LC*, 7/6/1901, 8; *LC*, 8/3/1901, 6; *NSJ*, 8/25/1901, 10; *LC*, 8/31/1901, 7.

70. L. Clark Seelye, *Annual Report of the President of Smith College 1899–1900*, 21–22 (recipient names were not published); Complete record of John S. Knox v. Henry E. Lewis et al., 34–238, District Court of Lancaster County.

71. Alice Duryee to Elizabeth Kimball, 10/9/1901, Elizabeth McGrew Kimball Papers, SCA; Mary A. Jordan, "The Teaching of English in Smith College from President and Professor Seelye to President and Professor Nielson," 45, Mary A. Jordan Papers, SCA; Olive Rumsey, "Faculty Notes," *SCM*, 2/1902, 333–34.

72. Helen Appleton Reed, in Van Voris, *College: A Smith Mosaic*, 17; EL, "Sonnet," *SCM*, 10/1901, 28.

73. *Class Book for 1901* and *Class Book for 1902* (Northampton, MA: Smith College) (graduating seniors are listed with their societies in the yearbooks and I cross-checked them with their hometowns as listed with their photographs); Faith Potter, 1902, and Dorothy Amy Young, 1902, Office of the Registrar, Transcripts, SCA.

74. Ethel Keeler Betts, "About College," *SCM*, 1/1902, 269; Charlotte Burgis De Forest, "College Societies," *SCM*, 12/1899, 159–60.

75. "About College," *SCM*, 10/1901, 135; "About College," *SCM* 1/1902, 241.

76. Seelye, *Early History*, 91; EL, "About College: College Independence," *SCM*, 2/1902, 330.

77. EL, "Sonnet," *SCM*, 5/1902, 501; EL, "Where Are You Going, My Pretty Maid?," *SCM*, 6/1902, 567–74.

78. Melnick, *Senda Berenson*, 66; Rachel Cohen, *Bernard Berenson* (New Haven, CT: Yale University Press, 2013); *Catalog of Officers, Graduates and Nongraduates of Smith College . . . 1875–1905* (Northampton, MA: Alumnae Association of Smith College, 1906), 76.

79. Document addressed by EL et. al. to Rachel Berenson, 5/9/1902, Rachel Berenson, Class of 1902 Individuals, SCA.

80. Mark J. Noonan, *Reading "The Century Illustrated Monthly Magazine": American Literature and Culture, 1870–1893* (Kent, OH: Kent State University Press, 2010); "Topics of the Time: 'The Century's' Prize Manuscripts," *Century*, 11/1899, 155–56.

81. Helen Fairbanks Hill, "Miss Caverno's Lecture," *SCM*, 6/1902, 606–607.

82. Smith College, *Class Book for 1902*, 103.

83. On Wicker and McClintock, "Alumnae Department," *SCM*, 10/1902, 59; "Miss Duryee a Suicide at Sea," *NYT*, 2/2/1911, 11; on Smith and Treat, Alumnae Association of Smith College, *Catalog of Officers, Graduates and Nongraduates of Smith College, Northampton Mass., 1875–1905* (1906), 79–80; on Barlow, "Alumnae Department," *SCM*, 11/1902, 125, and Marks and Porter, *Seeking Life Whole*, 35.

84. *Hoye's City Directory of Lincoln for 1903* (Lincoln: State Journal Company, 1903), n.p.; *All Souls Church (Unitarian)*, [1902], B1:F3, Unitarian Church Records; Lotos Club, Minute Books, vol. III, 2/26/1903 and 3/12/1903, and vol. IV, 5/23/1903; *Columbia University Catalogue*, 1900–1901, 328.

85. "Dartmouth Alumni Reunion," *Omaha Daily Bee*, 1/11/1903, 1, and "Women's Clubs," *Lincoln Daily Star*, 1/17/1903, 9 (text of EL's poem); EL to Rudolph Ruzicka, 11/22/1962, B1:F35, Rudolph Ruzicka Papers, Rauner MS-1078, Dartmouth.

86. "Prize Story Awards," *LC*, 11/22/1902, 6; EL, "The Fraternity Season," *Anchora of Delta Gamma*, 1/1/1903, 44–45.
87. Tour with docent at Fairview, 7/5/2016; EL, "Kappa Theta Alumnae: Lincoln, Neb.," *Anchora of Delta Gamma*, 7/1/1903, 221; "Society Notes," *LC*, 3/14/1903, 3; EL, "Kappa Theta," 222.
88. EL, "Kappa Theta," 222.
89. Solomon, *In the Company of Educated Women*, 119–21. Although these statistics come with many qualifications, marriage rates of women's college graduates did rise markedly after World War I.
90. Gertrude Willard Phisterer, "New York Alumnae Association, New York," *Anchora of Delta Gamma*, 4/1/1903, 142–43.

Chapter 2

1. Sarah Orne Jewett to WC, 12/13/[1908], *Letters of Sarah Orne Jewett*, ed. Annie Fields (Boston: Houghton Mifflin, 1911), 248–49.
2. On Jewett and the Boston marriage tradition, see Melissa J. Homestead, "Willa Cather, Sarah Orne Jewett, and the Historiography of Lesbian Sexuality," *Cather Studies* 10 (2015): 3–37.
3. "People You Know," *NSJ*, 8/27/1903, 6; "The Card Basket," *Lincoln Star*, 9/12/1903, 10; Harold Lewis's address is listed in the 1903–1904 Columbia student directory as 6 E. 32nd (photocopies from Columbia archives); on Mary Lewis, email from Joanna Rios, Columbia Archives, 4/10/2017; Helen Gregory, "Chi Upsilon Alumnae, New York City," *Anchora of Delta Gamma*, 11/1/1903, 46–47; "Personals from Kappa Theta," *Anchora of Delta Gamma*, 11/1/1903, 48.
4. "In Society," *NSJ*, 10/4/1903, 14; Oliver Pilat and Jo Ranson, *Sodom by the Sea: An Affectionate History of Coney Island* (Garden City, NJ: Doubleday, Doran, 1941), 141–60, and Robin Jaffee Frank, *Coney Island: Visions of an American Dreamland* (Hartford, CT: Wadsworth Atheneum, 2015), 3–6. As clerk of the U.S. district and circuit courts in Omaha, Dundy would have regularly spent time in Lincoln.
5. "New York. June 8, 1904," *NSJ*, 11/12/1904, 14 (although I have not located EL's sketches, there is no reason to mistrust the report); "Personals from Kappa Theta," 48; class secretary card for EL, Class of 1902 Individuals, SCA; Robert K. Barnhart, "Aftermath," *Dictionaries*, 17 (1996): 116–25; "Personals from Kappa Theta," 48; Emmeline Ruddy to William Koshland, 8/8/1973, B30:F5, Knopf Records, Addition to editorial files; Gertrude Willard Phisterer, "Chi Upsilon Alumnae, New York City," *Anchora of Delta Gamma*, 1/1/1904, 94.
6. Joanna Levin, *Bohemia in America, 1858–1920* (Stanford, CA: Stanford University Press, 2010), 13–69; Gerald W. MacFarland, *Inside Greenwich Village* (Amherst: University of Massachusetts Press, 2001), 171; Luther S. Harris, *Around Washington Square* (Baltimore: Johns Hopkins University Press, 2003), 28.

7. EL, *WCL*, xxxi; Lucy Marks and David Porter, *Seeking Life Whole: Willa Cather and the Brewsters* (Madison, NJ: Fairleigh Dickinson University Press, 2009), 33; Achsah Brewster, "Selections from 'The Child,'" in Marks and Porter, *Seeking Life Whole*, 165 (she misremembered details and confused dates but contemporary evidence corroborates some details); *List of Members, 1905–1906*, Smith College Club of New York City Records, SCA; *Fort Wayne (IN) Sentinel*, 12/24/1904, 12, 9/16/1905, 3, 6/29/1907, 3, and 12/14/1907, 3; Abby Merchant, Class of 1904 Individuals, SCA; Alumnae Department, *Smith College Monthly*, 2/1906, 328.

8. WC to Mariel Gere, 3/7/1899 (#0048); WC to Will Owen Jones, 5/7/1903 (#0084); WC to Dorothy Canfield, [3/1–4/30/1904] (#0097).

9. Brewster, "Selections from 'The Child,'" 165 (although she has WC already in New York in the fall of 1903, the recollection is consistent with WC's 1904 visit); Abby Merchant to EL, 10/10/1953, B7:F4, CECC.

10. Frederick Link, Charles Mignon, Judith Boss, and Kari Ronning, "Textual Essay," in *Youth and the Bright Medusa*, by Willa Cather (Lincoln: University of Nebraska Press, 2009), 462–64 (WC's conflict with Dorothy Canfield shifted the contents of *The Troll Garden*, but these two stories are logical candidates for EL to have taken to the office in 1904); EL, *WCL*, xxx; Ivan Turgenev, *On the Eve: A Novel*, trans. Constance Garnett (London: William Heinemann, 1903), inscribed in EL's hand, "Edith Lewis, August 1905, <u>W.S.C.</u>" (suggesting she was memorializing WC's gift to her of an uninscribed volume), HRC.

11. EL to E. K. Brown, 7/30/[1948], B5:F22, CECC. On their club memberships, see Chapter 1.

12. Frederick B. Adams, "Conversation with Edith Lewis, March 21, 1950," ADAMS 141, Drew. On WC and Canfield's friendship drawing on the Adams notes, Mark Madigan, "Edith Lewis, Dorothy Canfield Fisher, and the Scars of 'The Profile,'" in *Willa Cather: New Facts, New Glimpses, Revisions*, ed. John J. Murphy and Merrill Maguire Skaggs (Madison, NJ: Fairleigh Dickinson University Press, 2008), 252–59.

13. Henry James, *The Golden Bowl* (New York: Charles Scribner's Sons, 1904), inscribed "Willa Sibert Cather / <u>Dec. 1904</u> / E.L.L.," HRC; "Application for Employment," 11/27/1918, in Lewis, Edith—Personnel file, J. Walter Thompson Company, Personnel Records, RL 10998, Duke; *Lincoln Star*, 1/4/1905, 2; EL, *WCL*, xvii; James Woodress, Introduction to *The Troll Garden*, by Willa Cather (Lincoln: University of Nebraska Press, 1983), xvi; EL, "Aliens," *Scribner's*, 3/1905, 353. Sharon Hamilton suggests that EL's two poems establish that her sexual relationship with WC began in 1905. "Breaking the Lock: Willa Cather's Manifesto for Sexual Equality in 'Coming, Aphrodite!,'" *Women's Studies* 42 (2013): 857–885. Hamilton's aligning of "Coming, Aphrodite!" with the early stages of WC and EL's relationship has informed my thinking, but she relies on EL's faulty reconstruction of chronology in *WCL*. See also Andrew Jewell on "Coming, Aphrodite!" as set "around the years of Cather's first residence in the city." "Willa Cather's Greenwich Village: New Contexts for 'Coming, Aphrodite!,'" *Studies in American Fiction* 32, no. 1 (Spring 2004): 73.

14. WC to Mariel Gere, [9/30/1905] (#0107); EL, "At Morning," *Harper's Monthly*, 12/1905, 32; Woodress, *Willa Cather*, 182; Israel Zangwill, *Children of the Ghetto*

(New York: Macmillan, 1902), inscribed "Edith Lewis / Christmas / 1905. W.S.C.,", HRC; George Moore, *Modern Painting* (New York: Scribner's, 1898), inscribed "Willa Sibert Cather / E.L.L Jan. 1, 1906," HRC.

15. "$5,000 for a Short Story," *Collier's*, 3/19/1904, 22; "Results of the Collier's $5,000 Short Story Contest," *Critic*, 5/1905, advertising supplement, n.p.

16. Cather, *The Troll Garden*, [3], [2]; Woodress, Introduction, xvi–xviii; EL, "Chains of Darkness," *Collier's Weekly*, 11/18/1905, 24.

17. EL, "Chains of Darkness," 34.

18. WC, "Coming, Aphrodite!," in *Youth and the Bright Medusa*, 3, 6–7, 48.

19. Ibid., 61; EL, "Chains of Darkness," 24–25.

20. EL, "Chains of Darkness," 25–26.

21. Ibid. 26; WC to Will Owen Jones, 5/7/1903 (#0084).

22. "Personal," *NSJ*, 6/12/1904, 14. EL did not report the magazine's name to her parents, but the amount corresponds to the advertised rate.

23. Mildred Bennett, "At the Feet of Willa Cather: A Personal Account of Edith Lewis as Protector," *Willa Cather Pioneer Memorial Newsletter*, 33, no. 3 (Fall 1989): 19–22.

24. Ellen Gruber Garvey, Foreword to *Blue Pencils & Hidden Hands: Women Editing Periodicals, 1830–1910*, ed. Sharon M. Harris (Boston: Northeastern University Press, 2004), xi–xxiii.

25. "Miss Cather Entertains," *Pittsburgh Press*, 4/8/1906, 11; Peter Lyon, *Success Story: The Life and Times of S. S. McClure* (New York: Scribner's, 1963), 283–95; Harold S. Wilson, *"McClure's Magazine" and the Muckrakers* (Princeton, NJ: Princeton University Press, 1970), 168–89. Irwin kept a typed diary letter, which he sent periodically to Inez Haynes Gillmore. Will Irwin and Inez Haynes Gillmore Papers, YCAL MSS 603, B2, Beinecke. Irwin often exaggerates and distorts in order to impress Gillmore, and entries are often undated or were later dated erroneously. Nevertheless, Irwin's "log" (hereinafter cited as "Irwin") provides information never before used in Cather or *McClure's* scholarship. I cite the date information on each document, with corrected or surmised dates in brackets, followed by folder label information. See also Robert V. Hudson, *The Writing Game: A Biography of Will Irwin* (Ames: University of Iowa Press, 1982) (who accepts Irwin's log as entirely reliable).

26. James Woodress, *Willa Cather: A Literary Life* (Lincoln: University of Nebraska Press, 1987), 186 (thanks to Tom Gallagher for pointing out Woodress's error in calling it the Hotel Griffon); *Lincoln Star*, 3/4/1906, 8; "Among the Clubs," *NSJ*, 4/29/1917, 17; *Lincoln Star*, 3/7/1906, 2; *LC*, 12/3/1898, 7.

27. Henry E. Lewis and C. E. and E. F. Perkins, Agreement to Sell Real Estate, 10/1/1901, Dawson County (NE) Miscellaneous Records, vol. 7, 137; Midland Alfalfa Company, Articles of Incorporation, 11/15/1905, Nebraska Secretary of State Records, RG002, History Nebraska; "Addison Seabury Tibbets, C.E. Class of 1877," *Cornell Civil Engineer* 24 (10/1915–6/1916): 578–79; All Souls Unitarian Church, Ledger, 1900–, B4:F5, Church (Lincoln, Nebraska) Records, RG1054.AM, History Nebraska; "Death of Edward F. Pettis," *NSJ*, 9/3/1913, 9 (Pettis represented Henry Lewis in *Lewis v. Shinn*, *Knox v. Lewis*, *Cope v. Newport Savings Bank*, and *Tibbets v. Midland Alfalfa*);

Philip Holmgren, "The Watson Ranch—Part I," *Buffalo Tales* 2, no. 9 (1979); "Raise Alfalfa," *Elm Creek Beacon*, 11/18/1898, 1; Lillie G. Lewis and Henry E. Lewis to Paul H. Holm, Quit Claim Deed, 1/29/1906, Dawson County Deed Records, vol. 42, 564; Paul H. and Nora S. Holm to Lillie G. Lewis, Deed, 2/1/1906, Dawson County Deed Records, vol. 39, 637; Lillie G. Lewis and Henry E. Lewis to May Jansen, Mortgage, 5/28/1906, Dawson County Mortgage Records, vol. 44, 427.

28. EL class secretary card; "In Society," *NSJ*, 9/2/1906, 14; Monday morning, 5/17/1906 [5/15/1907], Irwin 1906 Mar–May F1 of 2; Monday 5 p.m. [6/1906], Irwin 1906 Mar–May F2 of 2.

29. Ellery Sedgwick, *The Happy Profession* (Boston: Little Brown, 1946), 142; Mark Sullivan, *The Education of an American* (New York: Doubleday, Doran, 1938), 194, 198; EL, *WCL*, 60, 60–61. Characterizations of McClure as crazy occur throughout Irwin's letters to Gillmore.

30. Wednesday at noon, probably 7/1906, Irwin 1906 July–Dec F1 of 2; EL, *WCL*, xxxiii.

31. Thursday morning, 5/10/1906, Monday morning, 5/17/1906 [5/21/1906], Wednesday morning, [5/23/1906], all Irwin 1906 Mar–May F2 of 2; WC to Harrison Dwight, 10/9/1906, B2:F5, Harrison Griswold Dwight Papers, Amherst College Archives and Special Collections.

32. Wednesday evening, [9/26/1906], Thursday night, [9/27/1906], and Sunday, 10/7/1906 [10/6/1906], all Irwin 1906 July–Dec F1 of 2; S. S. McClure to John S. Phillips, 10/17/1906, McClure mss. III, LMC 1689, Lilly Library, Bloomington, IN.

33. "In Society," 11/4/1906, *NSJ*, 20; Tuesday night, 10/24/1906 [10/ 23/1906], Irwin 1906 July–Dec F2 of 2; Thursday evening, [10/11?/1906], and Monday evening, 10/1906 [10/15/1906], Irwin July–Dec 1906 F1 of 2.

34. Thursday morning, 10/25/1906, 11/8/1906, 11/12/1906, Bechune, Saturday and Sunday, 11/12/1906 [11/10–11/1906], Tuesday, 12/4/1906, and Christmas Day, 12/25/1906, all Irwin 1906 July–Dec. F2 of 2. Ashley Squires persuasively debunks earlier attributions of Cather as sole author. "The Standard Oil Treatment: Willa Cather, *The Life of Mary Baker G. Eddy,* and Early Twentieth Century Collaborative Authorship," *Studies in the Novel* 45, no. 3 (Fall 2013): 328–48.

35. WC to Ida Tarbell, [1/4/1907 or 1/11/1907], Pelletier Library, Allegheny College, Meadville, PA; WC to Burton Hendrick, 1/18/1907 and [July 1907], B8:F14, Burton Jesse Hendrick Papers (MS 198), Beinecke; Thursday afternoon, 2/5/1907 [2/7/1907], Irwin 1907 Jan–Jun F1 of 2.

36. 2/2[2]/1907 and Friday morning, 2/1/1907, Irwin 1907 Jan–Jun F1 of 2.

37. WC identifies Mackenzie as managing editor in WC to Rose Standish Nichols, 11/29/1907, Nichols Family Papers, B2, Nichols House Museum, Boston; EL, *WCL*, 61, xxxiii; EL to E. K. Brown, 2/11/1950, B8:F14, CECC (EL does not date her acquiring of Terry photographs, but she clearly did so before 9/1908); Richard C. Cabot, "Christian Science Cures" ts., Milmine Collection, #103, Mary Baker Eddy Library, Boston.

38. Agreement between Lillie Lewis and William C. Shinn, 8/11/1904, Lancaster County (Nebraska) Deed Record Book 123, 126; Lillie Lewis v. William C. Shinn, Lancaster County District Court Appearance Docket vol. 33 and Court Journal vol. 45, and

Cope v. Newport Savings Bank complete record, 37–86, both District Court of Lancaster County, Nebraska, RG207, History Nebraska.

39. Henry Lewis to Lillie Lewis, 6/19/1907, private collection.

40. WC to Bess Seymour, 12/24/[1907], private collection; *Poems by Edgar A. Poe* (Aurora, NY: Roycrofters, 1901), copy inscribed "Edith Lewis / Christmas 1907 / W.S.C.," DFCF; WC to Roscoe Cather, 3/2/[1908] (#2057); WC to Charles F. Cather, 1/14/1908 (#1899); Sarah Orne Jewett, *A White Heron and Other Stories* (Boston: Houghton Mifflin, 1886), copy inscribed by Jewett to WC 3/29/1908, note on 151, HRC. On Jewett and McClure, Charles Johanningsmeier, "Sarah Orne Jewett and Mary E. Wilkins (Freeman): Two Shrewd Businesswomen in Search of New Markets," *New England Quarterly* 70, no. 1 (March 1997): 57–82.

41. WC to Alice Goudy, 3/31/1908, in EL "Notes for Biography," B7:F7, CECC.

42. WC to Roscoe Cather, 2/13/1910 (#2065); S. S. McClure to Robert Mather, 9/26/1908, B5, McClure mss, LMC 1687, Lilly Library.

43. WC to Annie Fields, "Sunday" [10/4 or 10/11/1908], private collection. WC's letters in the Nichols Family Papers establish the chronology for the letter to Fields.

44. WC to Sarah Orne Jewett, 10/24/[1908] (#0140).

45. Sharon O'Brien, *Willa Cather: The Emerging Voice* (New York: Oxford University Press, 1987), 342. In "Application for Employment," EL recounts that she was "successively proof reader, make-up editor, art-editor, literary editor & acting managing editor." The shift to makeup editor likely coincided with WC's promotion.

46. May Jansen order against Lillie G. Lewis et al., 9/2/1908 (entered 9/20/1909), Dawson County Deed Record vol. 32, 274; "City and County News Notes," *KDH*, 10/22/1908, 3; "Asks Court to Approve Feeding Hogs," *KDH*, 11/18/1908, 3; Tibbets v. Midland Alfalfa, Appearance Docket 41, District Court of Lancaster County.

47. Anne DeCorey, "Edgar Beecher Bronson, Nebraska's 'Ranchman,'" *Nebraska History* 81 (2000): 106–15.

48. Henry Lewis to Ruth Lewis, 4/19/1909, private collection; Henry Lewis to EL, 4/24/1912, B5:F25, CECC.

49. Elizabeth Shepley Sergeant to Witter Bynner, 5/16/1951, Elizabeth Shepley Sergeant Papers, YCAL MSS 3, B1, Beinecke (there are reasons to mistrust elements of Torrence's anecdote—he had WC and EL living at the Judson—but in the context of 1909, EL's emotions ring true); Sarah Orne Jewett, *Country of the Pointed Firs* (Boston: Houghton Mifflin, 1896), copy inscribed "Edith Lewis / June 1908," Duke; Jewett, *The Mate of the Daylight and Friends Ashore* (Boston: Houghton Mifflin, 1897), copy inscribed "Edith Lewis / Christmas 1908. W.S.C.," HRC; Jewett, *Strangers and Wayfarers* (Boston: Houghton Mifflin, 1890), copy inscribed "Edith Lewis / Christmas 1908. W.S.C.," Duke.

50. Sarah Orne Jewett, *Mate of the Daylight*, 213–14 (on this story in the context of Jewett and Fields's relationship, Homestead, "Willa Cather, Sarah Orne Jewett, and the Historiography of Lesbian Sexuality," 16–20); Esther Forbes, "Sarah Orne Jewett: The Apostle of New England," *Boston Evening Transcript*, Books section, 5/16/1925, 1.

51. EL to E. K. Brown, 8/10/1950, B5:F21, CECC; S. S. McClure to WC, 3/16/1909, and Viola Roseboro' to S. S. McClure, 11/16/1909, McClure mss., B5; *John Sloan's New York Scene: From the Diaries, Notes, and Correspondence, 1906–1913*, ed. Bruce St. John (New York: Harper, 1965), 426 (entry for 5/25/1910). Sloan reports visiting the *McClure's* office about illustrations for "His Father's Faith" but finding "Miss Lewis" out of town. The William Marcus McMahon story appeared without illustrations in 6/1911.

52. WC to Jessica Cather Auld, 12/17/1909, TWU Library, Denton, TX; WC to Alice Goudy, 2/10/1911, in EL, "Notes for Biography."

53. Earl Brewster to EL, 3/25/1948, B6:F9, CECC. EL was not at the small family wedding in New Haven but was at social events in New York City beforehand. See correspondence between Alpha Barlow and Early Brewster, 11/1908, BREWSTER 24, Drew.

54. WC to Roscoe Cather, 2/13/1910 (#2065); WC to Elizabeth Sergeant, [6/4/1911] (#0195).

55. WC, "The Swedish Mother," setting copy ts., McClure mss., and *McClure's Magazine* 9/1911, 541.

56. WC to Elsie Cather, 8/30/[1911] (#1982).

57. WC to Cameron Mackenzie, 11/3/1911 (#0207). WC submitted as "Miss Fanny Cadwallader" from St. Louis. Frederick Link, "Textual Essay," *Alexander's Bridge*, by Willa Cather (Lincoln: University of Nebraska Press, 2007), 247. Irwin followed this same "office etiquette" by submitting his own fiction to *McClure's* under "an assumed name." Friday morning, 5/20/1906, Irwin 1906 Mar–May F2 of 2.

58. WC to Zoë Akins, 2/6/[1912] (#0211); WC to Elizabeth Sergeant, [3/1/1912] (#0213); WC to Elizabeth Sergeant, [3/12/1912] (#0216).

59. WC to EL, 4/19/1912 (#2963), is addressed to EL at 60 Washington Square, as is Henry Lewis to EL, 4/24/1912, B5:F25, CECC.

60. Lyon, *Success Story*, 342; WC to S. S. McClure, 6/12/[1912] (#0235).

61. Cameron Mackenzie to WC, 9/19/1913, B1:F10, Rosowski-Cather; WC to Elizabeth Sergeant, 9/12/[1912] (#0242).

62. WC to Elizabeth Sergeant, 10/6/[1912] (#0244); EL, *WCL*, 86–7; *The Journal of Countess Françoise Krasinska*, trans. Kasmir Dziekonska (Chicago: McClurg, 1907), inscribed "Edith Lewis / September 1912 / W.S.C.," HRC.

63. EL to Alfred Knopf, 6/5/1952, B704:F6, Knopf Records; EL to Mrs. McClure, 1/23/1949, B11, McClure mss.; Editor of McClure's Magazine to W. J. Platka, 4/15/1913, McClure mss., B6 (declining membership in the Philippine Society for McClure and signed by EL). EL's name appears in letters and documents related to McClure's Montessori project dated 4–7/1912 in B6, McClure mss.

64. Managing Editor, "The Autobiography of S. S. McClure," *McClure's*, 8/1913, 77; WC to S. S. McClure, [12/10/1913] (#0271); William Morrow to S. S. McClure, 2/14/1914, B11, McClure mss.; Edith Wyatt to EL, 3/28/1914 (and adjacent materials documenting editing of letters for publication), B6, McClure mss.

65. WC to S. S. McClure, [12/10/1913] (#0271).

66. WC to Elsie Cather, [12/30/1913] (#1896).

67. Achsah Barlow Brewster, "The Child," 23–26, BREWSTER 26, Drew (reproduced in part in "Selections from 'The Child,'"152–53); EL to Stephen Tennant, n.d., B2:F30, Stephen Tennant Papers, OSB MSS 187, Beinecke; Earl Brewster to EL 7/15/1933, B6:F6, CECC.

68. EL, "Application for Employment."

69. Melissa J. Homestead, "Essays: Associated Sunday Magazines and the Origins of *Every Week*," http://everyweek.unl.edu/view?docId=AssociatedSundayMagazines. html.

70. According to EL's "Application for Employment," she wrote "captions, editorial notes & announcements, & short articles" at *Every Week*. I infer her authorship of anonymous *Every Week* content when it connects strongly to her life and WC's works. For more on EL's duties as managing editor, Melissa J. Homestead, "Edith Lewis as Editor, *Every Week* Magazine, and the Context of Cather's Fiction," *Cather Studies* 8 (2010): 325–52.

71. EL, *WCL*, xxxiii–xxxiv; WC to R. L. Scaife, 5/18/[1915] (#0306); WC to Ferris Greenslet [6/6/1915] (#308); "Two Women Wood-Choppers," *EW*, 6/28/1915, 4l; "They Come to Us from Every Nation," *EW*, 7/3/1916, 10–11.

72. WC, "Wireless Boys Who Went Down with Their Ships," *EW*, 8/2/1915, 3; "More or Less Personal," *NSJ*, 8/111915, 4.

73. Melissa Homestead, "Essays: *Every Week*'s Editorial Staff," http://everyweek.unl.edu/view?docId=EveryWeeksEditorialStaff.html; Anne Herendeen to Bruce Barton, 5/5/1960, Bruce Barton Papers, U.S. Mss. 44AF, B27, Wisconsin State Historical Society, Madison.

74. Brenda Ueland, *Me: A Memoir* (St. Paul, MN: Schubert Club, 1983), 158, 160, 158–59, 160–61.

75. Bruce Barton, "The Promise of Every Week," *EW*, 5/3/1915, 2; "A New Market," *Author's League Bulletin*, 4/1915, 9; "The Magazine Market," *Author's League Bulletin*, 7/1915, 18.

76. J. C. Waller to Mr. Kinney, 12/3/1918, in Lewis, Edith—Personnel File; "Writers of the Day," clipping from *Writer*, n.f., in B27, Philip Curtiss Papers, YCAL MSS 443, Beinecke (hereinafter cited as Curtiss Papers; see also finding aid). On Richter's career, David R. Johnson, *Conrad Richter: A Writer's Life* (University Park: Pennsylvania State University Press, 2001).

77. EL to Philip Curtiss, 3/18/1915, B27, Curtiss Papers; Philip Curtiss, "The Patrician," *EW*, 5/21/1915, 5–7 (the marked-up typescript in Curtiss's papers B10 predates both the submitted and published versions); EL to Philip Curtiss, 3/22/1915, Curtiss Papers, B27; Editor of McClure's to Philip Curtis, 10/16/1911 (signed by EL), Curtiss Papers, B27.

78. Bruce Barton to Conrad Richter, 5/8/1915, and EL to Conrad Richter, 7/2/1915, both B26:F2, Richter Papers, CO216, Princeton University Library Special Collections (hereinafter cited as Richter Papers).

79. EL to Conrad Richter, 10/27/1915, B26:F2, Richter Papers.

80. EL to Philip Curtiss, 2/19/1916, B27, Curtiss Papers; Philip Curtis, "Cather," *EW*, 3/6/1916, 6–9.

81. EL to Philip Curtiss, 2/19/1916, Bruce Barton to Philip Curtiss, 3/14/1916, and EL to Philip Curtiss, 2/26/1916, all B27, Curtiss Papers.

82. *Every Week*, Advertisement, *Author's League Bulletin*, 10/1916, [23]; Cora Paget to Conrad Richter, 5/17/1917, 7/6/1917, 8/15/1927, 8/23/1917, all B27:F18, Richter Papers; Conrad Richter, "Nothing Else Matters," *EW* 1/12/1918, 8–9, 18; Cora Paget to Conrad Richter, 1/14/1918, Richter Papers, B27:F18.

83. EL to Conrad Richter, 8/16/1917, B26:F2, Richter Papers.

84. EL to Conrad Richter, 8/28/1917, B26:F2, Richter Papers; Conrad Richter, "The Pippin of Pike County," *EW*, 3/16/1918, 8–10.

85. WC to Ferris Greenslet, 2/16/[1915] (#0375).

86. "They Come from Every Nation," *EW*, 7/3/1916, 11. Benda's name first appears in WC's correspondence with Houghton Mifflin in WC to R. L. Scaife, 4/17/[1917] (#0384). She sent Ferris Greenslet three "completed" Benda drawings in late 1917 (Lena Lingard not among these), but she also specified that Benda hired models and made many "sketches" for the whole series (11/24/[1917] [#0399]. Benda's images appear in *EW* with: Gertrude Brooke Hamilton, "The Doll Baby," 2/27/1915, 13–15; Charles Saxby, "The Sole Survivor," 2/21/1916, 7–8, 13; Katharine Tynan, "The Gardner," 2/5/1917, 4; George Elliott Howard, "What Will War Do to Marriage?," 9/3/1917, 3–4; "When the Prussians Came to Poland," 9/17/1917, 4. W. T. Benda, "The Most Interesting Man I Know: Ignace Jan Paderewski," *EW*, 11/19/1917.

87. WC to Ferris Greenslet, 10/18/1917 (#0394); WC to R. L. Scaife, 4/7/ [1917] (#0384); WC to R. L. Scaife 12/1/[1917] (#0400) (mentions Riis and lays out the conflict described below). For context, Evelyn Funda, "Picturing Their *Ántonia*(s): Mikolas Ales and the Partnership of W. T. Benda and Willa Cather," *Cather Studies* 8 (2010): 353–78, and Janis Stout, *Picturing a Different West: Vision, Illustration, and the Tradition of Austin and Cather* (Lubbock: Texas Tech University Press, 2007), 105–37.

88. WC to Ferris Greenslet, 11/24/[1917] (#0399); R. L. Scaife to WC, 11/26/1917, Houghton Mifflin Archive, bMS Am 1925 (341), Houghton Library, Harvard University.

89. Elizabeth Gaines Wilcoxson, "Morning," *EW*, 1/19/1918, 7.

90. WC to Ferris Greenslet, 11/24/[1917] (#0399).

91. Elizabeth Gaines Wilcoxson, "Mrs. Martin's Daughter-in-Law," *EW*, 9/17/1917, 5–7; "Something New in Short Stories," *EW*, 1/19/1918, 7.

92. WC, "Ardessa," *Century*, 5/1918, 105–16.

93. Donal Harris, *On Company Time: American Modernism in the Magazines* (New York: Columbia University Press, 2016), 31. Strangely, Harris also uses EL's description of her work as a *McClure's* proofreader to argue that as managing editor WC never left the office (43).

94. Homestead, "Edith Lewis as Editor," 335–42; Ueland, *Me*, 166; WC to Meta Schaper Cather, 12/14/[1917] (#2254).

95. WC to Meta Schaper Cather, 1/2/[1918] (#2255); WC to Carrie Miner Sherwood, 3/13/1918 (#0414).

96. WC to Ferris Greenslet, 6/20/[1918] (#0420); Conrad Richter to Bruce Barton, 5/28/1918, B88, Barton Papers; WC to Ferris Greenslet, 6/20/[1918] (#0420).

97. WC to Roscoe Cather, 7/14/[1918] (#2082); EL, *WCL*, 106.
98. EL, *WCL*, 106; WC to Elsie Cather, 5/4/[1917] (#2079) (mentions that she "blue-stone[s]" EL's eyes for her—copper sulfate crystals treat trachoma); EL, "Application for Employment"; WC to Elsie Cather, 11/11/[1918] (#1845); Harold Lewis to EL, 11/25/1918, B5:F26, CECC.

Chapter 3

1. EL to Virginia Cather Brockway, 3/22/1948, private collection.
2. EL to Stephen Tennant, [late 9/1947], B2:F30, Stephen Tennant Papers, OSB MSS 187, Beinecke.
3. Barbara Will, "The Nervous Origins of the American Western," *American Literature* 70, no. 2 (June 1998): 293–316; Owen Wister, "The Evolution of the Cow-Puncher," in *The Virginian*, by Owen Wister (New York: Oxford University Press, 1998), 344, 342.
4. On Cather resisting the masculine Western, Susan Rosowski, *Birthing a Nation: Gender and Creativity in the American West* (Lincoln: University of Nebraska Press, 1999), and Janis P. Stout, *Picturing a Different West: Vision, Illustration, and the Tradition of Cather and Austin* (Lubbock: Texas Tech University Press, 2007); on Westerns by women, Victoria Lamont, *Westerns: A Women's History* (Lincoln: University of Nebraska Press 2016); WC to Harriet Whicher, 10/16/[1925] (#0797). My thinking has been informed by John Swift's analysis in "Willa Cather in and out of Zane Grey's West," *Cather Studies* 9 (2011): 1–20. Audrey Goodman also places WC with Wister and Grey in a genealogy of touristic representations of the Southwest. *Translating Southwestern Landscapes: The Making of an Anglo Literary Region* (Tucson: University of Arizona Press, 2002).
5. WC to Alverda Van Tuyll, 5/24/1915, *SL*, 202; WC to Elizabeth Shepley Sergeant, 6/27/[1915], *SL*, 204; Sylvester Rawling, "Melanie Kurt Sings Lenore in 'Fidelio,'" *Evening World* (New York), 3/4/1915, 8; Douglas Johnson, "Fidelio," *Grove Music Online*.
6. On her shifting plans, WC to Ferris Greenslet, [7/24/1915] (#0315), and WC to Elizabeth Sergeant, 7/28/[1915], *SL*, 206; on McClure's association with the *Evening Mail*, ended with his being accused of pro-German propaganda, Peter Lynn, *Success Story: The Life and Times of S. S. McClure* (New York: Scribner, 1963), 352–60.
7. "More or Less Personal," *NSJ*, 8/11/1915, 4; EL, *WCL*, 94.
8. Brown Palace Hotel, Guest Register #75, Brown Palace Hotel Archive, Denver, CO; on ninth-floor rooms, conversation with hotel historian Debra Faulkner, 5/2018; on water supply, Corinne Hunt, *The Brown Palace: Denver's Grand Dame* (Pasadena, CA: Archetype Press, 2003), 29; EL, *WCL*, 101; Melissa Homestead, "Willa Cather in the *Denver Times* in 1915 and New Evidence of the Origins of *The Professor's House*," *Legacy* 35, no. 2 (2018): 205.
9. WC, "Mesa Verde Wonderland Is Easy to Reach," *Denver Times*, 1/31/1916, 7; Mary O. Griffits, *Guide to the Geology of Mesa Verde* (Mesa Verde National Park, CO: Mesa Verde Museum Association, 1990), 9; David Harrell, *From Mesa Verde to the Professor's House* (Albuquerque: University of New Mexico Press, 1992), 35–38 (Harrell did

not have the date information provided by Harvey's interview and the Brown Palace register, and he often overcorrects EL's errors in *WCL*); Duane A. Smith, *Mesa Verde National Park: Shadows of the Century*, rev. ed. (Boulder: University Press of Colorado, 2002), 86, 87-94. Smith provides a useful corrective to Harrell's overcorrection of EL.

10. Harrell, *From Mesa Verde*, ch. 3; U.S. Department of the Interior, *Rules and Regulations: Mesa Verde National Park, Colorado* (1927), 61.

11. EL, *WCL*, 95.

12. Harrell, *From Mesa Verde*, 60; EL, *WCL*, 97. As Harrell explains, the ruin EL calls "Tower House" could not be "Square Tower House," which was discovered earlier in 1915 (*From Mesa Verde*, 241-42n24). However, my own examination of the site substantiates elements of EL's account that Harrell identifies as misrepresentations.

13. EL, *WCL*, 95; Harrell, *From Mesa Verde*, 44.

14. Harrell, *From Mesa Verde*, 52-53; "Lost in Colorado Canon [*sic*]," *NYT*, 8/26/1915, 20.

15. On the train route, see system map in *Beautiful Historical Taos, A Wonderland for Tourists* http://www.library.arizona.edu/exhibits/pams/pdfs/f804t2b4.pdf; On Dunn, Mabel Dodge Luhan, *Edge of the Taos Desert: An Escape to Reality* (Albuquerque: University of New Mexico Press, 1987), 114.

16. Van Deren Coke, *Taos and Santa Fe: The Artist's Environment, 1882-1942* (Albuquerque: University of New Mexico Press, 1963), 27; Julie Schimmel, *The Art and Life of W. Herbert Dunton, 1876-1936* (Austin: University of Texas Press for the Stark Museum of Art, Orange, TX, 1984), 35; "Mrs. Blumenschein on Woman Artists," *EW*, 5/10/1915, 3 (EL's authorship in light of WC and EL's friendship with Ernest Blumenschein); Robert W. Larson and Carole B. Larson, *Ernest L. Blumenschein: The Life of an American Artist* (Norman: University of Oklahoma Press, 2013), 179-80, 185-87.

17. EL, *WCL*, 100.

18. Luhan, *Edge of the Taos Desert*, 56-57.

19. WC, "On *Death Comes for the Archbishop*," in *Death Comes for the Archbishop*, by WC, Willa Cather Scholarly Edition (Lincoln: University of Nebraska Press, 1999), 373-74. Scholars have long repeated WC's misspelling of the priest's surname as Haltermann. On EL's map, the handwriting of the word "Haelterman" is not entirely consistent with either EL's or WC's hand (although "Father" is certainly in EL's hand). I suspect EL first wrote the name and then WC erased and rewrote part of it to correct the spelling.

20. "Mesa Prieta—The Place," *Mesa Prieta Petroglyph Project*, https://www.mesaprietapetroglyphs.org/mesa-prieta---the-place.html, and Janet Mackenzie and Candie Bourdin, "Archaic Petroglyphs of Mesa Prieta, Northern New Mexico," https://www.mesaprietapetroglyphs.org/uploads/4/2/3/9/42390305/mppparchaic__final.pdf.

21. WC to Elizabeth Sergeant, 8/31/[1915] (#0320); WC to Ferris Greenslet, 9/5/[1915] (#0321); Homestead, "Willa Cather in the *Denver Times*," 192-93.

22. WC to Elizabeth Sergeant, 9/21/[1915] (#0323); Achsah Brewster to EL, 9/16/1915, B6:F2, CECC.

23. Larson and Larson, *Ernest L. Blumenschein*, 178; *Beautiful Historical Taos*, back cover, 8.

24. WC to Ferris Greenslet, 9/13/[1915] (#0322).

25. WC, "Mesa Verde Wonderland," 7; on WC's omission of the Wetherills' commercial motives, Matthias Schubnell, "From Mesa Verde to Germany: The Appropriation of Indian Artifacts as Part of Willa Cather's Cultural Critique in *The Professor's House*," in *Willa Cather and the American Southwest*, ed. John J. Swift and Joseph R. Urgo (Lincoln: University of Nebraska Press, 2002), 40.

26. "Lost Cities," *EW*, 11/8/1915, 12 (EL's authorship inferred from her recent experience there).

27. Achsah Brewster to EL, 8/9/1916, B6:F3, CECC; WC to Roscoe Cather, 7/8/[1916] (#2073).

28. WC to Ferris Greenslet, 6/30/1916 (#0359); WC to Douglass Cather, 7/8/[1916] (#1952); WC to Harrison Dwight, 7/10/[1916], B2:F5, Harrison Griswold Dwight Papers, Amherst College Archives and Special Collections; WC to Douglass Cather, 7/8/1916 (#1952).

29. WC to Roscoe Cather, 7/8/1916 (#2073).

30. Both WC and EL later merged and confused their travels in northern New Mexico in 1915 and 1916. Despite sparse documentation, the substantial gap between extant letters testifies to the length of their 1916 trip.

31. WC to Ferris Greenslet, 8/22/1916 (#0365); Ferris Greenslet to WC, 8/25/1916, Houghton Mifflin Archive, bMS Am 1925 (341), Houghton Library, Harvard University; WC to Ferris Greenslet, 10/23/[1916] (#0369); WC to R. L. Scaife, 3/8/ 1917 (#0382).

32. WC to Roscoe Cather, 12/8/[1918] (#2084); Grant Overton, *The Women Who Make Our Novels* (New York: Dodd Mead, 1928), 92.

33. WC to Roscoe Cather, 6/23/[1917] (#2077), and 7/4/[2017] (#2078); WC to Charles Cather, [7/27/1917] (#1907); Melissa J. Homestead, "Writing, Revising, and Promoting *The Professor's House*: New Evidence of Willa Cather at Work," *Willa Cather Review*, 62, no. 2 (2020): forthcoming.

34. Leon Edel, "Psychoanalysis," in *Literary Biography: The Alexander Lectures, 1955–56* (London: Hart-Davis, 1957), 56–80, revised as "A Cave of One's Own," in his *Stuff of Sleep and Dreams* (New York: Harper & Row, 1982), 216–40, and Doris Grumbach, "A Study of the Small Room in *The Professor's House*," *Women's Studies* 11 (1984): 327– 45. Queer readings of the novel are built on this foundation.

35. Elizabeth Sergeant, *Willa Cather: A Memoir* (Philadelphia: Lippincott, 1953), 212; Judith Fetterley, "Willa Cather and the Fiction of Female Development," in *Anxious Power*, ed. Carol J. Singley and Susan Elizabeth Sweeney (Albany: State University of New York Press, 1993), 221–34.

36. WC to Mary Virginia Boak Cather, 12/6/[1919] (#2416).

37. Lucy Marks and David Porter, *Seeking Life Whole: Willa Cather and the Brewsters* (Madison, NJ: Fairleigh Dickinson University Press, 2009), 94–97.

38. WC to Earl and Achsah Brewster, 2/21/[1923], *SL*, 337–78.

39. Sergeant, *Willa Cather*, 202.

40. Hannah Sullivan, *The Work of Revision* (Cambridge, MA: Harvard University Press, 2013), 39, 58. Sullivan acknowledges contributions made by others to the work of Henry James and T. S. Eliot.

41. For a full discussion and debunking of the idea that EL's role was "secretarial," see Melissa J. Homestead, "Willa Cather, Edith Lewis, and Collaboration: The Southwestern Novels of the 1920s and Beyond," *Studies in the Novel* 45, no. 3 (Fall 2013): 408–41.

42. Charles Mignon, "Willa Cather's Process of Composing," *Resources for American Literary Study* 29 (2003–2004): 165–84. Mignon gives the fullest account of WC's composing process and gives greater weight to EL's contribution than the Willa Cather Scholarly Edition but still underplays it. The most notable exception is *My Mortal Enemy*, which survives in one typed draft edited only by WC. Willa Cather Literary Manuscripts, MssCol 496, NYPL. Certainly another draft also edited by EL once existed.

43. Frederick Link, "Textual Essay," in *The Professor's House*, by WC, Willa Cather Scholarly Edition (Lincoln: University of Nebraska Press, 2002), 397–98 (hereinafter cited as WC, *PH*). Pages then missing were later located and added to WC, *The Professor's House*, ts., B9:F9–12, Southwick (hereinafter cited as WC, *PH* ts.); WC, *PH* ts., 132. The galley proofs, which were not available in the Willa Cather Scholarly Edition, are held by Smith College Special Collections, as described in my "Writing, Revising, and Promoting *The Professor's House*."

44. WC, *PH* ts., 18.

45. Ibid., 88; on the importance of the bells of Augusta's church to the novel's symbolic structure, John J. Murphy, "Holy Cities, Poor Savages, and the Science of Culture: Positioning *The Professor's House*, in Swift and Urgo, *Willa Cather*, 55–68.

46. WC, *PH* ts., 33, 52.

47. Ibid., 200; WC, *PH*, 257.

48. WC, *PH* ts., 229.

49. Ibid., 139, 140.

50. Ibid., 145, 156.

51. Caroline Fraser, *Prairie Fires: The American Dreams of Laura Ingalls Wilder* (New York: Metropolitan, 2017), 350.

52. WC, "The Novel Démeublé," *New Republic*, 4/12/1922, 6 (most readers are familiar with the revised version collected in *Not Under Forty*, and although no typescript has surfaced, EL may have been responsible for subtle differences between the two versions); WC, *PH*, 262. In *PH* ts., this passage is subtly different from the published version: "To the professor this plain account was almost beautiful, because of the stupidities it avoided and the things it did not say. If words had cost money, Tom couldn't have used them more sparingly. The adjectives were purely descriptive, relating to color and form, and were used to present the object under consideration, not the young explorer's emotions. Yet through this austerity one felt the kindling of imagination, the ardor and excitement of the boy, like the vibration in a voice when the speaker strives to restrain his emotion by permitting himself only conventional phrases" (206). Ann Romines traces Godfrey's resemblance to WC, in "The

Professor and the Pointed Firs: Cather, Jewett, and Problems of Editing," *Jewett & Her Contemporaries: Reshaping the Canon* (Gainesville: University Press of Florida, 1999), 153–66. My interpretive move is inspired by Sharon O'Brien's foundational work, although I take her argument in a different direction. "'The Thing Not Named': Willa Cather as a Lesbian Writer," *Signs* 9, no. 4 (1984): 576–99.

53. WC, *PH*, 210. In the typescript, EL had not finished disambiguating the names of two towns, Pardee and Tarpin (Pardee is where Tom and Roddy meet, and Tarpin is the closest town to the Mesa). The second sentence ends "an account of what we'd found that day, and of anything new or interesting that we'd noticed in Cliff City or its surroundings." *PH*, ts., 165.

54. WC, *PH*, 262.

55. "People You Know," *NSJ*, 6/10/1925, 10; giving the San Gabriel as WC's address before she departed, Memorandum re: Miss Cather, 6/4/1925, B30, Paul Reynolds Records, Uncatalogued Correspondence Series, MS #1065, Columbia University Rare Books & Manuscripts; WC to Mabel Dodge Luhan, 6/12/[1925], B6:F24, Mabel Dodge Luhan Papers, YCAL MSS 196, Beinecke (hereinafter cited as Luhan Papers); WC to Elizabeth Sergeant, 6/23/[1925] (#0787); Marta Weigle and Barbara Babcok, eds., *The Great Southwest of the Fred Harvey Company and the Santa Fe Railway* (Phoenix, AZ: Heard Museum, 1996), xv.

56. Lesley Poling-Kempes, *Ladies of the Canyons: A League of Extraordinary Women and Their Adventures in the American Southwest* (Tucson: University of Arizona Press, 2015), 201, 78–86, 194–95.

57. Ibid., 254, 256–57, 253, 281; San Gabriel Ranch, http://www.library.arizona.edu/exhibits/pams/pdfs/f804a39s1.pdf. The pamphlet is undated but has references to the Canjilon Camp, which the Pfäffles acquired in 1925.

58. WC to Robert Josephy, 6/26/[1925] (#2556) (sending him "the first half of the page proofs" from Alcalde and promising "the rest . . . in a few days").

59. On this terminology and evidence, Homestead, "Willa Cather, Edith Lewis, and Collaboration," 435.

60. WC, *PH*, 185, 189.

61. Ibid., 282.

62. EL, *WCL*, 139–40; WC, *PH*, 105.

63. On their possible earlier acquaintance in Greenwich Village, Janis P. Stout, "Modernist by Association: Willa Cather's New York/New Mexico Circle," *American Literary Realism*, 47, no. 2 (2015): 117–35; on Luhan generally, Flannery Burke, *From Greenwich Village to Taos: Primitivism and Place at Mabel Dodge Luhan's* (Lawrence: University of Press of Kansas, 2008), and Lois Rudnick, *Mabel Dodge Luhan: New Woman, New Worlds* (Albuquerque: University of New Mexico Press, 1984); David Ellis, *D. H. Lawrence: Dying Game, 1922–1930* (Cambridge: Cambridge University Press, 1998),7–23; Marks and Porter, *Seeking Life Whole*, 47–50; Earl Brewster to EL, 7/21/1923, B6:F4, CECC; D. H. Lawrence to Earl and Achsah Brewster, [7/19/1923], *Letters of D. H. Lawrence*, ed. James T. Boulton (Cambridge: Cambridge University Press, 1979), 4:471; Ellis, *D. H. Lawrence*, 122; D. H. Lawrence to Earl Brewster, 2/28/1924, *Letters of D. H. Lawrence*, 4:592.

64. Dorothy Brett, *Lawrence and Brett: A Friendship* (Philadelphia: Lippincott, 1933), 39. D. H. Lawrence to Harriet Monroe, 3/12/1924, *Letters of D. H. Lawrence*, 5:15; Brett, *Lawrence and Brett*, 39–40; EL, *WCL*, 138–39; WC to Elizabeth Vermorcken, 3/23/[1924] (#0727).

65. Frieda Lawrence to Baroness Anna von Richthofen [3/1/1925] and to Dorothy Brett 3/3/[1925], *Letters of D. H. Lawrence*, 5:215–16, 218.

66. WC to Mabel Luhan, 5/23/[1925], 6/12/[1925], and 6/25/[1925], B6:F24, Luhan Papers.

67. WC to Mabel Luhan, 6/25/[1925].

68. Lois P. Rudnick and MaLin Wilson-Powell, eds., *Mabel Dodge Luhan & Company: American Moderns and the West* (Santa Fe: Museum of New Mexico Press, 2016), 30, 77; Rauh appears on the fringes of most studies of Greenwich Village, getting the most coverage in Steven Watson, *Strange Bedfellows: The First American Avant-Garde* (New York: Abbeville, 1991).

69. EL, *WCL*, 142. I derive the chronology of their daily activities from EL's account in the Blue Jay notebook, B4:F8, CECC. This chronology calls into question Joseph Foster's representation of a solitary WC, "starched white, spinster-ish, wide-eyed, disdainful" at a party at Mabel Luhan's house at which Indians dance and white guests join them. *D. H. Lawrence in Taos* (Albuquerque: University of New Mexico Press, 1972), 180, partially collected in *Willa Cather Remembered*, ed. Sharon Hoover (Lincoln: University of Nebraska Press, 2002), 85.

70. Mabel Dodge Luhan, *Winter in Taos* (New York: Harcourt, Brace, 1935), 36. The backgrounds in Figures 3.12 and 3.13 are potentially consistent with both the San Gabriel Ranch and Mabel Luhan's place, although WC's pasting of them into a copy of *Death Comes for the Archbishop* (discussed below) strengthens the case for Taos over Alcalde.

71. Luhan, *Edge of the Taos Desert*, 198 (on Tony taking Mabel to Arroyo Hondo early in their relationship, 236).

72. Ellis, *D. H. Lawrence*, 183–84; Arthur J. Bachrach, *D. H. Lawrence in New Mexico: "The Time Is Different There"* (Albuquerque: University of New Mexico Press), 43–51; Kyle S. Crichton in *D. H. Lawrence: A Composite Biography*, ed. Edward Nehls (Madison: University of Wisconsin Press, 1958), 2:414; D. H. Lawrence to Earl and Achsah Brewster, 7/29/1925, *Letters of D. H. Lawrence*, 5:283; Crichton in *D. H. Lawrence*, 2:414.

73. Schimmel, *Art and Life*, 48, 60.

74. Ellis, *D. H. Lawrence*, 187; Luhan, *Winter in Taos*, 86.

75. EL to Mabel Luhan, [1934?], B23:F650, Luhan Papers. WC's and EL's letters to Luhan make clear that they both read her memoirs before publication. EL wrote that she read "Taos Seasons," which was clearly the working title for *Winter in Taos*. EL also placed Ida Rauh at the cave. Luhan calls it "Seco Mountain" (*Winter in Taos*, 86–89), but the proper name is Lucero Peak.

76. Luhan, *Winter in Taos*, 90–91; EL to Mabel Luhan, [1934?]. EL recorded the car accident in the composition notebook.

77. The more scurrilous parts of WC's fictional portrait of Martinez closely match Luhan's account in *Edge of the Taos Desert*, 85–87. Luhan credits her account to Tony Lujan and the Taos Pueblo community, but Luhan may have derived it from *Death Comes for the Archbishop* rather than vice versa.

78. WC, *PH*, 106; WC to Mabel Luhan, 8/7/[1925], *SL*, 372.

79. EL to Mabel Luhan, 7/20/[1925], B23:F650, Luhan Papers.

80. WC to Elizabeth Sergeant, 5/30/[1912] (#0230); WC to EL, [4/18/1912] (#2936).

81. WC to Mabel Luhan, [7/20/1925], *SL*, 372; Virginia L. Grattan, *Mary Colter: Builder upon the Red Earth* (Flagstaff, AZ: Northland, 1980), 22–25; Arnold Berke, *Mary Colter: Architect of the Southwest* (New York: Princeton Architectural Press, 2002), 77–78, 25.

82. EL, *WCL*, 144–46; WC to Mabel Luhan, 8/7/[1925]. EL consistently referred to the location of the hotel as Laguna, where, as she noted, the Santa Fe train stopped, while WC wrote that they spent three days at New Laguna. There was evidently no hotel Laguna Pueblo in the 1920s; perhaps they were driven back and forth between New Laguna and Laguna Pueblo during the rail delay.

83. WC to Mabel Luhan, 8/7/[1925], *SL*, 372; EL, *WCL*, 146.

84. Kate Wingert-Playdon, *John Gaw Meem at Acoma: The Restoration of San Esteban del Rey Mission* (Albuquerque: University of New Mexico Press, 2012), 34, 25; Courtney Lawton, "Willa Cather and Solastalgia: Yearning for a Lost, Invented Landscape," *Resources for American Literary Study* 38 (2015): 95–96.

85. WC to Mabel Luhan, 8/7/[1925] and 8/8/[1925], *SL*, 372–3.

86. Louise Guerber, Journal, 11/1/1925, Burroughs 25, Drew.

87. WC to Blanche Knopf, 9/19/[1925] (#0796); WC to Alfred Knopf, [10/6/1925] (#2561).

88. WC to Roscoe Cather, [12/29/1925] (#2086).

89. Guerber, Journal, 4/2/1926 and 4/26/1926; WC to Paul Reynolds, [4/19–26/1926] (#0826).

90. Guerber, Journal, 5/11/1926; WC to Blanche Knopf, 5/21/[1926] (#0831); Berke, *Mary Colter*, 127–41; WC to Mabel Luhan, 5/26/[1926], *SL*, 380.

91. WC to Mabel Luhan, 5/26/[1926], *SL*, 380; WC to Blanche Knopf, 5/28/[1926] (#0834).

92. Multiple snapshots taken from the canyon's rim suggest this scenario of entry (B4:F4, Southwick). Other observations based on my tour with a Navajo guide, 5/2018.

93. WC to Alfred A. Knopf, Inc., 6/3/1926 (#0835); WC to Elmer Adler, 6/8/[1926] (#2563).

94. WC to Mabel Luhan, 6/5/[1926], *SL*, 381. WC's and EL's correspondence with Luhan confirms Caroline Woidat's analysis of southwestern tourist tropes in WC's fiction. "The Indian-Detour in Willa Cather's Southwestern Novels," *Twentieth Century Literature*, 48, no. 1 (March 2002): 22–49.

95. Sharon Hoover, *Willa Cather Remembered* (Lincoln: University of Nebraska Press, 2002), 122–23.

96. Esther Lanigan Stineman, *Mary Austin: Song of a Maverick* (New Haven, CT: Yale University Press, 1989), 128; EL to Mary Austin, [4/8/1928], mssAU 3474, Mary Hunter Austin Collection, Huntington Library, San Marino, CA.

97. EL to Roscoe Cather, [6/27/1926], B1:F6, Roscoe and Meta Cather Collection, UNLASC.

98. WC to Roscoe Cather, [6/26/1926], (#2087); WC to Mary Austin, 6/26/[1926] (#0840).

99. WC to Louise Guerber Burroughs, [8/22/1926], *SL*, 384.

100. WC, *Death Comes for the Archbishop* (New York: Knopf, 1927), inscribed copy, CATHER15, Drew.

101. WC, *Death Comes for the Archbishop* (London: Heinemann, 1930), "personal copy," Robert and Doris Kurth Collection, MS 0076, UNLASC; describing the volume and its implications, Charles Mignon, "Cather's Copy of *Death Comes for the Archbishop*," *Cather Studies* 4 (1999): 172–86 (but misidentifies a photo of EL as one of WC); WC, *Death Comes for the Archbishop* (New York: Knopf, 1927), inscribed "Willa Cather," CECC.

102. Marilee Lindemann, *Willa Cather: Queering America* (New York: Columbia University Press, 1999), 116, 123; Melissa Homestead, "Willa Cather, Sarah Orne Jewett, and the Historiography of Lesbian Sexuality," *Cather Studies* 10 (2015): 23; Mabel Luhan, "Paso Por Aqui!," in *Santa Fe and Taos: The Writer's Era, 1916–1941*, ed. Marta Weigle and Kyle Fiore (Santa Fe, NM: Ancient City Press, 1982), 103.

103. WC to Eunice Chapin, 9/24/[1926], *SL*, 385–86.

Chapter 4

1. Caption for *My Mortal Enemy* by WC, *McCall's*, 3/1926, 8.

2. WC, *My Mortal Enemy*, *McCall's*, 3/1926, 72, 78, 116.

3. Woodbury's Facial Soap, "At the University," *McCall's*, 3/1926, 29; Woodbury's, "At the Colony Club," *McCall's*, 4/1926, 29.

4. Roland Marchand, *Advertising the American Dream: Making Way for Modernity: 1920–1940* (Berkeley, University of California Press, 1985), 217–18.

5. WC, "On the Art of Fiction," *The Borzoi, 1920* (New York: Knopf, 1920), 8; WC, "The Novel Démeublé," *New Republic*, 4/12/1922, 5. Tanagra figurines are priceless artifacts from fourth century BCE Greece, that, like plastic Kewpies, depict female figures.

6. Aaron Jaffe, *Modernism and the Culture of Celebrity* (Cambridge: Cambridge University Press, 2005), 7; Loren Glass, "Brand Names: A Brief History of Literary Celebrity," in David Marshall and Sean Redmond, eds., *A Companion to Celebrity* (Hoboken, NJ: Wiley, 2016), 41.

7. David Porter, *On the Divide: The Many Lives of Willa Cather* (Lincoln: University of Nebraska Press, 2008), 34.

8. WC to Douglass Cather, 7/8/[1916] (#1952); Melissa J. Homestead, "Willa Cather in the *Denver Times* in 1915 and New Evidence of the Origins of *The Professor's House*,"

Legacy 35, no. 2 (December 2018): 187–209; WC to Ferris Greenslet, 5/19/[1919] (#0461).

9. WC to Ferris Greenslet, 8/30/1919 (#0475); WC to Ferris Greenslet, [12/9/1917] (#0455) (portions of the *My Ántonia* blurb came from Greenslet's report on the manuscript—Porter, *On the Divide*, 39); WC to Alfred A. Knopf, [2/4/1922] (#2526).

10. "Application for Employment" in EL—Personnel file, J. Walter Thompson Company, Personnel Records, RL 10998, Duke (hereinafter in collection names, J. Walter Thompson Company is abbreviated JWT Co.). Asked "What suggested your making application to this company?" she responded, "Three years ago I was offered a job with you." Unless otherwise specified, additional information is from her application. "Application for Employment" in Maule, Frances—Personnel file, JWT Co., Personnel Records.

11. Richard M. Fried, *The Man Everybody Knew: Bruce Barton and the Making of Modern America* (Chicago: Ivan R. Dee, 2005), 53–54; Stephen Fox, *The Mirror Makers: A History of American Advertising and Its Creators* (New York: William Morrow, 1984), 104; EL to Aminta Casseres, 12/23/1918. EL mentions an employment offer from "a brother advertiser" in EL to Lucille Waller [12/1918], in EL—Personnel file.

12. Overview in Howard Kohl, "Getting Advertising 'Produced,'" *J. Walter Thompson News Bulletin*, 4/1922, 13–16; see Frances Maule's account of her experience at a cosmetics counter, "How to Get a Good 'Consumer Image,'" *J. Walter Thompson News Bulletin*, 3/1922, 9–11.

13. Kathy Peiss, *Hope in a Jar: The Making of America's Beauty Culture* (New York: Owl, 1998), 120. In addition, substantive treatments of the Women's Editorial Department appear in Simone Weil Davis, *Living Up to the Ads: Gender Fictions of the 1920s* (Durham, NC: Duke University Press, 2000); Stephen Fox, *The Mirror Makers: A History of American Advertising and Its Creators* (New York: Morrow, 1984); Jennifer Scanlon, *Inarticulate Longings: The "Ladies' Home Journal," Gender and the Promise of Consumer Culture* (New York: Routledge, 1995); Juliann Sivulka, *Ad Women: How They Impact What We Need, Want, and Buy* (Amherst, NY: Prometheus, 2009); Sivulka, *Stronger than Dirt: A Cultural History of Advertising Personal Hygiene in America, 1875 to 1940* (Amherst, NY: Humanity, 2001); Denise Sutton, *Globalizing Ideal Beauty: Women, Advertising, and the Power of Marketing* (London: Palgrave MacMillan, 2009). Scanlon and Sutton both erroneously place EL on the Ponds account as well; Sutton, *Globalizing Ideal Beauty*, 22.

14. "Mrs. Resor and Separation of Women's from Men's Editorial Groups," Biographical Files: Waldo, Ruth, B5, JWT Co., Bernstein Company History Files, RL 00667, Duke.

15. Earl Brewster to EL, 4/6/1950, B6:F9, CECC; John B. Watson, "Just a Piece of Key Copy," *J. Walter Thompson News Bulletin*, 8/1929, 12.

16. On EL's childhood association with Frances Maule and her sister Florence, "Social and Personal," *LC*, 5/7/1898, 8. See also "Frances Maule," *Nebraska Authors*, https://nebraskaauthors.org/authors/frances-maule; Judith Schwartz, *Radical Feminists of Heterodoxy, Greenwich Village, 1912–1940* (Norwich, VT: New Victoria, 1986), 123; Brenda Ueland to Clara Hampson Ueland, 3/1/1924, B3, Brenda Ueland Papers, Location 143.E.4.10 (F), Minnesota Historical Society, St. Paul.

17. F.M.W., Memo re Miss Helen Goodspeed, 12/18/1924, in Goodspeed, Helen—Personnel file, JWT Co., Personnel Records.
18. WC to Meta Cather, [Spring 1942] (#2271).
19. Qtd. in T. J. Jackson Lears, *Fables of Abundance: A Cultural History of Advertising* (New York: Basic Books, 1994), 233 (also placing Esty's comments in relation to the broader debate); Marchand, *Advertising*, 69.
20. Lears, *Fables*, 307, 358; Matthew J. Bruccoli, *Some Sort of Epic Grandeur: The Life of F. Scott Fitzgerald* (New York: Harcourt Brace Jovanovich, 1981), 6, and Kendall Taylor, *Sometimes Madness Is Wisdom: Zelda and Scott Fitzgerald, A Marriage* (New York: Ballantine, 2001), 54; on the analogy of advertising to literature, Ellen Gruber Garvey, *The Adman in the Parlor: Magazines and the Gendering of Consumer Culture, 1880s to 1910s* (New York: Oxford University Press, 1996), 12–13, and Marchand, *Advertising*, 24–26; Henry A. Beers, Jr., "Copy 'Novelettes,'" *Printers Ink*, 7/13/1916, 57; Charles Stirrup, "Ad Writer's Output Compared with That of Famous Authors," *Printers' Ink*, 3/22/1917, 75; WC, "On the Art of Fiction," 7; Newton A. Fuessle, "What Copy-writers Can Learn from Story-writers," *Printers' Ink*, 8/12/1915, 33.
21. In addition to documents cited below in relation to both Jergens and Woodbury's, an organization chart for the Women's Editorial Department establishes EL's unusual status as sole copy writer. "Copy Department," 10/27/1925, B5, Miscellaneous, JWT Co., Bernstein Company History Files; E. L., untitled, "Editorial Groups" section, *News Bulletin No. 73*, 3/29/1921, J. Walter Thompson Company Newsletter Collection.
22. WC, "The Novel Démeublé," 6.
23. EL, "The Emotional Quality in Advertisements," *J. Walter Thompson News Bulletin*, 4/1923, 11, 12.
24. Ibid., 13–14.
25. On the unsettled question of credit and first appearance of the slogan, documents collected in "The Story of Woodbury's Soap," JWT Co., Information Center Records, RL00714, Duke; Sutton, *Globalizing Ideal Beauty*, 113. See also Tom Reichert, *The Erotic History of Advertising* (Amherst, NY: Prometheus, 2003), 67–77.
26. Woodbury's, "You, too, can have the charm," *LHJ*, 10/1922, 63; Peiss, *Hope in a Jar*, 124.
27. Marchand, *Advertising*, 164–205, 208–17; Woodbury's, "Nothing quite effaces that momentary disappointment," *WHC*, 5/1922, 85; WC, "The Novel Démeublé," 6.
28. All Woodbury's in *LHJ*: "A man's first impression," 6/1921, 45; "His unspoken thoughts," 9/1922, 51; "All around you," 12/1922, 45; "Strangers' eyes," 1/1922, 42.
29. WC to Alfred Knopf, [2/4/1922] (#2526); typed draft of *One of Ours* jacket copy revised by EL in pencil, DFCF. In Alfred Knopf to WC, 2/6/1922 (DCFC), Knopf proposed revisions to EL's first paragraph but praised the second as "first rate." It is not clear whether the extant draft revised by EL was the version WC first sent or a later revision--it matches most, but not all of the jacket copy as published. In any event, the language I quote above appears both in the draft and published versions.

30. Statistical Department, "Woodbury's Facial Soap Consumer Investigation (Metropolitan New York, Lancaster, Pa. and Liberty, N.Y.)," 11/1922, [1], JWT Co., 16 mm. Microfilm Investigations, Duke; Statistical Department, "Woodbury's Facial Soap Investigation among College Women," 12/1922, [1]. JWT Co., 16 mm. Microfilm Investigations.

31. Marchand, *Advertising*, 97; Stanley Resor to William Groom, 11/2/1924, and William Groom to Stanley Resor, 11/19/1924, in "The Story of Woodbury's," 81–82, 85.

32. On the client's understanding of this relationship, William Groom to Stanley Resor, 12/31/1926, in "The Story of Woodbury's," 108–12; three 5/22/1923 memoranda on the Boston Woodbury investigation were addressed to Mr. [Paul] Cherington, Miss Lewis, and Miss [Ruth] Stocking (Cherington and Stocking were in the research department), but the scores of such memoranda dated from 11/26/1924 to 11/26/1927 were addressed only to EL. JWT 16 mm. Microfilm Investigations. Peiss discusses some of the consumer responses, which parrot the advertising copy. *Hope in a Jar*, 173.

33. "History of Jergens Lotion Advertising 1922 to 1929" and "History of Woodbury's Soap and Preparations 1903 to 1929," JWT Co., Information Center Records.

34. Woodbury's, "Five Hundred & Twenty Girls at Smith and Bryn Mawr," *LHJ*, 6/1925.

35. Special Production and Representatives' Meeting, 4/9/1928, 16–17, JWT Co., Staff Meeting Minutes, RL00749, Duke.

36. Woodbury's, "In the fashionable summer colonies", " *LHJ*, 7/1926, 31.

37. F. Scott Fitzgerald to WC, [4/1925], in Matthew J. Bruccoli, ' "An Instance of Apparent Plagiarism': F. Scott Fitzgerald, Willa Cather, and the First *Gatsby* Manuscript," *Princeton University Library Chronicle* 39, no. 3 (Spring 1978): 171–72; WC, *A Lost Lady*, Willa Cather Scholarly Edition (Lincoln: University of Nebraska Press, 1997), 163 (because Fitzgerald was in Italy he did not have access to Cather's novel, but he is clearly referring to this passage); WC to F. Scott Fitzgerald, 4/8/1925, *SL*, 370.

38. WC, *One of Ours*, Willa Cather Scholarly Edition (Lincoln: University of Nebraska Press, 2006), 193, 195; WC, *A Lost Lady*, 25, 33, 106–107.

39. WC, *The Professor's House*, Willa Cather Scholarly Edition (Lincoln: University of Nebraska Press, 2002), 37–38.

40. Davis, *Living Up to the Ads*, 2, 91.

41. Patricia Johnston, *Real Fantasies: Edward Steichen's Advertising Photography* (Berkeley: University of California Press, 1999), 210. Notably "Uncle Valentine" and *My Mortal Enemy* were both purchased by and published in women's magazines, which seemed to prefer the woman's point of view in fiction even as ads published in their pages deployed the male gaze. I depart from but have been influenced by Sharon O'Brien's influential text-subtext model for interpreting Cather's fiction through "The Novel Démeublé." " 'The Thing Not Named': Willa Cather as a Lesbian Writer," *Signs* 9, no. 4 (1984): 577.

42. WC, *A Lost Lady*, 25–26; WC, *The Professor's House*, 48, 257, 274–75.

43. Creative Staff Meeting Minutes, 10/26/1932, 2, and Staff Meeting Minutes, 10/6/1931, 5, JWT Co., Staff Meeting Minutes.

44. "Account Histories: The Andrew Jergens Company—Jergens Lotion," 1/12/1926, 3, JWT Co., Information Center Records. The preserved copy is an incomplete draft with many corrections and additions in EL's hand.

45. "Lotion Investigation, Consumer, Questionnaire by Mail," 6/1923, JWT Co., 16 mm. Microfilm Investigations (results from questionnaires sent out in March reported to Aminta Casseres, EL, and Miss Frisby—EL took entire responsibility soon thereafter).

46. "Account Histories: The Andrew Jergens Company—Jergens Lotion," 3; Johnston, *Real Fantasies*, 61–62.

47. Johnston, *Real Fantasies*, 36, 37.

48. Edward Steichen, *A Life in Photography* (Garden City, NY: Doubleday, 1963), n.p.; Representatives Meeting minutes, 1/31/1928, 10.

49. Penelope Niven, *Steichen: A Biography* (New York: Clarkson Potter, 1997), 501; Johnston, *Real Fantasies*, 55 (she points out that Steichen "pos[ed] hands with their props rather than stopping their action"; even the account history claims the latter; 48). Given typical lead times of six months and the fact that the first Woodbury's ad with a Steichen photograph ran in 9/1923, the photographs must have been taken in the spring.

50. Jergens Lotion, "If you want your hands to be beautiful," *LHJ*, 11/1923, 101. EL also used this fear to propel some Woodbury's ads, e.g. an ad headlined "After the age of thirty—can a woman still gain the charm of 'A Skin You Love to Touch?" *LHJ*, 2/1924, 39.

51. "Housework never yet spoiled the beauty of a woman's hands," *LHJ*, 12/1923, 48; Brent Bohlke, ed., *Willa Cather in Person* (Lincoln: University of Nebraska Press, 1990), 42.

52. Marchand, *Advertising*, 38.

53. On "sincerity," Johnston, *Real Fantasies*, 51–52; on EL's raise, WC to Achsah Brewster, 2/16/[1924], *SL*, 353; "Account Histories: The Andrew Jergens Company—Jergens Lotion," 4; Jergens, "No one would ever think she used her hands for housework," *LHJ*, 2/1924, 65. Johnston reproduces the beauty appeal from the *LHJ* (*Real Fantasies*, 61), but see also *WHC*, 2/1927, 75. According to Johnston, there was at least one other split run in 2/1924 in the *LHJ*, but she does not reproduce the Steichen version, and I have found only the beauty appeal version, "In the eyes of the world—a woman is as old as her hands," *LHJ*, 2/1924, 101.

54. Earl Brewster to EL, 3/25/1948, B6:F9, CECC; Earl Brewster to EL 8/26/1951, B6:F10, CECC; Harwood Brewster Picard, "To Frances and Claire Some Memories of Your Grandparents . . . July 1977," 35, BREWSTER 24, Drew. Some of Picard's details are confused (she remembered EL as working for a magazine), but the chronology and other details line up precisely with the Jergens campaign.

55. Qtd. In Johnston, *Real Fantasies*, 36; Jergens, "Usefulness, service for your hands," *LHJ*, 1/1925, 73.

56. Johnston, *Real Fantasies*, 43–44, 145; WC to Achsah Brewster, 2/16/[1924], *SL* 353.

57. Jergens, "A mother cannot 'save' her hands," *LHJ*, 3/1924, 77; Jergens, "She misses too much," *LHJ*, 4/1924, 109; Jergens, "Dozens of times a day," *WHC*, 10/1924, 111.

58. Jergens, "They can be exquisite—don't let them get in the drudge class!," *LHJ*, 11/1924, 95; "Account Histories: The Andrew Jergens Company—Jergens Lotion," 4;

Jergens, "Soft youthful hands that keep their power to charm," *WHC*, 3/1925, 79. Johnston analyzes the evolution of this campaign in great detail, focusing primarily on Steichen's photographs. *Real Fantasies*, esp. chaps. 3 and 6.

59. Jergens, "White Hands," *LHJ*, 9/1928, 55.

60. John Cawelti, "The Writer as a Celebrity: Some Aspects of American Literature as Popular Culture," *Studies in American Fiction* 5, no. 1 (1977): 164; on the photograph and modernist celebrity, Jonathan Goldman, *Modernism Is the Literature of Celebrity* (Austin: University of Texas Press, 2011); Dos Passos, quoted inLeo Braudy, *The Frenzy of Renown: Fame and Its History* (New York: Oxford University Press, 1986), 550, 550n40.

61. Melissa Homestead, "*Every Week*'s Editorial Staff," http://everyweek.unl.edu/vie w?docId=EveryWeeksEditorialStaff.html; John Chapin Mosher, "That Sad Young Man," *Conversations with F. Scott Fitzgerald*, ed. Matthew J. Bruccoli and Judith S. Baughman (Jackson: University Press of Mississippi, 2004), 77, 78, 80.

62. John Chapin Mosher, "Willa Cather," in Bohlke, *Willa Cather in Person*, 92.

63. Michael Schueth, "A Portrait of an Artist as a Cultural Icon: Edward Steichen, *Vanity Fair*, and Willa Cather," *Cather Studies* 7 (2007), 54–55; Faye Hammill, "In Good Company: Modernism, Celebrity, and Sophistication in *Vanity Fair*," in *Modernist Star Maps: Celebrity, Modernity, Culture*, ed. Aaron Jaffee and Loren Glass (Burlington, VT: Ashgate, 2010), 124; Lawrence Rainey, *Institutions of Modernism: Literary Elites and Public Culture* (New Haven, CT: Yale University Press, 1998), 77–106.

64. Melissa J. Homestead, "Willa Cather on 'A New World Novelist': A Newly Discovered 1920 *Vanity Fair* Essay," *American Literary Realism*, 50, no. 2 (2018): 164–79.

65. On Steichen meeting celebrities for the first time in his studio, Johnston, *Real Fantasies*, 201; WC to Mary Virginia Auld, [2/19/1927] (#0857). I have discounted the notion that WC's publishers were behind her *Vanity Fair* appearance because the Knopfs evidently did not know about the portrait until after it was published. Blanche Knopf to WC, 6/17/1927, Knopf Records, B689:F2; WC to Blanche Knopf, 6/19/1927 (#2497).

66. WC to Meta Cather, 3/19/[1927] (#2260); EL to Edward Steichen and Dana Desboro Glover Steichen, [3/1927], Edward Steichen papers, Museum of Modern Art, New York (EL's hospitalization is the logical occasion for the flowers, thus the dating of the letter). Standard reference works identify these photographs as having been taken in 1926, but WC's and EL's letters make clear they were taken in 1927.

67. "Harvesters in the Field of Fiction," *Vanity Fair*, 4/1927, 65.

68. "An American Pioneer—Willa Cather," *Vanity Fair*, 7/1927, 30. In a third, unpublished version, Steichen shot a seated and smiling Cather from the right.

69. All *Vanity Fair*: "America's Severest Critic—H. L. Mencken," 2/1927, 69; "A New Note—But Not a Blue One—for Gershwin," 5/1927, 77; "America's Most Distinctive Novelist—Sherwood Anderson," 12/1926, 88; "A Pugilistic Prodigy—William Lawrence Stribling, Junior, 8/1926, 69; "William Harrison ('Jack') Dempsey, of Colorado" and "James Joseph ('Gene') Tunney, of New York, 10/1926, 66–67; Schueth, "A Portrait of an Artist as a Cultural Icon," 51.

70. I depart here from Schueth ("Portrait," 59); Nebraska State Historical Society, *Willa Cather: A Matter of Appearances*, 2010 exhibition pamphlet, 17.

71. Representatives' Meeting, 1/31/1928, 5, JWT Co., Staff Meeting Minutes; Niven, *Steichen*, 511.

72. Inscribed copies at DFCF: WC, *Death Comes for the Archbishop* (New York: Knopf, 1927); WC, *A Lost Lady* (New York: Knopf, 1924); and WC, *My Ántonia* (Boston: Houghton Mifflin, 1926). While the inscriptions in the latter two are undated, WC inscribed later editions of the books, suggesting she also inscribed them in 1927.

73. "History of Woodbury's Soap and Preparations, 1901 to 1929, inclusive," [26], JWT Co., Information Center Records.

74. EL, "A New Kind of Beauty Contest," *JWT Co. News Letter*, 3/31/1929, [1].

75. Personals, *JWT Co. News Letter*, 10/15/1928, 3; Special Production and Representatives' Meeting, 4/9/1928, 5, JWT Co., Staff Meeting Minutes (commenting on campaigns for Ponds and Simmons, Aminta Casseres explained that part of the cost of each campaign was "the copywriter's time on photograph and arrangements," indicating that copywriters normally bore this responsibility).

76. Woodbury's, "Voted the Most Fascinating Young Sportswoman," *LHJ*, 4/1929, 85; Woodbury's, "Voted the Loveliest of Wives," *LHJ*, 5/1929, 43; Woodbury's, "Voted Most Beautiful Woman in the Arts," *LHJ*, 9/1929, 41.

77. See nickolasmuray.com/portraiture for the Fitzgerald portrait. I have not found the others credited to Murray, but he clearly took all three.

78. "Three distinguished judges," *LHJ*, 2/1929, 107; Bohlke, *Willa Cather in Person*, 77-78.

79. F. Scott Fitzgerald, "Ten Years in the Advertising Business," *Afternoon of an Author: A Selection of Uncollected Stories and Essays*, ed. Arthur Mizener (Princeton, NJ: Princeton University Library, 1957), 126; Kirk Curnutt, "Fitzgerald's Consumer World," *Historical Guide to F. Scott Fitzgerald*, ed. Kirk Curnutt (New York: Oxford University Press 2004), 87.

80. "The Story of Woodbury's," 137-61; Frances Maule, "The 'Woman Appeal,'" *J. Walter Thompson News Bulletin*, 1/1924, 1, 2.

81. R. V. Beucus to F. C. Adams, 12/5/1929, in "The Story of Woodbury's," 161.

82. WC, *The Professor's House*, 152, 30; White, quoted in Fox, *Mirror Makers*, 101; Louise Guerber, Journal, 4/2/1926, BURROUGHS 25, Drew.

83. "The Story of Woodbury's," 173.

84. Quotations from "Important Women (early days): Edith Lewis—1919-1948," B8, "Women," JWT Co., Bernstein Company History Files (Bernstein attributes these comments to Florence Baldwin, Bob Colwell, and Miss Reese).

85. WC to Alfred Knopf, 7/10/[1944] (#2730).

Chapter 5

1. EL, *WCL*, 129.

2. On Whale Cove: Theodore Jones, "Willa Cather in the Northeast: A Pictorial Biography, 1917-1947" (master's thesis, University of New Brunswick, 1968);

Robert Spiller, "The Cottage Girls and Whale Cove: An Oral History" (privately printed pamphlet, 1996); Marion Marsh Brown and Ruth Crone, *Only One Point of the Compass: Willa Cather in the Northeast* (Archer Editions Press, 1980); and Polly Duryea, "Memories of Grand Manan," *Willa Cather Pioneer Memorial Newsletter* 39, no. 4 (1995): 60–63. All rely on interviews conducted in the 1960s or later and depict Whale Cove women in ways implicitly shaped by homophobia. Both Jones and Brown and Crone rely heavily on Eloise Derby and on letters from Alice Mayo Hof to L. Keith Ingersoll (L. Keith Ingersoll Papers, Grand Manan Historical Society, New Brunswick, Canada). Although neither woman knew WC well, they claimed that she hid her identity and that she and EL stayed apart from the other women. I draw carefully and selectively on these sources, which are often contradicted by contemporaneous evidence, and draw on Brown and Crone's interview notes (Marion Marsh Brown Papers, Peru State College Library, Peru, NE) rather than their fanciful distortions of them in print.

3. George Chauncey, *Gay New York: Gender, Urban Culture, and the Making of the Gay Male World, 1890–1940* (New York: Basic, 1994), 240–42.

4. Martha H. Verbrugge, "Veritable Crusaders: The Early Graduates of the Boston Normal School of Gymnastics, 1189–1900," in *Able Bodied Womanhood: Personal Health and Social Change in Nineteenth-Century Boston* (New York: Oxford University Press, 1988), 162–91.

5. Email from Jane A. Callahan, Wellesley College Archivist, 3/5/2012, providing me with alumnae cards and entries in BNSG annual catalogs for Sarah Hayes Jacobus and Sarah McAllister Adams; "New from the Field," *New England Kitchen Magazine*, 8/1895, 235; U.S. Census, Newton Ward 4, Middlesex, MA, 1900 (Roll T623, p. 7B, Enumeration District 901) and 1910 (Roll T624_6043, p. 6B, Enumeration District 0968).

6. Alumna card for Alice Butler Coney, Wellesley College Archives; quotations from Marie Felix, "Whale Cove, 1900–1955," transcription courtesy of Gale Eaton (a transcription also appears in Spiller, "Cottage Girls," 27–18). Felix remembered buying the property in 1902, but see Thomas A. and Jennie F. Kendrick to Mary F. R. Felix, Sarah Hayes Jacobus, and Sarah McCallister Adams, 12/28/1901, Book 58, Deed 7222, Charlotte County, New Brunswick, Canada, Deed Books. On the additional acquisitions see (all Charlotte County Deed Books): William Kendrick to Mary R. Felix [*sic*], Alice B. Coney and Sarah H. Jacobus, 12/10/1909, Book 71, Deed 12758; and Omar P. Thomas and Amelia J. Thomas to Sarah H. Jacobus, Marie R. Felix, and Alice B. Coney, 8/20/1915, Book 81, Deed 17111; Alumna card for Sarah McAllister Adams, Wellesley College Archives. I located no deed transferring Adams's property to Coney, but see the 1909 and 1913 acquisitions to which Coney, not Adams, is a party.

7. Gale Eaton, *The Education of Alice M. Jordan: Navigating a Career in Children's Librarianship* (Lanham, MD: Rowman & Littlefield, 2014), chaps. 1 and 2 (I also rely on Eaton for Jordan's professional career); Helen Clark Fernald, "Alice Jordan at Grand Manan," *Horn Book Magazine*, 37, no. 1 (November 1961): 19, and quoted in Eaton, *Education of Mary Alice Jordan*, 74 (Eaton quotes Fernald's typescript, which includes the reference to Jordan's "famous knickers" omitted in the *Horn Book*);

Charlotte County Deed Book entries: Barbara J. Thomas and Stephen Thomas to Alice M. Jordan, 9/4/1922, Book 94, Deed 22305; Barbara J. Thomas and Stephen Thomas to Alice M. Jordan, 10/28/1924, Book 998, Deed 23862; Alice G. Brugger to Mary A. and Alice M. Jordan, 7/13/1939, Book 119, No. 33045.

8. Available information is contradictory. Spiller's summary ("Cottage Girls," 9) does not match legal records. Schwartz's name alone appears on deeds for land near the road acquired from the same people in 1924, 1925, 1926, and 1934. Charlotte County Deed Book entries: George W. Robinson and Ellen Robinson to Catherine M. Schwartz, 10/11/1924, Book 98, Deed 23837; 11/1/1925, Book 103, Deed 25775; 10/4/1926, Book 103, Deed 25776; 10/3/1934, Book 114, Deed 30366. Manning acquired "Sea Meadow" (on the water) in 1933. Adelia Thomas to Ethelwyn Manning, 6/27/1933, Book 112, Deed 29393. Nevertheless, Manning told Brown and Crone, "I was sitting on the porch and there [WC] had to go by to get to her little lot and one time she was quite laden down with groceries" (Interview notes, "Ethel Manning"). WC would not have walked past Sea Meadow on her way from the village to her cottage. "Entering Class, 1908," *Monthly Bulletin of the Carnegie Library of Pittsburgh*, 13, no. 8 (October 1908): 529–30; Carnegie Institute, *Catalog of the Carnegie Library School* (Pittsburgh: Carnegie Library, 1917), 44. Class secretary's card for Ethelwyn Manning, Class of 1908 Individuals, SCA.

9. Carnegie Institute, *Catalogue of the Carnegie Library School* (Pittsburgh: Carnegie Library, 1918), 61; NYPL, Minutes of the Committee on Circulation of the Board of Trustees, vol. 17 (1917), p. 332, NYPL Rare Books and Manuscripts; Smith College Class of 1908, *Decennial Class Book* (1918), 119, and *Twenty-Fifth Reunion* (1933), 62–63, Class of 1908 Reunion Records, SCA; *Report of the New York Public Library for 1922* (New York, 1923), 68; Spiller, "Cottage Girls," 17–18; U.S. Census, Manhattan, New York, New York, 1930 (Enumeration District 31-631, Roll 1562, p. 6B) and 1940 (Enumeration District 31-1005, Roll mt-0627-02648, p. 1B) (they lived on East Fifty-First Street).

10. Spiller, "Cottage Girls," 7, 9, 13 (because Felix already owned a third of the inn property and did not need to acquire land for her cottage, the date of her move is unclear); Brown and Crone, Interview notes, "Ethel Manning"; "Fatal Collision," *Scranton (PA) Republic*, 2/18/1929, 1. Alice Coney left her share to her sister Grace, but on the event of Grace's death, her share went to Felix and Jacobus. I infer Grace's death from the will of Alice B. Coney, dated 1/4/1928, recorded 2/4/1936, Book 115, p. 125, Charlotte County Deed Books; Marie F. R. Felix to Sarah Hayes Jacobus, 6/2/1931, Book 103, Deed 28311, Charlotte County Deed Books. Spiller, "Cottage Girls," 9.

11. "North Head," *Eastport (ME) Sentinel*, 6/11/1923, clipping, Grand Manan Historical Society; Brown and Crone, Interview notes, "Ethel Manning"; Bob Sink, "Florence Overton," 3/5/2011 blog entry, NYPL Librarians, nypl-librarians.blogspot.com; WC to Margaret and Elizabeth Cather, [August 1936] (#2341) (mentioning "Miss Bonnell," whom I have identified based on mentions of Margaret Bonnell as at the NYPL in *Smith College Monthly*, 10/1917, 168, and *Smith Alumnae Quarterly*, 11/1919, 83); *Report of the Pratt Institute Free Library and School of Library Science* (Brooklyn: Pratt

Institute, 1937), 18; Henrietta Quigley, "An Investigation of the Possible Relationship of Interbranch Loan to Cataloging, *Library Quarterly* 14, no. 4 (1944): 333–38; conversations with Laura Buckley, 5/17 and 5/19/2012 (Sarah Jacobus's address book places Osteen and Crissey at Whale Cove—"Appendix," Susan Hallgarth, *On the Rocks: A Willa Cather and Edith Lewis Mystery* [Albuquerque, NM: Arbour Farms Press, 2013], 25—but Buckley did not share this document with me).

12. "Studio of Willa Cather at Whale Cove," *St. Croix Courier*, 2/6/1930; Mary Ellen Chase, "Five Literary Portraits," *Massachusetts Review*, 3, no. 3 (Spring 1962): 512; WC to Chase, 11/23/1929 (#2005); Melissa Homestead and Anne Kaufman, "Willa Cather's Smith College Connection: Ten 'New' Cather Letters at Smith College Libraries," *Willa Cather Newsletter and Review*, 48, no. 2 (Fall 2004): 40–42; WC to Marion Edwards Park, president of Bryn Mawr College [1/25 or 2/1/1927], Bryn Mawr College Library; "Marion Edwards Park, 1922–1942," https://www.brynmawr.edu/about/history/past-presidents/park; Hallgarth, "Appendix," 251; Helen Clark Fernald to EL, 1/10/1954, B7:F2, CECC; Marjorie Harrison, *Saints Run Mad: A Criticism of the "Oxford" Group Movement* (London: John Lane, 1934), inscribed to Sarah Jacobus "With the author's love and best wishes . . . London 1935," Collection of Laura Buckley; *Social Register, Boston, 1906* 20, no. 6 (November 1905): 43; *On Duty and Off: Letters of Elizabeth Cabot Putnam Written in France, May 1917—September 1918* (Cambridge, MA: Riverside, 1919), 141; *Dau's Greater New York Blue Book, Winter Season, 1907–1908* (New York: Dau, 1907), 131.

13. Jones, "Willa Cather," 118–19; "Miss Sabra Jane Briggs," *Quoddy Tides* (Eastport, ME), 9/26/1975, 30.

14. The misrepresentation of Whale Cove as an "artists' colony" on the model of the McDowell Colony dates back to WC's time there (see Smith, "Studio of Willa Cather." Brown and Crone, Interview notes, "Miss Briggs." Ethelwyn Manning was also invited to visit (Brown and Crone, Interview notes, "Ethel Manning").

15. Brown and Crone, Interview notes, "Miss Derby" (the notes end before Frith's question is recorded, but see Brown and Crone, *Only One Point of the Compass*, 37).

16. WC to Meta Cather, 7/21/[1936] (#2264); Joan Marshall, "Prologue: Introducing Grand Manan," *Tides of Change on Grand Manan Island: Culture and Belonging in a Fishing Community* (Montreal: McGill-Queens University Press, 2009), 9–31 (although Marshall seriously misrepresents WC and Whale Cove later in the volume); see, e.g., responses of former dining room waitresses reported by Duryea, "Memories."

17. WC to Elizabeth Shepley Sergeant, 7/6/[1921] (#0547); WC, *One of Ours* (New York: Knopf, 1922), inscribed copy, CECC; WC to Dorothy Canfield Fisher, 9/1/1922 (#0615); WC, *A Lost Lady* (London: Heinemann, 1924). Inscribed copy, collection of Laura Buckley; WC, *Alexander's Bridge*, Willa Cather Scholarly Edition (Lincoln: University of Nebraska Press, 2007), 198.

18. WC to Dorothy Canfield Fisher, 9/9/1922 (#0615); WC to Mary Virginia Boak Cather, 9/6/[1922] (#1959). WC does not mention EL's presence in letters from or about Grand Manan in 1922, but see Henry Lewis to EL, 8/20/1922, B5:F25, CECC, which was addressed to her on Grand Manan.

19. WC to Alfred Knopf, 8/11/[1922] (#2531); WC to Frank Swinnerton, 9/18/[1924], *SL*, 361; WC to Alfred Knopf, [8/5/1922] (#2530); WC to Alfred Knopf, 8/26/[1922] (#2535).

20. WC to Ferris Greenslet, [6/2–4/1919] (#0465); Lillie Lewis to EL, 7/31/1924, B5:F25, CECC; WC to Mabel Dodge Luhan, [6/5/1926], *SL*, 381; WC to Frank Swinnerton, 9/18/[1924], *SL*, 361.

21. WC to Zoë Akins, 9/7/[1924] (#0743).

22. On 1925 and 1926, see Chapter 3; WC to Elizabeth Vermorcken, 9/19/[1928] (#0944); PHO-277-043, Elizabeth Shannon Collection, National Willa Cather Center, Red Cloud, NE.

23. Barbara Thomas to EL, 9/7/1926, Book 101, Deed 25114, Charlotte County Deed Books; WC to Carrie Sherwood, 7/25/[1929] (#0975). For the fullest account of the design and building of the cottage, see Phil Southwick, "The Cather Cottage," ts. 1983. Jones places WC on the island staking out the cottage ("Willa Cather," 91) but on 9/8/1926, WC wrote from the McDowell Colony to Samuel Knopf asking him to get her out of a request based on the fact "that I will be in Canada then . . . that is all true, except possibly Canada" (#2568).

24. Edward and Joy Johnston to EL, 9/5/1928, Book 105, Deed 26569, Charlotte County Deed Books. On layout, see Jones, "Willa Cather," 91–94 and plate 35, and Southwick, "Cather Cottage," 4. The shower shed is not mentioned in either, but see WC's story "Before Breakfast" (discussed later), set in a cottage modeled on theirs. Neither does anyone mention an outhouse, but see the preseason maintenance list from EL to the Beals in Southwick (10–11), which includes instructions for liming the "small house."

25. L. K. Ingersoll, "At the Turn of the Century (1877–1905)," *Grand Manan Historian* 13 (1969): 7, and "The Rich and the Lean Years, 1906:–1939," *Grand Manan Historian* 15 (1971): 11–12; Brown and Crone interview notes, "Ralph and Aggie Beals"; Southwick, "Cather Cottage," 8–9; EL to Howard Kohl, 8/7/1932, in EL—Personnel file, J. Walter Thompson Company, Personnel Records, RL 10998, Duke.

26. Mary Virginia Auld Mellen to WC, 8/15/1940, B2, Susan J. Rosowski Papers, RG 12-10-53, UNLASC; Jones, "Willa Cather," 95; Brown and Crone, Interview notes, "Ralph and Aggie Beal."

27. WC to Mary Virginia Cather, 6/22/1929 (#2425); WC to Blanche Knopf, 7/26/[1934] (#1230); WC to Mollie Ferris, 12/28/[1934] (#1778); WC to Lydia Lambrecht, 8/10/[1936] (#1321).

28. EL to Harwood Brewster Picard, 8/25/1938, LEWIS 1, Drew; Jones, "Willa Cather," plate 30.

29. EL to Rudolph Ruzicka, [7 or 8/1938], B1:F3, Rudolph Ruzicka Papers, Rauner Manuscript MS-1078, Dartmouth (hereinafter cited as Ruzicka Papers); WC to Zoë Akins, [7/1–31/1936] (#1322); WC to Mary Virginia Boak Cather, 10/17/[1928] (#2422); WC to Elizabeth and Margaret Cather, 5/22/[1937] (#2346); WC to Elsie Cather, 6/25/1934 (#1920); Jones, "Willa Cather," 135; Brown and Crone, Interview notes "Ralph and Aggie Beal."

30. WC to Charlotte Stansfield, 9/4/[1922] (#0617); WC to Dorothy Canfield Fisher, 8/14/[1931] (#1069); WC to Zoë Akins, 8/26/[1933] (#1189).

31. Howard Kohl to EL, 8/1/1932, and EL to Howard Kohl, 8/7/1932, in EL—Personnel File.

32. EL, *WCL*, 153.

33. *The Sargent School for Physical Education* (Cambridge, MA, 1915), 50, 54, B18:F16, Sargent College Archives, Boston University Special Collections; Lillie Lewis to EL, 2/14/1918, and Henry Lewis to EL, 2/3/1921, B5:F25, CECC.

34. "Brooklyn Heights Female Seminary Play at the Pouch," *Brooklyn Life*, 5/18/1919, 12; "People You Know," *NSJ*, 6/13/1920, 14; "Miss Dorothy Cobb, Hostess to Brooklyn Heights Team," *Brooklyn Daily Eagle*, 5/18/1925, 7; "People You Know," *NSJ*, 6/3/1920, 2–B; Lillie Lewis to EL, 4/24/1921, B5:F25, CECC; *Lincoln City Directory, 1922* (Lincoln, NE: Lincoln City Directory Co, 1922), n.p.; Personal interview with Martha Day, 4/6/2012; "People You Know," *NSJ*, 10/13/1921, 10; WC to Earl and Achsah Brewster, 2/21/[1923], *SL*, 337. Lillie Lewis's dislike for her daughter-in-law and son-in-law is evident in many letters to EL. Henry Lewis's earliest letter to EL from California is dated 9/21/1923, while Lillie's first extant letter from Brooklyn is dated 10/26/1924 (all B5:F25, CECC), but see the inscribed copy of *One of Ours* in the next note.

35. WC, *One of Ours* (New York: Knopf, 1922), inscribed copy, family of Ruth Lewis Trainor; Lillie Gould to EL, 10/26/1924 and 7/31/1924, B5:F25, CECC; Henry Lewis to EL, 9/11/1923, B5:F25, CECC; Books and photographs, Family of Ruth Lewis Trainor.

36. Information for the Dartmouth College Alumni Records on Henry Euclid Lewis, 1872, by Harold G. Lewis, 4/18/27, Dartmouth College Archives; WC to Mabel Luhan, 5/25/[1926], *SL*, 380; WC, *Death Comes for the Archbishop* (New York: Knopf, 1927), copy inscribed to Sarah Jacobus 8/29/1927, collection of Laura Buckley; WC to Mabel Dodge Luhan, 9/17/[1927], B6:F174, Mabel Dodge Luhan Papers, YCAL MSS 196, Beinecke.

37. EL to E. K. Brown, 10/19/1950, B5:F21, CECC; WC to Dorothy Canfield Fisher, 4/3/[1928], *SL*, 405; WC to Roscoe Cather, 4/11/[1928] (#2090). Lillie's name was added to Henry's tombstone at Union Cemetery in Claremont, New Hampshire. https://www.findagrave.com/memorial/50470929.

38. Jones, "Willa Cather," 68; WC to Mary Rice Jewett, 5/30/[1928] (#0936); WC to Carrie Miner Sherwood, [6/1928] (#0937); EL, *WCL*, 154; WC to Carrie Sherwood, 7/25/[1929] (#0975); EL, *WCL*, 156.

39. Jane Labaree, *History of the Descendants of Peter Labaree, Charlestown, New Hampshire* (Keene, NH: Darling, 1912); Henry Lewis, "Genealogy of Ruth Putnam, wife of Peter Labaree," B5:F26, CECC; email from Martha Day, 5/6/2009.

40. WC to Roscoe Cather, 8/26/1940 (#2171); WC to M. Manley Aaron, 7/30/[1929] (#2600); WC to Louise Guerber Burroughs, 7/30/[1929] (#2889). WC, *Shadows on the Rock*, ts., B1:F13–17, Southwick, and Willa Cather Literary Manuscripts, MssCol 496, NYPL (both marked extensively by WC and EL; the Southwick copy has the Grand Manan–typed segment spliced into it); Emmeline Ruddy to Alfred Knopf, B30:F5, Knopf Records. There is reason to mistrust Ruddy, EL's late-life nurse, but EL

herself wrote to the Brewsters that about writing on Grand Manan. Earl Brewster to EL, 10/12/1936, B6:F7, CECC.

41. Mary Ellen Chase, "Five Literary Portraits," 512; Homestead and Kaufman, "Willa Cather's Smith College Connections."

42. EL to Mabel Luhan, [1929], B23:F650, Luhan Papers.

43. WC to Ferris Greenslet, 5/5/1930 (#1012); WC to Carrie Miner Sherwood, 7/17/[1930] (#1015); WC to Elizabeth and Margaret Cather, 8/14/[1930] (#2314); WC to George Austermann, 9/14/[1930] (#1017); WC to Dorothy Canfield Fisher, 9/30/[1930] (#1018); WC, *Shadows on the Rock* (New York: Knopf, 1931), inscribed copy, DFCF.

44. WC to Roscoe Cather, [6/21/1931] (#2095); WC to Blanche Knopf, 7/10/[1931] (#1062).

45. I document the bases for these claims more fully in "The Composing, Editing, and Publication of Willa Cather's *Obscure Destinies* Stories," *Scholarly Editing* 38 (2017), http://scholarlyediting.org/2017/essays/essay.homestead.html.

46. EL, *WCL*, 6; WC, "The Novel Démeublé," *New Republic*, 4/12/1922, 6.

47. WC, "Old Mrs. Harris," ts., 3, 11, 69, B4:F6, Papers of Willa Cather, University of Virginia Special Collections.

48. WC to Alfred A. Knopf, 7/31/[1931] (#2628).

49. WC, "Two Friends" ts., 1, B1:F4, Willa Cather, Collected Materials, MS 0008, UNLASC.

50. WC to Helen McAfee, 8/24/[1931] (#2034).

51. WC, "Old Mrs. Harris" ts., 38/82, B1:F20, Southwick.

52. WC to Alfred Knopf, [8/30/1931] (#2634); Blanche Knopf to WC, 9/10/1931, B689:F4, Knopf Records.

53. WC to Elsie Cather, 9/2/[1931] (#3262).

54. WC to Alfred Knopf, 9/10/1931 (#2641).

55. WC, "Two Friends" ts., 1/121, B1:F21, Southwick.

56. WC, *Obscure Destinies* (New York: Knopf, 1932), inscribed copy, CECC.

57. "Alumnae Notes," *Smith Alumnae Quarterly*, 7/1931, 511, and Sally Frankenstein, Class of 1912 Individuals, SCA (small reproduction of a Grand Manan watercolor); Schwartz's Grand Manan watercolors in the Barnlet, visit 5/2012; Achsah Brewster to EL, 6/10/1932, B6:F6, CECC; WC to Zöe Akins, 9/9/[1934] (#1234); Earl Brewster to EL, 7/15/1933, B6:F6, CECC.

58. Jones, "Willa Cather," 70; Ingersoll, "The Rich and Lean Years," 25–26; "Grand Manan Had Fine Tourist Season," *Eastport (ME) Sentinel*, 9/13/1933 (clipping, Grand Manan Historical Society); WC to Alfred Knopf, 7/12/1936 (#2685).

59. NYPL, Minutes of the Committee on Circulation of the Board of Trustees, vol. 32, pp. 10–11, 33, NYPL Rare Books and Manuscripts; WC to Blanche Knopf, 7/24/[1932], B4:F14, Irving Kolodin Papers, JPB 06-40, Music Division, NYPL for the Performing Arts; WC to Meta Cather, [Spring 1942] (#2271). EL to Alfred Knopf, 4/27/1951, B704:F5, Knopf Records; WC to Roscoe and Meta Cather, 7/13/[1933] (#2107).

60. WC to Zoë Akins, 8/26/[1933] (#1189); WC to Elsie Cather 6/25/1934 (#1920) (mentioning "Edith Lewis's sister" as having brought a car to the island at a time when Helen Lewis Morgan was living in the West; see also Harold Lewis, envelope address of Ruth and Helen Lewis on Nova Scotia, 1933, family of Ruth Lewis Trainor); "Scholastic Highlights," *Brooklyn Daily Eagle*, 12/17/1932, 11; "Shore Road School Holds Field Day," *Brooklyn Daily Eagle*, 5/16/1933, 20.

61. WC to Elsie Cather, 6/25/1934 (#1920); WC to Elsie Cather, 7/9/[1934] (#1857).

62. EL to Rudolph Ruzicka, [7 or 8/1938] and 9/4/1938, B1:F3, Ruzicka Papers.

63. WC to Roscoe Cather [6/21/1931] (#2095) and [7 or 8/1931] (#2099); Margaret Cather Shannon, "Willa Cather Remembered," 4, Cather Family folder, Mildred Bennett Collection, National Willa Cather Center; WC to Roscoe Cather, 3/26/[1936] (#2133).

64. WC to Elsie Cather, 6/9/1936 (#1977); WC to Roscoe Cather, 5/16/1936 (#2122).

65. Shannon, "Willa Cather Remembered," 4, 5–6. Further details derived from both Shannon (5–6) and Jones, "Willa Cather" (107–17) (Shannon's letters to Jones were more detailed than her sketch).

66. EL, Travel Diary, 8/1936, B3:F6, Rosowski-Cather.

67. Shannon, "Willa Cather Remembered," 6.

68. WC to Zoë Akins, [7/1–31/1936] (#1322); WC to Margaret and Elizabeth Cather, 8/12/1936 (#2340).

69. WC to Blanche Knopf, 8/9/[1936], B4:F14, Kolodin Papers.

70. WC to Margaret and Elizabeth Cather, 5/5/1937 (#2345); WC to Alfred Knopf, 8/9/[1937] (#2490).

71. WC to Margaret and Elizabeth Cather [8/1937] (#2341).

72. WC to Margaret and Elizabeth Cather [10/1/1937] (#2349); WC to Margaret and Elizabeth Cather, 1/24/1938 (#2352); WC to Roscoe Cather, [3/12/1938] (#2132).

73. WC to Elsie Cather, 7/1/[1938] (#1983); EL to Harwood Brewster Picard, 8/25/1938, LEWIS1, Drew; WC to Roscoe Cather, [9 to 12/1938] (#2142); WC to Alfred A. Knopf, [9/2/1938] (#2702); Earl Brewster to EL, 12/1/[1938], B6:F7, CECC.

74. WC to Roscoe Cather, 7/17/1939 (#2152); EL, Travel Diary, 8/27/1939; WC to Roscoe Cather, 7/29/1939 (#2153); WC to Elizabeth Cather Ickis and Margaret Cather Shannon, 8/31/[1939] (#2318).

75. WC to Elizabeth Cather Ickis and Margaret Cather Shannon, 8/31/[1939] (#2318); Earl Brewster to EL, 12/26/1939, B6:F7, CECC; Achsah Brewster to EL, 11/21/1939, B6:F7, CECC.

76. L. K. Ingersoll, "M.D. for the Islands: The Life and Times of Dr. John Francis Macaulay," *Grand Manan Historian* 25 (1993); WC to John Macaulay, 9/23/1939, and WC to Marion Smith Macaulay, 10/14/[1939], Grand Manan Historical Society.

77. EL to Sarah Jacobus, [10/1939], Grand Manan Historical Society.

78. WC to Alfred A. Knopf, 8/29/1940 (#2713); WC to Roscoe Cather, 7/11–12/1940 (#2169); WC to Roscoe Cather, 10/5/1940 (#2172); WC to Alfred Knopf, 8/22/1940 (#2710).

79. WC to Roscoe Cather, 11/28/1940 (#2174).

80. WC to Mary Jordan, 9/18/[1942], private collection.

81. WC to Margaret Cather Shannon, 7/8/[1943] (#2400); WC to Alfred A. Knopf, 7/29/1943 (#2723); WC to Margret Cather Shannon, [8/1/1943] (#2384); WC to Margaret Cather Shannon, 8/3/1943 (#2385).

82. WC, *The Old Beauty and Others* (New York: Knopf, 1948), 141–42.

Chapter 6

1. WC to Alfred Knopf, 9/10/1936 (#2689); WC to EL, [10/4/1936] (#1328); EL, Travel Diary, 10/16/[1935], B3:F6, Rosowski-Cather.

2. Melissa Homestead, "Willa Cather's Letters in the Archive," *Tulsa Studies in Women's Literature* 40, no. 1 (Spring 2021): forthcoming.

3. WC to Roscoe Cather, 7/2/1934 (#2110); EL to Stephen Tennant, 4/18?/[1948], B2:F29, Stephen Tennant Papers, OSB MSS 187, Beinecke; WC, *Lucy Gayheart*, ts., 145, Willa Cather Literary Manuscripts, MssCol 496, NYPL.

4. Stephen Fox, *The Mirror Makers: A History of American Advertising and Its Creators* (New York: Morrow, 1984), 139–40, 291; "Personals," *J.W.T. News*, 12/1930, 5; Earl Brewster to EL, 2/24/1931, B6:F6, CECC.

5. EL to Howard Kohl, 9/27/1931, and Howard Kohl to EL, 10/3/1931, in Lewis, Edith— Personnel file, J. Walter Thompson Company, Personnel Records, RL 10998, Duke. In addition to placing many ads in the magazine, the *Journal* was a J. Walter Thompson client. Ads were seldom written for one venue, so EL was to write an ad *for* the magazine rather than to be placed in it.

6. Staff Meeting, 1/5/1932, 15, J. Walter Thompson Company, Staff Meeting Minutes, RL00749, Duke; Patricia Johnston, *Real Fantasies: Edward Steichen's Advertising Photography* (Berkeley: University of California Press, 1999), 301n5 (Johnston mentions only Steichen's work on Traveler's Aid, but Cather's letter suggests EL was also assigned to it); WC to Carrie Miner Sherwood, 5/2/[1932] (#1108).

7. WC to Blanche Knopf, 12/31/[1927] (#0916).

8. Sam Roberts, "One Hundred Years of Grandeur," *NYT*, 6/18/2013, Streeteasy.com/building/570-park-avenue-new_york; EL to Leon Edel, 5/21/1952, Leon Edel Collection, MSG 993, McGill University Special Collections, Montreal, Quebec.

9. WC to Mabel Luhan, 11/22/1932, *SL* 476–77.

10. Elizabeth Shepley Sergeant, *Willa Cather: A Memoir* (Philadelphia: Lippincott, 1953), 261–63.

11. Albert Donovan in 1940 U.S. Census, Manhattan Borough, New York, NY, Enumeration District 31-1366, Sheet 12A; John Chapin Mosher, World War II Draft Registration Card, 4/27/1942, and Philip W. Claflin, New York Military Service Card, 1/3/1941, both accessed through www.ancestry.com (and listing 136 E. 64th Street address); Esther Newton, *Cherry Grove, Fire Island: Sixty Years in America's First Gay and Lesbian Town* (Boston: Beacon, 1993), 23; Melissa Homestead, "Willa Cather Editing Sarah Orne Jewett," *American Literary Realism* 49, no. 1 (Fall 2016), 88n51;

Brenda Ueland to Bruce Barton, 11/24/1935, B68, Bruce Barton Papers, U.S. Mss 44AF, Wisconsin Historical Society, Madison.

12. WC to Roscoe Cather, 6/12/1935 (#2117); WC to Elsie Cather, 6/22/1935 (#1922).

13. WC to Virginia Cather, [12/10/1932] (#2328); WC to Elizabeth Seymour, [12/1932] (#1945); WC to Annetta Clark 3/7/[1931] (#2007); WC to Annetta Clark 3/1/[1933] (#2009).

14. WC to Roscoe Cather, 4/3/[1933] (#2105); Virginia Cather, 1933, Office of the Registrar, Transcripts, SCA; Mary Delia Lewis, Faculty, SCA (documenting her teaching at Smith from 1906 to 1937); WC to Virginia Cather, [6/9/1933] (#2331); WC to Virginia Cather, 5/22/1933 (#2329); WC to Elsie Cather, 6/21/[1933]) (#1862); Charlotte Wilder to EL, 5/27/1953, B6:F25, CECC (Virginia's son has many letters from Charlotte Wilder to his mother).

15. WC to Elsie Cather, 5/25/[1930] (#2257); Yehudi Menuhin, *Unfinished Journey* (New York: Knopf, 1977), 77–78; Jan Hambourg to EL, 2/14/[1931], B6:F13, CECC.

16. WC to Elsie Cather, 3/17/[1931] (#2263); Yaltah Menuhin to EL, 3/24/1931, B6:F13, CECC; WC to Helen McNeny Sprague, 3/20/[1932] (#1102); Marutha Menuhin to EL, 2/10/32, B6:F13, CECC.

17. WC to Carrie Miner Sherwood, 2/19/[1932] (#1097) and 2/12/[1935] (#1215); Yaltah Menuhin to EL, 2/17/1937, B6:F13, CECC.

18. Hephzibah Menuhin to WC and EL, 1/11/[1938], B6:F13, CECC; Humphrey Burton, *Yehudi Menuhin: A Life* (Boston: Northeastern University Press, 2000), 91–92, 4–5; Yaltah Menuhin to EL, 2/17/1937, B6:F13, CECC; Yehudi Menuhin to EL, 3/17/1937, B1:F10, Mary Lou Karch Collection on Edith Lewis, MS 0395, UNLASC.

19. WC to Carrie Miner Sherwood, 2/19/[1932] (#1097) and 2/12/[1935] (#1215); WC to Carrie Miner Sherwood and Mary Miner Creighton, 1/31/[1933] (#1159); EL to Harwood Brewster Picard, 2/22/[1938], LEWIS 1, Drew; WC to Elizabeth and Margaret Cather, 1/24/1938 (#2352); Marutha Menuhin to EL, 1/7/[1938], B6:F13, CECC; EL to Harwood Brewster Picard, 2/22/[1938], LEWIS1, Drew.

20. Marutha Menuhin to EL, 12/23/1936, Yaltah Menuhin to EL, 2/17/1937, and Marutha Menuhin to EL, 1/7/1939, all B6:F13, CECC.

21. EL, *WCL*, 173. See also John Flanigan, "A Collegial Friendship: Willa Cather and Ethel Herr Litchfield," *Cather Studies* 13 (2021): forthcoming.

22. Ruth Lewis Trainor, personal interviews with Anne L. Kaufman, 8/2004 and 8/2005; Achsah Brewster to EL, 3/8/1940, B6:F8, CECC; *Polk's Lincoln (Lancaster County, Neb.) City Directory, 1935*, 346. Disputes about the property boundaries and between creditors kept the Lewis house empty. The two duplexes currently on the lot were built in 1945.

23. WC to Elsie Cather, 12/22/[1937] (#1872).

24. WC to Vilhjalmur Stefansson, 2/24/1936 (#2025); EL to Vilhjalmur Stefansson, [8/10/1936], B39:F10, and EL to Vilhjalmur Stefansson, 4/3/[1936], B41:F15, Papers of Vilhjalmur Stefansson, Stefansson Mss-98, Dartmouth (hereinafter cited as Stefansson Papers).

25. EL to Vilhjalmur Stefansson, [5/30/1936], B41:F15, Stefansson Papers.

26. EL to Vilhjalmur Stefansson, 5/12/1937 and [7?/1937], B41:F15, Stefansson Papers.

27. WC to Helen Louise Cather, 6/2/[1930] (#1947); WC to Elizabeth and Margaret Cather, 7/14/[1930] (#2310); WC to Carrie Miner Sherwood, 7/17/[1930] (#1015); WC to Carrie Miner Sherwood, 7/26/[1935] (#1269).

28. WC to Elsie Cather, 7/14/1935 (#1923); WC to Mary Miner Creighton, 8/8/[1935] (#1270); WC to Alfred Knopf, 8/13/1935 (#2679) and 8/26/1935 (#2680); WC to Roscoe Cather 9/8/1935 (#2119); EL, Travel Diary, 9/25/[1935].

29. Lucy Marks and David Porter, *Seeking Life Whole: Willa Cather and the Brewsters* (Madison, NJ: Fairleigh Dickinson University Press, 2009), 52; EL, Travel Diary, 9/21 and 9/24/[1935]; Marks and Porter, *Seeking Life Whole*, 70; EL, Travel Diary, 9/26/[1935].

30. EL, Travel Diary, 9/23, 9/29, and 10/1[1935]; Marks and Porter, *Seeking Life Whole*, 70–72.

31. EL, Travel Diary, 10/14 and 10/22/[1935].

32. Ibid., 10/16, 10/22, 10/20, 10/24, and 10/28/[1935]; WC to Carrie Miner Sherwood, 11/12/1935 (#2055).

33. WC to Yaltah Menuhin, 10/23/[1935], *SL*, 509; Marutha Menuhin to EL, 12/10/1935, Karch Collection.

34. EL to Harwood Brewster Picard, [after 10/10/1938], Lewis 1, Drew.

35. WC to Roscoe Cather, 11/6/[1938] (#2137); WC to Margaret Cather, [11/9/1938] (#2359).

36. WC to Margaret Cather, [11/9/1938] (#2359); WC to Roscoe Cather, 10/23/1939 (#2155); Sergeant, *Willa Cather*, 275 (this one documented act of destruction is the kernel of the mythology of Cather as letter burner).

37. WC to Roscoe Cather, 5/23/1938 (#2134); WC, *Sapphira and the Slave Girl*, Willa Cather Scholarly Edition (Lincoln: University of Nebraska Press, 2009), 169; WC to Ferris Greenslet, [11/24/1940] (#1506).

38. WC to Roscoe Cather, 3/2/1941 (#2179); EL to E. K. Brown, 10/19/1950, B5:F21, CECC.

39. WC to Carrie Miner Sherwood, 5/16/1943 (#1541).

40. Unless otherwise specified, details from EL, Travel Diary; Sarah Bloom to Roscoe Cather, 6/[17]/1941 (#2183).

41. Roscoe Cather to Virginia Cather Brockway, 7/11/1941, private collection.

42. WC to Zoë Akins, 9/17/1941 (#1548); EL to Meta Cather, 6/15/[1947], private collection.

43. EL to Ruth Lewis, 5/17/1943, private collection; WC to Meta Cather, [Spring 1942] (#2271); *American Weekly*, BAW1, J. Walter Thompson Company, Domestic Advertisements Collection, RL.00687, Duke; WC to E. K. Brown, 10/7/1946, *SL*, 666.

44. WC to Meta Cather, [1942/1943] (#2468); WC to Meta Cather, [Spring 1942] (#2271); Art Directors Club "Award for Distinctive Merit" to Paul F. Berdanier, Jr., and EL, 6/17/1943, CECC; WC to Carrie Sherwood, 6/9/1943 (#1633); WC to Alfred Knopf, 12/30/1943 (#2726).

45. On Undset and WC, see Sherrill Harbison, "Sigrid Undset and Willa Cather: A Friendship," *Willa Cather Pioneer Memorial Newsletter & Review* 42, no. 3 (Winter–Spring 1999): 53–54, and "Willa Cather and Sigrid Undset: The Correspondence in

Oslo," *Resources for American Literary Study* 26, no. 2 (2000): 236–59 (though she presumes that EL typed WC's letters and falsely inserted herself into the friendship); Alfred Knopf to Willa Cather, 9/4/1940, B1:F1, Rosowski-Cather; "Alumnae Notes," *Sargent Quarterly* 27, no. 1 (1941): 15; "Miss Morgan Is Married on Heights," *Brooklyn Daily Eagle*, 5/11/1942, 4.

46. EL to Virginia Cather Brockway, 12/27/1949, private collection; WC to Sigrid Undset, [12/25/1943], *SL*, 623; WC to Sigrid Undset, 1/6/1945, National Library of Norway, Oslo. On Cather's mental state during the war, see Andrew Jewell, "Why Obscure the Record: The Psychological Context of Willa Cather's Ban on Letter Publication," *Biography* 40, no. 3 (Summer 2017): 399–424.

47. WC to Roscoe Cather, 8/15/[1942] (#2197).

48. WC to Irene Miner Weisz, 12/26/[1942] (#1605); WC to Meta Cather, 4/10/1942?] (#2278); WC to Roscoe Cather, 8/15/[1942] (#2197).

49. WC to Margaret Cather Shannon, 10/16/[1942] (#2379) and 11/13 and 16/1942 (#2380).

50. Thomas Vicniguerra, *Cast of Characters: Wolcott Gibbs, E. B. White, James Thurber, and the Golden Age of the "New Yorker"* (New York: Norton, 2016), 45, 266; Tim Page, Introduction to *The Happy Island*, by Dawn Powell (South Royalton, VT: Steerforth Press, 1998), viii.

51. Dawn Powell to Coburn Gilman, [summer of 1939], *Selected Letters of Dawn Powell, 1913–1965*, ed. Tim Page (New York: Henry Holt, 1999), 105; Vinciguerra, *Cast of Characters*, 266; EL to Brenda Ueland, 2/4/1961, B4, Brenda Ueland Papers, Location 143.E5.1 (B), Minnesota Historical Society, St. Paul.

52. Earl and Achsah Brewster to EL and WC, 12/27/1942, B1:F5, Karch Collection; Alpha Barlow to Mrs. Wheeler, 2/27/1945, Class of 1902 Individuals, SCA; "In Memoriam," *Smith Alumnae Quarterly*, 5/1945, 144.

53. WC to Roscoe Cather, [4/15/1945] (#2228); WC to Roscoe Cather, 5/26/[1945] (#2233).

54. Details from EL, Travel Diary. See also "Asticou Terraces," https://acadiamagic.com/asticou/terraces.html. On McKenzie (misspelled Mackenzie by EL), "McKenzie, Ethel O'Neil," in *Canada's Early Women Writers*, https://digital.lib.sfu.ca/ceww-556/mckenzie-ethel-oneil, and "Dedication of Joseph H. Curtis Memorial, Northeast Harbor, 1933," *Maine Memory Network https://www.mainememory.net/artifact/81109.*

55. WC to Meta Cather, 9/7/[1945] (#2273); WC to James Cather, 9/24/1945 (#2770).

56. Certificate of Death No. 9733 for Willa Sibert Cather, filed 4/25/1947, New York City Vital Records; WC to Meta Cather, 12/17/1945 (#2276). A conversation with Caroline Schimmel, granddaughter of Dr. William Crawford White, led to my discovering WC's cancer, and Byers ("Bud") Shaw, M.D., helped me to interpret the evidence.

57. On the diagnosis and treatment of breast cancer in the 1940s, James Patterson, *The Dread Disease: Cancer and Modern American Culture* (Cambridge, MA: Harvard University Press, 1987), James S. Olson, *Bathsheba's Breast: Women, Cancer & History* (Baltimore: Johns Hopkins University Press, 2002), and Ellen Leopold, *A*

Darker Ribbon: Breast Cancer, Women, and Their Doctors in the Twentieth Century (Boston: Beacon, 1999). Olson describes the diagnosis of Maude Louis Gilpatric in 1950, with a lapse of several days while she waited for biopsy results (99), a scenario best fitting WC's letters as evidence.

58. WC to Meta Cather, 1/14/1946 (#2279); WC to Meta Cather, 2/8/[1946] (#2280); WC to Helen Cather Southwick, [2/1946] (#2785); WC to James Cather, 3/26/1946 (#2775).

59. WC to Meta Cather, 4/13/[1946] (#2281).

60. Thayer Jaccaci to EL, 2/7/1946, and Thayer Jaccaci to Howard Kohl, 2/11/1946 (EL's response to Jaccaci was appended to his memorandum to Kohl) in EL—Personnel file; WC to Meta Cather, 7/22/1946 (#2463).

61. WC to Meta Cather, 10/17/[1946] (#2464); WC to Carrie Sherwood, 9/25/1946 (#1740).

62. WC, Engagement Calendar for 1946, B4:F13, CECC; EL to Ruth Lewis Trainor, 1/1/1947, private collection.

63. WC to Carrie Miner Sherwood, 11/3/1941 (#1553); WC to Meta Schaper Cather, 12/17/1945 (#2776); Engagement Calendar for 1946 and Engagement Calendar for 1947, B4:F14, CECC (single-word entries in both for "liver" thrice-weekly match her description of treatments in letters).

64. Details of WC's death and immediate aftermath from Ruth Putnam Lewis to Harold Gould Lewis, 4/24/1947, private collection. Ruth either did not know about or suppressed medical details. She identified their maid as a practical nurse and reported that WC was supposed to be admitted to Roosevelt Hospital the day she died but ostensibly because she needed "rest" because construction noise had been disturbing her sleep. According to White's report on the death certificate, however, he examined WC at 10 a.m. the same morning, suggesting he wanted WC admitted for medical reasons. EL, fragment of ts. of timeline produced from WC's "line-a-day" diary, B7:F13, CECC.

65. EL, *WCL*, 172; WC to E. K. Brown, 3/23/1947, *SL*, 669–70.

66. EL, *WCL*, 197.

67. EL to Stephen Tennant, 9/5/[1947], B2:F30, Tennant Papers; Elsie Cather to E. K. Brown, 9/23/1949, B1, Edward Killoran Brown Collection of Willa Cather, YCAL MSS 490, Beinecke.

68. Virginia Cather Brockway to Meta Schaper Cather, 4/30/[1947], *SL*, 674; Alfred Knopf, Diary, 1947, B626:F2, Knopf Records; Rudolf Ruzicka, Diaries, 1908–1958, B3:F1, Rudolph Ruzicka Papers, Rauner Manuscript MS-1078, Dartmouth (hereinafter cited as Ruzicka Papers); Virginia Cather Brockway to Meta Schaper Cather, 4/30/[1947], *SL*, 674.

69. Virgina Cather Brockway to Meta Schaper Cather, 4/30/[1947], *SL*, 675; Margaret C. Bean, *Willa Cather in Jaffrey* (Jaffrey, NH: Jaffrey Historical Society, 2005), 11–12; L. Brent Bohlke and Anders G. Lund in *Willa Cather Remembered*, ed. Sharon Hoover (Lincoln: University of Nebraska Press, 2002), 192–195. These sources either identify EL as WC's secretary or put Sarah Bloom, WC's actual secretary, at her side in death, but I draw on them for details supported by contemporaneous

documentation. Woodress wrongly puts Sarah Bloom, not EL, at WC's side as she was dying. *Willa Cather: A Literary Life* (Lincoln: University of Nebraska Press, 1987), 504.

70. EL to Meta Schaper Cather, 6/15/1947, private collection.

71. EL to Harwood Brewster Picard, 7/7/947, Lewis 1, Drew.

72. EL to Alfred Knopf, 8/7/1947, B704:F3, Knopf Records.

73. Marutha Menuhin to EL, [early September 1947], B1:F8, Karch Collection; EL to Charles Cather, 10/16/1947, B5:F11, CECC.

74. Earl Brewster to EL, 7/12/1947 and 12/3/1947, B6:F9, CECC.

75. Earl Brewster to EL, 1/13/1948 and 3/25/1948, B6:F9, CECC.

76. Philip Hoare, *Serious Pleasures: The Life of Stephen Tennant* (London: Hamish Hamilton, 1990), 211–13; Stephen Tennant to EL, 1/4/1948, B2:F22, Rosowski-Cather. Hoare did not have access to Tennant's letters to EL or EL's travel diary, and he relies on Patricia Yongue's mischaracterization of EL.

77. Hoare, *Serious Pleasures*, 171–77, 285; Stephen Tennant to EL, 8/19/1947, B2:F21, Rosowski-Cather.

78. EL to Stephen Tennant, 9/5/[1947], B2:F30, Tennant Papers; Stephen Tennant to EL, 9/19/1947, B2:F21, Rosowski-Cather; EL to Stephen Tennant, [late 9/1947], B2:F30, Tennant Papers; Stephen Tennant to EL, 1/4/1948, B2:F22, Rosowski-Cather.

79. Stephen Tennant to EL, 3/26/1948, B2:F22, Rosowski-Cather; EL to Stephen Tennant, 4/18?/[1948]; Stephen Tennant to EL, 4/22/1948, B2:F22, Rosowski-Cather.

80. Hoare, *Serious Pleasures*, 309; Tennant to EL, 4/22/1948.

81. EL, [Book 5], 4/3/[1949] and 4/5/[1949], B3:F4, Southwick.

82. EL mentions the Joshua trees in the Mohave in her travel diary for her 1941 trip with WC.

83. On Kates, Karl E. Meyer and Shareen Blair Brysac, *The China Collectors* (Basingstoke: Palgrave Macmillan, 2015). Kates mentions EL frequently in his letters to his sister. George N. Kates Letters, Archives of American Art, Washington, DC. Details of Ferry's life derived from EL's letters to him. Patrick Ferry Willa Cather Collection, Colby College, Waterville, ME.

84. According to paperwork in EL—Personnel file, her "resignation after leave of absence" took effect 3/31/1948; Stephen Tennant to EL, 8/19/1947, B2:F21, Rosowski-Cather; EL to Stephen Tennant, 9/5/[1947], B2:F30, Tennant Papers.

85. EL to Stephen Tennant, 4/18?[1948]; Alfred Knopf to EL, 1/27/1948, and EL to Alfred Knopf, 1/29/1948 and 2/9/1948, B704:F3, Knopf Records.

86. Alfred Knopf to EL, 3/3/1949, B704:F3, Knopf Records.

87. El, [Book 5], 4/3/[1949] and 4/4/[1949].

88. Alfred Knopf to EL, 4/13/1949, B704:F3, Knopf Records.

89. Meta Cather to EL, 3/13/[1953], B7:F4, CECC; Mabel Luhan to EL, 3/17/1953, B6:F25, CECC.

90. Louise Burroughs to EL, 3/9/[1953], B7:F1, CECC.

91. Earl Brewster to EL, 3/5/1953, B6:F10, CECC; Abby Merchant to EL, 10/10/[1953], B7:F4, CECC.

92. Laura Paxton to EL, 4/15/1953, B6:F25, CECC.

93. Mary A. Jordan to EL, 3/23/1953, Alice M. Jordan to EL, 3/23/1953, and Marie Felix to EL, 4/17/1953, all B6:F25, CECC.

94. EL to Alfred Knopf, 2/17/[1953], B5:F9, Irving Kolodin Papers, JPB 06-40, Music Division, NYPL for the Performing Arts; Earl Brewster to EL, 3/5/1953, B6:F10, CECC; Earl Brewster to EL, 8/8/1953, B6:F11, CECC.

95. EL to Leon Edel, 8/2/1953 and 12/26/1953, Edel Collection; Earl Brewster to EL, 1/14/1954, B6:F11, CECC.

96. L. Keith Ingersoll to EL, 12/5/1956, Grand Manan Historical Society, New Brunswick, Canada.

97. EL to L. Keith Ingersoll, 1/9/1957, Grand Manan Historical Society.

98. Earl Brewster to EL, 6/17/1951, B6:F10, CECC.

99. EL to Rudolph Ruzicka, 11/22/1962, B1, Ruzicka Papers; EL to Harwood Brewster Picard, 7/12/1962, LEWIS 1, Drew; EL to Alfred Knopf, 6/1/1962, and Alfred Knopf to EL, 6/5/1962, B705:F3, Knopf Records.

100. EL to Patrick Ferry, 11/26/1964, Ferry Cather Collection.

101. Phil Southwick, "The Cather Cottage," 2–3, Grand Manan Historical Society.

102. Marion Marsh Brown and Ruth Crone, Interview notes, "Mrs. James Buckley, 17 July 1967" and "Ralph and Aggie Beal," Marion Marsh Brown Papers, Peru State College Library, Peru, NE; Woodress, *Willa Cather*, 323.

103. "In the Matter of the Estate of Edith Lewis, Deceased," Surrogate's Court, New York County. The more than one thousand pages of documents include depositions of EL's doctor, Helen Southwick, Helen Morgan, and Emmeline Ruddy. Because the case was settled, there was no finding of fact, but I am inclined to believe the version of events advanced by Helen Southwick's lawyers. Ruddy also removed and sold books and manuscripts. See Homestead, "Willa Cather's Letters in the Archive."

104. Death announcement, *NYT*, 8/13/1972; "Edith Lewis, Friend of Willa Cather," *NYT*, 8/12/1972; Last Will and Testament of Edith Lewis, 7/31/1968, Surrogate's Court of the County of New York.

Epilogue

1. David K. Johnson, *The Lavender Scare: The Cold War Persecution of Gays and Lesbians in the Federal Government* (Chicago: University of Chicago Press, 2004), and see also John D'Emilio, "The Homosexual Menace: The Politics of Sexuality in Cold War America," in *Making Trouble: Essays on Gay History, Politics, and the University* (New York: Routledge, 1992), 57–73. Margot Canaday argues that attempts to purge homosexuals from government began before World War II, but the public panic after the war is most relevant here. *The Straight State: Sexuality and Citizenship in Twentieth-Century America* (Princeton, NJ: Princeton University Press, 2009).

2. Terry Castle, *The Apparitional Lesbian: Female Homosexuality and Modern Culture* (New York: Columbia University Press, 1993), 2, 4–5.

3. WC to E. K. Brown, 4/9/1937 and 10/7/1946, *SL*, 530, 664–67; Alfred Knopf to E. K. Brown, 5/8/1947, B1, Edward Killoran Brown Collection of Willa Cather, YCAL

MSS 490, Beinecke (hereinafter cited as Brown Collection). For background on Brown (and a different take on these events), Robert Thacker, "'A Critic Who Was Worthy of Her': The Writing of *Willa Cather: A Critical Biography*," *Cather Studies* 7 (2007): 303–28.

4. EL to E. K. Brown, 4/20/[1948], B1, Brown Collection; Margaret Brown to Dorothy Canfield Fisher, 4/28/[1951] and 8/11/1951, B6c:F8, Dorothy Canfield Collection, mss-975, University of Vermont Special Collections, Burlington (hereinafter cited as Canfield Collection).

5. EL to E. K. Brown, 8/2/[1948], B5:F20, CECC; on Fisher's life, Mark Madigan, Introduction to *Keeping Fires Night and Day: Selected Letters of Dorothy Canfield Fisher* (Columbia: University of Missouri Press, 1993), 1–22; Margaret Brown to Dorothy Canfield Fisher, 4/29/[1951].

6. Dorothy Canfield Fisher to E. K. Brown, 10/29/1949, Leon Edel Collection, MSG 993, McGill University Special Collection, Montreal, Quebec (hereinafter cited as Edel Collection); E. K. Brown to Dorothy Canfield Fisher, 11/12/1949, B6c:F8, Canfield Collection; E. K. Brown to Elizabeth Shepley Sergeant, 9/14/1949, B1:F2, Elizabeth Shepley Sergeant Papers, M10, Bryn Mawr College Special Collections (hereinafter cited as Sergeant Papers); E. K. Brown to Dorothy Canfield Fisher, 11/21/1949, Edel Collection.

7. Dorothy Canfield Fisher to E. K. Brown, 11/27/1949, Edel Collection.

8. James R. Shively to E. K. Brown, 3/2/1951, B1, Brown Collection. I give the story no credence—Ballard, who liked to spin tales, likely misconstrued Cather's pleasure in the presence at the MacDowell Colony of composer Arthur Nevin, brother of her deceased Pittsburgh friend Ethelbert Nevin.

9. Mildred Bennett to Moshe and Marutha Menuhin (copy), 8/19/1947, and EL to Marutha Menuhin, draft telegram, [8/21/1947], B6:F14, CECC; Mildred Bennett to Wilbur Bennet, 8/22/1947, Mildred Bennett Collection, Correspondence Files, National Willa Cather Center, Red Cloud, NE; Mildred Bennett to Alfred Knopf, 5/29/1948, and EL to Alfred Knopf, 6/12/[1948], B704:F3, Knopf Records.

10. Mildred Bennett to Dorothy Canfield Fisher, 6/22/1949, B6c:F9, Canfield Collection.

11. Dorothy Canfield Fisher to EL, 5/21/1948, B6:F23, CECC; Alfred Knopf to EL, 4/19/1948, and EL to James Shively, 4/25/1948, B704:F4, Knopf Records.

12. Dorothy Canfield Fisher to E. K. Brown, 3/27/1950, Edel Collection.

13. EL to E. K. Brown, 12/6/[1948], B5:F22, CECC; E. K. Brown to Dorothy Canfield Fisher, 1/15/1951, B6c:F8, Canfield Collection.

14. Dorothy Canfield Fisher, 1/21/[1951], Edel Collection (a typed transcription likely made by Margaret Brown before returning the original to Fisher).

15. Dorothy Canfield Fisher to E. K. Brown, 2/13/1951, Edel Collection (a typed transcription); Elizabeth Shepley Sergeant to E. K. Brown, 9/24/[1950], B1:F3, Sergeant Papers.

16. E. K. Brown to Elizabeth Sergeant, 7/16/1949, B1:F1, Sergeant Papers.

17. Ernest Sirluck to Margaret Brown, 9/23/[1951], Edel Collection.

18. Margaret Brown to Dorothy Canfield Fisher, 4/28/[1951]; Dorothy Canfield Fisher to Margaret Brown, 5/4/1951, B6c:F8, Canfield Collection.

19. Dorothy Canfield Fisher to Alfred Knopf, 12/31/1947, B704:F3, Knopf Records.

20. Dorothy Canfield Fisher to Margaret Brown, 7/8/1951, B6c:F8, Canfield Collection.

21. Margaret Brown to Dorothy Canfield Fisher, 8/11/1951, B6c:F8, Canfield Collection; Leon Edel, "Homage to Willa Cather," in *The Art of Willa Cather*, ed. Bernice Slote and Virginia Faulkner (Lincoln: University of Nebraska Press, 1974), 190–91.

22. "Agnes Rindge Wed to Captain," *Poughkeepsie Journal*, 1/5/1945, 8.

23. Mildred Bennett, "Friends of Willa Cather," *Willa Cather Pioneer Memorial Newsletter* 16, no. 1 (Spring 1997): 6.

24. Henry S. Gallup, Robert E. Bussier, and Howard O. Williams to Charles Bacon, 10/28/1977, and Randyl P. Cournoyer to Helen Lewis Morgan, 8/31/1973, B1:F7, Willa Cather Collected Materials, MS 0008, UNLASC.

25. Randyl P. Cournoyer, Jr., To whom it may concern, 3/22/1994, B1:F7, Willa Cather Collected Materials.

26. Helen Cather Southwick to Virginia Faulkner and Bernice Slote, 3/24/1960 [*sic*— more likely 1970], Bernice Slote Papers, RG 12-10-16, UNLASC; Helen Morgan Schulte to Hunter F. Riesenberg, 1/20/1992, and Helen Morgan Schulte to F. Roberts, 6/2/1992, B1:F7, Willa Cather Collected Materials.

27. Francis Murphy, "'That Is Happiness': A Note on the Final Resting Place of Willa Cather and Edith Lewis," *Willa Cather Newsletter and Review* 57, no. 2 (Summer 2014): 22–25. Murphy covers part of the story I tell here but repeats common errors, including misstating Lewis's birth year. Robert Stephenson (email, 11/29/2019) identified Murphy as responsible for the changes.

28. Mildred Bennett, "At the Feet of Willa Cather: A Personal Account of Edith Lewis as Protector," *Willa Cather Pioneer Memorial Newsletter* 33, no. 3 (Fall 1989): 20; WC to EL, [10/4/1936] (#1328).

Index

For the benefit of digital users, indexed terms that span two pages (e.g., 52–53) may, on occasion, appear on only one of those pages.

Figures are indicated by an italic *f* following the page number.